Ohio

Hopewell

Community

Organization

Ohio

Hopewell

Community

Organization

Edited by

William S. Dancey and Paul J. Pacheco

The Kent State University Press

KENT, OHIO, & LONDON, ENGLAND

© 1997 by The Kent State University Press, Kent, Ohio 44242

Library of Congress Catalog Card Number 96-27659

ISBN 0-87338-561-6

Manufactured in the United States of America

02 01 00 99 98 97   5 4 3 2 1

Library of Congress Cataloging-in-Publication Data

Ohio Hopewell community organization / edited by William S. Dancey and
    Paul J. Pacheco.

    p.   cm.

  Includes bibliographical references and index.

  ISBN 0–87338–561–6 (cloth : alk. paper) ∞

  1. Hopewell culture—Ohio.   2. Earthworks (Archaeology)—Ohio.
3. Land settlement patterns, Prehistoric—Ohio.   4. Subsistence
economy—Ohio.   5. Ohio—Antiquities.   I. Dancey, William S.
II. Pacheco, Paul J. (Paul Joe)

  E99.H69O55   1997

  977.1′01—dc20   96–27659

British Library Cataloging-in-Publication data are available.

Contents

Middle Woodland Habitations in the Ohio Hopewell Periphery

Thirteen   Beyond the Scioto Valley: Middle Woodland Occupations in the
            Salt Creek Drainage
            Flora Church and Annette G. Ericksen   331

Appendix to Chapter 13: The Ilif Riddle Sites
            Olaf H. Prufer   361

Fourteen   Living on the Edge: A Comparison of Adena and Hopewell
            Communities in the Central Muskingum Valley of Eastern Ohio
            Jeff Carskadden and James Morton   365

PART FIVE

Afterword

Fifteen   Interpretations of Ohio Hopewell 1845–1984 and the Recent
            Emphasis on the Study of Dispersed Hamlets
            James B. Griffin   405

            Contributors   427
            Index   363

Figures

Tables

Preface

The majority of the papers in this volume were originally presented in Pittsburgh on April 10, 1992, at the 57th Annual Meeting of the Society for American Archaeology at a symposium entitled "Testing the Prufer Model of Ohio Hopewell Settlement Pattern." The impetus for organizing the symposium came from our involvement with Middle Woodland deposits in the Raccoon Creek Valley, Licking County, Ohio. These deposits were close to the Newark Earthworks, and their significance for the settlement pattern of the builders and users of the earthworks was apparent. Olaf Prufer's position on this question was well known, yet as we searched the literature we found little published work that built on his research, which was conducted in the 1960s. We found master's theses, senior theses, contract reports, and unpublished manuscripts but few journal papers and no monographs. Furthermore, we learned that Prufer's proposition had never really been put to the test, although several small-scale surveys had been done with this in mind.

At first we worked on the symposium without informing Prufer, and by the time of the conference we still had not contacted him. Despite our neglect, he learned of the project and wrote a long letter expressing his surprise and concern to James B. Griffin, who we had invited, along with Bruce Smith, to serve as a discussant. This led to the dramatic reading, by Griffin, of parts of Prufer's letter to preface his own comments on the symposium papers. Following the meeting, we wrote Prufer an apologetic letter and sent him copies of the symposium papers. We also asked if he would care to contribute a foreword. With typical good humor, he forgave us our faux pas, and ultimately he became a major contributor to the published version of the symposium, writing two chapters and an appendix as well as helping out with much of the editorial work. The final product, therefore, owes a great deal to Olaf's enthusiasm for the project; this book is as much his as ours.

The original symposium presenters included Bruce Aument, Flora Church, Robert Connolly, Robert Genheimer, N'omi Greber, Sue Ellen Kozarek, Mark E. Madsen, and Dee Anne Wymer. To broaden the representation of case studies, we approached Jeff Carskadden and Jim Morton of the Muskingum Valley Archaeological Survey to contribute a paper on the central Muskingum River Valley. After the symposium we learned of Sean Coughlin's senior thesis research on Robert Harness's collections at the Liberty Works, which he completed at Kent State University under Mark Seeman's direction. Bradley Lepper's restudy of collections from a survey in the shadow of the Great Circle earthwork at Newark drew our attention for obvious reasons, and we asked him to contribute a paper. Annette Ericksen and Richard Yerkes had done specialized analyses of materials from the investigations of Flora Church and Bradley Lepper, respectively, and their addition to the project broadened the evidentiary base being described in the volume as a whole.

We are sorry that Bruce Smith, who was a discussant along with James B. Griffin, was unable to add his comments to the published version of the symposium. In a widely circulated manuscript, now published, evaluating the role of domestic plants in Middle Woodland, he portrayed Ohio as virtually unknown with regard to settlement archaeology. While recognizing this as true for the published literature, we knew it was false if one included theses, dissertations, and contract reports. We vowed to set the record straight.

Our intention in putting together this collection of papers was to accomplish at least three things. First, we wanted to fill the data gap described by Smith as hindering attempts to study the role of subsistence in Ohio Hopewell. Second, we wanted to confront the diversity of explanations in archaeology for the Hopewell phenomenon in general and settlement pattern specifically. Third, we wanted to suggest that a fruitful place to start solving the Hopewell problem(s) is in the construction of a simple model of the Hopewellian community which assumes that much of the complexity often assumed for Ohio Hopewell is actually the product of processes such as duration of occupation, bioturbation, or erosion. Above all, our objective in editing this book is to show that settlement data do exist and that systematic study of these data can lead to the resolution of some of the conflicting, or uncertain, positions current among archaeologists working on research problems associated with the Middle Woodland period.

Another objective of this collection is to show the historical development of archaeological thought and research on the Ohio Hopewell settlement question. While we attempted to do this in a paper introducing the symposium, our effort was not entirely successful. One of the benefits of drawing Olaf Prufer into the project is that one of his three contributions to this collection, chapter 4, describes his early career in archaeology and how he came to work on the Hopewell problem. Thus, for the Ohio area, at least, the historical background is laid by the founder of Hopewellian settlement studies. We are fortunate as well to be able to see the problem in an even larger temporal and geographic scope in James B. Griffin's contribution to the collection. In chapter 15, an extended version of his symposium comments for the present volume, Dr. Griffin chronicles the gradual, and often tortuous, process by which American archaeologists have wrestled with the Ohio Hopewell problem. His is the only chapter in Part V of the collection, an "afterword" that might better have been titled the "last word."

Many individuals have contributed to the production of this volume, and we thank them all for their efforts. In particular, our thanks to Robyn Geary, Felipe Avila and Jarrod Burks for peering long hours at the manuscript at various stages; to Susan Bean for her valiant efforts in getting this monster on her PC; to Ann Lee for her help with the Murphy investigation data recording and map making; to Paul Hooge, director of the Licking County Archaeology and Landmark Society, for making the Murphy investigations possible; and to all the volunteers who were in the field with Paul.

In the end, the final product is our responsibility, but it would not be the same without the help of these and other individuals every step of the way.

Ohio

Hopewell

Community

Organization

PART ONE

The Ohio Hopewell Settlement Problem

CHAPTER ONE

A Community Model
of Ohio Hopewell Settlement

William S. Dancey and Paul J. Pacheco

ABSTRACT

In the 1960s Olaf Prufer postulated that the Ohio Hopewell communities lived in dispersed households, or farmsteads, that were clustered around, but not in, areas containing burial mounds and ceremonial earthworks. These ceremonial precincts were essentially vacant in his view, and he borrowed the Mesoamerican concept of Vacant Ceremonial Center-Dispersed Agricultural Hamlet pattern to characterize Ohio Hopewell community organization. This idea is formalized in this paper and referred to as the Dispersed Sedentary Community model. We know of no data that would not support this conception of Hopewellian settlement and subsistence, although other authors have argued for nucleated communities living in villages, semi-sedentary lifeways with seasonal abandonment of permanent settlements, and even complete seasonal mobility. As summarized here, current evidence, in our view, points toward Hopewellian communities being made up of single- or multiple-family households scattered across the landscape but concentrated around the centrally located burial and ceremonial precincts. These households were the stable, long-term settlements of people who cultivated indigenous domesticated plants, collected a wide variety of edible plants and nuts, and hunted extensively.

Ohio archaeologists have often been chided for not investigating the settlement pattern associated with the spectacular earthworks and burial mounds of the Middle Woodland Hopewell. Most recently, while addressing the question of whether or not the nucleated village was the basic pan-eastern Middle Woodland settlement type, Smith (1992) lamented the paucity of settlement data from the Ohio Hopewell area. Like most, he resorted to citing Olaf Prufer's work and theories, which date back over thirty years. Prufer's ideas provided a powerful framework for understanding Ohio Hopewell, yet they were never fully evaluated beyond his own field studies. Upon publishing a report on the excavation of the McGraw site on the Scioto River in Ross County, he expected that additional work soon would follow (Prufer 1965:137). This did not happen.

Within the last decade, research has begun to accumulate that can provide the foundation for a systematic evaluation of the Prufer model. Our own eight-year Murphy project is an example (Dancey 1991; Pacheco 1993). Beyond this we have located reports on over ninety sites in southern Ohio that have been systematically surface collected, tested, or excavated. Many more are recorded in the Ohio Archaeological Inventory, and local collectors know of others (Converse 1993). While at one time few could be found, it seems now as though there is no limit to the number of Middle Woodland occupations.

Table 1.1 lists the major sites for which we have information, grouped according to their geographic locality and proximity to an earthwork. Table 1.2 summarizes these data with respect to geographical and environmental distributions and settlement type. Table 1.3 lists forty-five radiocarbon dates ranging largely between 200 B.C. and A.D. 500 that have come from eighteen of the excavated sites.

Looking more closely at the data of Table 1.1, it can be seen that the sample includes fair representation of environmental diversity. Drainage and physiographic coverage is excellent with samples from various locations in the Till Plain (n=23), the Glaciated Plateau, (n=37), and the Unglaciated Plateau (n=31). All the major drainages, including the Miami Rivers (n=20), Brush Creek (n=2), the Scioto River (n=37), the Hocking River (n=1), the Licking River (n=19), the Muskingum River (n=7), and the upper Ohio River (n=3) are included. Furthermore, as Table 1.2 shows, the sample includes assemblages from many different settings, including rockshelters (n=12), terraces (n=54), floodplains (n=9), bluff edges (n=1), hilltops (n=6), and uplands (n=9).

As can be seen from the geographical arrangement of Table 1.1 and from the map in Fig. 1.1, distribution along the Glaciated Plateau, the Ohio Hopewell heartland, is well covered. As expected, however, the sites in the sample come mostly from areas of obtrusive remains such as mounds and earthworks where modern farming is extensive. Settlement variability seems well represented, if our crude types (hamlet, specialized, and logistical; see Table 1.2) meaningfully reflect the degree of diversity in the artifact record. While scattered, the >90 sites listed can be considered a reasonably good measure of variation in artifact clusters. Furthermore, although the work on nearly all of them is done in a unique way, most was done by academic, contract, or organized amateur groups and the results constitute evidence.

In *Ohio Hopewell Community Organization* we bring together some of the information on Middle Woodland nonmortuary locations currently scattered in conference papers, master's theses, contract reports, and the like and assess the fit of the data with Prufer's conception. Out of this evaluation we anticipate renewed interest in the evolving settlement system of the Woodland populations of the Middle Ohio Valley between 1000 B.C. and A.D. 1000. In the remainder of this chapter, we sketch what we think a Middle Woodland cultural landscape would have looked like and identify how the following chapters in this book contribute to this understanding. Along the way we describe the current state of affairs in Middle Woodland settlement archaeology in Ohio. The sites discussed in detail in the book as a whole have been asterisked in Table 1.1 to show that all major areas of recent site discovery are represented here.

The title of the 1992 symposium at which most of the papers in this volume were presented was "Testing the Prufer Model of Ohio Hopewell Settlement Pattern." While not retained in the book title, that phrase captures the theme of this book. Each of the chapters addresses some aspect of the hypotheses advanced in the 1960s by Olaf Prufer in his construction of the culture history of the Ohio area. We now turn to the elements of his prehistory of Ohio that pertain to the Hopewell problem.

The Vacant Center Pattern

Prufer's conception of Hopewell settlement was created in the 1960s as part of a comprehensive study of Ohio Hopewell (Prufer 1964a, 1964b, 1965, 1968). His work includes an explanation of the culture history, which he referred to as the Dual Tradition, and a characterization of Middle Woodland settlement, which he termed the Vacant Ceremonial Center—Dispersed Agricultural Hamlet pattern (hereafter the Vacant Center pattern). Only the latter concerns us here although several aspects of the Dual Tradition influence the settlement pattern. One is the postulated existence of an intrusive, dominant minority (the Hopewell) who introduced a mortuary cult, another is the local production of Hopewell artifacts by specialized craftsmen, and a third is the role of exchange that Prufer thought was essential in maintaining the Hopewell cult.

In the Vacant Center pattern, Prufer envisioned swidden agriculturalists encircling but not directly occupying the geometric earthworks. Surveys in the Scioto (Prufer 1967) and Paint Creek Valleys of Ross County, Ohio, produced evidence that Middle Woodland domestic sites were small in size, modest in content, low in visibility and located away from, rather than in, or adjacent to, earthworks. In the conclusion of his report on the McGraw site, a domestic settlement on the Scioto River in Ross County, Ohio, he wrote that "the general settlement pattern during the Hopewellian period in Ohio seems to have been characterized by a system of semi-permanent shifting agricultural farmsteads or hamlets, clustered around a series of ceremonial centers and burial grounds with which a number of such settlements identified themselves" (Prufer 1965:137). This he contrasted with the prevailing view in which Hopewell settlements (if they could have been found) were large, adjacent to the earthworks, and based upon a nonagricultural economy.

There are at least three settlement types in Prufer's model: the hamlet, the earthwork with accompanying burial ground, and the specialized camp. Two other types are implied in his writing, elite residences and distinct burial grounds for common folk. But he does not define them formally, and we have elected not to include them. The pattern of settlement distribution, then, consists minimally of farm dwellings scattered across the landscape and centered on the vacant earthworks near which were located the camps of specialized activities.

A number of terminological ambiguities are present in Prufer's writing. Not the least of them is his use of the terms "farmstead," "hamlet," "village," and "household" interchangeably to refer to the same thing: the McGraw-like archaeological cluster. Also confusing is his use of "semi-permanent." At first glance this term suggests a short, unstable occupation span. But since he clearly refers to McGraw as semi-permanent while at the same time regarding this settlement to have been occupied for a generation, the term cannot mean what it seems. Instead, permanence takes on meaning in the context of shifting cultivation, the opposite of which is permanent field agriculture. In other papers (Dancey 1991; Pacheco 1988, 1993) we have chosen to use the term "hamlet" over all the others, and we will use it here in the same sense. It is flexible enough to allow variable numbers of households and variable populations, yet it expresses the concept of the community as being made up of a number of such social groups. Importantly, the common meaning of the term implies small size, below the scale of village. It also implies a residential group of related households (Blanton 1994).

Implied in most of Prufer's discussion is the idea that the contemporaneous hamlets around each earthwork constitute a community. In subsistence, hamlets are self-sufficient. Within the community, however, dependent relationships between farmers, craft specialists, and the Hopewell immigrants hold the households together. The earthwork is a focal point for community identity within the boundary of a distinct territory. Overall, this is an ecological concept and the McGraw report accordingly is subtitled "A Study in Hopewellian Dynamics." The community in Prufer's writing is an adaptational entity.

In order to evaluate and improve its heuristic value, we have generalized Prufer's pattern as shown in Fig. 1.2. Hamlets are shown as equidistant, with intersite spacing increasing toward the edge of a territory. Specialized camps are shown exclusively in the vicinity of the earthwork, although there would have been some in other parts of a territory as well. Because earthwork groups are located along river courses at equal intervals, territorial boundaries are shown as fixed on the valley floors but open on the margins facing upland terrain. Farming is conducted on the terraces and floodplain, hunting in the uplands.

In this depiction of the Ohio Hopewell settlement pattern, while no major domestic unit is considered to be located within an earthwork, these ritual places clearly are thought to have been the scenes of frequent human activity. They are vacant only in the sense of not having a permanent residential population. As Prufer explains in this volume (chapter 4), the term was in widespread use in Mesoamerican archaeology in the late 1950s and early 1960s in reference to Mayan ceremonial complexes. Subsequent field research has revealed Mayan pyramids and necropolises to have been surrounded by palaces and abundant, yet diffuse, domestic housing; thus the term "Vacant Center" no longer is used to refer to these complexes (Morley et al. 1983). In the Ohio area, however, similar evidence of directly associated residential remains has not been found and the term remains appropriate. Some may quibble that the evidence of ritual activity nullifies the term. We do not agree.

A Dispersed Sedentary Community Model

In updating the Prufer conception, we have drawn on advances in knowledge of the mortuary program, formation process theory, and perspectives on spatial organization to construct what we refer to as the Dispersed Sedentary Community model of Ohio Hopewell. Methodologically we view this more general construction as a case of model building within a hypothetico-deductive research strategy. Smith and Winterhalder (1992:12) point out that an "HD method distinguishes between the creative and evaluative components of scientific research; it acknowledges and draws our attention to differences between the processes of discovery and those of verification." Prufer's formulation of the Vacant Center pattern, as he explains in chapter 4, was a process of discovery that included initial steps toward verification. Our work is an attempt to continue the process of verification by employing a more formal hypothesis testing methodology. In keeping with the HD method, our model simplifies what, through advances in testing, undoubtedly will prove to be more complex.

The Model

According to this model, the foundation of the social order is the community, which consists of isolated households dispersed across the landscape in sedentary settlements. The dispersed pattern is thought to be the result of interaction between the sometimes contradictory demands of garden-level food production and intensive hunting and collecting. Such a pattern is not unlike Joseph Caldwell's Primary Forest Efficiency (Caldwell 1958). Residents of dispersed hamlets inhabit a niche made up of relatively homogeneous patches, usually defined by the regional drainage system. Along with household sites (hamlets) the settlement pattern consists of activity loci, specialized camps, public works, and symbolic places. At or near the center of the community is a ritual precinct—the sacred center of community life. Archaeologically, mortuary activities are most prominent in these central places, but other kinds of community affairs take place in them as well (as argued for Seip by Greber, chapter 8).

The household is a stable unit that does not vary significantly in size through time. However, the number of households may increase as children leave the parental household to form independent residences. Thus, variable household longevity creates a dynamic demographic history and a complex archaeo-logical record. This process is modeled in Fig. 1.3 to show how a local segment of the archaeological record of the Middle Woodland community might grow through time. Settlements A through E are inhabited for variable lengths of time. At any given time, therefore, one, two, or three settlements might be occupied by related households. Archaeologically, the number of settlement clusters increases through time, and because each one experiences different longevity, the quantity and condition of remains necessarily varies from one to another while preserving the basic residential layout.

Similarly, ritual precincts are spatially stable but have varied histories. They grow in size and complexity throughout the life of the community. A hypo-thetical history of a ceremonial complex is shown in Fig. 1.4. The process begins with construction of two burial mounds (Time 1). This is followed by the construction of a third burial mound that is encircled by an earthwork (Time 2). Subsequently (Times 3, 4, and 5), geometric earthworks are added, and finally (Time 6), these monuments are linked by an earthwork arc. Con-tinued use results in a size increase, a wider distribution of burials (mounded and other), and the joining of adjacent earthworks. Not shown are the ar-chaeological traces of activities related to earthwork and burial mound con-struction and use, as well as other activities of ritual significance.

Individual graves within the burial mound edifices exhibit differences in construction and in the kinds and amounts of accompanying artifacts. As Braun (1986) has observed, although graves often are spectacular, there is little reason to believe that anything more than individual achievement explains differences between them. He finds no evidence for institutionalized social classes. Along these same lines, it is highly likely that direct and down-the-road procurement rather than organized trade may explain the occurrence of nonlocal raw materials and craft products. This point was advanced years ago by Griffin (1965). Nevertheless, it seems unlikely that these burial mound sites are representative of the total population of the community using them, pro-moting a common belief that the burials are of elite members of the group, or leaders in some way. If that is true, the burial groups under the conjoined mounds at sites like Seip, Liberty, and Hopewell may represent the dominant lineages of several adjacent communities, as Greber argues (Greber 1979).

Above the scale of individual communities, functionally similar, contigu-ous communities may form peer polities (Braun 1986) anchored in centrally located public works, such as represented by the Hopewell, Newark, Ports-mouth, and Turner earthwork groups, to name a few. These polities are located at the intersection of major physiographic provinces and originate out of economic considerations. Thus, while adequate food resources can be found nearly everywhere within a community's catchment, long-term cycles of abundance and scarcity make for risks in the subsistence strategy. Intercommunity exchange balances out such fluctuations. Exchange also may link Hopewellian polities with communities located in peripheral regions. These are the communities that although dating to the Middle Woodland retain strong resemblance to the Adena Tradition (Greber 1991). At an even higher level are regional traditions and interaction spheres, such as envisioned by Caldwell (1958, 1964), which have given Hopewell its pan-eastern flavor (see also Prufer 1961).

A scheme such as this has the appearance of hierarchy: households are grouped to form communities, communities to form peer polities, and groups of polities to make up regional traditions with interaction spheres at the top. However, Seeman (1979) was unable to find support for the hierarchical model advanced by Struever and Houart (1972), and we have chosen to keep our model flat. If hierarchy is present, its form must have been sequential rather than simultaneous (Braun 1991; Johnson 1982).

Current Perspectives on the Hopewell Community

Let us turn now to the current state of knowledge about Hopewell in reference to the Dispersed Sedentary Community model. Of the many topics that need to be explored, the papers in this collection concern three: subsistence, settlement pattern, and earthwork function. This section is organized by these topics and identifies research bearing on each with particular reference to the chapters of this volume that contain expanded treatments of the topics.

Subsistence

An agricultural subsistence strategy had long been thought to feed Hopewellian communities, and maize was assumed to have been the principal staple (Willey 1966). Recent research has confirmed the agricultural status, but little evidence of tropical plants has been forthcoming. As a result of flotation sampling of settlement deposits beginning in the early 1970s (Watson 1976), it is now known that Hopewell subsistence included abundant wild foods and a suite of domesticated oily and starchy seed-bearing plants of local origin

(Watson 1988). These plants include sumpweed *(Iva annua),* sunflower *(Helianthus annuus),* chenopod *(Chenopodium berlandieri),* squash *(Cucurbita pepo),* erect knotweed *(Polygonum erectum),* maygrass *(Phalaris caroliniana),* and little barley *(Hordeum pusillum).*

Smith (1989) argues that this should be regarded as a farming adaptation centered on indigenous domesticated plants. He argues that if Hopewellians ate corn, it was only rarely, making this a nonmaize agricultural system. Maize was found in the midden deposit at McGraw (Cutler 1965), although suspicion has been cast on its stratigraphic integrity by an as-yet-unpublished AMS radiocarbon date (Ford 1987). Prufer comments on this discrepency in chapter 4. In chapter 6, Wymer summarizes current data on this question, arguing that the farming system had a major impact on the forest ecology, many aspects of which were managed by its human inhabitants at the time. And she sees dispersed households as the fundamental unit of settlement.

Settlement Pattern

A more complicated topic is settlement pattern, since no comprehensive regional surveys have been undertaken. Pacheco's review of reported sites in Licking County offers support for the Prufer model (Pacheco 1988), which he refers to as the Hamlet Hypothesis. In this region, most of the known, tested sites are small, functionally similar, structurally identical, and spatially dispersed. These are precisely the properties, or correlates, as he labels them, that Pacheco associates with the Prufer conception of Ohio Hopewell. Here and in other regions, in addition to the residential locations, special-purpose sites such as quarries, bladelet-use locations, ritual structures, and hunting camps have been documented. Furthermore, rockshelters within the rugged terrain of the Appalachian Plateau commonly contain Hopewellian components.

In chapter 5, Kozarek addresses the question of sedentism with data from the Jennison Guard site at the mouth of the Great Miami River. She argues for accepting the dispersed sedentary model of Hopewell settlement. This is an important Middle Woodland site which has been referred to also as the Whitacre Site (Whitacre and Whitacre 1986; see also Blosser 1989). Kozarek's analysis derives from her own master's thesis (Kozarek 1985) wherein she independently concluded on the basis of the evidence of chipped stone technology, faunal and floral remains, and the organization of cultural features that the local environment could and most likely did support individual households year round. Another Middle Woodland occupation has been documented 4 km from Jennison Guard in the stratified deposits of the Leonard Haag site (Reidhead and Limp 1974). Both are within view of Miami Fort which is considered a Hopewell site and which has Middle Woodland settlement debris near it (Fischer 1974).

In the unstable environment at the confluence of the Great Miami and the Ohio Rivers, where flooding undoubtedly forced the occupants of the Jennison Guard site from their home more than once, the archaeological record suggests a migration of settlement debris along the natural levee. The result is a series of similar, time-transgressive deposits, different segments of which have been sampled by Kozarek, Blosser and the Whitacres.

In chapter 2 Pacheco reports and analyzes the siteless survey coverage (Dunnell and Dancey 1983) of a tract of land encompassing a minor drainage channel on the floor of Raccoon Creek Valley in Licking County that includes the Murphy site (Dancey 1991; Pacheco 1993). Unlike the geomorphologically volatile setting of Jennison Guard, Pacheco's 30 ha sampling unit is on a stable outwash terrace well above flooding. What Pacheco documents on this terrace is dispersed population growth along the edge of a short, seasonal run draining into the Raccoon Creek Valley channel. The spacing of clustered chipped stone artifact clusters containing Middle Woodland artifacts conforms to the historical pattern of hamlet growth and abandonment described earlier in this chapter. Briefly, beginning with a founder household, offspring are depicted as establishing neolocal residence close to but spatially separate from the founder in a generational sequence that ultimately results in archaeological debris scattered along the entire length of the run. This process has been documented archaeologically and ethnographically in studies of Mayan house sites (Tourtellot 1983).

Theoretically, household history can vary radically from unit to unit. This is the reason for favoring use of the term "hamlet" for the fundamental Hopewell settlement unit. If a founder household is barren or suffers a catastrophe, the hamlet would consist of but one archaeological cluster. If it is highly fecund over many generations, a number of household clusters should result. "Hamlet," therefore, is preferred over "household" because it can accommodate variable numbers of spatially distinct households. "Farmstead" is rejected because it implies a function.

The methodological problem of contemporaneity, which plagues settlement archaeology in general, is magnified in the case of dispersed sedentary communities. The archaeological traces of the individual household units must be put in chronological order to enable study of demographic patterns, intracommunity interaction, and the processes of materials and artifact exchange. However, developing chronologies, even within hamlet groups, is severely hampered by the variable lifespans, often radically different, of the individual households. Pacheco confronts the problem in practice in summarizing his work on the Murphy Tract in chapter 2; Madsen tackles it theoretically in chapter 3.

Not far from the Liberty Works in the Salt Creek Valley is the Wade site reported on in chapter 13 by Church and Ericksen. Wade was discovered during a testing survey along a fiber optics cable right-of-way. The site is 15 km from Liberty Works and is discussed as a potential seasonal homestead occupied by members of a dispersed sedentary community that was not organized around a ritual precinct marked by earthworks.

Carskadden and Morton (chapter 14) summarize their twenty years of survey and excavation in Muskingum County. They marshal abundant evidence of small sites for the Early and Middle Woodland periods and document the presence of the dispersed sedentary pattern in the central Muskingum. The data reported for this county are the most extensive available and appear to support the community model's assumption that the archaeological record has the capability of mapping communities through time.

Earthworks

The earthwork sites (by which we mean sites with enclosures) are the most compelling of all Ohio Hopewellian archaeological remains. Within and around them are the graves and tombs of at least some of the Ohio Hopewell people. Most have been destroyed or degraded by deforestation, agriculture, road building, looting, and excavation, and it is often said that little or nothing remains for research. That this is not true can be seen in Greber's reexamination of portions of the Liberty Works (Greber 1983), along with Brown and Baby's excavations at Mound City (Brown 1979), among others. These projects, salvaging information from badly damaged deposits and poorly curated collections, have advanced understanding, yet there is even more to learn.

Reexamining the collections, notes, and a report of a highway survey conducted within the Newark Works in the early 1970s, Lepper and Yerkes attempt in chapter 7 to determine how two instances of settlement debris containing Middle Woodland diagnostics relate to Prufer's ideas. The sites are on terraces at the northeastern edge of the earthwork complex. The impoverished nature of the remains as well as the results of a microwear analysis suggest that both are the result of domestic activity related to the ritual use of the earthworks.

In attempting to understand the function of earthwork sites, it is important to address the question of the contemporaneity of the individual figures making up the enclosure groups. This is explored in chapter 8 by Greber, who takes a detailed look at the archaeological landscape in and around the Seip Works, as well as the neighboring Baum Works.

Coughlin and Seeman, in chapter 9, examine the distribution of surface-collected artifacts within and around the Liberty Works in southern Ross County on the lower Scioto River. The collection represents over twenty years of effort by the property owner, Mr. Robert Harness, who faithfully marked his finds with a number corresponding to the fields in which he collected the items. They conclude that with one exception the sample supports the Prufer pattern. The exception is a potential village that would have been occupied after active use and maintenance of the earthwork had passed, or very near the end of Ohio Hopewell.

Connolly, in chapter 10, reviews data from recent excavations of settlement debris adjacent to Fort Ancient to evaluate the nature of activity conducted on the margins of this classic earthwork complex. While finding that some of the settlement debris clusters to the northeast of the Fort Ancient Works fits Prufer's concept, he found the excavated structural remains immediately adjacent to the earthwork to be unique. Connolly argues that these remains imply some kind of specialized activity but are not complete enough to reveal what it was. Perhaps this is what dispersed "elite" residences or "caretaker" residences look like.

Based upon surface-collected and tested Middle Woodland sites near the Stubbs Mill Works on the Little Miami River in Warren County, Genheimer examines in chapter 11 the question of the density of settlement around an earthwork. His samples contain abundant bladelet technology debris that he uses to analyze functional variability among his clusters. As a result he is able to argue that clusters adjacent to the earthwork suggest specialized function while those away from, but within visibility of, Stubbs appear to represent households.

A contribution by Prufer (chapter 12), reporting an excavation at Fort Hill, represents an all-too-rare example of an attempt to learn something about the construction, maintenance, and rebuilding of an earthwork. Prufer refers to recent excavations of earthwork walls, such as conducted by Riordan (1984) at the Pollack Works in Greene County. In 1992 the Great Circle at Newark was trenched, revealing evidence of at least two episodes of construction (D. A. Wymer, Bloomsburg University, and B. T. Lepper, The Ohio Historical Society, personal communication), a finding duplicated at many other sites. The architectural design and constructional history of the segments of the earthworks potentially contributes to understanding of earthwork function.

Challenges to the Model

Because little systematic, regional scale field research has been conducted on the problem of Hopewell settlement pattern since Prufer's efforts in the 1960s, the door is open for alternative hypotheses. Some of these are alluded to or advocated explicitly in the present volume. As we see it, there are at least four possible hypotheses:

(1) Communities are nucleated and the major settlements are villages located adjacent to the earthworks (Nucleated Sedentary).
(2) Communities inhabit nucleated settlements adjacent to earthworks for part of the year but disperse seasonally to outlying camps (Semi-permanent Sedentary).
(3) Communities are residentially stable, but high-ranking households (chiefdoms?) reside in the shadows of the earthworks (Central Place).
(4) The households making up a community are seasonally mobile throughout the year (Seasonal Mobility).

In what follows we comment on these models in discussing nucleation, social type, and seasonality. These models are similar to the types formulated by Smith (1992).

Nucleation

The notion that Hopewell communities were nucleated has a long history, and Griffin (1967) retained this idea in his classic synthesis of eastern North American prehistory. Griffin's basis for claiming that nucleated communities were established adjacent to earthworks is based on references, largely anecdotal, in the older literature to settlement debris adjacent to earthworks. His argument, or supposition, is that the record of these villages either has since been destroyed or, if preserved, not investigated intensively. In Chapter 15 he remarks that recent excavations at the Fort Ancient site may provide support for this position. More recently, Converse (1993, 1994) has revived this claim in challenging the growing interest in Prufer's Vacant Center pattern. He cites collector reports of large Middle Woodland settlements in the Raccoon Creek Valley and incompletely reported observations on the Troyer site in western Franklin County, Ohio. Converse argues that a nucleated community is implied by the scale of construction of the earthworks and by the lavish nature of the grave goods accompanying Hopewell burials.

This notion, while it should remain a possibility, is rejected here for several reasons. First of all, surveys at several of the best-known earthwork sites have found no evidence of nucleated settlements coeval with the construction and use of the earthwork sites. For example, Lynott (1982) surveyed tracts adjacent to Mound City and found low-density clusters of Hopewellian artifacts but no nucleated village debris. In the final report of this work (Lynott and Monk 1985), he declared that the Prufer Vacant Center hypothesis had not been overturned by his survey. Similarly, a survey of the Hopewell site and environs by Seeman (1981) produced no evidence of nucleated sedentary village debris. In neither case has modern land use been intensive enough to have destroyed the evidence, at least not on the tracts surveyed. Nor does a nucleated settlement appear to be present at the Seip (Greber, chapter 8), Newark (Lepper and Yerkes, chapter 7), or Stubbs Works (Genheimer, chapter 11). Settlement debris is present northeast of the Fort Ancient Works (Connolly, chapter 10), but the size of individual clusters does not appear to exceed that of most Hopewell hamlets.

Another basis for rejecting this possibility comes from Rafferty's (1985) argument regarding the function of ceremonial precincts. Simply stated, if human populations are governed by principles of energy conservation, as are other animal species, there should be a direct relationship between the degree of local group (community in the anthropological sense) aggregation and the effort put into facilities for community interaction. At one extreme are communities of dispersed households whose members need a community center that is given or comes to contain permanent landscape features. At the other extreme is the aggregated set of households that, because they live in a single settlement, can dispense with construction of special facilities, eliminate certain classes of ritual altogether, and incorporate some elements of community center design into the domestic settlement. Along the continuum of aggregation (Leonard and Reed 1993) there are many variations. However, we feel that in the Middle Ohio Valley the data match the extreme patterns and that Rafferty's observation is appropriate. With nucleation of a community, many of the practices associated with the vacant ritual precinct are abandoned.

Finally, the assertion that Hopewellian villages have been observed adjacent to earthworks may result from a mistaken identity. Traditionally, the Middle Woodland period extends from circa 200 B.C. to A.D. 500 (Stoltman 1978), and earthwork construction appears to have terminated between A.D. 300–400. The artifacts associated with village scale residential debris represent styles prevalent after A.D. 400. Diagnostic ceramics from these villages include the thin-walled, cord-marked vessels of the Newtown Tradition (McMichael 1984), and diagnostic projectile points include the Lowe Flared Base type (Justice 1987). By considering settlements from late in the period as typical of the entire Middle Woodland, it is possible to say that Hopewellian groups were nucleated and lived in villages. However, a diachronic view suggests that within communities that once constructed earthworks in centrally located ritual precincts, nucleation postdates the construction, maintenance, and use of ceremonial and ritual architecture. Viewed in this way, it may not be legitimate to view it as Hopewell in the first place.

The analysis of Robert Harness's collection in the vicinity of the Liberty Works reported here by Coughlin and Seeman (chapter 9) provides an example of the above settlement pattern trend. Harness A, which Coughlin and Seeman suggest on the basis of the predominance of Lowe Flared Base projectile points constitutes a late Middle Woodland settlement, is large (ca. 5 ha) and may represent a nucleated community. Troyer (Converse 1993) may be another one of these villages, along with the Strait site in Fairfield County (Gehlbach 1993).

Social Type

It has been suggested by some archaeologists (Seeman 1979) that the Hopewell may have lived in chiefdom-type societies (Earle 1977). In such societies wealth is aggregated by a chief who redistributes portions to members of the community. Against this proposition is the failure to identify disparities in wealth among the known settlements. The well-defined postmold pattern of large posts at the Fort Ancient Works (Connolly, chapter 10) may be the remains of a durable structure built for a special purpose. However, the excavated strip did not expose enough of the postmold area to be able to infer the type of dwelling(s) represented.

A chiefdom pattern can be looked at as one kind of central place system because of the collecting practices of the paramount chief. Wealth is accompanied by increased interaction with members of the community, increased potential for aggregation of family members and laborers, and increased production of waste. Thus, a chief's residential unit predictably would be larger than those of the rest of the community. It also would be more visible and more complexly organized than the normal household deposit. There is no evidence of such disparities within the sample of known Middle Woodland habitation sites.

Seasonality

The foods that were eaten by these people were highly seasonal, and there is no question that seasonality played a role in their life cycle. However, the only two sites so far analyzed for plant and animal remains, McGraw (Prufer 1965) and Jennison Guard (Kozarek, chapter 5), point to year-round residence. Food waste, including most of the local food plants, was found in the middens and pit fill at these sites. Residentially, therefore, these are said to represent sedentary households.

Seasonality obviously governed the lives of these people, as it does ours today. The Hopewell data do not suggest that differential distribution of optimal foraging and residential resources forced them to relocate to different places throughout the year to be near available food and suitable shelter. In structure and content, the known assemblages are remarkably uniform, and, except for remote areas, tool types do not appear to be differentially distributed. Furthermore, rockshelter deposits containing Middle Woodland material usually are impoverished assemblages with little pit excavation or accumulation of organic material. In any case, for areas in the central part of the Till Plain, winter retreat to a rockshelter area would mean a long trek through neighbors' territories before establishing residence well away from home. Neither a logistics argument nor archaeological evidence favor a seasonal pattern for the Ohio Hopewell, although in saying so we want to be clear that this does not preclude the members of a household spending time away from home or seasonal plants and animals attracting people to them.

Conclusion

The chapters in this book present a much richer reporting of the above data, and more, in describing samples of Middle Woodland settlement debris from various locations throughout Ohio. Many of them use the Hamlet Hypothesis as articulated by Pacheco (1988) as their standard of evaluation as to whether or not they had recovered data on a McGraw-like settlement. As he expressed it, the Hamlet Hypothesis predicts that Middle Woodland settlement trash will conform to certain parameters, or "correlates." These correlates are: size at or below 1 ha, identical range of tools and tool-making debris, similar layout of archaeologically detected activity areas within a settlement, and higher densities in the vicinity of the ritual precincts. Adjusting for duration of occupation, controlling for the sample size-diversity relationship, and allowing for differential collecting by local people, the known, reported sites are mostly of the hamlet type and only a small percentage represent a specialized, seasonal activity.

The chapters in this book also represent a diversity of positions on the question of Hopewell settlement. Many abstain from taking a position due to lack of data either from their own settlement or from the region around it. Thus, even though we try to make a case for the dispersed sedentary nature of Hopewell settlement, there are many archaeologists taking a wait-and-see attitude and demanding more conclusive evidence. As did Olaf Prufer thirty years ago, we hope fervently that publication of this volume will stimulate systematic research on a local scale throughout the area of Ohio Hopewell distribution. Maybe then the issue can be laid to rest and research can proceed to investigate the dynamics of demographic change and adaptation.

Key to Site Numbers

1. Leonard Haag
2. Jennison Guard
3. Miami Fort
4. Turner
5. Stubbs Mill
6. Fort Ancient
7. Jonah's Run
8. Grimes
9. Fort Hill
10. Seip
11. Baum
12. Frankfort

13. Hopewell
14. Mound City
15. Hopeton
16. McGraw
17. Liberty
18. Newton, Morrison
19. Lynch
20. 33PK153
21. Rais-Swartz,
    Stanhope, Wise
22. Riddle
23. Wade

24. Ash Cave
25. Shaw
26. Marsh Run
27. DECCO
28. Pierce
29. Dow #2
30. Murphy
31. Newark Campus
32. NUWAY
33. Li-79
34. Digiondomenico
35. Locust

36. Apostolic #2
37. Dodson-Graham
38. Knight Hollow
39. Philo II
40. Cox
41. White Rocks
42. Raven Rocks
43. Fairchance
44. Gillies

1.1 Middle Woodland nonmortuary investigations.

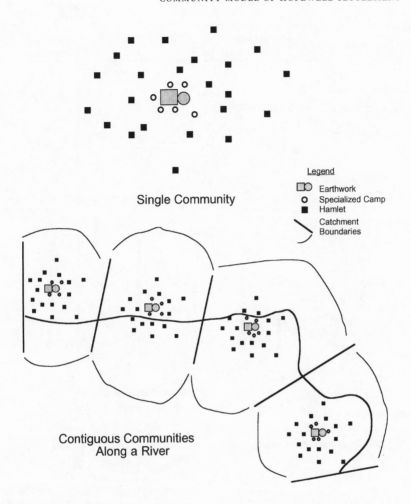

1.2 Generalized model of Hopewellian community structure.

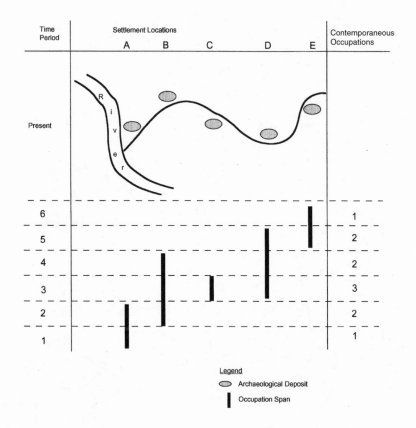

1.3 Model of hamlet evolution.

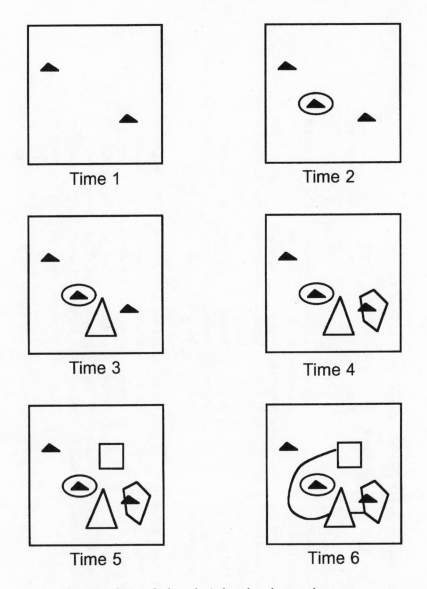

1.4 Growth in complexity of a hypothetical earthwork-mound group.

Table 1.1

Middle Woodland Habitation and Other Nonmortuary Sites in the Ohio Area

Associated Earthwork	Name	Topographic Setting	Site Type	Project Type	Size (ha)	Reference(s)
Till Plain: Lower Great Miami River						
Miami Fort	*Jennison Guard A	Floodplain	Hamlet	Academic	1.21	Kozarek 1987
Miami Fort	Jennison Guard B	Floodplain	Hamlet	Amateur	—	Whitacre 1986
Miami Fort	Jennison Guard C	Floodplain	Hamlet	Academic	—	Blosser 1989
Miami Fort	Headquarters	Hilltop	Hamlet	Contract	0.16	Lee and Vickery 1972
Miami Fort	Twin Mound Village	Hilltop	Hamlet	Contract	0.45	Fischer 1971
Miami Fort	Fort Miami EHA	Hilltop	Hamlet	Contract	0.34	Fischer 1968
Miami Fort	Leonard Haag	Terrace	Hamlet	Contract	—	Reidhead and Limp 1974
Miami Fort	Fort Miami WHA	Hilltop	Specialized	Contract	—	Fischer 1967
Till Plain: Middle Little Miami River						
Fort Ancient	*Fort Ancient Northeast	Upland	Hamlet	Academic	0.53	Connolly 1991
Fort Ancient	Fort Ancient 1146	Upland	Hamlet	Academic	0.5	Connolly 1991
Fort Ancient	Fort Ancient 519	Upland	Hamlet	Academic	—	Connolly 1991
Fort Ancient	Jonah's Run	Upland	Logistical	Contract	0.06	Brose and White 1979
Fort Ancient	Fort Ancient Middle Fort Pavement	Hilltop	Specialized	Academic	—	Connolly 1991
Fort Ancient	Fort Ancient Middle Fort Terrace	Hilltop	Specialized	Academic	—	Connolly 1991
Fort Ancient	Fort Ancient 518	Upland	Specialized	Academic	—	Connolly 1991

Table 1.1 Cont'd.

Stubbs Mill	*Hayner #3	Terrace	Hamlet	Academic	0.13	Genheimer 1984, 1992
Stubbs Mill	*Barnyard Smith	Terrace	Hamlet	Amateur	0.75	Genheimer 1984, 1992
Stubbs Mill	*Stubbs Mill Blade	Terrace	Specialized	Academic	4.8	Genheimer 1984, 1992
Stubbs Mill	*Smith	Terrace	Unknown	Academic	—	Genheimer 1984
Turner	Turner Blade	Terrace	Specialized	Academic	—	Greber et al. 1981
Till Plain: Middle and Upper Scioto River						
	Marsh Run	Upland	Hamlet	Academic	1.3	Aument and Gibbs 1991
Spruce Run	Pierce	Bluff	Hamlet	Contract	—	Drennan and Baby 1974
Orange	DECCO	Floodplain	Hamlet	Contract	0.74	Phagan 1977
Blue Grass: Brush Creek						
Fort Hill	Fort Hill Base	Floodplain	Hamlet	Academic	—	Baby and Goslin 1953
	Grimes	Terrace	Hamlet	Contract	0.12	Brose 1982
Glaciated Plateau: Central Scioto River and Paint Creek						
Hopewell	Hopewell Turtle Shell	Terrace	Specialized	Academic	0.06	Seeman 1981; Moorehead 1922
Hopewell	Hopewell West Village	Terrace	Specialized	Academic	0.8	Seeman 1981
Seip	Seip structures	Terrace	Specialized	Academic	0.15	Baby and Langlois 1979
Hopeton	Hopeton 1a6	Terrace	Unknown	Contract	—	Brose 1976:64
Hopeton	Hopeton 17A	Terrace	Unknown	Contract	—	Brose 1976:54–57
Hopeton	Hopeton 17B	Terrace	Unknown	Contract	—	Brose 1976:54
Hopeton	Hopeton 1a4	Terrace	Unknown	Contract	—	Brose 1976:64–67
Hopeton	Hopeton 1b	Terrace	Unknown	Contract	—	Brose 1976:60–62
Hopeton	Hopeton 7B	Terrace	Unknown	Contract	—	Brose 1976:57

Table 1.1 Cont'd.

Mound City	Mound City North	Terrace	Specialized	Academic	8.94	Lynott and Monk 1985
Mound City	Mound City Southeast	Terrace	Specialized	Academic	0.3	Brown 1982
Chillicothe II	McGraw 1	Floodplain	Hamlet	Academic	0.13	Prufer et al. 1964
Chillicothe II	McGraw 2	Floodplain	Hamlet	Academic	0.2	Prufer 1967:280
Unglaciated Plateau: Lower Scioto River, Salt Creek, and Lower Hocking River						
Liberty	Harness 28	Terrace	Unknown	Amateur	—	Greber et al. 1981
Liberty	Harness 6	Terrace	Unknown	Amateur	—	Greber et al. 1981
Liberty	Brown's Bottom 1	Terrace	Hamlet	Academic	0.3	Blank 1965
Liberty	Brown's Bottom 2	Terrace	Hamlet	Academic	0.3	Blank 1965
Liberty	Brown's Bottom 3	Terrace	Hamlet	Academic	0.2	Blank 1965
Liberty	Rus. Brown Mid. Ter. 2	Terrace	Hamlet?	Academic	—	Prufer 1967:284–286
Liberty	Rus. Brown Mid. Ter. 1	Terrace	Specialized	Academic	4.5	Prufer 1967:283–284
Liberty	Rus. Brown Mid. Ter. 3	Terrace	Specialized	Academic	—	Prufer 1967:286–287
Liberty	Rus. Brown Mid. Ter.	Terrace	Specialized	Academic	0.4	Prufer 1967:288
Liberty	Harness 14	Terrace	Specialized	Amateur	—	Greber et al. 1981
Liberty	Harness 18	Terrace	Specialized	Amateur	—	Greber et al. 1981
Liberty	Harness 25	Terrace	Specialized	Amateur	—	Greber et al. 1981
Piketon	33 PK 153	Floodplain	Hamlet	Contract	—	Baker 1994
(none)	Rais-Swartz Rockshelter	Steep valley	Logistical	Academic	0.006	Shane 1971
Rockshelter	Stanhope Cave	Steep valley	Logistical	Academic	0.01	Grunwald 1980
Rockshelter	Wise Rockshelter	Steep valley	Logisitical	Academic	—	Oplinger 1981
(none)	Newton Farm	Terrace	Hamlet	Academic	—	Prufer 1967:311–312

Table 1.1 Cont'd.

(none)	Morrison Farm	Terrace	Hamlet	Academic	—	Prufer 1967:305–306
(none)	*Wade	Terrace	Hamlet	Contract	0.9	Church 1989
(none)	Lynch 4	Terrace	Hamlet	Academic	0.81	Prufer 1967:310
(none)	Ash Cave	Steep valley	Logistical	Academic	—	Smith 1985
(none)	Harrison Rockshelter	Steep valley	Logistical	Amateur	—	Murphy 1989:379
Glaciated Plateau: Licking River Valley						
Hazlett	Dodson-Graham	Upland	Logistical	Amateur	0.47	Murphy and Morton 1984
Granville	Murphy I	Terrace	Hamlet	Academic	0.4	Dancey 1991
Granville	*Murphy III	Terrace	Hamlet	Academic	0.32	Pacheco 1993
Granville	*Murphy IV	Terrace	Hamlet	Academic	0.9	Pacheco 1993
Granville	*Murphy V	Terrace	Hamlet	Academic	0.21	Pacheco 1993
Granville	*Murphy VI	Terrace	Hamlet	Academic	0.33	Pacheco 1993
Granville	*Murphy Cluster 4	Terrace	Logistical	Academic	0.12	Pacheco 1993
Granville	*Murphy Cluster 5/8	Terrace	Logistical	Academic	0.15	Pacheco 1993
Granville	*Murphy Cluster 7	Terrace	Logistical	Academic	0.08	Pacheco 1993
Granville	*Murphy IVB/C1/C2	Terrace	Specialized	Academic	4.0	Pacheco 1993
Granville	Munson Springs	Terrace	Logistical	Academic	0.06	Pacheco 1991
Granville	Dow #2	Upland	Hamlet	Academic	0.32	Pacheco and Pickard 1992
Newark	Newark Campus	Terrace	Hamlet	Academic	—	Wymer 1987
Newark	NUWAY	Terrace	Hamlet	Academic	—	Pacheco 1991
Newark	Digiondomenico	Floodplain	Hamlet	Contract	—	Bernhardt 1979
Newark	*Li-79.1	Terrace	Specialized	Contract	0.65	Hale 1980, Lepper 1988

Table 1.1 Cont'd.

Newark	*Li-79.2	Terrace	Specialized	Contract	0.07	Hale 1980
(none)	Applewood	Terrace	Logistical	Contract	0.03	Hale 1979
(none)	Locust	Terrace	Hamlet	Academic	0.21	Seeman 1985
(none)	Apostolic #2 Rockshelter	Steep valley	Logistical	Contract	0.003	Pacheco 1983
Unglaciated Plateau: Central Muskingum River						
Dresden	*Cox A	Terrace	Hamlet	Amateur	0.27	Carskadden and Morton 1995
Dresden	*Cox B	Terrace	Hamlet	Amateur	0.21	Carskadden and Morton 1995
Dresden	*Cox C	Terrace	Hamlet	Amateur	0.36	Morton and Carskadden 1987
(none)	Gutridge Rockshelter	Steep valley	Logistical	Amateur	0.005	Pickenpaugh 1974
(none)	Knight Hollow Rockshelter	Steep valley	Logistical	Amateur	0.005	Felumlee 1983
(none)	Shaw Rockshelter	Steep valley	Logistical	Academic	—	Shane and Murphy 1967
(none)	Philo II	Terrace	Hamlet	Amateur	—	Morton 1989
Unglaciated Plateau: Upper Ohio River						
Grave Creek	Fairchance	Floodplain	Hamlet	Contract	0.40	Hemmings 1977
(none)	Raven Rocks Rockshelter	Steep valley	Logistical	Academic	0.07	Prufer 1981
(none)	White Rocks Rockshelter	Steep valley	Logistical	Academic	0.03	Ormerod 1980
Glaciated Plateau						
(none)	Gillies Rockshelter	Steep valley	Logistical	Academic	0.09	Bernhardt 1973

*Site discussed in detail in this book.

Notes: Published and contract report literature only.

The sites are grouped by geographic region and their spatial relationship to an earthwork.

Table 1.2
The Distribution of Known Middle Woodland Habitation Sites by Region, Environmental Setting, and Settlement Type

Region	N	Environmental Settings						Settlement Type				Other Data	
		Hilltop	Upland	Bluff	Terrace	Flood-Plain	Steep Valley	Hamlet	Special-ized	Logis-tical	Un-known	Rock-shelter	Struc-ture
Great Miami	8	4	—	—	1	3	—	7	1	—	—	—	2
Little Miami	12	2	5	—	5	—	—	5	5	1	1	—	2
Middle Scioto	1	—	1	1	—	—	—	1	—	—	—	—	1
Upper Scioto	2	—	1	—	—	—	—	2	—	—	—	—	2
Brush Creek	2	—	—	—	1	1	—	2	—	—	—	—	2
Paint Creek	3	—	—	—	3	—	—	—	3	—	—	—	1
Central Scioto	10	—	—	—	8	2	—	2	2	—	6	—	—
Lower Scioto	20	—	—	—	16	1	3	9	6	3	2	3	1
Salt Creek	1	—	—	—	—	—	1	—	—	1	—	1	—
Hocking	1	—	—	—	—	—	1	—	—	1	—	1	—
Licking	19	—	2	—	16	1	—	10	3	6	—	—	4
Upper Licking	1	—	—	—	—	—	1	—	—	1	—	1	—
Central Muskingum	7	—	—	—	4	—	3	4	—	3	—	3	2
Upper Ohio	3	—	—	—	—	1	2	1	—	2	—	2	1
Cuyahoga	1	—	—	—	—	—	1	—	—	1	—	1	—
TOTAL	91	6	9	1	54	9	12	43	20	19	9	12	18

Table 1.3
Middle Woodland C14 Dates from Ohio Sites

Site Name	Date	Date B.P.	Lab No.	Context	Reference	Calibrated Date
Cox B	A.D. 30	1920±90	I-16023	Feature 24	8	A.D. 77 (17 B.C.–A.D. 194)
Cox C	100 B.C.	2050±80	I-13963	Feature 2	17	92 B.C. (178 B.C.–A.D. 22)
DECCO	A.D. 370	1580±50	DIC-1077	Interior post 40	20	A.D. 441 (A.D. 415–544)
DECCO	A.D. 270	1680±45	DIC-1074	Wall post	20	A.D. 381 (A.D. 262–406)
DECCO	A.D. 250	1700±50	DIC-1075	Pit feature 3	20	A.D. 343 (A.D. 253–406)
DECCO	A.D. 240	1710±50	DIC-1078	Pit feature 1	20	A.D. 268, 273, 338 (A.D. 249–399)
Fairchance	A.D. 155	1795±80	UGA 1279	Feature 6	13	A.D. 31 (A.D. 120–336)
Fairchance	A.D. 135	1815±120	UGA 1280	Feature 12	13	A.D. 217 (A.D. 70–350)
Fort Ancient Village	A.D. 10	1960±80	Beta-15161	Feature 4/88	11	A.D. 28, 45, 51 (54 B.C.–A.D. 119)
Gillies Cave	A.D. 205	1745±130	GX-2455	Feature 2	3	A.D. 260, 290, 330 (A.D. 131–429)
Grimes	A.D. 520	1430±110	DIC-861	Feature 4	5	A.D. 640 (A.D. 544–681)
Heckleman	A.D. 470	1480±105	GX-1744	Feature 13	22	A.D. 600 (A.D. 448–661)
Jennison Guard	A.D. 290	1660±70	WIS-1745	Feature 2-top	4	A.D. 398 (A.D. 261–435)
Jennison Guard	A.D. 150	1800±70	WIS-1744	Feature 2-base	4	A.D. 227 (A.D. 123–328)
Jennison Guard	A.D. 140	1810±70	WIS-1746	Feature 3-base	4	A.D. 221 (A.D. 113–328)
Jonah's Run	A.D. 270	1680±400	DIC-887	F.2A/postmold	6	A.D. 381 (110 B.C.–A.D. 690)
Leonard Haag	A.D. 40	1910±225	GX-2929	Feature	25	A.D. 82 (180 B.C.–A.D. 380)
Leonard Haag	A.D. 335	1615±150	GX-2928	Feature	24	A.D. 422 (A.D. 250–600)
Leonard Haag	A.D. 280	1670±100	DIC-242	Burnt mat	25	A.D. 391 (A.D. 240–450)
Li 79.1	A.D. 105	1845±60	Beta 208062	Feature 10	14	A.D. 137 (A.D. 84–236)
Li 79.1	A.D. 310	1640±90	Beta-58450	Feature 1	16	A.D. 420 (A.D. 267–275)
Locust	A.D. 151	1799±118	SMU 1868	Feature 7	7	A.D. 216 (A.D. 59–364)

Table 1.3 Cont'd

Site	Date	Lab no.	Context	Age	n	Calibrated date
Locust	A.D. 115	ETH-3070	Feature 13	1853±80	7	A.D. 172 (A.D. 59–254)
Locust	A.D. 20	ETH-3487	Feature 19	1930±100	7	A.D. 60 (82 B.C.–A.D. 173)
Marsh Run	A.D. 200	Beta-48083	F.147/hearth	1750±70	1	A.D. 260, 290, 320 (A.D. 229–398)
Marsh Run	A.D. 60	Beta-48080	F.7/hearth	1890±70	1	A.D. 120 (A.D. 65–231)
Marsh Run	200 B.C.	Beta-48084	F.3/postmold	2150±70	1	180 B.C. (353–302 B.C.)
Marsh Run	380 B.C.	Beta-48082	F.128/hearth	2330±120	1	390 B.C. (518–346 B.C.)
McGraw	A.D. 481	OWU 61	Unit C-1/midden	1469±65	23	A.D. 601 (A.D. 541–646)
McGraw	A.D. 440	UCLA 679c	Unit C-1/midden	1510±80	23	A.D. 554 (A.D. 434–632)
McGraw	A.D. 435	OWU 62	Unit D-2/midden	1515±166	23	A.D. 551 (A.D. 380–660)
McGraw	A.D. 280	UCLA 705	Unit B-1/midden	1670±80	23	A.D. 391 (A.D. 253–435)
McGraw	A.D. 230	M 1558	Unit D/midden	1720±140	21	A.D. 265, 281, 333 (A.D. 130–440)
McGraw	A.D. 190	UCLA 679b	Unit D-1/midden	1760±80	23	A.D. 249 (A.D. 140–382)
McGraw	A.D. 160	ETH-2883	Unit D-1/residue	1790±115	7	A.D. 233 (A.D. 80–390)
McGraw	A.D. 140	UCLA 679a	Unit D-1/midden	1810±80	23	A.D. 221 (A.D. 113–328)
McGraw	A.D. 120	ETH-2884	Unit C-1/residue	1830±135	7	A.D. 146, 164, 190 (A.D. 20–350)
McGraw	30 B.C.	ETH-2885	Unit D-1/residue	1980±100	7	A.D. 15 (110 B.C.–A.D. 120)
McGraw	230 B.C.	UCLA 685	Unit B-1/bone	2180±80	23	200 B.C. (368–101 B.C.)
Murphy I	A.D. 210	Beta-16621	Feature 130	1740±60	10	A.D. 260, 280, 330 (A.D. 238–398)
Murphy I	A.D. 190	Beta-15520	Feature 100A	1760±55	10	A.D. 260, 300, 320 (A.D. 231–379)
Murphy I	A.D. 130	AA 2823	F.81/residue	1820±80	10	A.D. 230 (A.D. 118–264)
Murphy I	A.D. 60	Beta-16619	Feature 14/strat 2	1890±110	10	A.D. 120 (A.D. 11–249)
Murphy I	90 B.C.	Beta-15267	Feature 14/strat 3	2040±80	10	50 B.C. (169 B.C.–A.D. 51)
Murphy III	285 B.C.	Beta-36274	F.1/nutshell	2235±65	19	360, 280, 250 B.C. (385 B.C.–192)
Murphy III	360 B.C.	Beta-36277	Feature 1	2310±70	19	390 B.C. (403 B.C.–360)
Murphy III	410 B.C.	Beta-36272	Feature 2	2360±90	19	400 B.C. (518 B.C.–372)

Table 1.3 Cont'd

Newark Campus	40 B.C.	1990±100	ETH 3074	F.4/residue	7	11 B.C. (127 B.C.–A.D. 84)
NUWAY	100 B.C.	2050±70	Beta-190411	Feature 94	19	40 B.C. (157 B.C.–135)
Rais Rockshelter	A.D. 280	1670±95	GX 1245	Midden 15"	26	A.D. 391 (A.D. 246–444)
Rais Rockshelter	A.D. 360	1590±85	GX 1452	Midden	22	A.D. 435 (A.D. 385–558)
Rais Rockshelter	A.D. 395	1555±155	OWU 252	Midden 10"	18	A.D. 532 (A.D. 268–650)
Seip structure	A.D. 590	1360±105	DAL-281	Feature 13/house 5	12	A.D. 660 (A.D. 600–770)
Seip structure	A.D. 350	1600±60	DIC-289	House 4/postmold	12	A.D. 429 (A.D. 397–540)
Seip structure	A.D. 280	1670±55	DIC-281	Feature 7/house 4	2	A.D. 410 (A.D. 269–272)
Seip structure	A.D. 230	1720±80	DAL-116	Midden/houses 1–3	12	A.D. 265, 281, 333 (A.D. 227–412)
Seip structure	A.D. 90	1860±85	DAL-280	Feature 5/house 7	12	A.D. 128 (A.D. 61–242)
Seip Locale 20	A.D. 470	1480±55	DIC-1724	Feature 4/midden	12	A.D. 600 (A.D. 545–644)
Seip Locale 20	A.D. 350	1600±45	DIC-1725	Feature 2	12	A.D. 439 (A.D. 416–540)
Seip Locale 23	A.D. 430	1520±70	DIC-2471	Burned area/plaza	12	A.D. 550 (A.D. 444–629)
Wade	A.D. 150	1800±100	Beta-29446	Feature 3	9	A.D. 185, 186, 228 (A.D. 80–377)
Wade	100 B.C.	2050±170	Beta-29447	Feature 2/upper	9	91, 79, 71 B.C. (356 B.C.–A.D. 127)
Wade	220 B.C.	2170±120	Beta-29448	Feature 2/lower	9	341, 325, 204 B.C. (390–72 B.C.)

References

1. Aument and Gibbs 1991
2. Baby and Langlois 1979
3. Bernhardt 1973
4. Blosser 1986
5. Brose 1982a
6. Brose and White 1979
7. Carr, personal communication
8. Carskadden, personal communication
9. Church 1989
10. Dancey 1991
11. Essenpreis and Connolly 1989
12. Greber 1983
13. Hemmings 1977
14. Lepper 1988
15. Lepper 1989
16. Lepper and Yerkes, chapter 7
17. Morton and Carskadden 1987
18. Ogden and Hay 1969
19. Pacheco 1991
20. Phagan 1977
21. Prufer and McKenzie 1967
22. Prufer and McKenzie 1975
23. Prufer 1965
24. Reidhead 1981
25. Reidhead and Limp 1974
26. Shane 1971

References

Aument, B. W., and K. Gibbs
    1991   *Phase III and IV Data Recovery Survey of 33Fr895 and 33Fr901 on the Wal-Mart Property in Grove City, Franklin County, Ohio.* Archaeological Services Consultants, Columbus. Report submitted to Wal-Mart Stores, Inc.

Baby, R. S., and R. M. Goslin
    1953   Archaeological Field Work 1953. *Museum Echoes* 26(10):79–80.

Baby, R. S., and S. M. Langlois
    1979   Seip Mound State Memorial: Nonmortuary Aspects of Hopewell. In *Hopewell Archaeology: The Chillicothe Conference,* edited by D. Brose and N. Greber, pp. 16–18. Kent State University Press, Kent, Ohio.

Baker, S. W.
    1994   James Denny's Fieldnotes Regarding Piketon's Graded Way. *Ohio Archaeologist* 44(2):21–23.

Bernhardt, J. E.
    1973   *Gillie's Rockshelter: A Late Woodland Phase in Summit County, Ohio.* Unpublished master's thesis, Kent State University, Kent, Ohio.
    1979   *An Archaeological Survey of Licking County Route 343-0.00, Heath, Ohio. Phase IV.* Ohio Historical Society. Report submitted to the Ohio Department of Transportation, Columbus.

Blank, J. E.
    1965   The Brown's Bottom Site, Ross County, Ohio. *Ohio Archaeologist* 15(1):16–21.

Blanton, R. E.
    1994   *Houses and Households: A Comparative Study.* Plenum, New York.

Blosser, J. K.
    1989   *Mica Working at the Jennison Guard Site: A Middle Woodland Village in Southeastern Indiana.* Unpublished master's thesis, University of Cincinnati.

Braun, D. P.
    1986   Midwestern Hopewellian Exchange and Supralocal Interaction. In *Peer Polity Interaction and Socio-Political Change,* edited by C. Renfrew and J. Cherry, pp. 117–126. Cambridge University Press, New York.
    1991   Are There Cross-Cultural Regularities in Tribal Social Practices? In *Between Bands and States,* edited by S. Gregg, pp. 423–444. Center for Archaeological Investigations, Southern Illinois University, Carbondale.

Brose, D. S.
    1976   *An Historical and Archaeological Evaluation of the Hopeton Works, Ross County, Ohio.* Cleveland Museum of Natural History. Report submitted to the National Park Service.
    1982   The Archaeological Investigation of a Fort Ancient Community Near Ohio Brush Creek, Adams County, Ohio. *Kirtlandia* 34:69.

Brown, J. A.

1979   Charnel Houses and Mortuary Crypts: Disposal of the Dead in the Middle
        Woodland Period. In *Hopewell Archaeology: The Chillicothe Conference,* ed-
        ited by D. Brose and N. Greber, pp. 211–219. Kent State University Press,
        Kent, Ohio.

1982   Mound City and the Vacant Ceremonial Center. Paper presented at 47th
        Annual Meeting of the Society for American Archaeology, Minneapolis.

Caldwell, J. R.

1958   *Trend and Tradition in the Prehistory of the Eastern United States.* Memoir
        No. 88. American Anthropological Association, Washington, D.C.

1964   Interaction Spheres in Prehistory. In *Hopewellian Studies,* edited by J. R.
        Caldwell and R. L. Hall, pp. 133–143. Scientific Papers Vol. 12. Illinois State
        Museum, Springfield.

Church, F.

1989   *Phase IV Excavation at 33Vi315, Vinton County, Ohio.* Archaeological Ser-
        vices Consultants, Columbus. Report submitted to Bucher, Willis, and
        Ratcliff, Chillicothe, Ohio.

Connolly, R. P.

1991   *Prehistoric Site Structure at the Fort Ancient State Memorial: New Evidence
        from Lithic Analysis.* Unpublished master's thesis, Department of Anthro-
        pology, University of Cincinnati.

Converse, R. N.

1993   The Troyer Site: A Hopewell Habitation Site, and a Secular View of Hopewell
        Villages. *Ohio Archaeologist* 43(3):4–12.

1994   The Harness Hopewell Village Sites. *Ohio Archaeologist* 44(1):4–9.

Cutler, H. C.

1965   Cultivated Plants. In *The McGraw Site: A Study in Hopewellian Dynamics,*
        edited by O. Prufer, pp. 107–112. Scientific Publications, n.s. Vol. 4, No. 1.
        Cleveland Museum of Natural History.

Dancey, W. S.

1991   A Middle Woodland Settlement in Central Ohio: A Preliminary Report on
        the Murphy Site (33Li212). *Pennsylvania Archaeologist* 61(2):37–72.

Drennen, B. C., and R. S. Baby

1974   *Excavations of Pierce Site (22Di25) and Alum Creek Reservoir Mound (33Di21),
        Delaware County.* Ohio Historical Society, Columbus. Report submitted to
        the National Park Service.

Dunnell, R. C., and W. S. Dancey

1983   The Siteless Survey: A Regional Scale Data Collection Strategy. In *Advances
        in Archaeological Method and Theory, Vol. 6,* edited by M. B. Schiffer, pp. 267–
        288. Academic Press, New York.

Earle, T. K.
1987   Chiefdoms in Archaeological and Ethnohistorical Perspective. *Annual Review of Anthropology* 16:279–308.
Essenpreis, P. S., and R. P. Connolly
1989   Hopewellian Habitation at the Fort Ancient Site, Ohio. Paper presented at the 46th Southeastern Archaeological Conference, Tampa, Florida.
Felumlee, G.
1983   Report on the Knight Hollow Rockshelter. *Ohio Archaeologist* 33(4):22–28.
Fischer, F. W.
1968   *A Survey of the Archaeological Remains of Shawnee Lookout Park.* Report submitted to the Miami Purchase Association and the Hamilton County Park District.
1971   *Preliminary Report on the University of Cincinnati Archaeological Investigations, 1970.* Ms. on file, Department of Anthropology, University of Cincinnati.
1974   *Early and Middle Woodland Settlement, Subsistence and Population in the Central Ohio Valley.* Ph.D. dissertation, Washington University, St. Louis. University Microfilms, Ann Arbor.
Ford, R. I.
1987   Dating Early Maize in the Eastern United States. Paper presented at the Annual Meeting of the American Association for the Advancement of Science, Chicago.
Gehlbach, D. L.
1993   The Strait Site Revisited. *Ohio Archaeologist* 43(4):30–31.
Genheimer, R. A.
1984   A Systematic Examination of Middle Woodland Settlements in Warren County, Ohio. Report submitted to Ohio Historic Preservation Office, Columbus.
1992   *Bladelets at the Stubbs Earthwork Cluster: An Examination of Middle Woodland Settlement in the Little Miami River Valley.* Unpublished master's thesis, Department of Anthropology, University of Cincinnati.
Greber, N.
1979   A Comparative Study of Site Morphology and Burial Patterns at Edwin Harness Mound and Seip Mounds 1 and 2. In *Hopewell Archaeology: The Chillicothe Conference,* edited by D. Brose and N. Greber, pp. 27–38. Kent State University Press, Kent, Ohio.
1983   *Recent Excavations at the Edwin Harness Mound, Liberty Works, Ross County, Ohio.* Special Paper No. 5, Midcontinental Journal of Archaeology. Kent State University Press, Kent, Ohio.
1991   A Study of Continuity and Contrast Between Central Scioto Adena and Hopewell Sites. *West Virginia Archaeologist* 43(1&2):1–26.

Griffin, J. B.

    1965   Hopewell and the Dark Black Glass. *Michigan Archaeologist* 11(3-4):115–55.

    1967   Eastern North American Archeology: A Summary. *Science* 156:175–191.

Grunwald, R. R.

    1980   *Stanhope Cave: A Late Woodland Occupation in Jackson County, Ohio.* Unpublished master's thesis, Department of Anthropology, Kent State University, Kent, Ohio.

Hale, E. E.

    1979   *Archaeological Survey Report: Applewood Village, Newark, Ohio, Construction Project.* Wallick Construction Company. Report submitted to the Ohio Department of Transportation, Columbus.

    1980   *Archaeological Survey Report: Phase III, LIC. 79—12.55.* Report submitted to Eriksson Engineering Ltd., Columbus, Ohio.

Hemmings, E. T.

    1977   The Fairchance Site: Middle Woodland Settlement and Subsistence in the Upper Ohio Valley. *West Virginia Archaeologist* 21:41–55.

Johnson, G. A.

    1982   Organizational Structure and Scalar Stress. In *Theory and Explanation in Archaeology,* edited by C. Renfrew, M. J. Rowlands, and B. A. Segraves, pp. 389–422. Academic Press, New York.

Justice, N. D.

    1987   *Stone Age Spear and Arrow Points of the Midcontinental and Eastern United States.* Indiana University Press, Bloomington.

Kozarek, S. E.

    1987   *A Hopewellian Homestead in the Ohio River Valley.* Unpublished master's thesis, Department of Anthropology, University of Cincinnati.

Lee, A. M., and K. D. Vickery

    1972   Salvage Excavations at the Headquarters Site, a Middle Woodland Village Burial Area in Hamilton County, Ohio. *Ohio Archaeologist* 22(1):3–11.

Leonard, R. D., and H. E. Reed

    1993   Population Aggregation in the Prehistoric American Southwest: A Selectionist Model. *American Antiquity* 58:648–661.

Lepper, B. T.

    1988   An Historical Review of Archaeological Research at the Newark Earthworks. *Journal of the Steward Anthropological Society* 18:118–140.

    1989   Radiocarbon Date for a Hopewellian Habitation Site Associated with the Newark Earthworks. *Ohio Archaeologist* 39(4):12–13.

Lynott, M. J.

    1982   *An Archaeological Investigation of an Area Adjacent to Mound City Group National Monument: A Preliminary Report.* Midwest Archaeological Center, National Park Service, Lincoln, Nebraska.

Lynott, M. J., and S. Monk

    1985   *Mound City, Ohio, Archeological Investigations.* Occasional Studies in Anthropology No. 12. Midwest Archeological Center, National Park Service, Lincoln, Nebraska.

McMichael, E. V.

    1984   Type Descriptions for Newtown Series Ceramics. In *The Pyles Site (15Ms28), a Newtown Village in Mason County Kentucky,* edited by J. A. Railey, pp. 132–135. Occasional Paper 1. W. S. Webb Archaeological Society, Lexington, Kentucky. (Reprint of mimeographed original circulated in the early 1960s.)

Moorehead, W. K.

    1922   *The Hopewell Mound Group of Ohio.* Anthropological Series, Vol. 6, No. 5. Field Museum of Natural History, Chicago.

Morley, S. G., G. W. Brainerd, and R. J. Sharer

    1983   *The Ancient Maya.* 4th ed. Stanford University Press, Stanford, California.

Morton, J. F.

    1989   Middle and Late Woodland Components at the Philo II Site, Muskingum County, Ohio. *Ohio Archaeologist* 39(2):61–69.

Morton, J. F., and J. Carskadden

    1987   Test Excavation at an Early Hopewellian Site Near Dresden, Ohio. *Ohio Archaeologist* 37(1):8–12.

Murphy, J. L., and J. Morton

    1984   Dodson "Village": A Flint Ridge Habitation Site. *Ohio Archaeologist* 34(3):23–26.

Oplinger, J.

    1981   *Wise Rock Shelter: Multicomponent Site in Jackson County, Ohio.* Kent State Research Papers in Archaeology, No. 2. Kent State University, Kent, Ohio.

Ormerod, D.

    1980   *White Rocks Rockshelter.* Unpublished master's thesis, Department of Anthropology, Kent State University, Kent, Ohio.

Pacheco, P. J.

    1988   Ohio Middle Woodland Settlement Variability in the Upper Licking River Drainage. *Journal of the Steward Anthropological Society* 18:87–117.

    1991   Woodland Period Archaeology in Central Ohio: LCALS Contributions. *Ohio Archaeological Council Newsletter* 3(3):4–9.

    1993   *Ohio Hopewell Settlement Patterns: An Application of the Vacant Center Model to Middle Woodland Period Intracommunity Settlement Variability in Upper Licking River Valley.* Unpublished Ph.D. dissertation, Department of Anthropology, The Ohio State University, Columbus.

Pacheco, P. J., and W. H. Pickard

    1992   A Laterally Hafted Ohio Hopewell Bladelet From Dow Chemical #2 (33Li302). *Ohio Archaeologist* 42(2):12–15.

Phagan, C. J.

    1977   *Intensive Archaeological Survey of the S.R. 315 Wastewater Treatment Facility Location Known as the DECCO-1 Site (33Di28)*. Progress Report submitted to the Board of County Commissioners, Delaware County, Ohio.

Pickenpaugh, M. E.

    1974   The Fred Gutridge Cave. *The Redskin* 9(2):60–65.

Prufer, O. H.

    1961   *The Hopewell Complex of Ohio*. Unpublished Ph.D. dissertation, Peabody Museum, Harvard University, Cambridge, Massachusetts.

    1964a The Hopewell Cult. *Scientific American* 211(6): 90–102.

    1964b The Hopewell Complex of Ohio. In *Hopewellian Studies,* edited by J. R. Caldwell and R. L. Hall, pp. 35–83. Scientific Papers, Vol. 12, No. 2. Illinois State Museum, Springfield.

    1965   *The McGraw Site: A Study in Hopewellian Dynamics*. Scientific Publications, n.s. Vol. 4, No. 1. Cleveland Museum of Natural History.

    1967   The Scioto Valley Archaeological Survey. In *Studies in Ohio Archaeology,* edited by O. Prufer and D. McKenzie, pp. 267–328. Kent State University Press, Kent, Ohio.

    1968   *Ohio Hopewell Ceramics: An Analysis of the Extant Collections*. Anthropological Papers, No. 33. Museum of Anthropology, University of Michigan, Ann Arbor.

    1981   *Raven Rocks, a Specialized Late Woodland Rockshelter Occupation in Belmont County, Ohio*. Kent State Research Papers in Archaeology, No. 1. Kent State University Press, Kent, Ohio.

Prufer, O. H., and D. H. McKenzie (editors)

    1967   *Studies in Ohio Archaeology*. Kent State University Press, Kent, Ohio.

Rafferty, J. E.

    1985   The Archaeological Record of Sedentariness: Recognition, Development, and Implications. In *Advances in Archaeological Method and Theory, Vol. 8,* edited by M. B. Schiffer, pp. 113–156. Academic Press, New York.

Reidhead, V. A.

    1981   *A Linear Programming Model of Prehistoric Subsistence Optimization: A Southeastern Indiana Example*. Prehistory Research Series, Vol. 6, No. 1, pp. 1–277. Indiana Historical Society, Indianapolis.

Reidhead, V. A., and W. F. Limp

    1974   The Haag Site (12Di9): A Preliminary Report. *Indiana Archaeology Bulletin* 1:4–18.

Riordan, R. V.

    1984   *The Pollock Works: Report on the 1982 and 1983 Field Seasons*. Reports in Anthropology No. 7. Laboratory of Anthropology, Wright State University, Dayton, Ohio.

Seeman, M. F.

1979   *The Hopewell Interaction Sphere: The Evidence for Interregional Trade and Structural Complexity.* Prehistory Research Series, Vol. 5, No. 2, pp. 235–438. Indiana Historical Society, Indianapolis.

1981   *An Archaeological Survey of the Hopewell Site (33R027) and Vicinity, Ross County, Ohio.* Kent State University, Kent, Ohio. Report submitted to the Ohio Historic Preservation Office, Columbus.

1985   *The Locust Site (33Mu160): The 1983 Test Excavation of a Multicomponent Workshop in East Central Ohio.* Kent State Research Papers in Archaeology, No. 7, Kent State University Press, Kent, Ohio.

Shane, O. C. I.

1967   A Survey of the Hocking Valley, Ohio. In *Studies in Ohio Archaeology,* edited by O. H. Prufer and D. H. McKenzie, pp. 329–356. Kent State University Press, Kent, Ohio.

Smith, B. D.

1985   *Chenopodium berlandieri* ssp. *jonesianum:* Evidence for a Hopewellian Domesticate from Ash Cave, Ohio. *Southeastern Archaeology* 4:107–133.

1989   Origins of Agriculture in Eastern North America. *Science* 246:1566–1571.

1992   Hopewellian Farmers of Eastern North America. In *Rivers of Change,* by B. D. Smith, pp. 201–247. Smithsonian Institution Press, Washington, D.C.

Smith, E. A., and B. Winterhalder (editors)

1992   *Evolutionary Ecology and Human Behavior.* Aldine de Gruyter, New York.

Stoltman, J. B.

1978   Temporal Models in Prehistory: An Example from Eastern North America. *Current Anthropology* 19:703–746.

Struever, S., and G. L. Houart

1972   An Analysis of the Hopewell Interaction Sphere. In *Social Exchange and Interaction,* edited by E. Wilmsen, pp. 47–79. Anthropological Papers 46. Museum of Anthropology, University of Michigan, Ann Arbor.

Tourtellot, G.

1983   An Assessment of Classic Maya Household Composition. In *Prehistoric Settlement Patterns,* edited by E. Z. Vogt and R. M. Leventhal, pp. 35–54. University of New Mexico Press, Albuquerque.

Watson, P. J.

1976   In Pursuit of Prehistoric Subsistence: A Comparative Account of Some Contemporary Methods. *Midcontinental Journal of Archaeology* 1:77–100.

1988   Prehistoric Gardening and Agriculture in the Midwest and Midsouth. In *Interpretations of Culture Change in the Eastern Woodlands During the Late Woodland Period,* edited by R. Yerkes, pp. 39–67. Occasional Papers in Anthropology, Vol. 3. The Ohio State University, Department of Anthropology, Columbus.

Whitacre, D., and B. Whitacre

1986   The Whitacre Site (12D246). *Ohio Archaeologist* 36(3):24–36.

Willey, G. R.

1966   *An Introduction to American Archaeology, Vol. 1: North and Middle America.* Prentice-Hall, Englewood Cliffs, New Jersey.

Wymer, D. A. (editor)

1986   *Cultural Resource Assessment of the Black Hand Gorge Nature Preserve, Licking County, Ohio.* Licking County Archaeology and Landmarks Society. Report submitted to the Ohio Department of Natural Resources, Columbus.

1987   The Middle Woodland–Late Woodland Interface in Central Ohio: Subsistence Community Amid Cultural Change. In *Emergent Horticultural Economies of the Eastern Woodlands,* edited by W. F. Keegan, pp. 201–216. Occasional Paper 7. Center for Archaeological Investigations, Southern Illinois University Press, Carbondale.

CHAPTER TWO

Ohio Middle Woodland Intracommunity Settlement Variability

A Case Study from the Licking Valley

Paul J. Pacheco

ABSTRACT

Prufer's hamlet model has theoretical implications for interpreting Ohio Middle Woodland settlement variability. In this paper, working hypotheses derived from the Prufer model are applied to the results of a siteless survey conducted on 30 ha of glacial outwash terrace located 2.5 km west of the Newark Earthworks. A cluster of Middle Woodland hamlets was identified based upon these hypotheses. Other Middle Woodland locations were also identified occupying interhamlet space. Middle Woodland intracommunity settlement variability is explored by examining such topics as surface assemblage composition, cluster size and structure, dispersion, and contemporaneity.

Ohio Hopewell settlement patterns have long suffered from underexposure to archaeological research. When Olaf Prufer began his study of Ohio Hopewell more than three decades ago, there were only two candidates for domestic sites—Fort Ancient and Fort Hill. Despite a lack of data, the consensus of opinion prior to the 1960s was that the Ohio Hopewell resided in large complex villages adjacent to, or within, the monumental earthwork/mound centers (Griffin 1993). After extensive site survey and limited excavation in the central Scioto Valley, Prufer (1964:71; 1965:127) rejected the existence of such villages. Instead, he characterized the Ohio Hopewell settlement pattern as an example of what he termed the Vacant Ceremonial Center–Dispersed Agricultural Hamlet pattern (hereafter, Vacant Center pattern). By this he meant that the earthwork/mound complexes were isolated ceremonial centers surrounded by interacting networks of small farming settlements (Prufer 1967:137). The members of these dispersed "earthwork societies" (Greber 1979:36) interacted at the centers but did not live there on a permanent basis.

One could argue that the published literature on Ohio Hopewell settlement research has not progressed much beyond Prufer's central Scioto River Valley survey (Prufer 1967). There has been little additional research either explicitly or implicitly capable of evaluating Prufer's ideas about Ohio Hopewell settlement patterns. As noted recently by Smith (1992), despite at least 150 years of archaeological fascination with the mounds and earthworks, we still do not know much about the size, distribution, or organizational complexity of Ohio Hopewell domestic settlements.

This chapter summarizes the hypotheses, research strategy, results, and conclusions of a five-year study I conducted in the Licking River Valley of east-central Ohio (Fig. 2.1), undertaken in conjunction with a program of regional archaeology initiated by the Licking County Archaeology and Landmarks Society and coordinated by William S. Dancey of The Ohio State University. The explicit goal of the research was to test the implications of Prufer's Vacant Center pattern in a region outside the one where his ideas were formulated. Several prior accomplishments gave impetus to my research. One of these was the mapping of the spatial organization of surface and subsurface artifacts and cultural features at the Murphy site (Dancey 1991; hereafter Murphy I site). This provided a working model of the layout of this kind of settlement that could be used for locating and interpreting the archaeological traces of other local Hopewellian settlements (Pacheco 1988). A second significant finding came from Wymer's (1987) analysis of the paleoethnobotanical remains from the fill of cultural features excavated at the Murphy I site. The suite of wild and domesticated plants identified from the charred plant remains in these features suggested to her that the Murphy I residents were sedentary horticulturalists. Both findings fit the pattern formulated by Prufer and were stimuli to continued exploration of the record of Hopewellian occupation in this locality.

Of specific interest in expanding beyond the Murphy I excavation was the question of whether or not additional remains of Middle Woodland occupation were present along an abandoned runoff channel that once flowed past this settlement to empty in Raccoon Creek. With this in mind, and armed with a set of hypotheses, described below, as to what constitutes a Hopewellian hamlet, a 50 ha tract of land corresponding to the former Murphy Farm was blocked out and labled the Murphy Tract. Volunteers recruited through the Licking County Archaeology and Landmarks Society obtained surface collections from this tract in the manner described below in the spring months of 1989 and 1990. This research is described in greater detail elsewhere (Pacheco 1993).

Hypotheses

Working hypotheses or "correlates" were generated to predict the content and organization of the archaeological record for the three main types of Ohio Hopewell settlements expected for the Vacant Center pattern: hamlets, logistical or short-term activity areas, and specialized camps. For each settlement type, I generated expectations concerning measurable variables, such as settlement size, settlement layout, assemblage variability, and regional distribution characteristics (Pacheco 1988:92–93; 1993:83–89). Because these hypotheses represent statements about the archaeological record, they can be falsified by archaeological data. Thus, the research design is not only an application of the model but a test of its applicability to explain Ohio Hopewell settlement variability.

Central to these hypotheses is the repetitive or redundant nature of the dispersed hamlet residence pattern (Fuller 1981, 1986; Smith 1992). Because each hamlet is the sedentary residence of small, independent, self-supporting social groups, such settlement units tend to leave similar archaeological traces. Duration, in particular, appears to account for much of the known variation in Ohio Hopewell domestic settlements (Dancey 1992). The hypotheses that guided the analysis of the Murphy Tract archaeological sample are expressed formally below. They specify properties of the archaeological record to be expected from the surface traces of dispersed sedentary hamlets. Hypotheses 1, 2, and 3 are explored in detail in this paper; hypothesis 4 is discussed elsewhere (Pacheco 1993).

1. Hamlets are relatively small in size, usually covering no more than 1 ha. The size distribution of hamlets is distinctly unimodal.

2. The surface structure of hamlets is characterized by high-density areas of artifacts resulting from formal refuse disposal. Household garbage

dumps appear as sharply defined single-peak (uninodal) concentrations when mapped.

3. Hamlet artifact assemblages contain functionally equivalent, generalized tool kits necessary to maintain the day-to-day existence of the domestic unit. These assemblages will contain both the products and byproducts of the manufacturing and maintenance of the tool kits.

4. Hamlets are locally dispersed in the general vicinity of ceremonial centers. Clusters of hamlets form communities associated with particular center/burial mounds.

Acquisition and Classification of the Artifact Sample

The Murphy Tract surface collection strategy adopted for this research is a special case of the data recovery strategy known as siteless survey (Dunnell and Dancey 1983). Following this approach, artifacts were located and mapped over an entire block of land rather than identifying artifact concentrations and focusing recovery on them exclusive of artifacts occurring between the concentrations. The latter approach is the customary strategy of site survey. The Murphy Tract collection is a special case of siteless survey in that the recovery universe is a single block of land rather than a region. This approach is important to the test of hypotheses 1 and 2 because it permits size and density to be measured rather than assumed.

Coverage of the Murphy Tract was accomplished by the establishment of a 4 x 4 meter grid over the entire tract and the inspection of all grid units on the cultivated portion of the flat outwash terrace forming the valley floor of Raccoon Creek Valley. This process resulted in the recovery of 13,606 lithic artifacts. The collection was augmented by the inclusion of 3,772 artifacts that had been collected previously from a 520 m² area gridded in 1 x 1 m units on the Murphy I site (Dancey 1991), which falls within the Murphy Tract.

Spatial analysis of artifact distributions (Pacheco 1993) resulted in the identification of four dense clusters (labeled Murphy III through VI) and five low-density clusters (labeled Clusters 1, 2, 4, 5/8, and 7). Diagnostic Middle Woodland artifacts, such as corner notched projectile points and bladelet industry material (including 805 bladelets and 29 cores), were recovered from all nine of these clusters, which along with Murphy I comprise the analytic sample for this study. Artifacts from outside the clusters included in the analysis are referred to collectively as from intercluster space. Fig 2.2 shows the loca-

tion of the clusters in relation to the Murphy Tract grid, a general characterization of the tract's topography, and the layout of modern cultural features.

The surface collection produced 33 projectile points. Table 2.1 shows their
distribution in relation to the time period within which they were most likely
made and used along with the raw material from which they were manufactured. As can be seen, the Murphy Tract was utilized during many periods.
However, these data suggest that non–Middle Woodland occupants preferred
Upper Mercer and Columbus-Delaware cherts, while the Middle Woodland
occupants preferred Vanport (Flint Ridge) and Wyandotte (Harrison County)
cherts. The debitage fraction of the sample is similarly dominated by these
later chert types. Therefore, in order to narrow the sample to those artifacts
most likely to be related to the Middle Woodland occupation, the sample has
been limited to objects of Vanport and Wyandotte chert. This reduced the
sample from 17,378 to 15,991 artifacts.

My classification scheme emphasizes variability in chert production debris, rather than a strictly functional typology limited to tool types. The classes
are listed in Table 2.2 along with their representation in the Murphy Tract
sample. Their taxonomic relationships are shown in Fig. 2.3. The classes represent products and by-products of the independent trajectories of the Ohio
Hopewell biface and blade-core industries. The primary contrast between these
two industries is one of positive and negative flake-removal strategies (Pacheco
and Pickard 1992:13).

Research Results

The results of the analyses are broken into four main sections, including analyses of assemblage composition, artifact density, artifact diversity, and contempo-
raneity/duration. After partitioning the unit samples for these analytical purposes, the remaining 15,991 Vanport and Wyandotte chert artifacts were treated
as Middle Woodland in origin. Artifacts were counted and classified according
to the classification scheme described above.

Assemblage Composition

Artifact counts from the ten Middle Woodland clusters (combining spatially
adjacent Clusters 5 and 8 for sample size reasons) and intercluster space are

presented in Tables 2.3 and 2.4. These tables show raw counts for the defined 16-class taxonomy. Only one class had no members in the sum totals for all assemblages. This is Wyandotte/Class 9–Thinned broken bifaces. Within assemblages, many classes have zero values using the complete classification scheme, resulting in a need to collapse the classification scheme for statistical analyses to minimize sample size problems.

The frequency distribution that results from combining Tables 2.3 and 2.4 represents the sum of all assemblages and has been suggested by Kintigh (1984) as an estimate for the underlying population distributions of artifact classes. I used this distribution as the estimated population values in the calculation of Z-scores to test the significance of differences in Middle Woodland use of Vanport and Wyandotte cherts (Fleiss 1983).

Analysis of the artifact class frequency distribution for Vanport versus Wyandotte chert addresses the issue of combination of chert types in the assemblages. Sample sizes, though unequal, are large enough for both chert types to support evidence for different class frequency distributions for the two chert types.

The most outstanding visual difference is the reverse frequencies of bladelets with single or multiple dorsal spines or arrises. The number of arrises on a bladelet indicates the number of previous bladelets removed from a particular core. Single-arris bladelets are taken to be earlier in the manufacturing process, assuming that producing multiple-arris specimens was the objective of the industry. In cross-section, single-arris bladelets are triangular in shape, while multiple-arris bladelets are trapezoidal. Wyandotte has a higher proportion of multiple-arris bladelets relative to single-arris bladelets, while the ratio is reversed for Vanport bladelets. There are 339 (60 percent) single arris Vanport, 230 (40 percent) multiple arris Vanport, versus 89 (38 percent) single-arris Wyandotte, and 147 (62 percent) multiple-arris Wyandotte bladelets. Thus, for the Vanport sample the ratio of single to multiple arrises is 3:2, whereas for Wyandotte it is 2:3. The reversal of ratios of single- to multiple-arris bladelets for the two chert types is probably indicative of a higher success rate in sequential removal of bladelets from Wyandotte blade cores as compared to Vanport blade cores. The high-quality, homogeneous Wyandotte chert that was obtained by the local members of the Middle Woodland community may have been valued as a source for making bladelets because of this higher success rate.

Wyandotte chert may also have been valued because the edges produced with this chert source were superior to Vanport chert that had not been heat-treated. Another potential answer to the observed differences is the mixing of disposal contexts when forming the summed assemblages (see Cowgill 1989). Hopewell refuse deposits within domestic units may be expected to contain higher frequencies of triangular bladelets, representing possible manufacturing failures of earlier, less desirable stages of bladelet removal (Dancey 1991). Short-term or specialized Hopewell activity areas, on the other hand, are more apt to be loci of bladelet use (Greber et al. 1981). These contexts will be explored in the discussion of surface distributions of artifacts.

Statistical comparison of these proportions is based on a Z-test for unequal sample sizes proposed by Fleiss (1983). Z-scores and associated significance levels are listed in Table 2.5. Significant differences in proportions exist for several classes, notably medium debitage and multiple-arris bladelets. The value for classes such as bladelet cores and thinned bifaces are difficult to interpret because of potential sample size biases introduced by preferential collection by amateurs. In general, however, differences in the two chert types appear to result from differential use of Wyandotte chert for making bladelets. The Wyandotte material was used infrequently to make bifaces. This is supported by the lower representation of medium flakes (13 percent lower than Vanport) and the higher representation (22 percent higher) of multiple-arris bladelets.

Despite the somewhat different utilization patterns for these two chert types by members of the local Middle Woodland population, combining the chert types within assemblages is also logical. The combined chert types represent the residual of the sum of events at any particular locale, lending meaning to approaching the lithic assemblages as units. Wyandotte is concentrated in the Murphy IV and V assemblages (see Table 2.4); hence, separation only highlights these assemblages. It will be shown that these assemblages have different patterns of disposal and utilization for Wyandotte chert. Differences in chert types between clusters, however, are examined where appropriate.

Artifact Density

Artifact density was calculated by dividing the size of the partitioned assemblages by the size of the defined cluster. The results of estimation of cluster boundaries, assemblage size, and artifact density are presented in Table 2.6. This table provides an estimate of absolute artifact density within defined areas of cluster space. There are two groups of cluster sizes and artifact densities in addition to intercluster space, but there is a fairly direct linear relationship between surface assemblage size and cluster size (Spearman's rank-order correlation coefficient equals .78). On the average, the larger assemblages are from clusters with larger areas. The most conspicuous outlier in the group is Murphy IV, which is the largest cluster identified but has the lowest estimated artifact density of any of the large clusters. In contrast, Murphy I and III are one-half to two-thirds smaller in area but six times as dense. As will be shown in various discussions, Murphy IV, with a high frequency of Wyandotte bladelets, is a consistent outlier.

A generalization about absolute artifact densities is provided by comparing the two groups of assemblages. Not counting intercluster space, the five smallest assemblages have pooled average surface densities of .08 artifacts per m^2 with an average cluster size equaling .14 ha, while the five largest assemblages have pooled average surface densities of 1.85 artifacts per m^2 with an average cluster size of .45 ha. The overall average estimated size of the ten Middle Woodland clusters defined by the survey is 2,930 m^2 or .29 ha. This figure is almost twice as small as the figure calculated for twenty-one other Middle Woodland sites with size data from the Licking Valley (Pacheco 1988:94–95). The reason for this discrepancy can probably be sought in the more precise methods of size estimation utilized in this study. Nonetheless, taking into account possible expansion of surface scatters by plowing (Odell and Cowan 1987), the general trend for Middle Woodland clusters in the Licking Valley is toward small size, and the data collected in this study support the direction of that trend.

Unit level artifact densities are illustrated through the analysis of surface structure of the artifact clusters. Murphy I, III, V, and VI have very similar uninodal surface artifact distributions, which are interpreted as formal refuse deposits. While the Murphy I, III, and VI assemblages are composed of over 94.5 percent Vanport chert, the Murphy V assemblage is composed of 80.3 percent Wyandotte chert. Murphy VI will be used to illustrate the structural pattern of this group of clusters.

The structural pattern of the surface lithic distribution for Murphy VI is distinctly uninodal (Fig. 2.4). Absolute density for Murphy VI is about four times lower than for either Murphy I or III; however, inclusion of over 1,000-plus m^2 of lower-density space on the west-southwest side of the cluster may have doubled the differences in density for these otherwise structurally similar Middle Woodland clusters.

Wyandotte chert in the Murphy VI cluster has a patchy surface distribution pattern, although the highest concentration corresponds to the peak distribution of Vanport chert artifacts. Several contiguous units along the west margin of Murphy VI have Wyandotte artifacts, also corresponding to a moderately dense outlier Vanport chert concentration. This area includes bladelets in addition to the Wyandotte chert, supporting a Middle Woodland origin. Potentially this location was some type of activity area related either to the Murphy VI occupation or to the nearby Murphy IV occupation, 50 m distant. Another likely explanation is that recent plowing has truncated a feature, since features may be expected in this lower-density area in complimentary distribution to the refuse dump.

Bladelets have a similar patchy distribution, but the bulk of these also correspond spatially to the uninodal Vanport concentration (Fig. 2.5), supporting the interpretation that the observed structural pattern at Murphy VI is attributable to a Middle Woodland occupation. Bladelets were also distributed in low densities along the northwest-to-southwest margin of Murphy VI, parallel to the terrace edge. The collection includes forty single-arris bladelets and twenty-nine multiple-arris bladelets. The frequency of Wyandotte bladelets was 24.6 percent of the total, which is five times higher than the frequency of Wyandotte as a chert type in the assemblage. Four bladelet cores were recovered, two from the uninodal concentration and two from the west-central portion of the cluster.

The smaller clusters, 4, 5/8, and 7, had generally dispersed low-density surface distributions. Cluster 5/8 is used here as an example of these smaller clusters. The artifact distribution for the combined Cluster 5/8 shows a distinct lack of clustering, probably indicative of casual discard from overlapping but unrelated short-term activities (Fig. 2.6). Three bladelets were recovered in this cluster, two made out of Wyandotte chert. Short-term duration is suggested by the relative density within the smaller concentrations being much lower than the concentrations interpreted as formal refuse deposits in the larger clusters.

The surface distribution pattern for Murphy IV stands in direct contrast to Murphy I, III, V, and VI. Murphy IV is the largest cluster identified in the study area at 9,000 m² (.9 ha). Its absolute artifact density is the lowest of any of the large clusters, estimated at .29 artifacts per m². The Murphy IV locality shows significant evidence for multiple occupations, minimally extending from the Early Archaic through the Middle Woodland periods. The location of the cluster on the terrace edge near the point where the paleostream emptied over the terrace can, no doubt, be attributed to the favored reuse of the Murphy IV locality throughout prehistory. Diagnostic evidence for the multiple

occupations is provided by the recovery of fifteen out of the thirty-three projectile points from the Murphy IV cluster.

Only two of the fifteen projectile points are Middle Woodland types. A
minimum of ten are attributable to other occupations; they are made of either
Upper Mercer (90 percent) or Columbus cherts (10 percent). Murphy IV had
the highest frequency of other cherts for any cluster (21.9 percent). A distinct
cluster of Upper Mercer identified along the northwest margin of Murphy IV
represents a spatially distinct non–Middle Woodland occupation (not mapped).
Three Late Archaic projectile points were recovered in this area.

While prehistoric occupations that favored the use of other cherts were
partitioned out of the assemblage to eliminate one source of bias, the Murphy
IV assemblage of Vanport material is also at least partially attributable to a
non–Middle Woodland occupation. Evidence for this occupation is provided
by the three Late Archaic projectile points made out of Vanport chert. These
points are all morphologically similar examples of the Late Archaic variety
Matanzas Side Notch (locally called Fishspears). These points were recovered
in the northeast quadrant of Murphy IV from within an area of approximately
1,000 m². Potentially the spatial proximity of these points documents the lack
of spatial overlap between the main Vanport Late Archaic component at Murphy IV and the Vanport distribution attributable to the Middle Woodland
occupation.

The surface distributions for Murphy IV were graphed at a scale that includes an area (called the South Block during the survey) of approximately 4
ha, which encompasses not only Murphy IV, but Clusters 1 and 2 and a large
portion of the Intercluster Space with recovered artifacts. Maps were constructed at this larger scale to provide a broader comparison for the cluster
and because Middle Woodland activities in the South Block potentially do
not correspond to defined cluster boundaries.

The surface distribution of Vanport chert in the South Block is shown in
Fig. 2.7. Vanport chert represents approximately 65 percent of all recovered
artifacts, with Wyandotte and other chert providing roughly equal portions
of the remaining 35 percent. The Vanport chert distribution in the South Block
is complex, with both nodal and dispersed qualities. The margins of the
Murphy IV cluster have a fairly uniform low-density distribution of Vanport
chert. There is one distinct high-density node in the south-central portion of
the cluster paralleling the terrace edge and up to five lower-density nodes,
although spatial proximity suggests two of these may be associated with the
highest-density area.

The moderately dense node along the northeast margin of the cluster is located in the area associated with the Vanport chert Late Archaic points, and the slight node along the northwest margin of the cluster is located in the area where the Upper Mercer chert cluster was noted. Within the highest-density node, density peaked at 2.3 artifacts per m². The overall crisp spatial boundaries of the concentration suggest that this area of the cluster represents a formal refuse deposit. A Middle Woodland origin for the deposit is suggested by the corresponding association of bladelets (discussed below). Thus, at Murphy IV, the Vanport chert distribution provides evidence for both a probable Middle Woodland refuse deposit and a general low-density scatter at least partially attributable to multiple non–Middle Woodland occupations.

The Wyandotte chert surface distribution in the South Block is generally concordant with the Vanport chert distribution but is considerably more patchy and scattered (Fig. 2.8). Wyandotte chert artifacts comprised about 18 percent of the total sample in the South Block, approximately 25 percent of which were bladelets. The main concentration of Wyandotte chert is to the west of the potential Murphy IV Vanport lithic refuse deposit. There is only a slight overlap in these concentrations. Nonoverlapping distributions potentially stem from a lack of contemporaneity between the Vanport refuse deposit and the depositional events responsible for the disposal of the Wyandotte chert.

Wyandotte bladelets are distributed in a scattered pattern over the entire South Block, including Cluster 2 and the intercluster area south, north, and west of Cluster 1 (Fig. 2.9). Most of the Wyandotte bladelets were located in the southwest quadrant of Murphy IV, including a few within the high-density Vanport node. There were only a few small concentrations of bladelets within the South Block, with the highest-density concentration located on the northern margin of the Vanport chert nodal concentration.

The overall scattered distribution of Wyandotte bladelets suggests that these items were deposited primarily by a drop or toss discard pattern as opposed to systematic disposal (the kind of disposal pattern expected from short-term activities). Hence, within the South Block, Wyandotte chert and at least one concentrated area of Vanport chert in the Murphy IV cluster probably represent different disposal patterns. The high frequency of scattered Wyandotte bladelets in the South Block points to an activity that relied heavily on bladelets. Following this activity, bladelets were casually discarded as opposed to being disposed of in a formal refuse zone. The widespread activities that resulted in the scattered distribution of bladelets was matched by an equally scattered distribution of utilized debitage.

To summarize, four large clusters had distinct high-density concentrations that were interpreted as formal refuse zones of sedentary households. The smaller clusters are characterized by low-density scatters lacking distinct concentrations. These probably represent short-term activity areas. In the South Block, the Middle Woodland distribution of Vanport and Wyandotte artifacts is attributable to at least two unrelated disposal contexts. Vanport chert has a distinct uninodal concentration in the Murphy IV cluster, which probably is also a household refuse zone. Wyandotte chert including bladelets partially overlap in distribution within this concentration, but primarily they are widely scattered. This pattern of discard is associated with short-term activities or occupations that, because of the preponderance of exotic bladelets and because of the size of the scatter, may have been deposited by an interhousehold "specialized" camp. The limited overlap in the distributions of Wyandotte and the uninodal concentration of Vanport was probably fortuitous.

Artifact density is also related to the issue of spatial dispersion of clusters since it is necessary to define what the measured distance between two points represents. The large clusters within the study area, except for Murphy V, are located along the course of a former stream that traversed the terrace (see Fig. 2.2). Murphy V is located along the terrace margin of the Raccoon Creek. Smaller clusters are located between the larger clusters in a complimentary distribution.

The distances between the larger clusters were calculated using U.T.M. coordinates measured from the southwest corner of the potential refuse deposits. Even for the clusters located along the terrace edge, a distance of greater than 100 m apart was observed for all possible nearest-neighbor pairs. The average distance is 480.4 m. The spatial distribution of the large clusters represents a dispersed pattern. There was no evidence for multinodal Middle Woodland clusters in close spatial proximity to each other anywhere within the study area. In other words, a village was not observed.

Diversity Results: Assemblage Variability

Diversity analysis addresses issues of functional variability between assemblages. Functional variability in spatially separated assemblages implies creation by different activities or events. For this study, I have assumed that diversity in the defined classes should be indicative of different types of settlements. Specific activity reconstructions are not attempted since the goal of the study is differentiation of types of place outlined by the model. Unfortunately, the differentiation of places with diversity analysis is linked intrinsically to artifact density by the sample size requirements necessary to produce valid estimates of the proportional representation of classes within assemblages, or evenness. Potentially there may be no meaningful diversity comparisons between certain small and large assemblages. Such issues are linked to the aspect of diversity referred to as richness—the number of classes in an assemblage (regardless of what the classes represent). Heterogeneity measures, like the Shannon-Weaver statistic, combine evenness and richness into a single value. Such statistics are of little value in archaeological research (Bobrowsky and Ball 1989).

Richness was examined for combinations of the classification scheme and chert-type dimensions in order to explore the analytical contexts under which class richness has been influenced by sample size. Simple linear regression coefficients, using log-log transforms as suggested by Jones et al. (1983), were calculated for various combinations of the two dimensions. The correlation coefficients for the calculated relationships are moderately to strongly related to sample size for all the combinations of data analyzed. In general, the greater the number of classes in a regression model, the stronger the positive correlation coefficient. This was especially true after removing an outlier, Cluster 1, from the data. Correlation coefficients for these combinations ranged between .82 and .95.

The collapsed classification in general showed a minor sample size effect on richness, except for Wyandotte, which showed a strong correlation between sample size and richness R=.81. The correlation coefficients prior to removal of the outlier ranged between .47 and .65. There was also less improvement following the removal of the outlier with these models. The relationship between class richness and sample size proved to be weakest in the models with a collapsed classification and separated or combined chert types (.67 and .48, respectively, after removal of the outlier). The weaker relationship is directly related to the reduction in the number of classes. Nonetheless, the collapsed data structures were utilized for statistical analyses because they minimize variation attributable solely to sample size. Visual examination of evenness, by looking at frequency distributions, provides an intuitive perspective of assemblage variability (see Tables 2.3 and 2.4). Four of the largest and densest assemblages, Murphy I, III, V, VI, have very similar frequency distributions. Class frequencies document the dual Middle Woodland reduction sequences. There is abundant debitage from primary production of bifaces and bladelet cores. Biface rejects and thinned bifaces document the complete stages of the biface manufacturing process for the assemblage. Likewise there are single-arris bladelets and cores representing the bladelet manufacturing process. Multiple-arris bladelets, the assumed products of the industry, are also present. Utilized debitage is present that shows within-cluster expedient use and discard of fortuitously shaped flakes or debris. These assemblages document a wide range of domestic production, maintenance, and use activities.

The similarity of Murphy V to this group was surprising given the high frequency of Wyandotte chert in the assemblage. Murphy V was initially considered to have been a staging area for producing Wyandotte bladelets that are scattered across the South Block. Instead, Wyandotte appears to have been used at Murphy V in a manner similar to the use of Vanport at Murphy I, III, and VI.

The frequency distribution of the Murphy IV assemblage supports the interpretation of this place as fundamentally different from the other large assemblages. The most striking contrast is between the frequency distributions of the two chert types. The high frequency of multiple-arris Wyandotte bladelets suggests activities emphasizing the use and manufacture of exotic chert bladelets. The frequency distribution of Vanport chert, on the other hand, is similar to that of the other large assemblages. Because of density relationships, the profile of Vanport chert primarily measures the class frequency distribution of the uninodal surface concentration of Vanport chert artifacts located on the southwest margin of the cluster. Thus, assemblage variability at Murphy IV may also be explained as resulting from the overlap of two sets of noncontemporaneous activities or events. The frequency distribution of Vanport chert at Murphy IV is similar to that of the other four clusters considered candidates for households, matching their similarities in surface distribution. The Wyandotte chert frequency and surface distributions are more characteristic of short-term special activities. Activities producing such scatters did not involve formal refuse clearing or dumping.

The frequency distributions of the smaller clusters and Intercluster Space are all somewhat unique. Clusters 1 and 2 are consistent with Murphy IV, although Cluster 1 has the lowest richness of any assemblage. Intercluster Space includes a high frequency of thinned bifaces, suggesting use and discard of broken or lost bifaces in the spaces in between domestic units. At least one of these thinned bifaces is an example of a Middle Woodland Snyders projectile point made of Vanport chert. The tip and base of this point exhibit snap fractures.

Cluster 4 includes a high proportion of utilized debitage from both chert types, multiple-arris Wyandotte bladelets, and a very low frequency of small debitage. Cluster 5/8 has a unique frequency distribution of Wyandotte chert, with high proportions of finished products from both trajectories (bifaces and bladelets), utilized debitage, and low frequencies of small to medium debitage. Cluster 7 includes a high frequency of Wyandotte biface rejects. Both Cluster 7 and Cluster 5/8 have small sample sizes containing less than one hundred artifacts. The potential for misrepresentations among class frequencies is high. Nonetheless, the scattered nature of these clusters located in the community space between potential domestic units suggests that they represent short-term localized activity areas. In other words, while the sample size problem may preclude statistical demonstration of significant differences between smaller and larger assemblages, the distinct contrast in density properties, size, location, and surface structure strongly suggests that the smaller clusters represent activity areas distinct from the household activities and refuse areas. The potential for functional variation in the small clusters is documented by the class frequency distributions, despite possible biases.

A number of correspondence analyses (Greenacre 1984) were performed on various combinations of the data in an attempt to determine the stability of the data set in a multidimensional space. Analyses performed with the raw or untransformed data proved to be seriously affected by the mass of the small and medium debitage class. A series of transformations were performed in an attempt to provide a stable data structure for the analysis. One possible transformation is to divide assemblage size by area in order to produce a density figure, thus, in effect, standardizing the observation unit. This transformation, unfortunately, makes little intuitive sense in this context, because the important assemblage differences are not necessarily measured by the density of an artifact type within a unit area. Likewise, the lack of a completely linear relationship between assemblage size and settlement size compounded the problems of interpreting the results.

Greenacre and Vrba (1984) suggested equalization of the weights of the samples as a possible transformation, treating all assemblages as if they were the same size. For the assemblage data of this study, equalization of the sample weights provided the most consistent results. The transformation has the added value of providing a statistical comparison of evenness, using the standardized class frequency distributions as the data matrix. Enhancing the interpretive value of the model is the graphical comparison of the variation pattern provided by correspondence analysis. The most successful correspondence analysis, which is presented here, made use of a collapsed classification with eight classes instead of nine (small and medium debitage were combined into a single class). Murphy IV was split into the two chert-type assemblages, and Clusters 5/8 and 7 were combined.

The results of the chosen correspondence analysis are presented in Table 2.7A–E. The first three eigenvalues are provided by the program. The first eigenvalue accounts for 68.8 percent of the total variation and the second eigenvalue accounts for another 20.72 percent of the variation for a cumulative 88.08 percent. The third eigenvalue adds another 5.6 percent of explained variation, increasing the cumulative total to 94.46 percent. A plot of the model in three-dimensional space is provided in Fig. 2.10.

The three-dimensional graphical display of the correspondence analysis illustrates the similarity in assemblage composition between Murphy I, III, V, VI and Murphy IV-Vanport. These assemblages are contrasted with the remaining assemblages and are furthest removed from the intercluster space, Murphy IV-Wyandotte, and Cluster 2. Cluster 4 and the Cluster 5/7/8 combination are midway between the large assemblages and Murphy IV-Wyandotte. Cluster 1 is close to the large assemblages, but because of low richness it has a weak correlation with all of the first three principal axes.

The loadings and correlations of each class and assemblage with the principal axes of variation define similarities and differences in the data structure. The small and medium debitage class is associated with the large assemblages, all of which have high correlation with the first axis. Directly opposed on the first axis are thinned bifaces and multiple-arris bladelets and the assemblages from the South Block. The first axis appears to contrast domestic production with specialized use. Utilized debitage and single-arris bladelets also are positively correlated with the first axis. Both classes of bladelets loaded positive on the second axis, as did the South Block assemblages. These were contrasted with large debitage, biface rejects, utilized debitage, and the other small clusters. The second axis shows a contrast between specialized use of bladelets in the South Block and the use of large-edge or expedient tools in smaller assemblages and clusters. To summarize, the first axis contrasts sedentary domestic units and short-term specialized use. The domestic assemblages are signified by clear association with the by-products of primary production, including Murphy IV-Vanport.

The results of the correspondence analysis present a consistent pattern of variation with that exhibited by the other analyses. As measured in this research, the large assemblages exhibit almost identical patterns of assemblage variability. These assemblages were spatially dispersed and of similar size and exhibit similar surface distributions. The South Block assemblages were characterized by the scattered distribution of Wyandotte chert artifacts, especially multiple-arris bladelets and utilized debitage. Finally, the smaller clusters located in the space between the large clusters were similar to each other in structure and size and possessed divergent assemblages emphasizing use over production.

Confounding Issues: Contemporaneity and Duration

Evidence for contemporaneity and duration in the collected data are examined in this final section of the analysis. The issues of contemporaneity and duration have an undetermined, but important, confounding effect on the conclusions of this study. The observed Middle Woodland settlement variability represents a conflation of multiple activities and events that took place over an extended period of time, possibly as much as four hundred years. Aspects of the analysis, such as the investigation of settlement dispersion, assume the contemporaneity of the phenomena being measured.

One possible approach to contemporaneity is provided by the presence of Wyandotte chert in the assemblages. Approximately 2 kg of this material were recovered during the survey. If we can assume that this amount is somewhat less than 5 percent of the total Wyandotte population within the plowzone (Lewarch and O'Brien 1981), then the total weight of Wyandotte chert in the study area is between 40 and 50 kg. This amount is no more than one or two canoe-loads-full in terms of transportability and exchange (Brose 1990). If we consider the acquisition of the Wyandotte chert to have been a single event rather than a process of long-term procurement, then Wyandotte chert in the assemblages can serve as time markers. The homogeneity of the Wyandotte chert used in the study area supports the single acquisition theory. An absolute date for this event can be extended through the radiocarbon date for Murphy I Feature 100A. A Wyandotte biface and a bladelet were recovered from this feature, which has a date of A.D. 190±60 (Dancey 1991).

These and other inferences presented during the study imply contemporaneity for at least some of the Middle Woodland clusters in the study area. Murphy V and IV-Wyandotte (and the rest of the Wyandotte chert in the South Block) have a high probability of contemporaneity. Murphy IV-Vanport presumably would predate the Wyandotte event, based on the partially over-lapping surface distribution. Murphy I is likely contemporaneous with Murphy V and the Wyandotte event, based on the radiocarbon date and the evidence for manufacturing of Wyandotte artifacts. Both Murphy III and VI contained a preponderance of finished Wyandotte artifacts, while four Wyandotte bladelet cores were recovered during the excavations and surface collections at Murphy I. Murphy VI, as noted, has a light scatter of Wyandotte chert on its west margin that may be related to nearby Murphy IV-Wyandotte, although, like Murphy III, there are such bladelets in the central refuse deposit. Murphy VI and III probably postdate the Wyandotte event, with Wyandotte presence in these assemblages a result of recycling of bladelets discovered during later occupations of the study area. Ceramic evidence from the Murphy III fea-tures supports a late–Middle Woodland position, overlapping the end of the Murphy I occupation (Pacheco 1991). Of the smaller clusters, Clusters 1, 4, 5/8, and 7 all contained Wyandotte artifacts, including bladelets. These four short-term activity areas should be contemporaneous with or postdate the Wyandotte event. Partial overlap of Vanport and Wyandotte cherts in Cluster 2 suggests that this cluster, like Murphy IV-Vanport, may predate the Wyan-dotte event. All of these proposed relationships require explicit testing be-yond the hints of evidence found in this study. Seriation and chert analysis are two possible independent avenues to test the validity of this hypothetical reconstruction.

The Murphy V assemblage is puzzling because of the typical household characteristics of the settlement. Wyandotte was not used at Murphy V in any special manner, duplicating use of local Vanport in the other household clus-ters. I would speculate that the Murphy V household was the member of the local community that acquired the Wyandotte chert, either through exchange or as a result of an expedition to southern Indiana. Wyandotte was channeled into the blade-core industry everywhere else in the study area, but at Murphy V it was used for all kinds of mundane purposes.

One possible solution to the duration issue is provided by the relationship between absolute artifact density and duration. As people stay in one place for longer periods of time, we can expect the accumulation of more trash (Kozarek 1987). Since the pattern of household clusters in the study area has redundant traces, and similar dimensions, the intervening variable of differ-ences in the number of people involved is less likely to affect the density/duration relationship. By this argument, Murphy I and III represent the longest-term settlements observed.

Conclusion

Putting together all the information gathered during this study, I propose that the Middle Woodland remains within the study area represent several genera- tions of an evolving social unit's (perhaps a family) utilization of the valley floor. The data includes evidence for five household areas, short-term activity areas between households, and a specialized camp in which exotic bladelets were used.

A time series diagram of the evolutionary process of accumulating Middle Woodland settlements in the study area is shown in Fig. 2.11. This diagram not only incorporates all available evidence discovered during the study, but it is also, at another level, a testable hypothesis. Comparison of the diagram to the hypothetical models of Ohio Hopewell community organization presented in Dancey and Pacheco (chapter 1) demonstrates a close match to the pattern observed in the study area. Based on the results of this study in the Licking Valley, the Dispersed Sedentary Community model can be considered a valid characterization for the local Ohio Hopewell community settlement pattern.

Broad acceptance of the Dispersed Sedentary Community model for all Ohio Hopewell communities will ultimately, I believe, lead to a shift from site-oriented research to studies of local communities and regional systems. Ohio Hopewell communities are fundamentally linked to the vacant center- dispersed hamlet dichotomy. The spectacular aspects of Hopewell societies stem from the social relationships created by interacting dispersed house- holds at vacant centers. If the communities were not dispersed, the earthwork/ mound centers would cease to function in the same manner. Thus, stability in community organization should be considered a standard feature of Ohio Hopewell settlement systems. No change should be expected within the settle- ment pattern, except to the extent that the entire Hopewell system evolves and then ultimately disappears from the record (near the Late Hopewell/Early Late Woodland boundary ca. A.D. 400). From this argument, I would expect major disjunction in settlement patterns prior to and after Ohio Hopewell, but not during the use of the vacant centers—these existed for and by the efforts of dispersed communities. The various dispersed Ohio Hopewell com- munities that used the vacant centers, however, had their own individual his- tories of success and failure. These communities and the dispersed house- holds that formed them were the social units on which evolutionary processes were acting. Thus, community scale analysis provides the focus on which an evolutionary approach to Ohio Hopewell settlement archaeology can be based.

The Ohio Hopewell were mysterious people only because the lives of the people who built the earthworks and mounds are not well understood. The Dispersed Sedentary Community model provides these communities with tangible homes, placing the mound-building activities within a social framework that unites the domestic and corporate spheres of Hopewellian life.

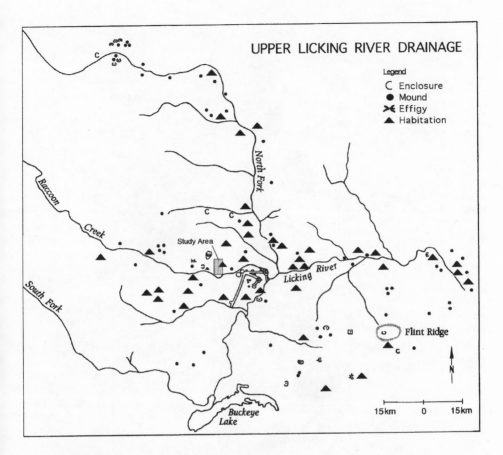

2.1 Distribution of known Ohio Hopewell settlements, earthworks, and Woodland period mounds in the upper Licking River Valley. Adapted from Pacheco (1988:102–103).

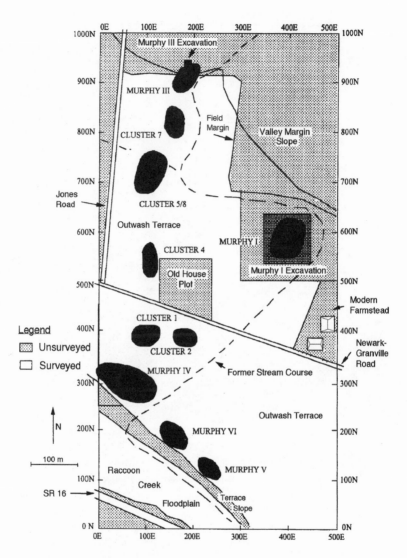

2.2 Map of the Murphy Tract showing major artifact clusters. The U.T.M. coordinate of the field grid point of origin is Zone 17, 37300E443450N.

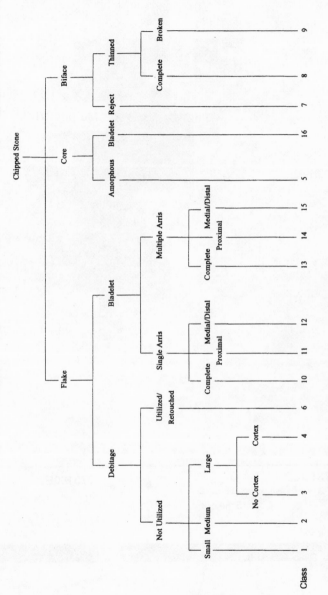

2.3 Taxonomy of technological-functional chert debris classification.

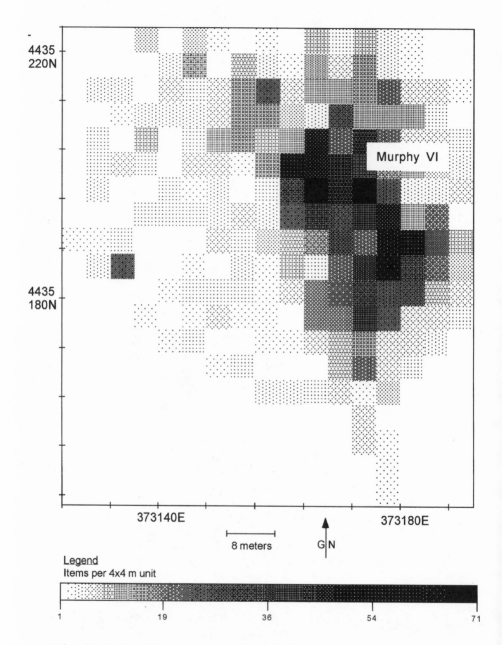

2.4 Surface distribution of Vanport chert artifacts, Murphy VI cluster, by 4 x 4 m units (datum shown is 373132 east, 4435180 north).

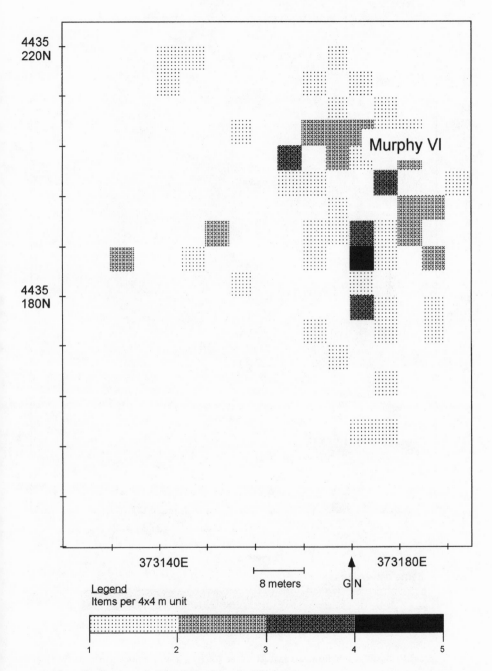

2.5 Surface distribution of all bladelets, Murphy VI cluster.

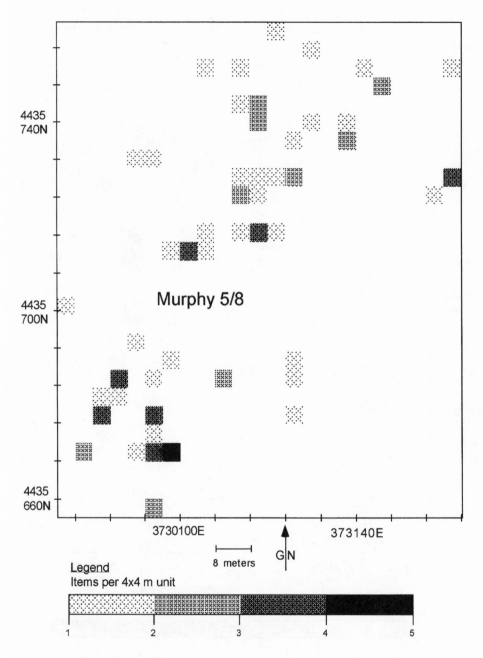

2.6 Surface distribution of all lithic artifacts, Cluster 5/8, by 4 x 4 m units (map's southwest corner is 373072 east, 4435656 north).

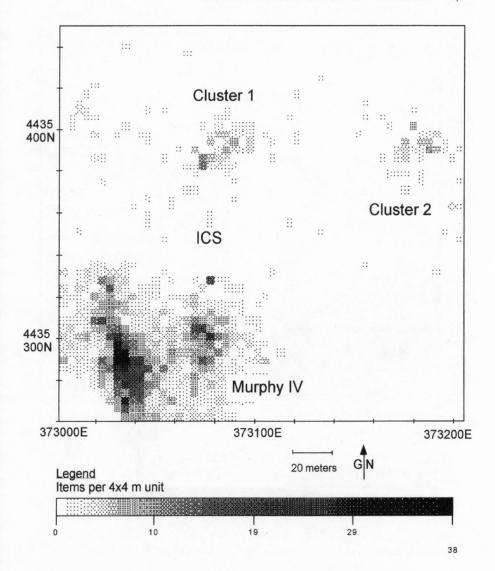

2.7 Surface distribution of Vanport chert artifacts, South Block, by 4 x 4 m units (map's southwest corner is 373000 east, 4435260 north).

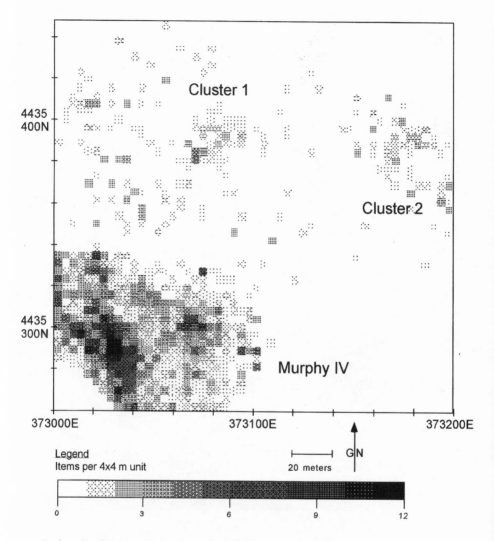

2.8 Surface distribution of Wyandotte chert artifacts, South Block.

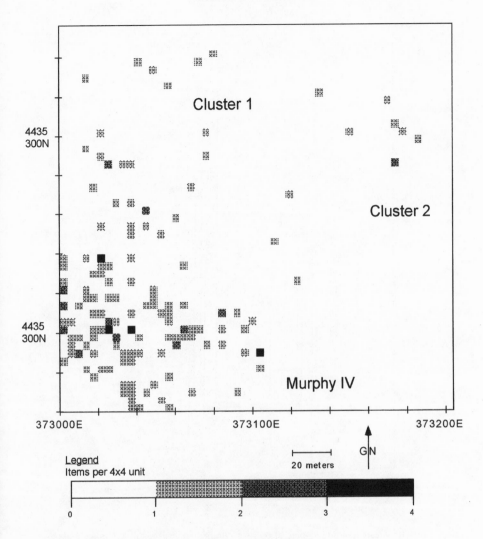

2.9 Surface distribution of Wyandotte bladelets, South Block.

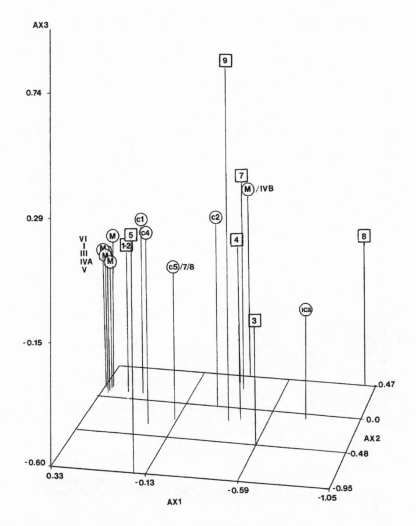

2.10 Three-dimensional display of correspondence analysis results. (Circles = assemblages; squares = artifact classes. The display was rotated 80 degrees and tilted 80 degrees.)

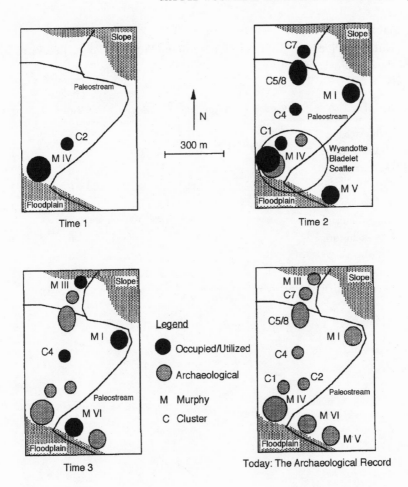

2.11 Reconstruction of the history of the Ohio Hopewell hamlet in Murphy Tract.

Table 2.1

Numerical Frequency of Chert Types Among Projectile Points Recovered by
the Murphy Farm Survey

Period	Vanport	Wyandotte	Upper Mercer	Columbus-Delaware	TOTAL
Early Archaic	2	1	4	1	8
Middle Archaic	1	0	0	0	1
Late Archaic	3	0	4	0	7
Early Woodland	1	0	2	0	3
Middle Woodland	3	1	0	0	4
Late Woodland	0	0	2	2	4
Late Prehistoric	1	0	3	0	4
Unknown	0	0	2	0	2
TOTAL	11	2	17	3	33

Table 2.2

The Technological-Functional Classes Used to Compare Assemblages

	Vanport Chert		Wyandotte Chert	
Classes	Number	Percentage	Number	Percentage
1 Small flake	7161	50.91	1000	51.95
2 Medium flake	5434	38.63	488	25.35
3 Large flake	76	0.54	6	0.31
4 Large decortication flake	46	0.33	24	1.25
5 Amorphous core	23	0.16	1	0.05
6 Utilized/retouched flake	570	4.05	144	7.48
7 Biface reject	115	0.82	7	0.36
8 Thinned biface (complete)	3	0.02	0	0.00
9 Thinned biface (broken)	49	0.35	10	0.52
10 Single-arris bladelet (complete)	34	0.24	8	0.42
11 Single-arris bladelet (proximal)	79	0.56	13	0.68
12 Single-arris bladelet (medial/distal)	226	1.61	68	3.53
13 Multiple-arris bladelet (complete)	25	0.18	20	1.04
14 Multiple-arris bladelet (proximal)	55	0.39	27	1.40
15 Multiple-arris bladelet (medial/distal)	150	1.07	100	5.19
16 Bladelet core	20	0.14	9	0.47
TOTAL	14066	100.00	1925	100.00

Table 2.3
Total Assemblage Artifact Counts Within Technological/Functional Classes, Vanport Chert Only

	Class 1	Class 2	Class 3	Class 4	Class 5	Class 6	Class 7	Class 8	Class 9	Class 10	Class 11	Class 12	Class 13	Class 14	Class 15	Class 16	TOTAL
Murphy I	2043	1060	20	10	1	147	14	0	4	8	26	72	4	18	44	7	3478
Murphy III	3007	2216	6	3	6	146	54	2	16	17	35	91	7	24	78	6	5714
Murphy IV	884	851	11	15	6	98	10	1	12	4	8	29	7	5	11	1	1953
Murphy V	97	111	0	2	1	12	2	0	3	0	0	2	0	2	0	2	234
Murphy VI	1002	967	28	12	4	104	28	0	4	0	9	24	4	3	12	3	2204
Cluster 1	42	64	0	0	0	15	0	0	0	0	1	2	3	0	0	0	127
Cluster 2	30	29	2	1	0	11	1	0	1	2	0	4	0	3	0	0	84
Cluster 4	23	52	1	1	1	12	4	0	1	2	0	2	0	0	0	1	101
Cluster 5/8	14	32	1	1	2	8	1	0	1	1	0	0	0	0	0	0	62
Cluster 7	8	16	0	0	0	5	0	0	0	0	0	0	0	0	2	0	31
Intercluster	11	36	4	1	2	12	1	0	7	0	0	0	0	0	3	0	77
TOTAL	7161	5434	76	46	23	570	115	3	49	34	79	226	25	55	150	20	14066

Table 2.4

Total Assemblage Artifact Counts Within Technological/Functional Classes, Wyandotte Chert Only

	Class 1	Class 2	Class 3	Class 4	Class 5	Class 6	Class 7	Class 8	Class 9	Class 10	Class 11	Class 12	Class 13	Class 14	Class 15	Class 16	TOTAL
Murphy I	14	5	2	0	0	1	0	0	0	0	0	1	0	0	0	0	23
Murphy III	1	1	0	0	0	1	0	0	0	0	0	2	0	0	3	0	8
Murphy IV	191	147	0	5	0	48	1	0	6	3	8	30	12	14	57	6	528
Murphy V	720	249	2	14	0	48	3	0	0	2	4	18	2	6	9	0	1077
Murphy VI	54	42	1	1	0	11	0	0	1	2	0	5	0	3	7	1	128
Cluster 1	1	4	0	0	0	3	0	0	0	0	0	2	0	0	1	0	11
Cluster 2	4	8	1	0	0	6	0	0	0	0	0	1	2	0	4	1	27
Cluster 4	0	2	0	0	1	3	0	0	0	0	0	0	0	0	1	0	7
Cluster 5/8	1	1	0	0	0	2	1	0	2	0	0	0	1	1	1	1	10
Cluster 7	1	5	0	0	0	1	2	0	0	1	0	1	0	0	0	0	11
Intercluster	13	24	0	4	0	20	0	0	1	0	1	8	3	4	17	0	95
TOTAL	1000	488	6	24	1	144	7	0	10	8	13	68	20	27	100	9	1925

Table 2.5

Statistical Tests Comparing Proportional Differences in Artifact Class Frequencies by Chert Types, for Collapsed Classification Scheme

Class	Value of Z	Significance Level
Small debitage	0.56	.55<p<.6
Medium debitage	6.09	p<.0001
Large debitage	0.66	.5<p<.55
Utilized debitage	1.55	.11<p<.13
Biface reject	-2.07	.04<p<.05
Thinned biface	-2.69	.007<p<.009
Single-arris bladelet	0.77	.42<p<.48
Multiple-arris bladelet	3.37	.0007<p<.001
Bladelet core	4.3	p<.0001

Table 2.6

Assemblage Size, Estimated Surface Area, and Density

Cluster Identification	M. Woodland Surface Lithics Collected	Estimated Surface Area of Lithics Scatter (m²)	Estimated Percentage of Surface Area Sample	Estimated Surface Assemblage Size (number of total lithics)	Estimated Density (number/sq m)
Intercluster	172	265,000	50	344	0.002
Cluster 1	138	1,800	75	173	0.1
Cluster 2	112	2,000	75	140	0.7
Cluster 4	108	1,200	75	135	0.11
Cluster 5/8	72	1,500	75	90	0.06
Cluster 7	42	800	75	53	0.07
Murphy IV	2,481	9,000	95	2,605	0.29
Murphy V	1,311	2,100	95	1,377	0.66
Murphy VI	2,332	3,300	75	2,915	0.88
Murphy III	5,722	3,200	50	11,444	3.58
Murphy I*	3,501	4,400	10	17,000	3.86

*A 520 m² area was collected from the densest concentration at Murphy I. The estimate reflects known areas of lower density within the MI cluster (Cowan et al. 1981).

Table 2.7A

Results of Correspondence Analysis: The First Three Eigenvalues

	Eigenvalue	*Percentage*	*Cumulative Percentage*
1.	0.011846691	68.08	68.08
2.	0.03605876	20.72	88.80
3.	0.00984742	5.66	94.46

Table 2.7B

Results of Correspondence Analysis: Coordinates of the Columns

				Coordinates		
Class	*Grouping*	*Mass*	*Distance*	*First Axis*	*Second Axis*	*Third Axis*
1/2	Small & medium debitage	0.768	0.03	0.18	-0.03	-0.01
3	Large debitage	0.024	0.70	-0.59	-0.51	-0.15
4	Utilized debitage	0.096	0.31	-0.46	-0.24	-0.07
5	Biface reject	0.011	1.18	-0.08	-0.95	-0.24
6	Thinned biface	0.011	1.62	-1.05	-0.32	-0.60
7	Single-arris blade	0.037	0.25	-0.39	-0.19	-0.23
8	Multiple-arris blade	0.049	1.21	-0.99	-0.47	-0.02
9	Bladelet core	0.004	1.00	-0.39	-0.20	-0.74

Table 2.7C

Results of Correspondence Analysis: Absolute Contributions and Squared Correlations
of the Columns

Class	Absolute Contributions			Squared Correlations		
	First Axis	Second Axis	Third Axis	First Axis	Second Axis	Third Axis
1/2	20.1	1.3	1.4	0.97	0.02	0.03
3	7.2	17.9	5.5	0.50	0.38	0.03
4	17.0	14.7	5.3	0.69	0.18	0.02
5	0.1	27.9	6.3	0.01	0.76	0.05
6	9.9	3.0	38.1	0.69	0.06	0.22
7	4.8	3.9	20.3	0.61	0.15	0.21
8	40.4	30.8	0.2	0.80	0.19	0.00
9	0.5	0.4	2.99	0.15	0.04	0.54

Table 2.7D

Results of Correspondence Analysis: Coordinate of the Rows

Cluster	Mass	Distance	Coordinates		
			First Axis	Second Axis	Third Axis
Murphy I	0.091	0.09	-0.29	-0.10	-0.01
Murphy III	0.091	0.13	-0.33	-0.10	-0.05
Murphy IVA-VP*	0.091	0.09	-0.28	-0.03	-0.08
Murphy IVB-Wy*	0.091	0.33	-0.39	-0.38	-0.14
Murphy V	0.091	0.10	-0.30	-0.05	-0.05
Murphy VI	0.091	0.09	-0.29	-0.01	-0.04
Cluster 1	0.091	0.07	-0.11	-0.05	-0.07
Cluster 2	0.091	0.12	-0.30	-0.03	-0.12
Cluster 4	0.091	0.14	-0.01	-0.35	-0.12
Cluster 5/7/8	0.091	0.13	-0.14	-0.32	-0.01
Intercluster	0.091	0.62	-0.76	-0.00	-0.20

*VP=Vanport chert; Wy= Wyandotte chert

Table 2.7E

Results of Correspondence Analysis: Absolute Contributions and Squared Correlations of the Rows

Cluster	Absolute Contributions			Squared Correlations		
	First Axis	Second Axis	Third Axis	First Axis	Second Axis	Third Axis
Murphy I	6.4	2.4	0.2	0.89	0.10	0.00
Murphy III	8.5	2.8	1.9	0.86	0.08	0.02
Murphy IVA-VP*	6.0	0.2	6.5	0.90	0.01	0.08
Murphy IVB-Wy*	11.9	36.4	16.9	0.47	0.44	0.06
Murphy V	7.0	0.7	2.5	0.93	0.03	0.03
Murphy IV	6.4	0.0	1.8	0.94	0.00	0.02
Cluster 1	1.0	0.7	3.9	0.18	0.04	0.06
Cluster 2	6.7	0.2	14.4	0.75	0.01	0.13
Cluster 5/7/8	1.5	25.3	0.1	0.15	0.76	0.00
Intercluster	44.5	0.0	37.8	0.93	0.00	0.07

*VP=Vanport chert; Wy=Wyandotte chert

References

Bobrowsky, P. T., and B. Ball
   1989   The Theory and Mechanics of Ecological Diversity in Archaeology. In *Quantifying Diversity in Archaeology,* edited by R. Leonard and G. T. Jones, pp. 4–12. Cambridge University Press, Cambridge, England.
Brose, D. S.
   1990   Toward a Model of Exchange Values for the Eastern Woodlands. *Midcontinental Journal of Archaeology* 15:100–136.
Cowgill, G. L.
   1989   The Concept of Diversity in Archaeological Theory. In *Quantifying Diversity in Archaeology,* edited by R. Leonard and G. T. Jones, pp. 131–141. Cambridge University Press, Cambridge, England.
Dancey, W. S.
   1991   A Middle Woodland Settlement in Central Ohio: A Preliminary Report on the Murphy Site (33Li212). *Pennsylvania Archaeologist* 61:37–72.
   1992   Small Site Formation Process and the Hopewell Problem. Paper presented at the 49th Southeast Archaeological Conference, Little Rock, Arkansas.
Dunnell, R. C., and W. S. Dancey
   1983   The Siteless Survey: A Regional Scale Data Collection Strategy. In *Advances in Archaeological Method and Theory, Vol. 6,* edited by M. B. Schiffer, pp. 267–287. Academic Press, New York.
Fleiss, J. T.
   1983   *Statistical Methods for Rates and Proportions.* John Wiley, New York.
Fuller, J. L.
   1981   *Developmental Change in Prehistoric Community Patterns: The Development of Nucleated Village Communities in Northern West Virginia.* Unpublished Ph.D. dissertation, Department of Anthropology, University of Washington, Seattle.
   1986   The Development of Sedentary Village Communities in Northern West Virginia: The Test of a Model. In *Plowzone Archaeology: Contributions to Theory and Technique,* edited by M. J. O'Brien and D. Lewarch, pp. 187–214. Publications in Anthropology 27. Vanderbilt University, Nashville.
Greber, N.
   1979   A Comparative Study of Site Morphology and Burial Patterns at the Edwin Harness Mound and Seip Mounds 1 and 2. In *Hopewell Archaeology: The Chillicothe Conference,* edited by D. S. Brose and N. Greber, pp. 27–38. Kent State University Press, Kent, Ohio.
Greber, N., R. S. Davis, and A. S. DuFresne
   1981   The Micro-Component of the Ohio Hopewell Lithic Technology: Bladelets. *Annals of the New York Academy of Sciences* 376:489–528.

Greenacre, M. J.
    1984   *Theory and Applications of Correspondence Analysis.* Academic Press, East Kilbride, Scotland.
Greenacre, M. J., and E. S. Vrba
    1984   Graphical Display and Interpretation of Antelope Census Data in African Wildlife Areas, Using Correspondence Analysis. *Ecology* 65:984–997.
Griffin, J. B.
    1993   The Hopewell Housing Shortage in Ohio, A.D. 1–350. Paper presented at the Ohio Archaeological Council 2nd Annual Conference on Ohio Archaeology, Chillicothe.
Jones, G. T., D. K. Grayson, and C. Beck
    1983   Artifact Class Richness and Sample Size in Archaeological Surface Assemblages. In *Lulu Linear Punctate: Essays in Honor of George Quimby,* edited by R. C. Dunnell and D. K. Grayson, pp. 55–73. Anthropological Papers 73. Museum of Anthropology, University of Michigan, Ann Arbor.
Kintigh, K.
    1984   Measuring Archaeological Diversity by Comparison with Simulated Assemblages. *American Antiquity* 49:44–54.
Kozarek, S. E.
    1987   *A Hopewellian Homestead in the Ohio River Valley.* Unpublished master's thesis, Department of Anthropology, University of Cincinnati.
Lewarch, D. E., and M. J. O'Brien
    1981   Effect of Tillage Patterns on Artifact Patterning: A Preliminary Assessment. In *Plowzone Archaeology: Introduction to Theory and Technique,* edited by M. J. O'Brien and D. E. Lewarch, pp. 7–49. Publications in Anthropology 27. Vanderbilt University, Nashville.
Odell, G. H., and F. Cowan
    1987   Estimating Tillage Effects on Artifact Distributions. *American Antiquity* 52:456–484.
Pacheco, P. J.
    1988   Ohio Middle Woodland Settlement Variability in the Upper Licking River Drainage. *Journal of the Steward Anthropological Society* 18:87–117.
    1991   Woodland Period Archaeology in Central Ohio: Licking County Archaeology and Landmarks Society Contributions. *Ohio Archaeological Council Newsletter* 3(3):4–9.
    1993   *Ohio Hopewell Settlement Patterns: An Application of the Vacant Center Model to Middle Woodland Period Intracommunity Settlement Variability in the Upper Licking River Valley.* Unpublished Ph.D. dissertation, Department of Anthropology, The Ohio State University, Columbus.
Pacheco, P. J., and W. Pickard
    1992   A Laterally Hafted Ohio Hopewell Bladelet from Dow Chemical #2 Site (33Li302). *Ohio Archaeologist* 42(2):12–15.

Prufer, O. H.

    1964   The Hopewell Complex of Ohio. In *Hopewellian Studies,* edited by J. R. Caldwell and R. L. Hall, pp. 35–84. Scientific Papers 12, No. 2. Illinois State Museum, Springfield.

    1965   *The McGraw Site: A Study in Hopewellian Dynamics.* Scientific Publications, n.s. 4(1). Cleveland Museum of Natural History.

    1967   The Scioto Valley Archaeological Survey. In *Studies in Ohio Archaeology,* edited by O. H. Prufer and D. H. McKenzie, pp. 267–328. Western Reserve University Press, Cleveland.

Smith, B.

    1992   Hopewellian Farmers of Eastern North America. In *Rivers of Change: Essays on Early Agriculture in Eastern North America,* by B. Smith, pp. 201–248. Smithsonian Institution Press, Washington, D.C.

Wymer, D. A.

    1987   The Middle Woodland–Late Woodland Interface in Central Ohio: Subsistence Continuity Amid Cultural Change. In *Emergent Horticultural Economies in the Eastern Woodlands,* edited by W. F. Keegan, pp. 201–216. Occasional Paper 7. Center for Archaeological Investigations, Southern Illinois University Press, Carbondale.

CHAPTER THREE

Problems and Solutions in the Study of Dispersed Communities

Mark E. Madsen

ABSTRACT

When analyzing settlement patterns or community organization, archae-ologists must either demonstrate or assume that deposits being compared were synchronous. Typically, contemporaneity is assumed or poorly dem-onstrated, and much of this paper is devoted to examining the concept. Equally important is the concept of formation process, since the history of an archaeological deposit is critical to unraveling it. Operationalizing contemporaneity requires selection of dating methods, and these are con-sidered here in relation to the nearly intractable problem of correlating the occupational history of spatially independent households.

Since 1772, when missionaries David Zeisberger and David Jones observed mounds in the Muskingum and Scioto River Valleys of Ohio (Anonymous 1775; Zeisberger 1910), the earthworks and burial mounds of the Hopewell archaeological complex have been a source of interest and contention among professionals and the public alike. Beginning in the nineteenth century, a huge amount of archaeological effort has been devoted to the excavation and de-scription of earthworks, mounds, and their contents. Attributes of burial fea-tures have been used to define separate cultural groups, to create chronologies, and to infer something about the lifeways of the groups that created the earthen features. Fascination with mounds and earthworks has rightly led to an emphasis on documenting these sites as they disappear (Squier and Davis 1848). In turn, however, this emphasis on burial sites has meant that our knowledge of other aspects of Hopewell is far weaker than it might otherwise have been.

Ohio Hopewell was defined entirely from burial contexts. Subsequent trait lists continue this focus on burial contexts to the exclusion of other kinds of sites (Webb and Snow 1945). In part, existing data are derived from mounds and burial because the majority of the large-scale excavations of Hopewellian sites occurred between 1880 and 1930, during a period when monumental structures rather than portable artifacts were central to archaeological research. Additionally, a bias favoring the study of large, obtrusive sites has slowed the accumulation of information about the domestic sphere. Until recently, Hopewellian settlement was assumed to take the form of nucleated villages (Griffin 1967, 1983; Morgan 1952).

During the past thirty years, fieldwork at small sites has begun to fill the gaps in our knowledge of domestic sites and the Hopewellian economy. Prufer (1964, 1965) argued that settlement was dispersed around intermittently utilized ceremonial centers. His hypothesis has since been supported by data from individual domestic settlements, or "hamlets," throughout the Middle Ohio River Valley (Blank 1965; Church, chapter 13; Dancey 1991; Fuller 1981a&b; Genheimer 1984, chapter 11; Kozarek, chapter 5; Pacheco 1988, 1993a, 1993b, chapter 2; Prufer 1965; Shane 1971; contra Converse 1993; Griffin 1993). Through investigations at hamlets in diverse regions and ecological contexts, we are beginning to understand something of the domestic economy of Ohio Hopewell groups (e.g., Wymer 1992, 1993, chapter 6).

However, many phenomena of interest simply cannot be studied using data from single hamlets or small groups alone. Burial ceremonialism is a group activity conducted by the members of a local community at a location separate from the normal domestic sphere. Redistribution, postulated as one of the driving forces of the Hopewellian phenomenon (e.g., Hall 1973; Seeman 1979), occurs between hamlets in a community. Because single sites do not represent whole communities in a dispersed settlement pattern (Fuller 1981 a&b), studies of community structure and function in dispersed systems require regional-scale, multiple-site efforts. We must be able to associate hamlets and occupations of hamlets with the larger corporate units of which they are a part, without the benefit of close spatial proximity or superposition. Therefore, methods of creating comparable assemblages and measuring their contemporaneity are crucial to studying the economics and ceremonial behavior of Hopewellian communities.

The purpose of this paper is to explore methods for studying dispersed settlement systems. The history of Hopewellian archaeology as well as formation process research demonstrate that the way in which assemblages are constructed can have a significant effect on our eventual knowledge of the record. Following a brief review of the effects of traditional site concepts on our knowledge of Hopewell, I propose to review some methods by which comparable assemblages can be created. In the final section of this paper, I will review the contemporaneity "problem" in archaeology and suggest an approach to dating that yields contemporaneous sets of hamlets.

Hopewellian Settlement Patterns: History and Biases

History of Research

Hopewellian settlement research does not have a long history in comparison to the history of mound and earthwork research. Until Prufer's (1964, 1965) work at the McGraw site, discussion focused on the fact that no "village" sites had been found and excavated (e.g., Morgan 1952; Prufer 1964), despite occasional references to village sites in the earlier literature. However, as Fuller (1981a&b) and Smith (1992) have pointed out, the term "village" in early writings does not mean any specific kind of community organization but simply distinguishes concentrations of portable artifacts from earthwork and mound locations.

By the early 1960s the framework of discussion about Hopewellian settlement was firmly in the domain of culture-history, carrying with it a traditional concept of how domestic sites "should" appear in the record (Griffin 1967, 1978, 1983). The traditional view holds that only high-density aggregates of artifacts are worth investigation, given that only high-density aggregates had "materials of sufficient quality and quantity . . . to sustain interpretation" (Plog et al. 1978:389). Griffin's (1978, 1983) idea that the Hopewellian domestic sphere must be represented by high-density, "village" sites has influenced his interpretations of commonplace artifacts. Concentrations within or near earthworks are seen as evidence of villages that were not recognized by previous investigators (Griffin 1983). Such interpretations enjoy little empirical support. Size, rather than functional patterning, is the criterion by which archaeological deposits are defined as "sites."

It is worth noting that not all areas of low artifact density were completely ignored by earlier researchers. Moorehead (1892) seems to have been aware of the relatively low-density deposits in the Murphy site area in Licking County, Ohio, and it is common knowledge that artifacts of Hopewellian manufacture can be picked up in agricultural fields throughout regions where earthworks are found (Bell 1959; Dunkel 1956). Despite this fact, the low-density portion of the record was virtually ignored until the 1960s. The high-density bias of the traditional systematics seems to have prevented recognition that low-density portions of the archaeological field record are, in fact, the equivalents of our common-sense idea of "villages." The bias toward high-density aggregates quite clearly carries a bias against the remainder of the archaeological record.

In response to the lack of high-density deposits representing "villages," Prufer (1964, 1965) finally suggested that the Hopewell community pattern consisted of small farmsteads whose archaeological record would not produce high-density "sites" at all. Only recently have intensive, often "siteless," surveys documented what Prufer believed to be the case (Dancey and Pacheco 1992, chapter 1; Pacheco 1993a). Occupational remains of the Ohio Hopewellians appear to be small, low-density scatters of artifacts that likely were not considered "sites" under many survey regimes (Church and Ericksen, chapter 13; Dancey 1991; Kozarek, chapter 5; Genheimer 1984, chapter 11; Pacheco 1988, 1993a; chapter 2; Whitacre and Whitacre 1986). Once fieldwork focused on low-density sites of the kind represented at McGraw, our knowledge of Hopewellian settlement and subsistence patterns has grown substantially. The effect of traditional thinking about sites and communities is strong, however. Despite growing empirical evidence that Prufer's model is correct in its essentials, Griffin (1993) and Converse (1993) continue to argue against the dispersed community model in favor of nucleated villages as the primary Hopewellian settlement form, demonstrating that traditional thinking about sites and communities is still influential.

The contrast between Hopewellian studies since Prufer's critical work and the older views on Hopewell settlement patterns demonstrates the thoroughness with which a particular algorithm for defining sites can affect our knowledge. The traditional site concept, with its focus on large, high-density deposits, has had two significant effects on Hopewell archaeology. The first, discussed above, is that small and low-density deposits were not considered significant until relatively recently, creating a systematic bias in our knowledge of the record. The second effect is that the traditional approach to fieldwork equated two concepts that refer, as far as Hopewell is concerned, to distinct phenomena: site and community.

Sites and Communities in Dispersed Settlement Systems

At the most fundamental level, concepts for describing settlement systems are built up from single domestic units, which are the minimal functional units of human occupation (Steward 1977:390). Groups of interacting domestic units are often referred to as communities (Beardsley et al. 1956; Steward 1977) and represent the fact that human populations virtually always appear to be organized into groups of varying sizes (Birdsell 1957; Krzywicki 1934; Steward 1977).

Community groups are structured in space as well as through the annual cycle. At a fundamental level the settlement structure of a community is responsive to resource structure since all ecosystems are spatially and temporally heterogenous. Structured resources mean that human groups cannot be arbitrarily organized and still exploit needed resources. The spatio-temporal organization of community groups has been called the "settlement system" (Winters 1969) and includes two dimensions of variability. Settlement system organization denotes the spatial pattern taken by a group at a particular point in time (Fuller 1981a&b). At the most general level, groups may take one of two forms. If all of the domestic units comprising a community are concentrated into a single location, the community pattern is "nucleated" or "contagious" (Flannery and Coe 1968; Fuller 1981b). If, on the other hand, the domestic units comprising a community are not concentrated into a single location but are distributed across regional space, the community pattern is "dispersed." The second dimension, scheduling, denotes the placement of communities throughout the annual cycle with respect to resource availability and is not considered further here.

Community organization is significant to settlement pattern analysis because different organizational modes change the spatial scale at which the community group will be recognizable in the archaeological record. In nucleated communities the entire community group is recognizable as a single, contiguous archaeological deposit. The traditional focus within Hopewellian archaeology on large sites resulted in an implicit assumption that Hopewellian communities were nucleated. Sites were assumed to be coeval with communities. In dispersed communities, on the other hand, the community group is represented by numerous discrete archaeological deposits, often separated by considerable distances. The dispersed community has no common-sense correlate such as "village." As Fuller (1981b) argued, archaeological communities are synthetic units recognized as groups of functionally identical assemblages that interacted as cohesive units. Communities, and all other high-level synthetic units, are built up as groups of assemblages. The critical step, then, is the creation of assemblages that are composed only of those artifacts that are historically related as part of the same depositional events. Assemblages built according to a common criterion of historical relatedness rather than size or shape will then be comparable for purposes of settlement-pattern analysis.

Building Comparable Assemblages

Archaeologists never "discover" assemblages in the field. Some algorithm always conditions what we call an assemblage for analytic purposes, whether rules are based on size or function. Thus, how we create assemblages is crucial if we want to compare assemblages across space for community pattern studies. The usual procedure for forming assemblages is to rely on the time-honored concept of spatial proximity; that is, objects close together in space are likely to be historically related as part of the same depositional events. The traditional procedure is an argument of association.

The concept of association is a fundamental one in archaeology. Every basic textbook in archaeology discusses the importance of association for dating artifacts, deposits, and sites (e.g., Fagan 1978). In common usage, the term "association" refers to two or more objects in close proximity to one another, often within the same stratigraphic unit (Jones and Beck 1992). Contemporary observation as well as formation studies show that the archaeological record is created by a continuous series of overlapping depositional and erosional events active on surfaces. Consequently, "assemblages" or "sites" formed by putting together objects from arbitrary spatial units will be, in almost all cases, a mix of objects from multiple depositional events and several time periods. This conclusion holds true for buried deposits as well, since nearly all buried materials begin as depositional events on surfaces that are further modified by sedimentation and burial (Lewarch and O'Brien 1981; Dunnell and Dancey 1983). Since much archaeological analysis consists of comparing frequencies or occurrences of artifact classes between assemblages, it is critical that assemblages represent archaeologically meaningful groups of artifacts, or frequencies will not be meaningful. If artifacts are grouped into assemblages on spatial grounds, it is important to know what processes resulted in the spatial proximity of such artifacts.

Spatial proximity, in fact, can result from at least four potential causes. First, artifacts may be close together because of accidental proximity of different depositional events. This situation can be expected to occur regularly on surfaces of great stability, where artifacts from ancient depositional events are exposed. Second, unrelated artifacts may be found in close proximity because of their common relationship to a third environmental factor that conditioned cultural deposition for both objects. A common example is streambanks, which are common foci for artifact deposition throughout prehistory; artifact assemblages from streambanks are often palimpsests of unrelated artifacts from long spans of time. Third, earlier deposition of artifacts may create environmental factors that create foci for later artifact deposition. Tells, in the Near East, or artificial mounds in swampy areas of eastern North America, are excellent examples of this phenomenon, where cultural deposition is focused on areas where previous deposition has created significant landscape features. Finally, artifacts may be found together because they were deposited by the same group of people and are therefore historically related.

In order for frequencies of artifact classes within an assemblage to be meaningful for archaeological purposes, assemblages should include only those artifacts related by common depositional history. At present, there are no tried-and-true methods for subdividing artifacts into groups that represent deposition by the same group of people. What I present here are a number of methods that are being tested by workers in several different contexts (e.g., Dunnell 1988; Jones and Beck 1992; Teltser and Kovachik 1991). Because the goal of creating assemblages for analysis is to put together those artifacts that are derived from the same depositional contexts, I am focusing here on techniques that measure attributes that are sensitive to depositional history (Stein 1987; Stein and Rapp 1985). Since artifacts are altered by people or natural processes through straightforward physical and chemical processes, we can work backwards from the attributes found on artifacts to the processes that created the attributes during an object's depositional and use history (Schiffer 1987; Stein 1987).

Depositional events often differ in terms of their effects on artifact size. The effect of depositional processes on size has been exploited to determine the depositional history and potential relatedness of artifact classes across large areas, principally through the combination of information on large-size classes and microartifacts (e.g., Dunnell and Simek 1995; Madsen 1992; Madsen and Dunnell 1989; Stein and Teltser 1989; Teltser and Kovachik 1991). Artifact size is affected by weathering and may exhibit variations that are depositionally significant in some contexts. Dunnell and Simek (1995) have demonstrated that ceramics, in plowzone contexts, retain indications of original stratigraphic distinctions in artifact size and shape. Artifacts that formerly resided in shallower deposits are incorporated into the plowzone first and are subjected to plowzone weathering (breakage and rounding) for a longer period of time. Deeper deposits are only occasionally impacted by the plow. Thus, ceramics from such deposits have a shorter mean residence time in the plowzone. Ceramics from deeper deposits are larger than those from shallower deposits. Dunnell and Simek (1995) successfully exploited this fact to separate materials from formerly distinct depositional events from plowzone materials alone.

The weathering history of deposits offers a great deal of potential information about depositional association. Weathering is often considered an approach to absolute dating. The chief utility of weathering, however, may be that it can be used to separate otherwise-indistinguishable events. Jones and Beck (1992) and Raymond (1984–85) used obsidian hydration widths to understand the depositional history of lithic scatters in the arid West with great success. A weathering approach appears promising for chert as well. Chert hydrates in a manner similar to obsidian, with the result that the width of the hydration layer can indicate the time elapsed since exposure of a surface (Purdy and Clark 1987). It is possible to sort artifacts into weathering classes that represent different age episodes of manufacturing and use, although this will frequently require destructive thin-sectioning and microscopic examination. Weathering rates may not be fast enough in some environments to produce useful chronological distinctions over the period of interest, but at least one study by Sheppard and Pavlish (1992) in Polynesia has found resolvable differences over the last two thousand years.

Another potential method of establishing depositional association is refitting, which provides the strongest possible evidence of historical relatedness. Several archaeologists have used refitting to study the depositional history of deposits (e.g., Lindauer 1992; Rapson and Todd 1992) and have found the method to be of considerable utility. The value of refitting fades, however, proportionate to the number of artifacts under consideration and as distances between refittable pieces increases. Because refitting is an extremely labor-intensive method at present, it is best deployed as a means to test hypotheses concerning association generated using size, shape, or chronological information.

It is impossible at this point to specify an absolute flowchart of techniques whereby artifacts and clusters may be sorted into assemblages that represent only those artifacts that are historically related. Rather, the techniques discussed here, as well as others under development, will have to be applied where appropriate in order to sort out the particular history of each set of deposits. Once information on depositional history has led to the creation of meaningful assemblages, though, chronological information is necessary in order to assess the possible contemporaneity of assemblages.

Contemporaneity

In order to study community-scale phenomena, we must be able to distinguish between those assemblages that represent different time periods and those that are synchronous. This problem has plagued archaeology ever since the field began to take a serious interest in chronology and change. "Contemporaneity" is an English word used in archaeology to denote the situation where two or more objects, assemblages, or "sites" represent the same period of time (e.g., Schacht 1984). Because archaeological time is traditionally dissected into intervals using phases, the contemporaneity problem has been simplified to an issue of sites that do not last for the duration of a phase, or spill over into adjacent phases (Adams 1965; Wright and Johnson 1975). In modern regional analysis, this problem is principally an issue because of its potential effect on population reconstruction, where contemporaneity problems can cause "overcounting" of sites and thus inflated population estimates (Ammerman 1981; Schacht 1981, 1984; Weiss 1977). In broader terms, the real issue in settlement-pattern analysis is establishing that, for analytic purposes, several assemblages represent the same period of time.

As Binford (1968) noted, however, the archaeological record is a contemporary phenomenon. All artifacts are thus "contemporaneous" in the trivial sense that they represent the same period of time: the present. The purpose of this section, then, is to consider how artifacts and assemblages can represent particular periods in the historical past and how sets of artifacts can be formed that demarcate the same period of historical time. The common usage would, in fact, be appropriate if time were a physical dimension of the archaeological record, observable in the same manner as are location and form. Because, however, the archaeological record is a contemporary phenomenon, historical time is an inference from formal and relational properties of artifacts (Dean 1978; Dunnell and Readhead 1989; Spaulding 1960). For example, physical and chemical dating methods derive ages from measurements of compositional or structural attributes of artifacts, such as the concentration of carbon-14 atoms or the intensity of stored thermoluminescence. Similarly, seriation derives temporal orderings from measurements of the frequencies of formal attributes within a group of objects. Dating methods focus on one specific kind of event, measuring the elapsed time since the event occurred on a particular artifact. Radiocarbon dating, for example, measures the elapsed time since a sample was isolated from atmospheric exchange.

Artifacts undergo many episodes of deposition, modification, and transport during their use-lives and during their residence in the archaeological record. Each episode changes some attributes of an artifact and represents a configuration of attributes that came together at some point in the historical past. The time over which a particular set of attributes assumed its configuration is an event (Dunnell 1981). Because artifacts have undergone many physical transformations, there are typically many events represented on each object. Of the large number of different events represented, only a limited number are capable of yielding chronological information. Only events that result in attribute configurations that are temporally dependent are amenable to dating. Typically, several general classes of events are temporally dependent: weathering events, which alter the physical properties of an artifact progressively through time; radioactive decay events, utilized in radiocarbon dating; and radioactive storage events, typified by thermoluminescence.

Different dating methods target different kinds of events and therefore can return widely divergent dates even for the same object or assemblage. A classic example is the potential difference between radiocarbon dates for wood charcoal and thermoluminescence dates for broken ceramics from the same hearth feature. The dates can easily be grossly different because the events dated are different. In the case of the radiocarbon dates, the event being dated is the death of the tree that provided the wood. In the case of the thermoluminescence dates for ceramics, the event being dated is either the firing of the vessel during manufacture or the last heating event during use. Each date may be correct, but since each dating method targets a different kind of event, the archaeologist must select which events, and thus which dates, are most relevant to a research problem. Once a specific kind of event is selected, there exists a real basis for evaluating the differing dates in terms of requirements set forth for a given research problem. For example, if the research problem involves building a ceramic chronology for a particular area, the thermoluminescence dates on ceramics are clearly more relevant to this problem than radiocarbon dates. The first steps in assembling contemporaneous sets of objects or assemblages must establish what kinds of events are of interest, taking care to select the proper dating method for these kinds of events and ensuring that comparisons of dates utilize comparable events.

In order to establish contemporaneous sets we must define the temporal resolution required by a research problem. If, for example, we are interested in examining the evolution of nucleated from dispersed settlement systems, and if this change is assumed to have occurred over a period of several centuries, then presumably we will require a resolution of events that is fine-tuned to periods of fairly short duration, certainly much less than several hundred years apart, in order to distinguish competing hypotheses. The requirements for such a research problem define a tolerance limit, which is the resolution required in order to distinguish between alternative explanations (Lewontin 1974). Achieving this resolution is a matter of manipulating both the dating method itself and the process of forming assemblages: the first in order to obtain an acceptable error range from the dating methods used, and the second to create assemblages of the necessary duration and range.

All dating methods are measurement processes. Measurement procedures always involve errors; no method is perfectly accurate and precise. It is usually possible to control the measurement process to minimize systematic errors in accuracy at a cost in precision. At the same time, precision controls resolution. Thus, if the error range of radiocarbon dates decreases, we are better able to distinguish closely spaced events (see Barford 1985 for an introduction to measurement error statistics). All dating methods have parameters that can be modified to control either precision or accuracy or both, although in most cases an increase in sample size is the only way to increase both precision and accuracy at the same time. For example, in radiocarbon dating greater precision can be obtained by lengthening counting times (Taylor 1987). Similarly, seriations can produce better precision, and therefore resolution, by two manipulations: increases in sample size and inclusion of a larger number of classes in the seriation (Dunnell 1970, 1981).

When the problem is creating contemporaneous sets of assemblages, the events used must be at the scale of the assemblage. That is, we must use events that represent the interval of time during which the artifacts that form an assemblage came together. As Dunnell (1981) has shown, seriation measures precisely these kinds of events. There are two principal kinds of seriation, distinguishable by the methods used to produce chronological orderings. "Probabilistic" seriations, which includes most statistical methods, are those that assign assemblages to a unique position in a chronology based on a "best fit" algorithm (Dunnell 1970). "Deterministic" methods, on the other hand, yield paired, indistinguishable assemblages if the classes used in the seriation cannot discriminate the intervals of time represented by the assemblages (Dunnell 1970). The latter method, most often implemented by the use of Ford's manual technique, is the method most suited to assessment of contemporaneity. Within the framework of the seriation, contemporaneous assemblages are those that cannot be distinguished and thus generate ties.

From the results of the seriation alone, it is impossible to determine what kind of temporal resolution is represented by sets of assemblages that are tied in a deterministic seriation. For this task, absolute dating methods such as radiocarbon or thermoluminescence are indispensable. By measuring the duration of assemblages that generated ties in the seriation, the temporal resolution achieved can be measured. For assemblages composed principally of ceramics or heat-treated lithics, thermoluminescence is the dating method of choice since it directly measures an archaeological event (Aitken 1985; Valladas 1992).

If the measured temporal resolution for a group of potentially contemporaneous assemblages is less than required by the tolerance limits set for a research problem, seriation can be tuned to give finer discrimination. First, seriation can be made finer-grained by the inclusion of more classes. As Dunnell (1981) notes, this may be achieved either by including more stylistic classes with the same number of defining attributes or by subdividing existing classes using additional attributes. Either method yields finer distinctions between assemblages in a seriation. Second, finer distinctions can always be achieved by the inclusion of larger sample sizes of artifacts, although this method entails greater analytic expense (Dunnell 1981).

In summary, two or more assemblages are contemporaneous when they are comparably defined from historically related depositional events and when they cannot be distinguished in a seriation within problem-specific tolerance limits. The most significant difference between this usage of the term "contemporaneity," as opposed to its standard English meaning, is the focus on events, not objects. Changing the focus of analysis from objects to the events represented by (and on) artifacts is the primary means by which we can avoid the biases of traditional means of defining assemblages, such as spatial proximity.

Conclusion

Historically, the study of settlement patterns and subsistence in Hopewellian archaeology has been hampered by preconceived notions of how domestic sites "should" look. This normative bias led investigators to search for many years for high-density villages that simply are not a part of the Hopewellian record. Recent studies of small, low-density hamlets support the view that Hopewell domestic sites are not represented by high-density villages. At the same time, the work of Dancey, Pacheco, and others underscores the need for studies of communities at regional scales. Many of the fascinating questions concerning Hopewell virtually require data at regional scales ranging from isolated to multiple hamlets, including the nature of redistribution networks and the evolution of burial and other ceremonial configurations. Because hamlets are not spatially contiguous, community groupings are not immediately apparent from survey data. Rather, communities are synthetic units that must be formed from comparable assemblages defined on the basis of historically related depositional events, not classical notions of "association." Once defined, communities must be delineated using those assemblages that are contemporaneous with respect to a given research problem.

Implementing a regional research program meeting these requirements is a critical task for Hopewellian studies. The purpose of this chapter has been to review some of the emerging methods for creating depositionally related assemblages and measuring their contemporaneity, in order to answer questions about community organization and economic functioning. Answers to these questions are prerequisites for addressing questions about redistribution and trade, subsistence, and sociopolitical organization. The approach outlined here represents at least the beginnings of a research program capable of studying the evolution of dispersed communities and ultimately solving some of the enduring mysteries of the Hopewellians.

Acknowledgments

The author would like to thank W. S. Dancey and P. Pacheco for the opportunity to participate in the symposium that gave rise to this chapter and for their patience during its preparation. I gratefully acknowledge W. S. Dancey, R. C. Dunnell, P. Pacheco, S. Sterling, C. P. Lipo, P. T. McCutcheon, and K. Wilhelmsen for reading several versions of this work with a critical eye; this paper is much improved due to their assistance. C. M. Woods, of Woods Cultural Research, Inc., encouraged me during the transformation of my conference paper into this chapter and generously provided the time and a place to work. Finally, the conference paper on which this chapter is based was produced during the author's tenure as a NSF Graduate Research Fellow, and the author's initial fieldwork in Ohio was begun with assistance from Sigma Xi, The Scientific Research Society.

References

Adams, R. M.
1965 *Land Behind Baghdad: A History of Settlement of the Diyala Plains.* University of Chicago Press, Chicago.
Aitken, M. J.
1985 *Thermoluminescence Dating.* Academic Press, London.
Ammerman, A. J.
1981 Surveys and Archaeological Research. *Annual Review of Anthropology* 10:63–88.
Anonymous
1775 A Plan of an Old Fort and Intrenchment in the Shawnese Country, Taken on Horseback, by Computation Only. *Royal American Magazine,* January 1775, pp. 29–30.
Barford, N. C.
1985 *Experimental Measurements: Precision, Error and Truth.* 2nd ed. Wiley, New York.
Beardsley, R. K. (editor)
1956 *Seminars in Archaeology: Functional and Evolutionary Implications of Community Patterns.* Memoirs 11. Society for American Archaeology, Washington, D.C.
Bell, R. E.
1959 Snyders Points. *Ohio Archaeologist* 9(4):128–129.
Binford, L. R.
1968 Archaeological Perspectives. In *New Perspectives in Archeology,* edited by S. R. Binford and L. R. Binford, pp. 5–32. Aldine, Chicago.
Birdsell, J. B.
1957 Some Population Problems Involving Pleistocene Man. *Cold Spring Harbor Symposium on Quantitative Biology* 22:47–69.
Blank, J. E.
1965 The Brown's Bottom Site, Ross County, Ohio. *Ohio Archaeologist* 15(1):16–21.

Converse, R. N.
1993   The Troyer Site: A Hopewellian Habitation Site, and a Secular View of Ohio Hopewell Villages. *Ohio Archaeologist* 43(3):4–12.

Dancey, W. S.
1991   A Middle Woodland Settlement in Central Ohio: A Preliminary Report on the Murphy Site (33Li212). *Pennsylvania Archaeologist* 61:37–72.

Dancey, W. S., and P. J. Pacheco
1992   The Ohio Hopewell Settlement Pattern Problem in Historical Perspective. Paper presented at the 57th Annual Meeting of the Society for American Archaeology, Pittsburgh.

Dean, J. S.
1978   Independent Dating in Archaeological Analysis. In *Advances in Archaeological Method and Theory, Vol. 1,* edited by M. B. Schiffer, pp. 223–265. Academic Press, New York.

Dunkel, R. E.
1956   Local Finds on the Old Home Place. *Ohio Archaeologist* 6(4):116–118.

Dunnell, R. C.
1970   Seriation Method and Its Evaluation. *American Antiquity* 35:305–319.
1981   Seriation, Groups, and Measurement. In *Manejos de Datos y Methods Mathematicos de Arqualogia,* edited by G. L. Cowgill, R. Whallon, and B. S. Ottaway. Union Internacional de Ciences Prehistoricas y Protohistoricas, Mexico DF.
1988   Low Density Archaeological Records from Plowed Surfaces: Some Preliminary Considerations. *American Archaeology* 7:29–38.

Dunnell, R. C., and W. S. Dancey
1983   The Siteless Survey: A Regional Scale Data Collection Strategy. In *Advances in Archaeological Method and Theory, Vol. 6,* edited by M. B. Schiffer, pp. 267–283. Academic Press, New York.

Dunnell, R. C., and M. L. Readhead
1989   The Relation of Dating and Chronology: Comments on Chatters and Hoover (1986) and Butler and Stein (1988). *Quaternary Research* 39:232–233.

Dunnell, R. C., and J. F. Simek
1995   Artifact Size and Plowzone Processes. *Journal of Field Archaeology* 22:1–15.

Fagan, B. M.
1978   *In the Beginning: An Introduction to Archaeology.* 3rd ed. Little, Brown, Boston.

Flannery, K. V., and M. D. Coe
1968   Social and Economic Systems in Formative Mesoamerica. In *New Perspectives in Archeology,* edited by S. R. Binford and L. R. Binford, pp. 267–284. Aldine, Chicago.

Fuller, J. W.
1981a   *Developmental Change in Prehistoric Community Patterns: The Development of Nucleated Village Communities in Northern West Virginia.* Unpublished

Ph.D. dissertation, Department of Anthropology, University of Washington, Seattle.

1981b   The Development of Sedentary Village Communities in Northern West Virginia: The Test of a Model. In *Plowzone Archaeology: Contributions to Theory and Technique,* edited by M. O'Brien and D. Lewarch, pp. 187–214. Publications in Anthropology No. 27. Vanderbilt University, Nashville.

Genheimer, R. A.

1984   A Systematic Examination of Middle Woodland Settlements in Warren County, Ohio. Report submitted to Ohio Historic Preservation Office, Columbus, Ohio.

Griffin, J. B.

1967   Eastern North American Archaeology: A Summary. *Science* 156:175–191.

1978   Late Prehistory of the Ohio Valley. In *Northeast, Vol. 15,* edited by B. Trigger, pp. 547–559. Handbook of North American Indians. W. C. Sturtevant, general editor. Smithsonian Institution, Washington, D.C.

1983   The Midlands. In *Ancient North Americans,* edited by J. D. Jennings, pp. 243–302. W. H. Freeman, New York.

1993   Major Hopewell Sites Without People and Minor Hopewell Sites Without Goodies. Paper presented at "A View from the Core: A Conference Synthesizing Ohio Hopewell Archaeology," Chillicothe, Ohio.

Hall, R. L.

1973   An Interpretation of the Two-Climax Model of Illinois Prehistory. Paper presented at 9th International Congress of Anthropological and Ethnological Sciences, Chicago.

Jones, G. T., and C. Beck

1992   Chronological Resolution in Distributional Archaeology. In *Space, Time, and Archaeological Landscapes,* edited by J. Rossignol and L. Wandsnider, pp. 167–191. Plenum Press, New York.

Kryzwicki, L.

1934   *Primitive Society and its Vital Statistics.* Macmillan, London.

Lewarch, D. E., and M. J. O'Brien

1981   The Expanding Role of Surface Assemblages in Archaeological Research. In *Advances in Archaeological Method and Theory, Vol. 4,* edited by M. B. Schiffer, pp. 297–342. Academic Press, New York.

Lewontin, R. C.

1974   *The Genetic Basis of Evolutionary Change.* Columbia University Press, New York.

Lindauer, O.

1992   Ceramic Conjoinability: Orphan Sherds and Reconstructing Time. In *Piecing Together the Past: Applications of Refitting Studies in Archaeology,* edited by J. Hofman and J. G. Enloe, pp. 210–216. International Series 578. British Archaeological Reports, Oxford.

Madsen, M. E.
    1992   Microdebitage Analysis of Lithic Material from a Northwest Coast Shell
           Midden. In *Deciphering a Northwest Coast Shell Midden: Geoarchaeological
           Approaches to Site Formation,* edited by J. K. Stein, pp. 193–210. Academic
           Press, New York.
Madsen, M. E., and R. C. Dunnell
    1989   The Role of Microartifacts in Deducing Land Use from Low Density Records
           in Plowed Surfaces. Paper presented at 53rd Annual Meeting of the Society
           for American Archaeology, Atlanta.
Moorehead, W. K.
    1892   *Primitive Man in Ohio.* G. P. Putnam's Sons, New York.
Morgan, R. G.
    1952   Outline of Cultures in the Ohio Region. In *Archeology of Eastern North
           America,* edited by J. B. Griffin, pp. 83–98. University of Chicago Press, Chicago.
Pacheco, P. J.
    1988   Ohio Middle Woodland Settlement Variability in the Upper Licking River
           Drainage. *Journal of the Steward Anthropological Society* 18:87–117.
    1993a Ohio Hopewell Regional Community and Settlement Patterns. Paper pre-
           sented at "A View from the Core: A Conference Synthesizing Ohio Hopewell
           Archaeology," Chillicothe, Ohio.
    1993b *Ohio Hopewell Settlement Patterns: An Application of the Vacant Center Model
           to Middle Woodland Period Intracommunity Settlement.* Unpublished Ph.D.
           dissertation, Department of Anthropology, The Ohio State University, Co-
           lumbus.
Plog, S., F. Plog, and W. Wait
    1978   Decision Making in Modern Surveys. In *Advances in Archaeological Method
           and Theory, Vol. 1,* edited by M. B. Schiffer, pp. 383–421. Academic Press, New
           York.
Prufer, O. H.
    1964   The Hopewell Complex of Ohio. In *Hopewellian Studies,* edited by J. Caldwell
           and R. Hall, pp. 37–83. Scientific Papers 12, No. 2. Illinois State Museum,
           Springfield.
    1965   *The McGraw Site: A Study in Hopewellian Dynamics.* Scientific Publications,
           n.s. 4(1). Cleveland Museum of Natural History.
Purdy, B. A., and D. E. Clark
    1987   Weathering of Inorganic Materials: Dating and Other Applications. In *Ad-
           vances in Archaeological Method and Theory, Vol. 11,* edited by M. B. Schiffer,
           pp. 211–254. Academic Press, New York.
Rapson, D. J., and L. C. Todd
    1992   Conjoins, Contemporaneity, and Site Structure: Distributional Analyses of
           the Bugas-Holding Site. In *Piecing Together the Past: Applications of Refitting*

Studies in Archaeology, edited by J. Hofman and J. G. Enloe, pp. 238–263. International Series 578. British Archaeological Reports, Oxford.

Raymond, A. W.

1984–85 Evaluating the Occupational History of Lithic Scatters: Analysis of Obsidian Hydration Measurements. *North American Archaeologist* 6:115–133.

Schacht, R. M.

1981 Estimating Past Population Trends. *Annual Review of Anthropology* 10:119–140.

1984 The Contemporaneity Problem. *American Antiquity* 49:678–695.

Schiffer, M.

1987 *Formation Processes of the Archaeological Record.* University of Arizona Press, Tucson.

Seeman, M. F.

1979 Feasting with the Dead: Ohio Hopewell Charnel House Ritual as a Context for Redistribution. In *Hopewell Archaeology: The Chillicothe Conference,* edited by D. Brose and N. Greber, pp. 39–46. Kent State University Press, Kent, Ohio.

Shane, O. C. III

1971 The Scioto Hopewell. In *Adena: The Seeking of an Identity,* edited by B. K. Swartz, pp. 142–145. Ball State University Press, Muncie, Indiana.

Sheppard, P. J., and L. A. Pavlish

1992 Weathering of Archaeological Cherts: A Case Study from the Solomon Islands. *Geoarchaeology* 7:41–53.

Smith, B. D.

1992 Hopewellian Farmers of Eastern United States. In *Rivers of Change: Essays on Early Agriculture in Eastern North America,* edited by B. D. Smith, pp. 201–248. Smithsonian Institution Press, Washington, D.C.

Spaulding, A. C.

1960 The Dimensions of Archaeology. In *Essays in the Science of Culture,* edited by G. E. Dole and R. L. Carneiro, pp. 437–456. T. Y. Crowell, New York.

Squier, E. G., and E. H. Davis

1848 *Ancient Monuments of the Mississippi Valley.* Contributions to Knowledge 1. Smithsonian Institution, Washington, D.C.

Stein, J. K.

1987 Deposits for Archaeologists. In *Advances in Archaeological Method and Theory, Vol. 11,* edited by M. B. Schiffer, pp. 337–395. Academic Press, New York.

Stein, J. K., and G. Rapp

1985 Archaeological Sediments: A Largely Untapped Reservoir of Information. In *Contributions to Aegean Archaeology,* edited by N. Wilkie and W. D. E. Coulson, pp. 143–159. Publications in Ancient Studies 1. Center for Ancient Studies, University of Minnesota, Minneapolis.

Stein, J. K., and P. A. Teltser
　　1989　Size Distribution of Artifact Classes: Combining Macro- and Micro-Fractions. *Geoarchaeology* 4:1–30.
Steward, J.
　　1977　The Foundations of Basin-Plateau Shoshonean Society. In *Evolution and Ecology: Essays on Social Transformation*, edited by J. Steward and R. Murphy, pp. 366–401. University of Illinois Press, Urbana.
Taylor, R. E.
　　1987　*Radiocarbon Dating: An Archaeological Perspective*. Academic Press, New York.
Teltser, P. A., and J. Kovacik
　　1991　Plowzone Structure of a Middle Woodland Settlement from Microartifacts. Paper presented at 56th Annual Meeting of the Society for American Archaeology, New Orleans.
Valladas, H.
　　1992　TL Dating of Flint. *Quaternary Science Reviews* 11:1–5.
Webb, W. S., and C. E. Snow
　　1945　*The Adena People*. Reports in Anthropology and Archaeology 6. University of Kentucky, Lexington.
Weiss, H.
　　1977　Periodization, Population and Early State Formation in Khuzestan. In *Mountains and Lowlands: Essays in the Archaeology of Greater Mesopotamia*, edited by L. D. Levine and T. C. Young, Jr., pp. 347–370. Bibliotheca Mesopotamica, Undena Publications, Malibu, California.
Whitacre, D., and B. Whitacre
　　1986　The Whitacre Site (12D246). *Ohio Archaeologist* 36(3):24–36.
Winters, H. D.
　　1969　*The Riverton Culture*. Museum Monographs 1. Illinois State Museum, Springfield.
Wright, H. T., and G. A. Johnson
　　1975　Population, Exchange, and Early State Formation in Southwestern Iran. *American Anthropologist* 77:267–289.
Wymer, D. A.
　　1992　Trends and Disparities: The Woodland Paleoethnobotanical Record of the Mid-Ohio Valley. In *Cultural Variability in Context: Woodland Settlements of the Mid-Ohio Valley*, edited by M. F. Seeman, pp. 65–76. Special Paper 7, Midcontinental Journal of Archaeology. Kent State University Press, Kent, Ohio.
　　1993　The Ohio Hopewell Econiche: Human-Land Interaction in the Core Area. Paper presented at "A View from the Core: A Conference Synthesizing Ohio Hopewell Archaeology," Chillicothe, Ohio.
Zeisberger, D.
　　1910　David Zeisberger's History of North American Indians. *Ohio Archaeological and Historical Publications* 19:30–31.

CHAPTER FOUR

How to Construct a Model

A Personal Memoir

Olaf H. Prufer

ABSTRACT

Prufer's much-debated Ohio Hopewell settlement model was not the result of formal "model construction" but a wholly casual by-product of an attempt between 1959 and 1963 to organize and synthesize the massive chaotic data on Ohio Hopewell into a coherent pattern. This paper describes, largely in autobiographic, historic, and contextual terms, how the Prufer model came into being.

Most of the papers published in this volume were originally presented in Pittsburgh on April 10, 1992, at the 57th Annual Meeting of the Society for American Archaeology at a symposium entitled "Testing the Prufer Model of Ohio Hopewell Settlement Pattern." I did not attend these meetings, but I was greatly surprised to learn that some of my ideas, first articulated some thirty-three years ago, had by now been elevated to the lofty status of a "model." I certainly never had considered them in such formal terms. The way they came into being, together with a number of other tentative concepts on Ohio Hopewell that I toyed with in the early 1960s, was wholly casual. At no time had I intended to construct "models" of any kind; I merely tried to understand and explain certain obscure points (among many) that had struck my fancy regarding the Ohio Hopewellian phenomenon.

Upon learning what was going to happen in Pittsburgh, I wrote, somewhat alarmed, to James B. Griffin, who served as a symposium discussant, requesting that he read certain portions of my letter to the assembled participants. In this letter—from which I will quote at a later point in this narrative—I tried to set the record straight as to what I really had done.

Subsequent to the Pittsburgh meetings, when the editors of this volume began to contemplate its publication, I agreed, as the alleged culprit of the model-building crime, to provide the readers with a somewhat more detailed account of what, in those ancient days, I had actually intended to do and how I had arrived at whatever is now considered to be my "Model of Ohio Hopewell Settlement Pattern." Such an account, of necessity, has to be somewhat autobiographical. I thought it of possible interest to the profession to present in some detail how (at least in the case of one investigator) archaeological concepts are actually arrived at. In this particular case, although I do not consider my work and ideas particularly earthshaking, there may also be some additional merit in presenting the facts as I recall them, because, to the best of my knowledge, it was my Ph.D. dissertation of 1961, and the work it subsequently generated, that rekindled general professional interest in Ohio Hopewell after a long period of dormancy. The issue, then, is not whether the "model" is right or wrong—it probably is neither—but how it was arrived at.

I have always been suspicious of official versions of the "great genius at work." Many such accounts seem to be overly pat, as if the "great ideas and concepts" had been arrived at by systematic, inspired, almost teleological, conceptualizing. Although this may, on occasion, be the way it happens, in my experience and in cases I had opportunity to observe, the process is usually quite unsystematic, accidental, and less than elegant and orderly. Occasionally it can be shown that, clearly, the official version is at variance with reality. Lewis Binford's ecstatic account (1972) of his progress to archaeological enlightenment is an example of such creativity (Griffin 1976; Walker 1974).

I have, of course, been aware that the question of Ohio Hopewellian settlements—as opposed to ceremonial or other public centers—has been debated off and on ever since I came up with my so-called "model." In fact, I am surprised how often this "model" has stirred up tempers pro and con, encompassing arguments that range from the sublime (Pacheco 1988) to the ridiculous (Converse 1993). In order to set forth the record of what actually happened and what this is all about, let me, then, start at the beginning.

When, in 1958, I passed my Ph.D. qualifying examinations at Harvard University, I was as uninterested in American archaeology as I was ignorant of this subject.

I had arrived at Harvard in 1954, scholarship in hand, from India, by way of a brief sojourn in Germany, the land of my birth. Harvard had taken a considerable risk in admitting me to undergraduate studies, because I had no secondary schooling whatsoever. Due to the vagaries of World War II, I had to quit regular school in 1942, at age 12. I thus never even got close to anything resembling a high school diploma. Again, due to the uncertainties of the times, in 1948 I found myself, for reasons that are of no concern to this narrative, in India, where I became interested in archaeology and prehistory simply because in that country one could hardly fail to stumble over the massive archaeological remains of a most colorful and varied past. After a brief stint in broadcasting with All India Radio, through the good offices of a friend, who happened to be a superintendent in the Indian government's Department of Archaeology, I was employed, in 1950, by that organization as a research assistant of sorts. This is how I gained my first field experience, surveying and excavating at a variety of sites.

The major event of this period was my participation in the government's expedition, on the traces of the redoubtable Sir Aurel Stein of *Serindia* fame, into the Thar Desert of Rajasthan in search of traces of the Indus Valley civilization.

By the end of 1950, I became a research scholar at the Jamia Millia Islamia (National Muslim University), which gave me all the leeway I could possibly want to deal with Indian archaeological problems of my choice. From this point in time up to my departure from India in 1953, and always under the auspices of the Jamia Millia, I was hectically involved in fieldwork and research enterprises involving the Lower Palaeolithic, the Indus Valley civilization, and medieval archaeology. In the course of these operations, I also was sponsored by the Maharajah of Patiala in the Punjab and by the Sir Ruttan Tata Trust of Bombay. Much of this work was published at the time and later (Prufer 1952a, 1952b, 1956).

Early in 1953 it became apparent to me that, in order to develop any kind of career in the domain of the mind, I needed some formal academic qualifications. Because of my discovery of numerous Lower Palaeolithic localities in the Himalayan foothills, I had established contact with the then only major authority in the field of Asian palaeolithic studies, Hallam L. Movius at Harvard University. Movius took a lively interest in my labors and travails, and, through his most generous efforts, I was admitted in the fall of 1954 on a scholarship as a belated undergraduate student in anthropology at Harvard University. As these negotiations were going on, I had traveled, with Indian wife in tow, to Germany to see my parents and to do some auditing at the University of Tübingen.

When I arrived at Harvard, the university was at a loss as to where to place me in the student rank order. Finally, it was decided that I should be granted junior status, and thus I became a member of the class of '56. Thus far my anthropological interests were wholly in the domain of Old World archaeology, and they were to remain so for some time to come. In fact, upon completion of my studies, I intended to return to India to continue working at the Jamia Millia Islamia, from which, technically, I was merely on a leave of absence.

My senior honors thesis, which was published at a later date (Prufer 1958–59), dealt with the Upper Palaeolithic of the Lower Austrian Loess Region. Subsequently, I became involved in a number of other Old World archaeological projects that ranged from the Lebanese Middle Palaeolithic (Prufer and Baldwin 1957) via the Neolithic of Kansu in China (Prufer 1957) to the Mesolithic of East Germany (Prufer 1961a).

After graduation, Harvard University offered me (and I eagerly accepted) a scholarship to continue my studies toward a Ph.D. degree in anthropology, specifically in Old World palaeolithic studies under Movius. From many a student's point of view, Movius was a difficult man to get along with. He was single-mindedly dedicated to his field and demanded a similar devotion from his chosen disciples. I was neither the first nor the last of his students who was unable or unwilling to submit to his all-encompassing control, which, in addition to its professional aspects, tended to spill over into the personal domain. Thus, by the end of 1957, we came to a rather painful parting of the ways.

At this point Clyde Kluckhohn, then chairman of the Department of Anthropology, came to my rescue and became my adviser. He decided that I was almost ready for my Ph.D. qualifying examinations, that I should prepare myself for these ordeals within some six months or so while at the same time I should broaden my general anthropological horizons beyond the confines of Old World archaeology. To achieve this noble goal, he arranged for me to be employed by the Navaho Tribe to do ethnographic research on Navaho land claims cases; he also suggested that I coauthor with him a study on the early life of Franz Boas, which was to be published in a volume celebrating the centennial of Boas's birth in 1859 (Kluckhohn and Prufer 1959). He further asked me to do some work on the taxonomy of Navaho material culture. In retrospect I find it difficult to believe that I was able to do all of this in addition to preparing for my examinations—but I evidently managed to do so. In May 1958, I successfully passed the dreaded general examinations, and in October the special examinations.

To add to these crowded months, I was divorced and remarried between taking my generals and specials. My new wife, a Radcliffe graduate (but mercifully not in anthropology), hailed from Cleveland, Ohio, where her family was well connected in academic and cultural circles. At the time of our wedding, the issue of my future career was raised as casually as it was solved, then and there, on the spot. It so happened that the various Cleveland museums and institutions of higher learning were, at the time, drawing together into a large, loosely cooperative venture. In this context, and simply on the basis of a few well-placed phone calls, I was offered a joint position as Curator of Anthropology at the Cleveland Museum of Natural History and Instructor in Anthropology at Case Institute of Technology, then not yet part of Case Western Reserve University. Upon completion of my Ph.D. degree, this position was to be transformed into a full-time and tenured assistant professorship at Case and ex-officio consultancy at the museum. The job was to begin immediately, in midacademic year, January 1959.

By today's standards, this method of recruiting, without competitive advertising or elaborate affirmative action rules, etc., would seem highly unorthodox. At the time it was common. As late as 1964, I recruited faculty to the Case anthropology program in the same wholly casual fashion. In any event, it is in this essentially accidental manner that I ended up in Ohio and, as will be seen, Ohio archaeology.

Immediately after I had passed my special exams in October 1958, having thus become A.B.D., the question of my dissertation topic was raised by Kluckhohn. I briefly contemplated a topic in cultural anthropology but was dissuaded from pursuing this venture because of my lack of grounding in that branch of the field. Kluckhohn also thought, and in retrospect correctly so, that "out there" in the Midwest, library facilities to pursue a dissertation in Old World archaeology were likely to be inadequate. What then was I to do?

In discussions with Kluckhohn and Stephen Williams, it was casually suggested that I might do a dissertation on some aspect of American archaeology. It was Stephen Williams who narrowed this down to the argument that, now that I was to go into the Ohio wilderness, it might not be a bad idea if I were to reexamine and try to solve the vexing and perennial problem of Ohio Hopewell that had been stagnating ever since the days of Richard Guy Morgan. Morgan, who had made some efforts to deal with Ohio Hopewell in the

wider context of eastern North American archaeology, had been spectacu-
larly dismissed in 1948 from the Ohio Historical Society for political reasons.
Ever since that time, Ohio Hopewell and Ohio archaeology in general had
been lying fallow. As Williams put it to me, there was some fellow down there
in Columbus, at the Ohio Historical Society, by the name of Ray Baby who
may know something about this sort of stuff and who may be helpful; who
knows, things had been pretty dead in Ohio for years, which was surprising,
given the pivotal significance of the area to an understanding of many an
archaeological problem of eastern North America. Since my principal aim
was to complete my Ph.D. degree, I accepted this suggestion and thus, wholly
by accident, got into Ohio archaeology and, more specifically, into the thorny
area of Hopewellian studies. My main dissertation advisers were to be Stephen
Williams and Philip Phillips.

There was no further discussion on how I should proceed. I had to prepare
no thesis prospectus or any other document laying the foundations for what
I was to do. Basically I was told: go out there and see what you can come up
with. I was given carte blanche.

Up to this time, I had no interest whatsoever in North American archaeology. My preparation in this area had been minimal. Throughout my entire
Harvard career, I had taken only two relevant courses—a survey course by
Willey, covering all of Meso- and North America, and one by Stephen Williams, dealing with the archaeology of eastern North America. The former was
inspiring to me, especially because it introduced me to Willey and Phillips's
ideas on method and theory in American archaeology; the latter was, as I recall,
rather didactic, moving with military precision from subarea to subarea in
covering the endless archaeological sequences and their interrelationships.

I thus embarked upon my dissertation unburdened by any knowledge and
without any notable enthusiasm. It was a job that had to be done. Nor did I
find formative societies and their archaic predecessors particularly inspiring;
in fact (and apart from the question of origins), I still find the "pre-
civilizational" stages and cultural configurations of mankind rather boring
and essentially monotonous.

Upon my arrival in Cleveland, I dutifully contacted Raymond S. Baby, who
proved to be of little help, apparently thinking of me as an intruder on his
turf. At the time, as de facto State Archaeologist, he had been for more than a
decade the only individual in the state who could lay claim to some (*very*
modest) expertise in the field he supposedly represented. I also contacted James
B. Griffin at the University of Michigan, then arguably the greatest authority

in eastern North American prehistory, who gave me a first and very sobering idea of how complex a topic had been chosen for me to deal with in my dissertation.

Much chastened, I proceeded to procrastinate and did nothing to pursue the Hopewellian chimera. Instead, and in addition to teaching, I organized a joint venture between the Cleveland Museum of Natural History and the University of Erlangen in Germany to conduct, in the summer of 1959, excavations at an Upper Palaeolithic rockshelter in the classic Altmühl Valley of Bavaria (Prufer 1961b). Upon my return to Cleveland I began to devote a great deal of (as it turned out, productive) time in an attempt at defining and clarifying the nature of the palaeoindian sequence(s) of Ohio. This was the closest I could get to linking my new career with my former Old World palaeolithic interests.

By the summer of 1960, the administration of Case Institute pointedly asked me about the status of my dissertation, suggesting that I had better get moving if I wanted to receive tenure and promotion. I told them that I would have my Ph.D. degree in hand by the end of the 1960–61 academic year, in time (barely) for my subsequent contracts to be changed as originally agreed upon.

I immediately plunged into the Ohio Hopewell problem and found, to my dismay, that not only was the literature on this topic vast but that, with few laudable exceptions, much of the work done in the past was, by any standards, on an incredibly low level. In addition, and again with exceptions, museum and other institutional collections were curatorially defective. Much of the material that once seemed to have existed could no longer be traced; cataloging in many cases proved chaotic to the point where large numbers of objects recovered from numerous locations within and between sites were subsumed under single accession numbers; field notes, if they existed at all, were often minimal and totally incomprehensible. Also, in many cases artifact proveniences given in publications could not be matched with data contained in the catalogs; often, too, published quantitative information markedly differed from the reality as represented in the actual collections.

Some years later, Douglas McKenzie and I characterized this all-pervasive misery in Ohio archaeology as follows:

> Ohio did not participate in the awakening of scientific archaeology in the early 1930's or in the depression-born projects later in the decade. While Cole in Illinois and Ritchie in New York were experimenting with modern techniques and turning away from the "mound-builder" style of theorizing

while Webb in the Southeast was beginning salvage programs Ohio was firmly within the tradition of Moorehead and Mills. In method, theory, and scope of research it stagnated. (1967:v)

I now had to decide what to do with this vast array of disorganized and defective information on which, as I began to realize, hinged much of the interpretation of eastern Middle Woodland archaeology. None of this archaeologically crucial material had ever been pulled together into a coherent compendium.

With neither suggestions nor help forthcoming from Harvard, I had to formulate the actual thrust of my dissertation based upon what I found at hand. Its limits were set by available time and the quality of the database. I thus decided that the only feasible way to deal with Ohio Hopewell had to be

... based upon the vast body of published literature on the subject and on the extensive Museum collections . . . to present as rounded a picture as possible of Hopewell traits in Ohio and their distribution within known sites. On a higher level of abstraction, this bulky compendium—the first of its kind, to this writer's knowledge—forms the basis for a final discussion of the Ohio Hopewell [Complex] in the broader framework of Eastern archaeology. This synthesis primarily serves the purpose of clarifying external and internal chronological relationships of the Ohio Hopewell Complex. (Prufer 1961c:i–ii)

I approached this chaotic mass of information without any research design whatsoever, let alone any notion of constructing some sort of "model" or "models." I proceeded, step by step, in gathering and organizing the available information in terms of somewhat modified trait categories derived from the hallowed analyses of Adena by Greenman (1932) and Webb (Webb and Snow 1945; Webb and Baby 1957). The categories then became the headings of my dissertation chapters. No doubt, the Binfordian proponents of the "New Archaeology" shortly to be a-birthing, would have been appalled by such an antiquated approach.

Viewing Hopewell as part of a developmental continuum, I then assumed that sites and assemblages containing materials reminiscent of Early Woodland affiliations should be placed early within the Hopewell chronological sequence, whereas those with elements I viewed as foreshadowing subsequent Late Woodland/Mississippian developments should date from late in the sequence. At the time, radiocarbon dates were virtually nonexistent; hence, all chronological constructs had to be based upon typology. Finally, I attempted to tie the resultant Hopewell construct into the structure of Hopewellian manifestations in other regions of eastern North America. None of these operations, I should emphasize, was in any way planned; they developed as I plowed through the extant literature and collections.

As I had promised the Case administration, I completed this dissertation, which turned out to be a massive tome of 775 pages (not to mention volumes of illustrations), in time for the summer graduation of 1961. At no time in the course of researching and writing did I have any contact with Phillips. All Williams knew of my progress was that, late in 1960, I sent him a copy of my lengthy chapter on *Hopewell Metal Working* in order to ascertain whether my approach to the problem was acceptable. His brief response was in the affirmative, and thus I proceeded at breakneck speed to carry my labors to their conclusion. The original version was accepted without revisions. There was no dissertation defense.

While researching Ohio Hopewell, it became dramatically apparent that virtually all of the information available dealt with the ceremonial, more specifically the mortuary, aspects of this cultural phenomenon. Clearly I was not dealing here with a "culture" in toto (however one might wish to define an archaeological "culture"). There was no meaningful record of any settlements, certainly not of settlements that were commensurate with the huge earthwork and burial mound complexes characteristic of the southern Ohio Hopewell heartland. Neither did substantial habitational remains seem to be located around the great ceremonial ("public") structures nor, most assuredly, within their confines. This stood in sharp contrast to Hopewellian manifestations in, say, Illinois, where substantial Hopewellian settlements, such as Steuben Village (Morse 1963) and Pool and Irving (McGregor 1958), to mention only a few, were quite common.

At first I thought that the absence of habitational debris other than very occasional thin scatters at such sites as the eponymous Hopewell earthworks was a matter of sampling error or, rather, selective collecting and excavating by people blinded by the splendid burial mounds and the riches they contained. Closer examination established that, indeed, occupational debris of any substance appeared to be lacking, not for want of searching but because in the anticipated form of substantial villages it simply did not exist.

Reflecting on this situation, I became convinced that any speculations on the nature of Ohio Hopewell settlements must start with a consideration of the economic background of the Hopewellians. At the time, it was practically a matter of dogma that Hopewell could not really have been involved in food production, even though occasionally feeble reference was made (because on the evidence, it was unavoidable to do so) to the infrequent occurrence of maize kernels at Hopewellian localities. (For a relatively generous assessment of this situation, see, for instance, Caldwell [1958:30].) Hunting and collecting was typically considered to be the basis of the Hopewellian economy. I found myself unable to accept this obdurate position for the simple reason that the large numbers of enormous mound and earthwork complexes in southern and central Ohio (not to mention the very considerable riches many of these structures contained) could not possibly, by my reasoning, have been constructed and maintained on the basis of simple (or even developed) hunting-and-gathering economies. Virtually all archaeological and ethnographic evidence argued against such a proposition. As a result, I was firmly convinced that food production was an essential element of the Hopewellian way of life.

Having worked through to that proposition, I took a closer theoretical look at the many, apparently uninhabited, burial mound groups and earthworks of southern and central Ohio. I vividly recalled Gordon Willey's classroom discussions at Harvard, not only of Mesoamerican vacant ceremonial centers on the archaeological horizon but also of their catholically transformed, ethnographic survivals in this region.

For purposes of my dissertation in 1961, I summarized the results of these wholly casual reflections in the following sentences that constitute the first tentative formulation of what is now called "Prufer's model":

There is little doubt that Hopewell society was economically based upon agriculture. Two sites, Harness and Turner, have yielded remains of corn. The absence of substantial village refuse within or in the vicinity of the great ceremonial centers strongly suggests that the people lived in relatively small settlements away from the centers, congregating there only on special occasions. One might well conceive of the settlement pattern as consisting of a ceremonial center upon which a number of villages were dependent. The fact that few village sites have been identified thus far may of course reflect merely the preoccupation of professional archaeologists and their less reputable amateur brethren with the more obvious earthwork and mound structures. On the other hand, it is possible that village sites are difficult to identify because of their flimsiness. This may reflect a pattern of shifting agriculture. (Prufer 1961c:729)

At the time this was written, all prehistoric food production in North America was considered to have been derived from Mesoamerica, the principal cultigens being maize, beans, and squash. Hence, those of us willing to consider an agricultural base, or at least component, for the Hopewellian communities of eastern North America were looking for evidence of such plants. Such evidence, although clearly present (Prufer 1965:127), was usually ignored or deemphasized because it did not fit current thinking. Actually, although in time evidence for the presence of Hopewellian corn was noted with increasing frequency, in the aggregate, such evidence (even now) remains minimal and less than impressive. Still, corn is present not only in Hopewellian Middle Woodland contexts but also at Early Woodland sites such as the Daines Mound 2 in Athens County, Ohio. Here an ear of Tropical Flint corn was recovered in an impeccable context dated from 280 B.C. ± 140 (Murphy 1975:157–163). So great is the power of denial that James B. Griffin once wrote to me, without giving any reasons for his judgment, that although he thinks " . . . there was a minuscule amount of Zea in Ohio and Illinois, maybe less than 3–5%, . . . I do not have confidence in the Daines Mound find" (Griffin to Prufer, March 25, 1982). If the evidence does not fit the theory, it must be ignored. In this and other ways the significance of corn finds, if they were acknowledged as legitimate at all, was relegated to the back burner of the debate. Elsewhere in this paper I will have more to say about the rejection of this and other discoveries of relatively early maize.

As it happens, at the time, our preoccupation with classic Mesoamerican cultigens was, in a way, beside the point. As we now know with reasonable assurance, Hopewellian Middle Woodland communities were involved to a considerable degree in food production, albeit principally in the cultivation of various kinds of native starchy seed plants subsumed under the term "Eastern Agricultural Complex." Indeed, corn (and squash) was present in the region, but not to any major extent. I once argued that what is truly important about corn in Hopewellian contexts is not its apparent rarity but the very fact that it was present and had been so for several centuries (Prufer 1982:13–14). In any event, the presence of some corn, in addition to other cultivated plants, indicates an even broader reliance on food production than I had dared to postulate in the old days when I was merely arguing in terms of maize.

What I had in mind in 1961 when I referred to "villages" were *nucleated* villages; the notion of tiny hamlets or farmsteads had not yet entered my mind, except for the suspicion that Ohio Hopewellian villages may have been "flimsy" rather than substantial.

In the fall of 1961, I presented some of the results of my dissertation work at the Annual Meeting of the American Anthropological Society in Philadelphia. This paper was part of a symposium on "Hopewell Culture and Its Extensions," which, including my somewhat modified contribution (Prufer 1964a), was later on published by the Illinois State Museum under the title *Hopewellian Studies* (Caldwell and Hall 1964). This was also the session at which Joseph Caldwell introduced his concept of the "Hopewellian Interaction Sphere" (Caldwell 1964). On our way to the railroad station, after the AAA meetings, Caldwell suggested to me that I should apply to the National Science Foundation for funds in order to pursue some of the many Hopewellian problems that I had touched upon in my presentation. He also asked me what I thought of his Interaction Sphere. I told him that, offhand, I thought the concept to be vague and thus probably open to much potential abuse, but that I would think more about it and let him know, in due time, in the event that I should change my mind.

When *Hopewellian Studies* was in the editorial stages, Caldwell told me he was surprised at how his Interaction Sphere, which he had originally thought of in rather casual terms, had been so readily accepted by the younger generation of eastern North American archaeologists, who were, as it turned out, by and large cohorts of Lewis Binford and his "New Archaeology." Noting that I only used his concept rather sparingly, he wrote almost self-mockingly, "I notice you say nothing about the Hopewellian Interaction Sphere in the opening sections of your paper where you say what you mean by [Hopewell] 'Complex.' Yet, in the body of the paper you use the term interaction sphere more than once. You do this no doubt because it is such a magnificent concept and so convenient to use" (Caldwell to Prufer, March 19, 1963).

Although I did, as he noted, occasionally use the term, I did so (and have done so since) only halfheartedly. Perhaps I can best express my own views on this matter by quoting from a letter written to me by James B. Griffin after I had bemoaned the fact that there still was no consensus as to what Hopewell actually was, if indeed it ever had any reality: "If there is no such thing as Hopewell how can you find reality in the Hopewell Interaction Sphere. The latter term has caused more misinterpretations than the former one" (Griffin to Prufer, March 25, 1982).

Notwithstanding our disagreements on the Interaction Sphere, I followed Caldwell's advice and applied for a National Science Foundation grant. This document had, in retrospect, rather grandiose objectives, one of which was to establish the nature of Hopewellian habitation sites in Ohio. By the time I applied for this grant, I had spent some time in Mexico, where, among other things, I had presented a paper on "Hopewell versus Meso-America and Asia" at the 35th International Congress of Americanists held in Mexico City in 1962. In preparing this paper, I formulated, for the first time in public and on the basis of no material evidence, the hypothesis that was subsequently to become "Prufer's model":

> Another specific situation in Ohio, the heartland of the eastern North American Hopewell Complex, may also suggest Meso-American influence—unless this be interpreted as a case of parallel development. I here refer to the settlement pattern of Ohio Hopewell. It is notorious that in Ohio the evidence for Hopewell rests almost exclusively on the basis of innumerable large and complicated earthworks and burial mounds. Very few village sites have, by contrast, been identified. Certainly the villages that must have been inhabited by those responsible for the massive earthwork structures, were not located at the earthworks themselves. I suggest that this situation may reflect a settlement pattern similar to that characteristic of the vacant ceremonial center pattern in Meso-America. Whether or not we are here in the presence of a genetic link I dare not say. Certainly the situation seems to be typical of Ohio only. (Prufer 1964c:117)

Except for the small "hamlets" or "farmsteads," this passage contains all the ingredients of the version of the "model" that was to be formulated after my 1963 excavations at the McGraw and Brown's Bottom sites. It was added to the original text of the Americanists Congress paper (which was essentially no more than an excerpt from the concluding section of my Ph.D. dissertation) as an off-the-cuff idea, because it seemed a good possibility and because, after all, it fit well into the general topic of the symposium, which dealt with various external influences upon diverse American archaeological complexes.

After having been granted (to my surprise) the NSF funding I had requested, I became much concerned about my ability to produce the field data in support of my various ideas, which, at least in the case of habitation sites, were based wholly upon negative evidence; that is to say, I envisaged the possible reality of Hopewellian settlements in Ohio on the basis of what apparently did *not* exist, namely nucleated villages in or around the earthworks and mounds. My surviving notes and correspondence indicate that, as the field season of 1963 drew near, I became more and more concerned with how I might locate habitation sites and what they would turn out to be—if they should show up at all. What in theoretical discussions, far removed from the realities in the field, seemed plausible, took on a wildly visionary hue, as the zero hour approached.

My uneasiness is reflected in many letters. I really did not know what I was looking for and was even afraid that I might not identify the "real McCoy" if I should stumble upon it; thus, in connection with surveying for sites, I wrote to one correspondent just a few weeks before the start of the 1963 field season:

> If villages of any size exist, they must be near the great centers. But the crucial areas have been surveyed (how well??) from time to time, apparently without results. This, of course, is ludicrous. There must be some kind of settlements. The only possibility I can see (apart from the possibility that for some strange reason Hopewell villages have simply been overlooked) is that Hopewell villages—paradoxically—are not Hopewell villages, i.e. that the village material contains no classic Hopewell ceramics and other accoutrements and is therefore not readily identifiable as being linked to the stuff in the great mounds. This, if it is so, ought to [be] verifiable simply by a close survey around a number of the great centers. (Prufer to Elisabeth E. Baldwin, April 17, 1963)

I thought this passage worth quoting because it illustrates my uncertainties as to what, if anything, I was going to find, and because in it are contained the seeds for my subsequent formulation of the Middle Woodland Scioto Tradition—the notion that Hopewellian settlements may be part of a local cultural tradition of considerable time depth, showing few elements traditionally identified as Hopewell, and which, at a particular point in time, was intersected by the appearance of the Hopewellian Tradition, a supraregional, ceremonial phenomenon that found its expression in a pan–Middle Woodland mortuary complex (Prufer 1964b).

Be all that as it may, once our team was in the field, we located a promising locality on the Scioto River floodplain near the famed Harness (a.k.a. Liberty) earthworks in Ross County. This, Brown's Bottom, was a very small but clearly Hopewellian locality; it covered an area of less than 35 x 15 m. Unfortunately, it had been completely decapitated by recent agricultural activities, which had destroyed all in situ archaeological evidence below the plowzone. In short, extensive testing merely proved its Hopewellian affiliation as exemplified by large numbers of Flint Ridge bladelets, some Middle Woodland projectile points, mica specks, and quantities of simple cord-marked pottery (Blank 1965). There were numerous similar sites in the vicinity of Brown's

Bottom. We did not attempt to excavate any of these localities, because precedent suggested that they, too, had been destroyed by the plow.

However, it was at this point in time that I began to formulate in my mind the notion that (at least southern) Ohio Hopewell was assuredly not characterized by large nucleated villages but by small, presumably agriculturally based hamlets or farmsteads. In short, I began to reify the Mesoamerican aspect of the "model." The problem was, what next? The field season had hardly begun, and we had no viable site to excavate. As luck would have it, we were rescued, as if on cue, by Alva McGraw, a local farmer and most knowledgeable amateur archaeologist, who suggested that we attack an area on his property, again on the floodplain, that he considered promising. This led to the discovery of the McGraw site, which not only proved to be a prolific small farmstead (or hamlet, if you will) buried under substantial flood deposits but which also yielded, in the form of an ear of maize and a few isolated kernels, evidence of food production and, but for numerous bladelets, only small amounts of "classic Hopewellian" material. The recovery of the ear of corn was, by a fluke, witnessed by Richard A. Yarnell, then a student of ethnobotany at the University of Michigan; at my request, he actually removed the ear from the archaeological deposit. This corn did not belong to the Northern Flint varieties common on later archaeological sites of the Upper Midwest (Cutler 1965). The rest of the McGraw saga is a matter of record (Prufer 1965).

A word is in order regarding the age of the McGraw corn and other relatively early finds of maize such as that from the Daines Mound 2. A little over a decade ago, Richard I. Ford of the University of Michigan subjected a number of such finds, including those from Daines and McGraw, to accelerator radiocarbon dating. The result of this was that both of these finds yielded essentially modern values. Ford, curiously, never published this information, but it did, of course, enter the literature without critical evaluation (see, for instance, Wymer 1987). Murphy, clearly perplexed, reluctantly accepted the downgrading of his corn from the Daines Mound 2, even though neither stratigraphy, a standard radiocarbon date of the mound that agreed with its content, nor the taxonomic status of this maize supported the accelerator dates (Murphy 1989). The same holds true for the McGraw material. The argument follows:

1. The McGraw corn belonged to a variety of maize not found in local late-prehistoric contexts in which maize occurs in great abundance; in short, it does not fit the local context.

2. The McGraw midden represents unambiguously a single-component deposit.

3. With the exception of a single (then) experimental bone date (UCLA-685), which came out earlier than expected, all other radiocarbon dates, by now numbering ten, are internally consistent, placing the midden into Middle Woodland times.

4. These dates were run by four different labs, UCLA (679–A, 679–B, 679–C, 688), OWU (61, 62), M (1558), and ETH (2883, 2884, 2885).

5. The McGraw midden was sealed from the surface by massive flood deposits, as can readily be seen from the published photographs (Prufer 1965:17, Fig. 2.3).

6. The corn was found in this midden, in direct association with Hopewellian pottery, at a depth of 37 inches (94 cm), from which it was removed by Richard Yarnell.

Many years ago Griffin told me musingly that radiocarbon dates are tricky. If we like them we accept them; if we dislike them we reject them. Clearly, those who dislike Middle Woodland (let alone Early Woodland) corn accept Ford's dates. Equally clearly, I do not. We *all* know that radiocarbon dating is less of a science than an art plagued with explainable and unexplainable errors. There are, in short, far too many plainly wrong and inconsistent dates. This allows us to fish in troubled waters and to indulge our own prejudices. I plead guilty to being no different from anyone else, but I should like to add my own (hopefully mitigating) rule of thumb: if *all* the circumstantial evidence indicates that the radiocarbon dates are wrong, I will reject them as erroneous. I will accept them only if the contextual data support the assays. In the cases of Daines 2 and McGraw, *none* of the contextual evidence supports Ford's assays; therefore, I reject them. But to return to the narrative. . . .

The McGraw site excavations in 1963 and some additional survey work that year and in the summer of 1964 confirmed my previously formed basic impressions of the relationship between Ohio Hopewell ceremonial centers and the elusive habitation sites that, after McGraw and at least in the Hopewellian heartland of southern Ohio, did not appear to be nucleated villages but very small hamletlike farmsteads. Very clearly, these settlements in no way resembled the substantial nucleated villages of the later Fort Ancient Tradition as exemplified by the Baum (Mills 1906), Gartner (Mills 1904), or Blain Village sites (Prufer and Shane 1970) or the large, late-prehistoric villages of northern Ohio such as Fairport Harbor (Morgan and Ellis 1943) or

Riker (Vietzen 1974). If large Hopewellian villages actually existed, they should by now have been located; such sites are not difficult to identify.

This is not the place to answer questions such as "What do we mean by and how do we define 'villages,' 'hamlets,' 'farmsteads'?" Although at various meetings and in various publications these "profound" questions are occasionally and disingenuously raised, from my operational point of view this is not a particularly meaningful problem. The point is not to define the specific sociocultural content of such occupational entities but to establish whether such ethnographic entities *in general* fit the archaeological record. Suffice it to say that in the present context all relevant settlement units are within the parameter of food production, exhibit a certain degree of sedentism or permanency, and represent a level of sociocultural and demographic complexity above the level of hunters and gatherers/foragers. In interpreting the archaeological record, I might go so far out on a limb as to speculate that farmsteads and (probably) small hamlets are socially based upon kin groups alone, whereas larger nucleated villages are structured on levels that transcend mere kinship organization.

Although it is fun to speculate on the nature and precise structure of prehistoric settlement units, this can rarely be done with any degree of reliability, even if the record of archaeological recovery were superb, which, in the case of Ohio Hopewell, it is not. To quote Griffin again, with specific reference to Hopewell, this cannot be done because "in most areas the excavations have been either too restricted or bungled" (Griffin to Prufer, March 25, 1982). In any event, I have no great faith in such reconstructions, which are only too often underpinned by dubious statistical manipulations and faulty knowledge of social organization and social structure. The limits of archaeological inference are set by the hard fact that to jump from material archaeological culture to nonmaterial culture involves an unbridgeable quantum gap, because the specific nature of the former is not inevitably predetermined by the multitude of possible configurations of the latter. Dead men, after all, tell no tales; they merely leave material traces that can be interpreted in many different ways. The archaeological record can be likened to empty, unmarked bottles. We know that they contained liquids. But, once empty, the kinds of liquids they contained cannot be established but only guessed at by often imprecise analogy.

As far as the archaeological precipitates of "live" villages, hamlets, or farmsteads are concerned, we can infer something of their nature from their dimensions and locations. We can also test our perceptions by ethnographic analogies. Thus, we know something of the physical nature of nucleated villages such as those in the Brazilian rainforest or the early historic Indian villages of the southeastern United States. Physically, such settlements differ sharply from the small southern and central Ohio Hopewellian hamlets. Their ethnographic analogs can be found all over the place in Yucatan beyond the confines of Hispanic foundations such as Merida and among the Ifugao of Luzon in the Philippines (Goldman 1961; Barton 1930).

My immediate reaction to the discoveries at the McGraw site was contained in a letter to Stuart Struever, dated September 7, 1963:

> Just back from the field. In a great hurry, here is the news, nutshell-wise: Found spectacular Hopewell village, or rather farmstead. Dimensions of site no more than 100x100 feet. Farmstead. Found other similar farmsteads around earthworks in lower Scioto Valley where dig took place. Remember my hypothesis? The thing is classic as classic can be. Drilled bear teeth, gorgets, tens of thousands of sherds including Pike rocked, other rocked, dentate rocked, simple stamped, probably complicated stamped, cord marked & plain wares. Bone tools and flint tools galore inc. the most superior kinds of flake knives. But the greatest thing of all: 2 corn cobs [there actually was only one], charred, with rows of kernels in them. Association indubitable; 37 inches below ground, in Hopewell midden which was sealed off from surface by two clearly recognizable layers of flood deposit. Find of corn was witnessed by Yarnell and Jim Brown.

Almost immediately after our return from the field we began the analysis of the McGraw material. Barring some minor problems, and notwithstanding another season in the field, this was completed by the fall of 1964; by the end of the year the manuscript was ready to go to press, as was an article for the *Scientific American* (Prufer 1964b) and the revised version of the 1961 paper for *Hopewellian Studies* (Prufer 1964a).

Throughout the period of formal analysis of the McGraw data, I was bemused by the problem of organizing my thoughts into a coherent picture of what I perceived Ohio Hopewell to have been all about. I finally did this in the way I described in my letter of March 8, 1992, to James B. Griffin, and from which I asked him to read certain passages to the assembled symposium, because I was nonplussed by the fact that my various speculations had now been elevated to the level of a formal "model." Here is what I had to say:

There never was such a thing as a "Prufer Model of Ohio Hopewell Settlement Pattern," certainly nothing that in any way, shape or form, resembled or was intended to be a formal model. Back in 1959–1961, when I wrote my dissertation, and in 1963, when I dug at McGraw, I tried, like everybody else, to explain the scarcity of Hopewellian settlements in the Ohio Valley. Like everybody else too, I operated on the basis of absolutely minimal hard data of any kind . . .

So, with McGraw in hand, I speculated ex nihilo. I never took these speculations seriously. I based them on the application of Occam's Razor—the principle that given available knowledge, the simplest and most elegant explanations of phenomena ought to be the best. In other words, I played around on paper, long-hand, with the help of many martinis in the bar of Fred Harvey's Restaurant in Cleveland's huge Terminal Tower while waiting for a train to New York. The more I imbibed, the better I liked what I wrote. Anybody who seriously thinks that this was intended to be a formal model in the pompous sense of present archaeological practitioners is sadly mistaken.

What I produced one day in the late summer of 1964 was a manuscript of twenty-eight pages (typed) of pure text without bibliographic references. In this opus, which was never published, I incorporated all of my more or less casual ideas on Hopewell. It was entitled "Hopewell: The Dynamics of a Prehistoric Ceremonial System." In bits and pieces, and with slight rephrasings, these ideas were then incorporated into the formal reports intended for, or already in the process of, publication. Here is what I wrote on the nature of Hopewellian occupations in Ohio:

One of the many disturbing problems of Ohio Hopewell has been for many years the seeming lack of habitation sites to which the great tumuli could be linked. Well over a century of research has produced next to no evidence on this point and, by implication, no evidence on the cultural totality of those responsible for the erection of the mortuary monuments. This is the more surprising, since other Hopewellian areas, notably Illinois, have yielded very large villages indeed which could clearly be associated with local Hopewell mounds. Still, in Ohio years of patient fieldwork did not produce any site that could legitimately be called a settlement. Most surprising, the great ceremonial centers, the massive earthworks with their associated clusters of burial mounds, contained no village refuse to

speak of. If anything was found at all, it was in the nature of a thin squat-
ters' occupation that may have been associated at best with the construction of the burial mounds or with the ceremonies performed from time to
time at the great ceremonial centers. Clearly, the nature of Hopewell Society in Ohio must have been markedly different from that of its counterpart
in, say, Illinois.

Previous investigators appear to have approached this problem with the
preconceived notion that such large earthworks and wealthy burial mounds
as those in Ohio must of necessity reflect relatively large populations gathered in sizable villages perhaps similar to the great Mississippian village
sites of the post-Hopewell Fort Ancient Culture. Moreover—even though
this seems in contradiction to the big village–large population concept—
it was widely supposed that Hopewell represented a pre-agricultural level
of economic organization. Consequently, such attempts as were made to
locate Hopewellian settlements, were restricted largely to the immediate
vicinity of the great earthworks and mounds which usually are located on
high terraces above the river bottoms.

In 1962, on the basis of a thorough study of the then available data, the
author formulated a tentative hypothesis that might serve as a point of
departure for the search for Hopewell habitation sites in Ohio. The central
premises of this hypothesis were (a) that Ohio Hopewell was largely based
upon agriculture and that habitation sites should therefore be located in
the agriculturally most suitable bottom lands along rivers, and (b) that
such settlements probably were very small, in the nature of farmsteads
rather than villages, and were related to the great ceremonial centers in a
manner similar to the classic *Meso-American Vacant Ceremonial Center—
Semi-permanent Agricultural Village* type. In this view, a large ceremonial
center and its burial mounds would have been the socio-spiritual nucleus
of a series of small adjacent farm communities. The latter, in turn, were
responsible for the maintenance of their center. This does not necessarily
imply small numbers of people, but a population living in dispersed, small
hamlets.

In the situation here postulated, the ceremonial center served [as] an
overt symbol of the component settlements' social cohesion. Structurally,
this cohesion which ties a series of farmsteads into a unit with a ceremonial center at its core, probably was based upon a network of kinship relations, perhaps of a lineage type, for which the ceremonial center provided
the ancestral burial ground. (Prufer 1964d:x–xii)

Since I did not write this paper for publication, but for the purpose of clarifying my own ideas, the sequence of events narrated above does not quite follow a precise chronological order. Thus, although hinted at earlier, the specific formulation of small hamlets or farmsteads as forming the core of the southern Ohio Hopewellian settlement pattern did not enter my mind until after the excavation of the Brown's Bottom and McGraw sites.

The above, then, is an account of how haphazardly the so-called "Prufer model" came into being. It was a matter of educated guesswork, by elimination and analogy, guesswork that was verified—or so it seemed at the time—wholly by accident in the field. "Model" or not, what do I think of all this now? On the basis of the evidence that has come to light in the past thirty years, I see no special reason to abandon the core of my original hypothesis. I would add that modifications are obviously required in terms of the nature of Hopewellian food production, but the occurrence of maize combined with the now-recognized Eastern Agricultural Complex takes care of that. Further, I would argue today that the "model" is probably more restrictive in geographic application than I had envisaged at the time. To the extent to which any substantial new evidence has been gathered, I suggest that it may not apply to the Turner mounds and earthworks in extreme southwestern Ohio (Willoughby and Hooton 1922). Here there are some, albeit very imprecise, indications that the attendant settlement or settlements were of a larger order than those I envisaged for the Hopewellian heartland further east. Turner, in more than one respect, may be more closely related to such Hopewellian manifestations as the huge and very complex Mann site in Indiana and the settlement system(s) typical of southern and central Illinois.

References

Barton, R. F.
    1930   *The Half-Way Sun*. Brewer and Warren, New York.
Binford, L. R.
    1972   *An Archaeological Perspective*. Seminar Press, New York.
Blank, J. E.
    1965   The Brown's Bottom Site, Ross County, Ohio. *Ohio Archaeologist* 15(1):16–21.
Caldwell, J. R.
    1958   *Trend and Tradition in the Prehistory of the Eastern United States*. Memoir No. 88. American Anthropological Association, Washington, D.C.

1964   Interaction Spheres in Prehistory. In *Hopewellian Studies,* edited by J. R. Caldwell and R. L. Hall, pp. 133–144. Scientific Papers 12, No. 6. Illinois State Museum, Springfield.

Caldwell, J. R., and R. L. Hall

1964   *Hopewellian Studies.* Scientific Papers 12. Illinois State Museum, Springfield.

Converse, R. N.

1993   The Troyer Site: A Hopewell Habitation Site and a Secular View of Ohio Hopewell Villages. *Ohio Archaeologist* 43(3):4–6.

Cutler, H. C.

1965   Cultivated Plants. In *The McGraw Site: A Study in Hopewellian Dynamics,* by O. H. Prufer, pp. 106–112. Scientific Publications, n.s. 4(1). Cleveland Museum of Natural History.

Goldman, I.

1961   The Ifugao of the Philippine Islands. In *Cooperation and Competition Among Primitive Peoples,* edited by M. Mead, pp. 153–179. Beacon Press, Boston.

Greenman, E. F.

1932   Excavation of the Coon Mound and an Analysis of the Adena Culture. *Ohio State Archaeological and Historical Quarterly* 41:366–523.

Griffin, J. B.

1976   Some Suggested Alterations of Certain Portions of "An Archaeological Perspective." *American Antiquity* 41:114–119.

Kluckhohn, C. M., and O. H. Prufer

1959   Influence During the Formative Years. In *The Anthropology of Franz Boas: Essays on the Centennial of His Birth,* edited by W. Goldschmidt, pp. 4–28. Memoir 89. American Anthropological Association, Washington, D.C.

McGregor, J. C.

1958   *The Pool and Irving Villages: A Study of Hopewell Occupation in the Illinois River Valley.* University of Illinois Press, Urbana.

Mills, W. C.

1904   The Exploration of the Gartner Mound and Village Site. *Ohio State Archaeological and Historical Quarterly* 13:129–189.

1906   Baum Prehistoric Village. *Ohio State Archaeological and Historical Quarterly* 15:45–136.

Morgan, R. G. and H. H. Ellis

1943   The Fairport Harbor Village Site. *Ohio State Archaeological and Historical Quarterly* 52:3–64.

Morse, D. F.

1963   *The Steuben Village and Mounds: A Multicomponent Late Hopewell Site in Illinois.* Anthropological Papers 21. Museum of Anthropology, University of Michigan, Ann Arbor.

Murphy, J. L.
  1975   *An Archaeological History of the Hocking Valley.* Ohio University Press, Athens.
  1989   *An Archaeological History of the Hocking Valley.* 2nd ed. Ohio University Press Athens.
Pacheco, P. J.
  1988   Ohio Middle Woodland Settlement Variability in the Upper Licking River Drainage. *Journal of the Steward Anthropological Society* 18:87–117.
Prufer, O. H.
  1952a *Interim Report on the Excavations Carried out at Dher Majra.* Publications 1. Jamia Millia Islamia Historical Research Foundation, New Delhi.
  1952b *Report of the Trial Excavations Carried out at Khilokhri.* Publications 2. Jamia Millia Islamia Historical Research Foundation, New Delhi.
  1956   The Prehistory of the Sirsa Valley, Punjab, India. *Quartär* 7/8:91–123.
  1957   The Neolithic of Kansu Province, China. *Anthropology Tomorrow* 5(2):6–27.
  1958–59 The Upper Palaeolithic Cultures of the Lower Austrian Loess Region. *Quartär* 10/11:79–114.
  1961a The Mesolithic Industries of Fienerode: A Controlled Restudy. *Quartär* 13:31–65.
  1961b The Abri Schmidt: An Important Upper Palaeolithic Site in Bavaria. *Ohio Journal of Science* 61(1):45–49.
  1961c *The Hopewell Complex of Ohio.* Unpublished Ph.D. dissertation, Department of Anthropology, Harvard University, Cambridge, Massachusetts.
  1964a The Hopewell Complex of Ohio. In *Hopewellian Studies,* edited by Joseph R. Caldwell and Robert L. Hall, pp. 35–84. Scientific Papers 12, No. 2. Illinois State Museum, Springfield.
  1964b The Hopewell Cult. *Scientific American* 211(6):90–102.
  1964c Hopewell Versus Meso-America and Asia. In *Actas y Memorias* 1:113–120. XXXV Congreso Internacional de Americanistas, Mexico.
  1964d Hopewell: The Dynamics of a Prehistoric Ceremonial System. Unpublished manuscript in the author's possession.
  1965   *The McGraw Site: A Study in Hopewellian Dynamics.* Scientific Publications, n.s. 4(1). Cleveland Museum of Natural History.
  1982   Hopewell Archaeology. *Reviews in Anthropology* 9(1):7–16.
Prufer, O. H., and E. E. Baldwin
  1957   Mechmiche and Meyrouba: Two Palaeolithic Stations in Lebanon. *Quartär* 9:61–84.
Prufer, O. H., and D. H. McKenzie (editors)
  1967   *Studies in Ohio Archaeology.* The Press of Western Reserve University. Cleveland.
Prufer, O. H., and O. C. Shane
  1970   *Blain Village and the Fort Ancient Tradition in Ohio.* Kent State University Press, Kent, Ohio.

Vietzen, R. C.

1974   *The Riker Site of Tuscarawas County, Ohio*. Ohio Archaeological Society, Sugar Creek Chapter.

Walker, I. C.

1974   Binford, Science, and History: The Probabilistic Variability of Explicated Epistemology and Nomothetic Paradigms in Historical Archaeology. In *Conference on Historic Site Archaeology Papers 1972*, edited by Stanley South, pp. 159–201. South Carolina Institute of Archaeology and Anthropology 7, Charleston.

Webb, W. S., and R. S. Baby

1957   *The Adena People No 2*. The Ohio State University Press. Columbus.

Webb, W. S., and C. E. Snow

1945   *The Adena People*. Reports in Anthropology and Archaeology 6. Department of Anthropology, University of Kentucky, Lexington.

Willoughby, C. C., and E. A. Hooton

1922   *The Turner Group of Earthworks, Hamilton County, Ohio*. Papers 8(3). Peabody Museum. Harvard University, Cambridge, Massachusetts.

Wymer, D. A.

1987   The Middle Woodland–Late Woodland Interface in Central Ohio: Subsistence Continuity Amid Cultural Change. In *Emergent Horticultural Economies of the Eastern Woodlands*, edited by William F. Keegan, pp. 201–216. Occasional Papers 7. Center of Archaeological Investigation. Southern Illinois University, Carbondale.

PART TWO

The Issue of Sedentism

CHAPTER FIVE

Determining Sedentism in the Archaeological Record

Sue Ellen Kozarek

ABSTRACT

The Jennison Guard site is a Hopewellian habitation situated on the Ohio River floodplain in southeastern Indiana. Preliminary analyses of the floral and faunal remains suggested the site was occupied on a year-round basis. The research presented here focuses on the evidence for organization and maintenance of life space at the site. By comparing this evidence with expectations for the use and maintenance of space among groups that are highly mobile, seasonally migratory, and sedentary, it is demonstrated that this site was occupied for a relatively long, uninterrupted period by a residentially stable group.

The objective of my research was to determine the duration or permanence of the Hopewellian occupation of the Jennison Guard site (12D29S) in southeastern Indiana. In other words, was the site occupied on a seasonal basis, or does it represent a permanent settlement, one that was occupied on a year-round basis?

The impressive mounds and earthworks built by the Hopewell have long been an important feature of Midwestern archaeology. Most of our current knowledge of this tradition in the Ohio Valley region has been the result of archaeological investigations focusing on these ceremonial sites. At the 1978 Chillicothe Conference on Hopewell Archaeology, James B. Griffin issued a plea for investigations focusing on Hopewell village sites. He also said that "Someone ought to investigate where many of these populations *hibernated* because they seem to have operated only in the spring, summer, and fall" (Griffin 1979:278).

Fifteen years later we still know very little about the nature of Ohio Valley Hopewell settlements. This is true largely because of a lack of research emphasis on nonceremonial sites. Thus, while artifact and burial typologies are extensive, we know very little about subsistence strategies, settlement patterns, and the secular lives of the Hopewell people in this region.

In contrast, Hopewell archaeology in the Illinois region has focused on subsistence and settlement patterns since the 1950s (e.g., Farnsworth and Koski 1985; Stafford and Sant 1985; Wiant and McGimsey 1986). Several types of habitation sites have been identified in that region: large villages concentrated in major river valleys; other villages and homesteads along secondary streams; and small, isolated habitation sites (perhaps single extended families) in the uplands. All of these settlements appear to have been permanent residences occupied throughout the year. On the other hand, bluff-base sites, associated with ceremonial or mortuary activities, appear to have been short-term or seasonal occupations. Additional short-term occupations have been identified as specialized resource procurement camps.

It is difficult to make comparisons between Ohio Hopewell and the neighboring Havana Hopewell because the data sets are so different; there is a great deal more settlement evidence available for Havana, particularly from the lower Illinois River (Farnsworth 1973; Asch et al. 1979; Asch and Asch 1982; Bender 1985:47). I think we need to make these comparisons, and I suggest we begin by adopting a broader perspective with a new focus directed to investigation of the nonceremonial sites. This approach will provide a much-needed basis for comparison with Hopewellian subsistence and settlement studies of other regions and may shed new light on the nature of interregional relations.

The Jennison Guard site is situated on the floodplain of the Ohio River in Dearborn County, Indiana, approximately 1.6 km southwest of the Great Miami and Ohio River confluence (Fig. 5.1). I conducted excavations at the site as part of my master's thesis research at the University of Cincinnati (Kozarek 1987). As shown in Table 5.1, analyses of the floral and faunal assemblages from the site indicate that a variety of habitats, including wooded areas and forest-edge, aquatic, and riparian habitats, were exploited. All these habitats are in close proximity to the site. Although minor amounts of cultivated goosefoot *(Chenopodium)* and sunflower *(Helianthus)* were present at the site, the core of the subsistence economy consisted of animal species (particularly deer) that were available throughout the year. Evidence of multiseasonal exploitation of animals, combined with the presence of seasonally available species, strongly suggested that the Jennison Guard site was a permanent settlement. However, it is difficult to determine through floral and faunal analyses alone whether a given site was occupied during each season of the year. While identified species may indicate each season respectively, food could be stored and/or transported from a distant area. Moreover, it is nearly impossible to define a particular floral or faunal species that would have been available only in the winter.

I approached the problem from a somewhat different angle. First, I examined the lithic assemblage of the site. Analysis of this assemblage revealed a great variety of tool types, including bifaces, unifaces, projectile points, lamellar bladelets, and retouched and utilized flakes. Also present were numerous biface blanks, preforms, flake cores, and approximately 21,000 pieces of nonutilized debitage.

The major raw material represented in this assemblage was Harrison County (Wyandotte) chert, a variety that outcrops approximately 160 km from the Jennison Guard site (Seeman 1975). Several strategies could have been employed to obtain this nonlocal resource: regional exchange; direct acquisition as part of a seasonal, or migratory, round; direct acquisition incidental to procurement of other resources; and direct acquisition via logistical mobility (i.e., task force) specifically executed for the purpose of obtaining this particular resource. We would expect certain traits in lithic assemblages resulting from these different procurement strategies.

In a strategy employing regional exchange, the resource can be procured from producers through a network of trade partners or other forms of exchange (Ericson 1984:6). We do know that the Hopewell had an established exchange network that involved nonlocal raw materials and finished products. Although unmodified lithic materials do occasionally pass through exchange systems, these materials are usually modified at one or more points along the system, beginning at the source. The reasons for this are simple. Since chert is a heavy, bulky commodity, transportation of unprepared raw material would be costly. Moreover, the interior quality of nodules or blocks cannot be determined unless some flakes are removed; thus, it seems that "unchecked" nodules would be less desirable to consumers, particularly if

alternative chert sources were available as they were for the Jennison Guard
occupants. Typically, when such a resource is a commodity of exchange, it is
in the form of blanks, preforms, or finished products. Consequently, we would
expect little or no evidence of early-stage reduction at the consumer site. Even
blanks or preforms would pose constraints on the form of the finished product; therefore, if procurement was through the mechanism of exchange, we
would expect a relatively high degree of *standardization* in morphology among
the finished implements.

If the occupants of the Jennison Guard site were residentially mobile,
nonlocal chert varieties could have been procured during the course of their
seasonal round. The source area for Harrison County chert, near the confluence
of the Blue and Ohio Rivers, is ecologically the same as the setting of the
Jennison Guard site. Both areas would have offered the same potential for
food resources: fish and freshwater mollusks from the rivers, floodplain and
upland flora, as well as avian and terrestrial fauna. Therefore, a subsistence
strategy involving seasonal migrations between these two areas seems unlikely. If, however, the site's occupants did go to this area on a seasonal basis,
and Harrison County chert procurement occurred within this context, there
would have been ample time to reduce the raw material into at least blanks or
early-stage preforms. Given the amount of domestic paraphernalia they would
have had to transport, it seems that reduction of the nodules would have been
highly desirable. Accordingly, we would again expect very little early-stage
reduction debris to be present at the Jennison Guard site. Further, if lithic
resources were procured during the course of events at one seasonal occupation, then I would certainly expect to find evidence of exploitation of lithic
resources at the other occupation, assuming an alternate chert was available
in that vicinity. Several alternative sources of chert were indeed more readily
available to the Jennison Guard occupants, and an abundant supply of chert
cobbles and pebbles would have been immediately accessible in alluvial and
glacial deposits. These alternative sources were *not* exploited, however, even
for the production of expedient tools.

Direct acquisition of resources may also occur incidental to logistical
mobility strategies designed for procurement of other subsistence needs. Logistical mobility refers to movements of individuals or small groups from a
residential location; this can be in the form of one-day forays or of task-
specific journeys of longer duration. For example, among the Nunamiut,
Binford (1979) observed that lithic resources are normally obtained incidentally to basic subsistence tasks such as hunting forays. The source area for

Harrison County chert is nearly 160 km from the Jennison Guard site. While we could expect such a distance to be traveled during residential mobility, a roundtrip of over 300 km would *not* be undertaken as a logistical strategy for procurement of food resources. Moreover, as stated previously, the ecological settings of the chert source area and the residential site are quite similar, and it is unlikely that one would offer substantially different subsistence resources than the other.

The final means of direct acquisition is a task force organized specifically for the purpose of procuring the nonlocal resource. In order to limit the disruption to daily activities, relatively few individuals would have been involved in such a specific task; these individuals may or may not have been the same as those responsible for tool production. They could simply have quarried (or gathered) a number of nodules and transported them back to the site. If Harrison County chert was procured by such task forces, we would expect the Jennison Guard lithic assemblage to show evidence of initial reduction of nodules, a wide range of chert quality due to the lack of preparing the chert at its source area, early-stage manufacturing rejects reflecting interior flaws in the raw material, and evidence of intentional conservation of the resource, such as a relatively high frequency of expedient tools and formal tool refurbishing. The portion of the lithic assemblage consisting of Harrison County chert fits perfectly the expectations for an assemblage resulting from a procurement strategy involving specific task forces (logistical mobility) sent to procure a particular resource. The lithic assemblage does not reflect traits expected in an assemblage procured incidentally along with other resources obtained through a subsistence strategy based on logistical mobility. More importantly, the assemblage totally contradicts expectations of one procured as the result of residential mobility.

At this point in the investigation, the accumulated data strongly suggested that the Jennison Guard site was not a seasonal occupation. Rather than trying to pinpoint site occupation during each specific season, I next looked at how different groups of people use space—the site structure, or organization of space, and the evidence for site maintenance that would be expected for short-term, seasonal, and permanent occupations. Maintenance of life space (that is, cleaning up and disposing of refuse) is an integral part of a cultural system. It is *not* a distortion of past activities but an important activity in itself. Removal of refuse from an area is highly predicated on the intended future use of that area. Thus, the degree of maintenance activities evidenced at a site have a strong correlation with the permanence of the occupation.

With increased sedentism, one can expect to see greater care taken in refuse removal and disposal. Schiffer (1972:162) notes that "with increasing site population (or perhaps site size) and increasing intensity of occupation, there will be a decreasing correspondence between the use and discard locations for all elements used in activities and discarded at a site." This conclusion is consistent with Murray's cross-cultural study of refuse disposal. She concluded, "Migratory groups that use outdoor living spaces seem to be the only ones likely to discard elements [all types of refuse] at their use [or manufacturing] locations, though they also discard some elements outside their use locations" (Murray 1980:498).

In short-term occupations, such as those of migratory hunter-gatherers, we would expect very little systematic redeposition of refuse. Instead, we would expect most refuse-clearing activities to be of the expedient variety (Binford 1983:144–192; Stevenson 1985:75; Stafford and Sant 1985), with the majority of refuse left in primary context. An example of this type of site structure is shown in the lithic debitage distribution at the Campbell Hollow site (Fig. 5.2), an early Middle Archaic site in west-central Illinois (Stafford and Sant 1985). It shows that this debris class was as likely to be found near hearths as away from them. This distribution is also noted for other debris classes such as bone and carbonized nutshell. No evidence for secondary refuse disposal was found in this occupation. Such a site structure would be expected from a settlement strategy wherein residential camps were frequently moved, as has been proposed for the early Middle Archaic in the region by Brown and Vierra (1983).

A pattern of return occupation (such as a single group occupying a specific site for one or more seasons per year for consecutive years) would be expected to produce blurred areas. For instance, accidental overlapping of activity areas may occur when a base camp is annually reoccupied by the same local group but the camp is set up in a slightly different arrangement each year (Carr 1984:131). An example of overlapping features can be seen in the pattern of Late Archaic features at the Labras Lake site in Illinois (Fig. 5.3) (McElrath et al. 1984). Middens at seasonally occupied sites may be large but are basically homogeneous in content and relatively amorphous.

Sedentary, or permanent, occupations would be expected to show considerable evidence of organizational effort in the site structure, refuse disposal areas with relatively sharp parameters, and deep, dense middens spatially segregated from central activity areas.

Although no structural remains have been recovered from Jennison Guard, indirect evidence of a structure does exist in the form of more than 80 gm of twig-impressed daub. The map in Fig. 5.4 shows the total units excavated during two field seasons at the Jennison Guard site. Two fire features were located in Area B, and Areas C and D were part of a dense midden deposit. Area F is a very large midden, approximately 15 m in diameter and almost 80 cm in depth. A portion of this midden (F-1) yielded a copious amount of refuse and was particularly rich in ceramics and faunal remains. Nearly all the freshwater mussel shell (in excess of 7 kg) from the 1985 field season, as well as 9 kg of bone and over 15 kg of pottery, were recovered from F-1. Through controlled surface surveys and excavated test units, we were able to determine that the area between Transect A and the large midden (F) contained additional fire features. Between the large midden and Area B a dense concentration of chert debitage was located.

Transect A, the focus of my 1985 excavation, measures approximately 30 m by 9 m. Horizontal exposure of this transect revealed an extramural area consisting of a cluster of several types of cooking features, a highly maintained area within this cluster, and spatially discrete refuse disposal zones. Contemporaneity of the features was established through cross-mend analysis of ceramics recovered from them. Figs. 5.5 through 5.9 illustrate the distributions of various artifact classes relative to the features (shown as shaded areas) in this transect.

If the settlement were short-term, we would expect to find the greatest concentration of those materials directly associated with the construction and/ or use of the cooking facilities within the cluster of features. However, very little debris of any kind was found within this area. Note particularly the absence of those materials that may have been directly associated with the use of the cooking facilities (Figs. 5.5–5.8). While some small pottery sherds were found within this area, the average length of these sherds was less than 3 cm, suggesting that they were ground into the living surface.

Very little fire-cracked rock was recovered within the feature cluster, even though a substantial amount was retrieved from within the individual features. Floral and faunal remains were conspicuously absent from this area as well. Small ceramic fragments, floral and faunal remains, and microdebitage were recovered from within each individual feature, suggesting that these items were the products of activities conducted in the feature area. Within the transect, ceramics, fire-cracked rock, and faunal remains were found in concentrations to the west and east of the feature cluster. However, the majority of these debris types was recovered from the midden deposits outside the transect. The overall absence of debris within the ring of features suggests that this area was a highly maintained surface that was repeatedly swept, picked up, and otherwise kept free of debris.

As I have shown, refuse materials were concentrated in two disposal zones marked by crisp, clear-cut boundaries. The soil in these areas exhibited little or no evidence of organic staining; nevertheless, the presence of a wide variety of debris types, as well as several whole and fragmented tools, indicates that these areas were indeed dumps representing secondary deposits of refuse. As would be expected, organic refuse was concentrated in two discrete areas more remote from the central activity area.

Chert debitage was by far the most abundant type of debris within the transect, with a total of 15,723 pieces. This material was also concentrated in one of the refuse disposal areas to the west of the features (Fig. 5.9). Very small flakes or fragments were recovered from within the cleared area as well as from within the individual features. As with the small ceramic fragments, it is likely that these pieces were trampled into the ground. However, no pattern of size-sorting was evident since many more small flakes were recovered from the refuse disposal areas.

The distributions for utilized debitage, bladelets, bifacial blanks, preforms, manufacturing failures, and finished implements coincide with the distribution of nonutilized debitage. I should also note here that "Hopewell Interaction Sphere" items, such as exotic pottery, miniature vessels, and ornaments of mica and copper, were recovered from the refuse disposal areas within the transect as well as from the middens outside the transect. The context from which these items were recovered—along with typical domestic refuse—suggests that the use of these items permeated the daily lives of the Hopewell people, rather than being reserved for ceremonial purposes.

Ethnoarchaeological studies, such as those by Yellen (1977) on the Dobe !Kung, Binford (1983) on the Nunamiut, and O'Connell (1987) on the Alyawara, have shown that outdoor hearths or cooking areas tend to be the focus for a wide range of activities other than cooking and eating. These centrally located areas provide the social context within which a variety of activities may be conducted in the company of others. The cleared area within the ring of features at Jennison Guard appears to have been a centralized, communal activity area in which a variety of tasks was performed, even though very little direct evidence of specific activities was found there. The absence of this evidence is due to the basic behavioral processes of maintenance of life space and refuse disposal. The composition of nearby refuse disposal areas indicates that production of chert implements was among the activities conducted in this area. This activity requires little space, and, while it does produce potentially hazardous debris, this refuse may be swept or picked up fairly easily, particularly if the knapper worked over a basket or hide.

Considerable evidence of community planning is apparent at the Jennison Guard site. The arrangement of several cooking facilities in a large cluster provided a centralized, communal area for food preparation and eating; other activities such as flint knapping also appear to have taken place within this social context.

Refuse disposal at the site appears to have been very systematic; the central activity area was highly maintained, and all refuse items except some of the smallest were removed. Debris was disposed of in several distinct areas; each disposal area is characterized by exceptionally crisp parameters. Those areas near the central activity area contained only small quantities of organic refuse, although they did contain an abundance of potentially hazardous debris (chert debitage and fire-cracked rock). On the other hand, two distant refuse areas (middens) each contained a large amount of debris overall and were particularly rich in organic debris.

I have discussed how archaeological evidence of spatial organization and site maintenance activities may be correlated with expectations for three different types of occupations—short-term, seasonal, and permanent sedentary occupations. Both the short-term and seasonal occupations reflect a residential mobility subsistence strategy, whereas a sedentary occupation reflects residential stability. On the other hand, logistical mobility may enter into the subsistence strategies practiced by any group.

At the Jennison Guard site, in addition to floral and faunal analyses indicative of multiseasonal exploitation, we have evidence for logistical mobility employed for the procurement of a nonlocal lithic resource; great density and volume of middens; a great variety of refuse types; considerable organizational effort in the layout of features, refuse disposal areas, and activity areas; and a high degree of site maintenance. These data indicate that the site was occupied for a relatively long, uninterrupted period of time and that the occupants of the site were residentially sedentary.

The Ohio Valley Hopewell are generally considered to have been somewhat migratory (or seasonal) hunter-gatherers. This consensus may largely be due to our preoccupation with the obvious ceremonial sites. Archaeological investigations focusing on the ceremonial sites and associated habitation "localities" have resulted in a biased data base; these areas would likely have been occupied on a seasonal or short-term basis. Moreover, occupation of these areas at a given time could have been by a select few from a number of individual communities. Accordingly, we should not expect the archaeological remains at these sites to accurately reflect the lifeways of the Hopewell. While the occupants of the Jennison Guard site may have been highly mobile on a logistical scale, they were residentially stable. The Jennison Guard site is but a single example from a complex tradition whose settlements in the Ohio Valley remain poorly documented. The hypotheses and conclusions presented here are not intended to suggest a pattern of settlements for this tradition; rather, they are offered as a basis for much-needed future comparisons.

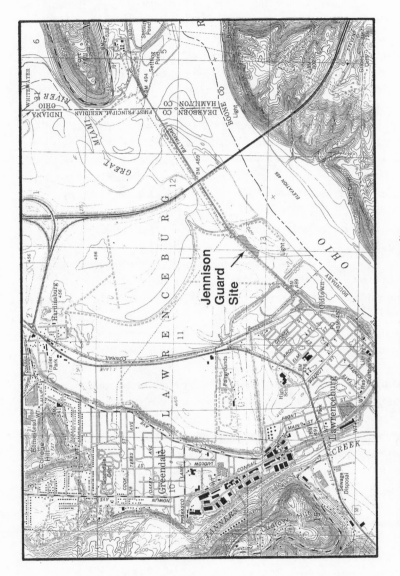

5.1 Location of the Jennison Guard site in Dearborn County, Indiana.

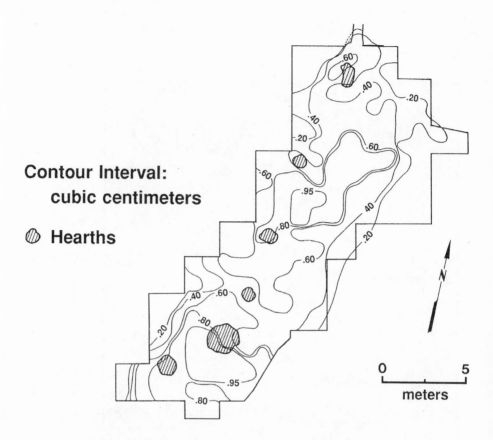

Contour Interval: cubic centimeters

⊘ **Hearths**

5.2 Debitage distribution at the Campbell Hollow site. Adapted from Stafford (1985:Fig. 7.7).

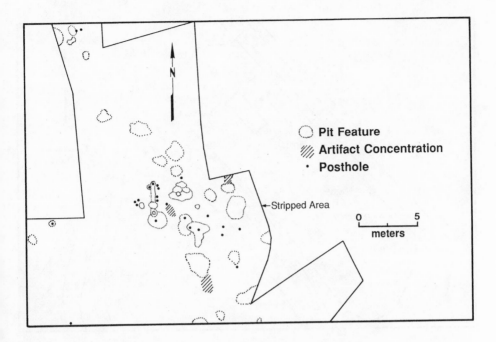

Pit Feature
Artifact Concentration
Posthole

←Stripped Area

0   5
meters

5.3 Debitage distribution at the Labras Lake site. Adapted from McElrath et al. (1984:Fig. 16).

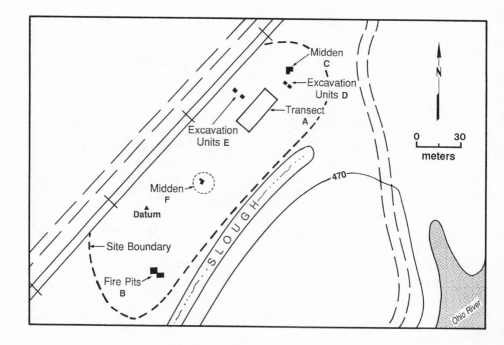

5.4 Excavated areas at the Jennison Guard site.

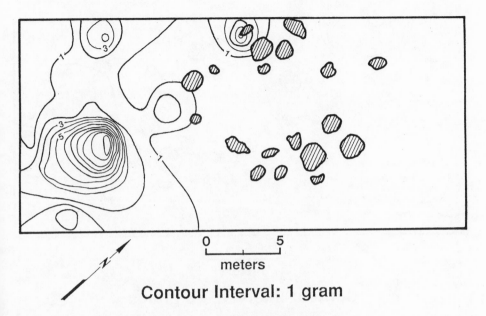

Contour Interval: 1 gram

5.5 Distribution of floral remains in Transect A: 1 gm contour interval.

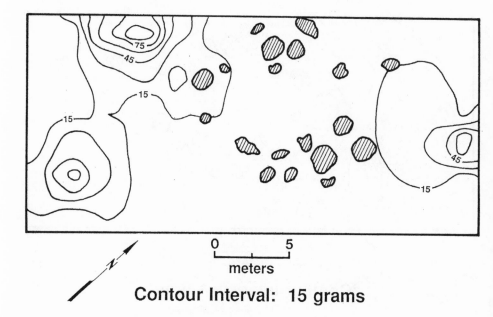

0   5
meters

Contour Interval: 15 grams

5.6 Distribution of faunal remains in Transect A: 15 gm contour interval.

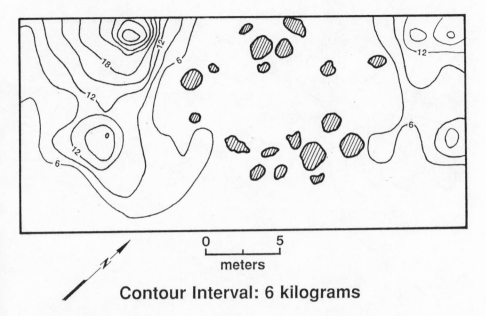

0   5
meters

Contour Interval: 6 kilograms

5.7 Distribution of fire-cracked rock in Transect A: 6 kg contour interval.

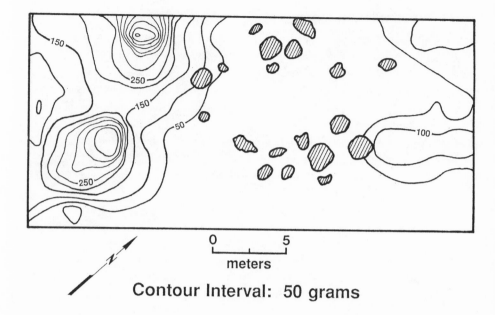

Contour Interval: 50 grams

5.8 Distribution of ceramics in Transect A: 50 gm contour interval.

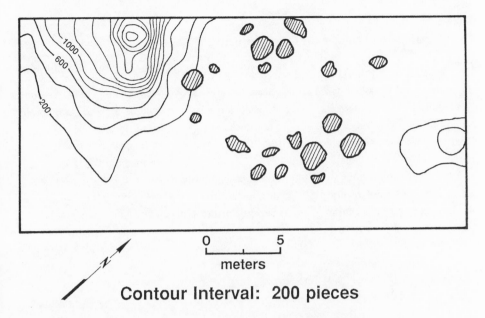

Contour Interval: 200 pieces

5.9 Distribution of chert debitage rock in Transect A: 200 piece contour interval.

Table 5.1

Identified Fauna and Flora at the Jennison Guard Site

Forest	Forest-Edge	Aquatic	Areas Near Water	Cultivated
Raccoon	White-tailed deer	Beaver	Wild onion	Goosefoot
Gray squirrel	Eastern elk	Canada goose	Wild bean	Sunflower
Oppossum	Bobcat	Teal duck	Honey locust	—
Passenger pigeon	Groundhog	Mallard duck	Hackberry	—
Hickory nut	Rabbit	Fish	Knotweed	—
Acorn	Turkey	Freshwater mollusks	—	—
Hazelnut	Bobwhite	Snapping turtle	—	—
Black walnut	Box turtle	Softshell turtle	—	—

References

Asch, D. L., and N. B. Asch

1982   Middle Woodland Archeobotany of West Central Illinois. Paper presented at the 54th Annual Meeting of the Midwest Archaeological Conference, Cleveland.

Asch, D. L., K. B. Farnsworth, and N. B. Asch

1979   Woodland Subsistence and Settlement in West Central Illinois. In *Hopewell Archaeology: The Chillicothe Conference*, edited by D. S. Brose and N. Greber, pp. 80–85. Kent State University Press, Kent, Ohio.

Bender, B.

1985   Prehistoric Developments in the American Midcontinent and in Brittany, Northwest France. In *Prehistoric Hunter-Gatherers: The Emergence of Cultural Complexity*, edited by T. D. Price and J. A. Brown, pp. 21–57. Academic Press, New York.

Binford, L. R.

1979   Organization and Formation Processes: Looking at Curated Technologies. *Journal of Anthropological Research* 35:255–273.

1983   *In Pursuit of the Past: Decoding the Archaeological Record*. Thames and Hudson, New York.

Brown, J. A., and R. Vierra

1983   What Happened in the Middle Archaic? An Introduction to an Ecological Approach to Koster Site Archaeology. In *Archaic Hunters and Gatherers in the American Midwest*, edited by J. Phillips and J. Brown, pp. 165–195. Academic Press, New York.

Carr, C.

1984   The Nature of Organization of Intrasite Archaeological Records and Spatial Analytic Approaches to their Investigation. In *Advances in Archaeological Method and Theory, Vol. 7*, edited by M. B. Schiffer, pp. 103–222. Academic Press, New York.

Ericson, J. E.

1984   Toward the Analysis of Lithic Production Systems. In *Prehistoric Quarries and Lithic Production*, edited by J. E. Ericson and B. A. Purdy, pp. 1-10. Cambridge University Press, New York.

Farnsworth, K. B.

1973   *An Archaeological Survey of the Macoupin Valley*. Reports of Investigations 26. Illinois State Museum, Springfield.

Farnsworth, K. B., and A. L. Koski

1985   *Massey and Archie: A Study of Two Hopewellian Homesteads in the Western Illinois Uplands*. Research Series 3. Center for American Archaeology, Kampsville Archaeological Center, Kampsville, Illinois.

Griffin, J. B.

 1979   An Overview of the Chillicothe Hopewell Conference. In *Hopewell Archae-
        ology: The Chillicothe Conference,* edited by D. S. Brose and N. Greber, pp.
        226–279. Kent State University Press, Kent, Ohio.

Kozarek, S. E.

 1987   *A Hopewellian Homestead in the Ohio River Valley.* Unpublished master's
        thesis, Department of Anthropology, University of Cincinnati.

McElrath, D. L., T. E. Emerson, A. C. Fortier, and J. L. Phillips

 1984   Late Archaic Period. In *American Bottom Archaeology,* edited by C. J. Bareis
        and J. W. Porter, pp. 34–58. University of Illinois Press, Urbana.

Murray, P.

 1980   Discard Location: The Ethnographic Data. *American Antiquity* 45:490–502.

O'Connell, J. F.

 1987   Alyawara Site Structure and Its Archaeological Implications. *American An-
        tiquity* 52:74–108.

Schiffer, M. B.

 1972   Archaeological Context and Systemic Context. *American Antiquity* 37:156–
        165.

Seeman, M. F.

 1975   The Prehistoric Chert Quarries and Workshops of Harrison County, Indi-
        ana. *Indiana Archaeological Bulletin* 1(3):47–61.

Stafford, B. D., and M. B. Sant

 1985   *Smiling Dan: Structure and Function at a Middle Woodland Settlement in the
        Lower Illinois Valley.* Research Series 2. Center for American Archaeology,
        Kampsville Archaeological Center, Kampsville, Illinois.

Stafford, C. R. (editor)

 1985   *The Campbell Hollow Archaic Occupations: A Study of Intrasite Spatial Struc-
        ture in the Lower Illinois Valley.* Research Series 4. Center for American Ar-
        chaeology, Kampsville Archaeological Center, Kampsville, Illinois.

Stevenson, M. G.

 1985   The Formation of Artifact Assemblages at Workshop/Habitation Sites:
        Models from Peace Point in Northern Alberta. *American Antiquity* 50:63–
        81.

Wiant, M. D., and C. R. McGimsey

 1986   *Woodland Period Occupations of the Napoleon Hollow Site in the Lower Illi-
        nois Valley.* Research Series 6. Center for American Archaeology, Kampsville
        Archaeological Center, Kampsville, Illinois.

Yellen, J. E.

 1977   *Archaeological Approaches to the Present: Models for Reconstructing the Past.*
        Academic Press, New York.

CHAPTER SIX

Paleoethnobotany in the Licking River Valley, Ohio

Implications for Understanding Ohio Hopewell

Dee Anne Wymer

ABSTRACT

The past decade has seen the establishment of an extensive and intensive paleoethnobotanical record for Hopewell habitation and ceremonial sites in the Ohio Licking River Valley. The paper explores the implications these data have for the larger theoretical issues of prime importance for understanding Ohio Hopewell. Thus, the paper addresses the nature of the native gardens and the impact of Hopewell subsistence practices on the local ecology and how both aspects relate to arguments centered on settlement sizes, population dispersion, and degree and type of sedentariness and explores niche width and diversity.

The purpose of this paper is to present an outline of a decade of research into Middle Woodland paleoethnobotany in the Licking River Valley of central Ohio. We now have enough information to be fairly confident regarding the role of collected and cultivated plants in the subsistence practices of Middle Woodland populations of this area. This is the only region in Ohio with well-documented, relevant botanical samples. Rather than merely listing the obvious—what has been found and identified in flotation samples, I am here attempting to utilize the recovered archaeobotanical material in order to address some of the larger issues in Hopewell archaeology, issues such as those pertaining to the nature of Middle Woodland settlements, the degree of sedentariness, and the level of integration of the corporate-ceremonial aspects of Middle Woodland culture with their presumed dispersed populations. These are the very issues that still lie at the heart of much of the impetus driving recent research in Ohio Hopewell archaeology.

Background

The data base for Middle Woodland archaeobotany in the Licking River Valley continues to yield quantitatively and qualitatively productive information. The present study is based on data principally derived from four Middle Woodland habitation areas: the Murphy (33Li212), Murphy III (33Li211), Campus (33Li250), and NUWAY (33Li267) sites. These localities have been thoroughly investigated and documented in recent years (Table 6.1), and we are now beginning to explore not only the domestic but also possible ceremonial uses of plant material at the corporate-ceremonial centers and ritual spaces (Wymer in press). Research at the Murphy site has documented an extensive and intensive paleoethnobotanical record, substantiated by analysis of samples from adjacent Middle Woodland habitation sites (Fig. 6.1; Table 6.1; also see Dancey 1991; Wymer 1987a, 1987b, 1992, 1993).

The analysis of samples from ceremonial sites outside the valley proper suggests possible uses of plant material, particularly the ritual use of certain specific tree taxa. This aspect of the problem is currently under investigation through the analyses of samples from ceremonial contexts in the area immediately adjacent to the Murphy site (Wymer 1984; Reustle 1993). Lastly, the paleoethnobotanical records of Early Woodland (1,000–100 B.C.) and Late Woodland (A.D. 300–900) sites in the region have been investigated. Thus, rather than standing in isolation, the Middle Woodland botanical data can be viewed in the larger context of the entire Woodland temporal framework (Wymer 1992). The Licking River Valley materials can also be compared to those from other Midwestern regions with substantial data bases suitable for paleoethnobotanical analysis.

As will be seen below, broad similarities emerge among these various regions, including similarities in the utilization of the same indigenous garden system (the Eastern Agricultural Complex), the reliance on gathered resources such as nut masts and shrubby fruits, and the initial impact of human economic activities on the local environments (Asch and Asch 1985; Crites 1987; Ford 1985; Johannessen 1982, 1984; Fritz 1986; Wymer 1989, 1992). Although regional differences do occur, including distinctions in the dominance of individual crop species by region, overall similarities are most striking. This is perhaps even more noteworthy when one considers the different environments represented by the regions; they range from the Illinois prairie-floodplain biome to the dense deciduous forests of central Ohio (Wymer 1989, 1992).

Licking River Valley Middle Woodland: The Paleoethnobotanical Record

Overall, the same basic categories of archaeobotanical materials such as wood charcoal, nutshell, nutmeat, squash rind, and seeds/achenes, have been identified in the various site assemblages. While, as will be explored below, fundamental similarities in the density and diversity of botanical data are evident, sometimes dramatic differences between sites have also been noted. Future work will be geared toward broadening the data base in order to investigate intra- and interregional distinctions. At this time, some obvious causes for such differences are the uneven sampling size, as well as certain depositional distinctions among feature classes from which the evidence has been derived (Wymer and Pacheco 1987). For example, the NUWAY site sample comes from a single large pit that contained unusually large quantities of sherds and carbonized matter. By contrast, the Murphy sample consisted of material derived from approximately half of all the site's features, which, moreover, included all feature classes (Table 6.1).

Density Values for Botanical Classes

The four primary botanical classes—wood charcoal, nutshell, squash rind, and seeds—occur in distinctive densities among the four sites (Figs. 6.2 and 6.3). Wood charcoal and carbonized nutshell are common components of site features, with wood charcoal always appearing at higher densities than the remains of other classes (Fig. 6.2). To place this in a broader perspective, Early Woodland densities of wood charcoal and nutshell are similar to, albeit slightly lower than, the densities of Middle Woodland samples, whereas the densities of these two plant classes are moderately to significantly higher in Late Woodland samples (Wymer 1992).

Seed densities at the Licking River Valley Middle Woodland sites are, with the exception of the Murphy III locality, quite high, typically clustering around twenty seeds per liter (Fig. 6.3). These seed densities are much higher than those noted at Early Woodland sites, and they match or (typically) exceed values for Late Woodland sites. Squash rind, although definitely present and at high ubiquities (it was recovered from 30 percent to 90 percent of features), occurs in low to moderate quantities. It is more common at Middle than Early Woodland sites; on the other hand, Late Woodland rind densities are much greater (Wymer 1992). Taxonomically the squash rind specimens are the same for all Woodland periods. They represent a warty variety of the yellow-flowered gourd squash (*Cucurbita pepo* cf. var. *ovifera*).

Nutshell

Hickory (*Carya* spp.), hazelnut (*Corylus* cf. *americana*), acorn (*Quercus* spp.), and black walnut (*Juglans nigra*) are the nut types recovered from the Licking River Valley Middle Woodland sites (Fig. 6.4). In all cases, hickory is the most common nut class, with either hazelnut or acorn in second position. The same pattern holds true for Late Woodland sites. Although hickory nutshell is prevalent in eastern North America for all time periods, hazelnut is not. This taxon is only recovered in moderate to large quantities in the mid–Ohio River Valley in Middle and Late Woodland sites (Wymer 1989, 1992).

Wood Charcoal Identification

A limited range of tree taxa was identified in the wood assemblages of the Middle Woodland sites (Fig. 6.5). Hickory and oak, particularly the white group, was the most commonly utilized firewood resource at these localities, with mesic taxa, such as elm (*Ulmus* spp.), ash (*Fraxinus* spp.), walnut (*Juglans* spp.), maple (*Acer* spp.), and sycamore (*Platanus occidentalis*) occurring in moderate to minor quantities. This use of local "climax" genera is indicative of Early Woodland fuel preferences as well. However, diversity of wood taxa increases substantially at Late Woodland sites, and a significant component (e.g., 25 percent) of the wood assemblages here consists of second-growth taxa such as, *inter alia*, red mulberry (*Morus rubra*), black cherry (*Prunus serotina*), black locust (*Robinia pseudoacacia*), and pine (*Pinus* spp.). (For further discussion of this point, see Wymer [1990].)

Carbonized Seeds/Achenes

The Eastern Agricultural Complex is present at all four sites and clearly represents the dominant portion of the seed assemblages (Fig. 6.6). The starchy, high-carbohydrate members of the Complex identified in the samples include maygrass (*Phalaris caroliniana*), erect knotweed (*Polygonum erectum*), and goosefoot (*Chenopodium* spp.). The oil-rich members of the Complex—domesticated sumpweed (*Iva annua* var. *macrocarpa*) and sunflower (*Helianthus annuus*)—were recovered in samples from the Murphy site, and sumpweed from the Campus site (Wymer 1987a). In fact, with 154 specimens, sumpweed is quite common at Murphy, constituting 6.6 percent of the site's identified seed assemblage. Only eleven sunflower achenes were noted in the Murphy samples. The Campus site material yielded five sumpweed specimens, or .8 percent of the identified seed assemblage.

Fruit and berry seeds and achenes were also frequently encountered in the samples; raspberry (*Rubus* sp.), elderberry (*Sambucus* cf. *canadensis*), and sumac (*Rhus* sp.) are the most common genera. Seeds of ruderal taxa, such as Graminae, spurge (*Euphorbia* sp.), and black-seeded plantain (*Plantago regulii*), are ubiquitous but numerically unimportant in the seed spectra.

Erect knotweed and maygrass are the most prevalent of the Eastern Agricultural Complex taxa at the sites; goosefoot consistently appears at around 25 percent of the total starchy counts (Fig. 6.7). It should be noted that goosefoot specimens from the Murphy, Campus, and NUWAY samples have been morphologically confirmed through scanning–electron microscopy analysis as representing the domesticated form (*C. berlandieri* spp. *jonesianum*). (For a discussion of this point, see Smith [1985a, 1985b].)

The Eastern Agricultural Complex also occurs at Early Woodland sites, although at lower percentages of the identified seed assemblages. With approximately 70–80 percent of the identified seeds, the importance of the Eastern Agricultural Complex at Late Woodland localities either matches or exceeds that noted for the Middle Woodland localities (Wymer 1987b, 1990). The same three taxa of erect knotweed, maygrass, and domesticated goosefoot appear at the Late Woodland sites, with the addition, at some localities, of little barley (*Hordeum pusillum*) (Wymer 1990). Overall, the diversity of seed types increases dramatically in Late Woodland times, particularly as far as fruit and ruderal taxa are concerned (Wymer 1990, 1992).

Implications of the Paleoethnobotanical Record

Going beyond mere numerical indices, what does the paleoethnobotanical record tell us about Middle Woodland settlement systems? This material should have implications regarding the choice of settlement locations, the nature of the settlements themselves, and patterns of intrasite social integration. Following are some basic conclusions drawn from the available information.

There is no doubt that Licking River Valley Hopewell populations had been farmers—not maize agriculturalists, but farmers nonetheless. The presence of squash rind, domesticated members of the Eastern Agricultural Complex, and evidence for land-clearing activities fully support this conclusion. Furthermore, I would suggest that these agricultural products had been a major (if not the primary) component of Hopewellian diet. This assertion is based on the pattern of archaeobotanical materials found at Middle Woodland sites, as well as on comparisons with the evidence from subsequent nucleated Late Woodland villages. For example, seed density and the numerical importance of the Eastern Agricultural Complex members is quite comparable to the values calculated for several large Late Woodland sites such as Water Plant, Zencor, and Childers (Wymer 1987a, 1990, 1992). This same assertion—that Middle Woodland populations had been based on a nonmaize agricultural subsistence economy—has recently been described for other regions (Smith 1987).

Licking River Valley Hopewell populations were sophisticated in their horticultural activities, and these activities are only one component of a system that purposefully manipulated local habitats, sometimes on a large scale. The term "sophisticated" here refers to the variety and types of cultigens and other domesticates utilized in the Hopewellian system; it also refers to the nature of the gardens themselves. The plants involved (sunflower, sumpweed, erect knotweed, maygrass, goosefoot, and squash) have different life history characteristics, lengths of growing season, and moisture requirements. All of these factors must have entailed careful management within garden spaces. They must also have had implications for the cultural aspects of harvesting, processing for consumption, and surplus storage.

Additionally, reconstruction of the prehistoric floral communities (Fig. 6.8) reveals that all four sites were located within what must have been a dense white oak–hickory forest (Wymer 1987a). Thus, some of the area surrounding the sites must have been cleared for gardens as well as for living space. The evidence also suggests that the cultivation strategy employed a swidden system. This is based not only on the identification of cultigens in the samples but also on the ubiquitous presence in the assemblages of elderberries, raspberries, sumac, and hazelnut. All of these genera are only common in relatively open areas with high light intensities; today such areas are frequently associated with overgrowth at forest edges or within fields. The co-occurrence of garden products and these collected genera in the same depositional contexts and in the same features implies artificially created plots of land in varying stages of regrowth close to the human habitation sites.

The system of habitat modification, which originated in Middle Woodland times, expanded in the subsequent Late Woodland period. There is evidence that Late Woodland populations, as inferred from second-growth wood and seed taxa, had severely affected their local environments (Wymer 1990). The differences observed between Middle and Late Woodland habitation sites may well reflect the increasing impact of land clearance and utilization on the structure of the local environment. The evidence from surveys and excavations indicates that Middle Woodland populations occupied small (0.5–1 ha) hamlets evenly dispersed across the valley floor (Dancey 1992; Pacheco 1990, chapter 2). These settlements appear to be systematically distributed on specific glacial or other outwash features that are characterized by the best agricultural soils in the county (Pacheco 1988, 1990; Wymer 1987a).

On the other hand, Late Woodland populations in central and southern Ohio apparently congregated in extensive (3–4 ha) nucleated villages (Dancey 1991, 1992; Pacheco 1988, 1990, chapter 2; Shott 1990). It seems plausible to assume that the greater population size of the Late Woodland villages undoubtedly required larger garden plots and an increased draw upon locally collected resources.

Middle Woodland manipulations of the environment were characterized by a unique aspect that may, moreover, have implications for investigations aimed at elucidating how these small and scattered local household clusters were integrated on a supraregional basis—for what these people did on a small scale at their habitation sites, they also did on a grand scale at their ceremonial centers. The Newark Earthworks are located on the same glacial outwash terrace as are many of the Hopewellian habitation sites. Available data indicate that, if left undisturbed by human populations, a rich and dense white oak forest would have once covered this terrace environment. To put it quite simply, it seems likely that a large number of trees must have been removed prior to the architectural planning and construction of the immense embankments and mounds. Not only does this imply a great expenditure of energy on the part of the Hopewellians, but it also raises a number of intriguing questions. When and in what manner was the land clearance initiated? What does this tell about the timing and degree of planning that went into the construction of the Newark Earthworks? What did the inhabitants do with all those trees cleared from the land? Was the space created by such deforestation kept deliberately clear by purposeful prevention of the natural reforestation process? Is it significant that the earthworks were built surrounding a natural marshy pond that may (even) have been artificially expanded? Given the apparent Hopewellian habit of placing their hamlets adjacent to marshes, this point is of more than passing interest.

The paleoethnobotanical data also have implications for illuminating the nature of Middle Woodland hamlets. There is currently an ongoing debate in the literature about the degree of sedentariness of Ohio Hopewell populations (Dancey 1991; Kozarek 1987, chapter 5; Pacheco 1988; Yerkes 1988; Smith 1987; Prufer, chapter 4). Specifically, the debate focuses on how "permanent" these settlements had been: were they nearly or completely permanent or merely seasonal and, if "seasonal," to what extent? A closely related point can be raised by questioning the life span of any or all of these habitation sites. The botanical material implies that people must have invested considerable amounts of time and energy in the creation, maintenance, and harvesting of the garden plots and in the processing of the products derived from these gardens. Furthermore, if hazelnut, elderberries, and other taxa recovered from the samples do represent abandoned garden plots, this may further imply that at least some (albeit unspecified) span of time was involved during which the local area had been utilized. It should also be noted that hazelnut, in order to avoid the heavy faunal predation characteristic for this genus, must be closely monitored by humans if they effectively desire to make use of this late-summer resource (Wymer 1983).

One can conclude from the above considerations that, at a minimum, some individuals must have been occupying these and other such sites during spring planting, summer maintenance, and fall harvesting of horticultural products. This implies some degree of sedentism. Given the small dimensions of the sites involved, this suggests low populations. It is not improbable that the people, in addition to their spring, summer, and fall stays, also wintered at these sites—although the lack of significant remains of house structures at the well-documented Murphy site is puzzling. Certainly, the formal plan of the living space at Murphy, with well-defined feature clusters based on probable function, suggests some degree of site maintenance during the period of occupation (Dancey 1991).

As noted above, the Middle Woodland populations were creating, in the immediate vicinity of their living spaces, limited, but deliberately induced, open environments by cutting and maintaining clearings in the dense forest. These clearings in the local ecosystem resulted in an artificial patchy environment and enhancement of local resource diversity. Abandoned and overgrown gardens would have increased the diversity of both floral and faunal resources, hence making them more attractive to humans. Furthermore, these second-growth shrubby areas would have been much easier to reclear for garden renewal than the virgin oak forest. It is not inconceivable that some of the Middle Woodland habitation sites were periodically used, or reused, after a period of abandonment, perhaps over several generations. Thus, although the horticultural activities at each individual hamlet were relatively small-scale (certainly when compared to the later and larger Late Woodland settlements), the cumulative effects of a dispersed series of hamlets throughout the valley may have created a significant impact on the resource base of the Licking Valley.

Conclusion

The data presented here have answered some questions and raised a few others. The Hopewellians were farmers, apparently occupying year-round, or nearly so, settlements, which can be called "hamlets." But even as the Hopewell corporate-ceremonial sphere is somewhat unique in the archaeological record, because Hopewellian monumental "architecture" seems to be of a kind usually associated with more complex, stratified societies, so is the Hopewellian horticultural system unique; it was a deciduous forest-based swidden system making use of a wide variety of diverse taxa. The next phase of research should address the precise nature of this horticultural system within the environmental context of eastern North America. Perhaps this can be done by testing and replicating garden plot formation and maintenance in similar situations in order to generate a better understanding of the impact this type of farming may have had on human populations and on the ecosystems within which they operated. Ultimately it is hoped that such information can be integrated into a broader and deeper understanding of the intrahamlet and hamlet-ceremonial center linkage within central Ohio Hopewellian contexts.

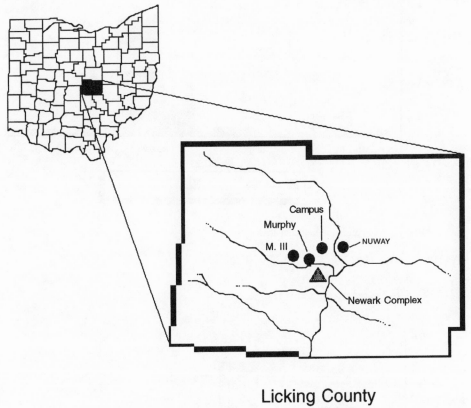

Licking County

6.1 Middle Woodland sites in Licking County with archaeobotanical samples.

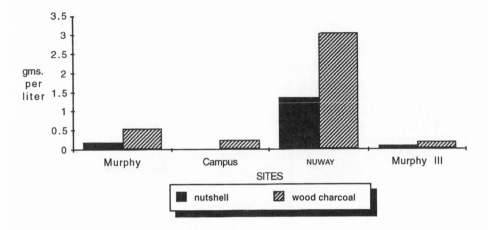

6.2 Wood charcoal and nutshell densities.

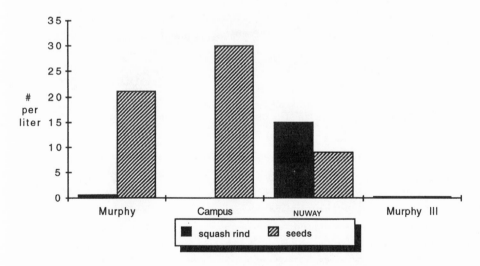

6.3 Squash rind and seed densities.

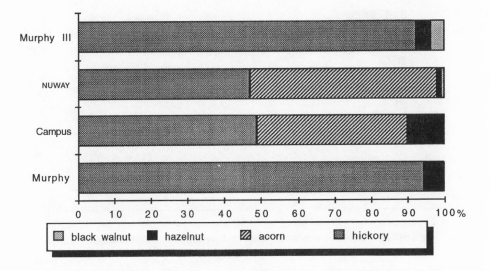

6.4 Identified nutshell percentages by fragment numbers.

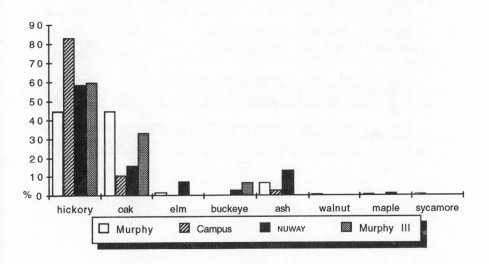

6.5 Percentage of identified wood taxa by fragment numbers.

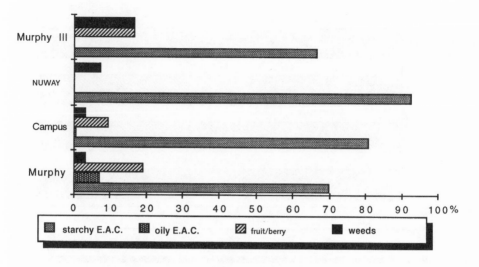

6.6 Seed groups: percentage of identified seeds.

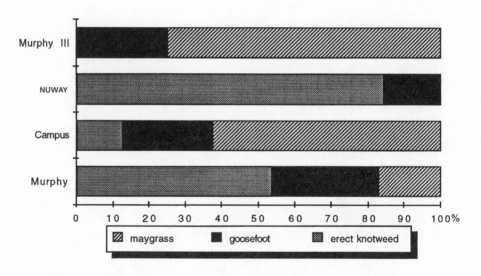

6.7 Starchy Eastern Agricultural Complex taxa: percentage each taxon contributes
to total.

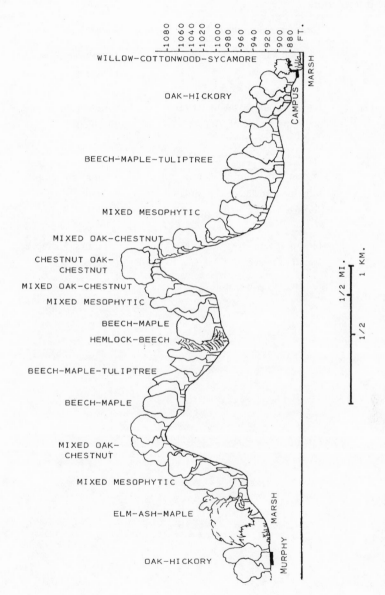

6.8 Vegetation transect of Licking Valley Middle Woodland sites.

Table 6.1

Site and Sample Information

Sites	Locations/Environment	Sample Size
Murphy (33LI212) A.D. 100–200	Raccoon Valley; Vanata Terrace— glacial outwash	18 features; 37 samples; 135 liters
Murphy III (33LI311) —artifacts similar to 33LI212	Raccoon Valley; Vanata Terrace— 400 m northwest of 33LI212	4 features; 9 samples; 25.6 liters
Campus (33LI250) 10 B.C.	Sharon Valley run; Wisconsin end moraine associated with Vanatta Terrace	3 features; 7 samples 25 liters
NUWAY (33LI267) 100 B.C.	Licking River—north branch; Vanatta Terrace	2 features; 3 samples; 12 liters

References

Asch, D. L., and N. B. Asch
    1985   Prehistoric Plant Cultivation in West-Central Illinois. In *Prehistoric Food Production North America,* edited by R. I. Ford, pp. 149–203. Anthropological Papers 75. Museum of Anthropology, University of Michigan, Ann Arbor.

Crites, G. D.
    1987   Human-Plant Mutualism and Niche Expression in the Paleoethnobotanical Record: A Middle Woodland Example. *American Antiquity* 52:725–740.

Dancey, W. S.
    1991   A Middle Woodland Settlement in Central Ohio: A Preliminary Report on the Murphy Site (33L1212). *Pennsylvania Archaeologist* 61:37–72.
    1992   Village Origins in Central Ohio: The Results and Implications of Recent Middle and Late Woodland Research. In *Cultural Variability in Context: Woodland Settlements of the Mid-Ohio Valley,* edited by M. F. Seeman, pp. 24–29. Special Paper 7, Midcontinental Journal of Archaeology. Kent State University Press, Kent, Ohio.

Fritz, G.
    1986   *Prehistoric Ozark Agriculture: The University of Arkansas Rockshelter Collections.* Unpublished Ph.D. dissertation, Department of Anthropology, University of North Carolina, Chapel Hill.

Ford, R. I.
    1985   Patterns of Prehistoric Food Production in North America. In *Prehistoric Food Production in North America,* edited by R. I. Ford, pp. 341–364. Anthropological Papers 75, Museum of Anthropology. University of Michigan, Ann Arbor.

Johannessen, S.
    1982   Paleoethnobotanical Trends in the American Bottom: Late Archaic through Mississippian. Paper presented at the 47th Annual Meeting of the Society for American Archaeology, Minneapolis.
    1984   Paleoethnobotany. In *American Bottom Archaeology,* edited by C. A. Bareis and J. W. Porter, pp. 197–214. University of Illinois Press, Urbana.

Kozarek, S. E.
    1987   *A Hopewellian Homestead in the Ohio River Valley.* Unpublished master's thesis, Department of Anthropology, University of Cincinnati.

Pacheco, P. J.
    1988   Ohio Middle Woodland Settlement Variability in the Upper Licking River Drainage. *Journal of the Steward Anthropological Society* 18:87–117.
    1990   Hopewell Settlement Patterns as Revealed by Siteless Survey. Paper presented at the 57th Annual Meeting of the Eastern States Archaeological Federation, Columbus, Ohio.

Reustle, C.

   1993   The Paleoethnobotanical Record of the Munson's Spring Site (33Li251): Plant Utilization of Ceremonial and Habitation Contexts. *Ohio Archaeologist* 43(4): 37–40.

Shott, M. J. (editor)

   1990   *Childers and Woods: Two Late Woodland Sites in the Upper Ohio Valley, Mason County, West Virginia.* Archaeological Report 200. Cultural Resource Assessment Program, University of Kentucky, Lexington.

Smith, B. D.

   1985a The Role of *Chenopodium* as a Domesticate in Pre-Maize Garden Systems of the Eastern United States. *Southeastern Archaeology* 4:51–72.

   1985b *Chenopodium berlandieri* sp. *jonesianum*: Evidence for a Hopewellian Domesticate from Ash Cave, Ohio. *Southeastern Archaeology* 4:107–133.

   1987   Hopewellian Farmers of Eastern North America. Paper presented at the Plenary Session, Eleventh Congress, International Union of Prehistoric and Protohistoric Sciences, Mainz, Germany.

Wymer, D. A.

   1983   An Investigation of Hazelnut: Its Archaeological Utilization, Ecology, and Mast Production. Manuscript on file at The Ohio State University, Department of Anthropology, Columbus.

   1984   The Archaeobotanical Assemblage from the Connett Mounds #3 and #4, the Wolf Plains Project, Athens County, Ohio. Report submitted to the Department of Contract Archaeology, Ohio Historical Society, Columbus.

   1987a *The Paleoethnobotanical Record of Central Ohio—100 BC to AD 800: Subsistence Continuity Amid Cultural Change.* Unpublished Ph.D. dissertation, Department of Anthropology, The Ohio State University, Columbus.

   1987b The Middle Woodland–Late Woodland Interface in Central Ohio: Subsistence Continuity Amid Cultural Change. In *Emergent Horticultural Economies of the Eastern Woodlands,* edited by W. F. Keegan, pp. 201–216. Occasional Papers 7. Center for Archaeological Investigations, Southern Illinois University, Carbondale.

   1989   The Middle Woodland–Late Woodland Cultural Shift in the Midwest: The Paleoethnobotanical Record. In *Anthropology: Unity in Diversity,* edited by M. H. Sidky, J. Forados, and P. Pacheco, pp. 34–52. Occasional Papers in Anthropology 4. Department of Anthropology, The Ohio State University, Columbus.

   1990   Archaeobotany. In *Childers and Woods: Two Late Woodland Sites in the Upper Ohio Valley, Mason County, West Virginia,* edited by M. J. Shott, pp. 402–535. Archaeological Report 200, Cultural Resource Assessment. University of Kentucky, Lexington.

   1992   Trends and Disparities: The Woodland Paleoethnobotanical Record of the

Mid-Ohio Valley. In *Cultural Variability in Context: Woodland Settlements of the Mid-Ohio Valley,* edited by M. F. Seeman, pp. 65–76. Special Papers 7, Midcontinental Journal of Archaeology. Kent State University Press, Kent, Ohio.

1993   Cultural Change and Subsistence: The Middle and Late Woodland Transition in the Mid-Ohio Valley. In *Foraging and Farming in the Eastern Woodlands,* edited by C. M. Scarry, pp. 138–156. University Presses of Florida, Gainesville.

in press   The Ohio Hopewell Econiche: Human-Land Interaction in the Core Area. In *A View From the Core: A Synthesis of Ohio Hopewell Archaeology,* edited by P. J. Pacheco, pp. 47–68. The Ohio Archaeological Council, Columbus.

Wymer, D. A., and P. J. Pacheco

1987   Correspondence Analysis: Paleoethnobotanical Data and the Middle Woodland to Late Woodland Transition. Paper presented at the 32nd Annual Midwestern Archaeological Conference, Milwaukee.

Yerkes, R. W.

1988   The Woodland and Mississippian Traditions in the Prehistory of Midwestern North America. *Journal of World Prehistory* 2:307–357.

PART THREE

Archaeological Studies In and Around the Hopewell Earthworks

CHAPTER SEVEN

Hopewellian Occupations at the Northern Periphery of the Newark Earthworks

The Newark Expressway Sites Revisited

Bradley T. Lepper and Richard W. Yerkes

ABSTRACT

Artifacts, feature plans, and other data from a testing program performed in the 1970s along the right-of-way of State Route 79 as it passes through the remnants of the Newark Earthworks are reexamined in this chapter. Two clusters of postmolds and pit features, named Hale's House (33LI252) and Meridian Alley (33LI260), were encountered during the testing; each contained artifacts suggestive of a Middle Woodland age. Microwear analysis and other properties of these sites suggest that they were used as seasonally occupied camps. Their closeness to the earthworks argues against the idea that these public works were uninhabited.

The purpose of this paper is to review the archaeological investigations of Everett Hale at the Newark Earthworks. Apart from a summary treatment by Lepper (1988) and Pacheco (1988), this work has not heretofore been presented in a widely accessible form. The Newark expressway sites warrant the attention of students of Hopewell archaeology. The evidence for Hopewellian habitation sites in such close proximity to a major earthwork complex casts doubt on the very idea of a vacant ceremonial center. The present volume offers an opportunity to review these important data in the broader context of Hopewell settlement archaeology.

This paper goes beyond a simple review and includes the results of a microwear analysis of lithic artifacts and radiocarbon dates for features from the Newark expressway sites. These data contribute to our understanding of the role played by the great earthwork complexes in Hopewell societies.

The Newark Earthworks

The reports of my death are greatly exaggerated.
—*Mark Twain*

There have been few scientific explorations undertaken at the Newark Earthworks in spite of the long-recognized preeminence of this site as the largest complex of geometric earthworks ever built in Ohio (Lepper 1988). One reason for this neglect is the long-standing and widespread assumption that virtually all evidence of a prehistoric presence here was obliterated (or at least hopelessly compromised) by Euro-American development in the early nineteenth century. This assumption was a logical extension of the progressive destruction of the mounds and embankments of the Newark complex throughout the nineteenth century (compare Figs. 7.1 and 7.2).

The devastation wrought upon the earthworks was graphically portrayed in emotional appeals for the preservation of the site: "The ancient lines can now be traced only at intervals, among gardens and outhouses. . . . A few years hence, the residents upon the spot will be compelled to resort to this map [Fig. 7.1], to ascertain the character of the works which occupied the very ground upon which they stand" (Squier and Davis 1848:71). "The 'Octagonal Fort,' . . . is suffering a vandalism much more destructive. . . . The circular wall . . . has been torn up by the plow. . . . A wagon road is biting off a portion of the octagonal walls on the other side, and ambitious potato patches are creeping over them wherever it suits their convenience. In a few more years the complications of this truly wonderful structure . . . will be wholly destroyed" (Fulton 1868).

The authors might have expected such accounts to awaken the sympathies of a neglectful citizenry. Indeed, ultimately the Great Circle as well as the Observatory Circle and Octagon were acquired and preserved by the Ohio Historical Society, but the square enclosure, the burial mounds, the numerous small circular earthworks, and the parallel walls that connected the major enclosures were plowed flat, dug through, and forgotten. Yet, contrary to antiquarian hyperbole, they were not utterly destroyed. Although little could be seen from the surface, much of Hopewellian Newark slept beneath a veneer of nineteenth-century architecture: "Everywhere we seem to be walking upon the dust of the departed. The workmen engaged in excavating for the building of the Agricultural Works in West Newark, and at a point where it is said some ancient mounds were removed years ago, found portions of a human skeleton and a stone image supposed to be of ancient manufacture" (Dragoo and Wray 1964:197, quoting from an 1881 Newark newspaper).

The Newark Expressway Project

In October 1977 consultant archaeologist Everett E. Hale initiated an archaeological reconnaissance of the proposed corridor for the Newark expressway project (LIC 79–12.55). Hale's literature review was perfunctory, though he did recognize that the project would cross the heart of Ohio's "largest and most elaborate" Hopewellian earthwork complex (Hale 1978:9).

After a brief review of a few early maps of the Newark Earthworks, Hale (1980:13) claimed that "no early site plan is any more accurate or useful today then [sic] any other site plan." This is an odd claim. Belt's (1925) cartoonish sketch for a newspaper article clearly is not as useful today as are the scholarly efforts of Whittlesey, Squier, and Davis (1848) and Wyrick (1866). Moreover, at another point in his review, Hale noted that Wyrick's rendering of "the north and south parallel mounds near the entrance to the Great Circle are much more representative of the extant mounds than are the parallels drawn by Squier and Davis" (Hale 1980:7). Instead of concluding that Wyrick's map was more accurate in representing this feature, Hale alleged that the reason why the modern converging walls do not closely match those drawn by Squier and Davis (1848) is that the present configuration reflects "the handiwork of the W.P.A. laborers" who assisted in the restoration of the earthworks at Moundbuilders Park (Hale 1978:15; 1980:12). Hale refered to discussions with Charles Frizzell, a lifelong resident of Newark, who "witnessed the W.P.A. restoration" of the park, and he further states that Frizzell "argued that the North Parallel Mound inside the memorial did not exist prior to the W.P.A. work" (Hale 1978:14–15). However, Frizzell indicated to Lepper (personal interview, May 3, 1988) that he never told Hale that the north wall did not exist in the 1930s, merely that it was much reduced and that the restorations had been extensive. This statement is supported by the blueprints prepared for the W.P.A.

restoration work, which are on file at the Ohio Historical Society and which had been viewed by Hale (1978:15).

Hale's cursory literature review and the interpretations he drew from his limited background research indicate that, from the earliest phases of the project, he was working under the assumption that the Newark Earthworks, and any associated archaeological record, had been destroyed and that the remnants which had been preserved in archaeological parks were, more or less, the products of modern reconstruction efforts (Hale 1980:12). This assumption was to be challenged at every subsequent stage of Hale's field work, but he never abandoned it. Hale's methods, interpretations, conclusions, and recommendations were all colored by this unfortunate misconception.

Methods

Archaeological investigations along the "proposed" corridor of the Newark expressway were preceded by the razing of houses and other modern structures within this corridor. It is regrettable that this extensive landscape modification occurred prior to the initial archaeological reconnaissance. The bulldozing, cutting, and filling must have destroyed much, if not most, of the surviving archaeological record within the corridor; it certainly did make Hale's job more difficult.

Hale began his investigation of the LIC-79 corridor with a futile surface examination of a 1 percent random sample of real estate lot parcels that had been "freshly dozed exposing large portions of bare earth" (Hale 1978:15). In addition, the affected portions of Moundbuilders State Memorial and White Athletic Field were walked, although the vegetation had not been cleared from these areas. Those lot parcels that had not been "freshly dozed" were "shovel tested," but the shovel testing only consisted of "cutting through the vegetation to view an area of top soil . . . from one to five square feet in area" (1978:16). For some reason, shovel testing apparently was never undertaken at White Field, where "the carpet of lawn grasses" with "no bare spots or erosion cuts" must have impeded "the search for artifacts" (1978:16). Therefore, the actual area subjected to adequate archaeological survey was far less than the 1 percent claimed by Hale. Not surprisingly, Hale concluded that "partially due to vegetation cover and partially due to recent churning up of the land in the razing process the examination of the sample parcels proved fruitless" (1978:17).

Nevertheless, there were two important results of the 1977 field work. First of all, the "surface examination of the corridor did reveal that the original land contours are amazingly well preserved considering the extent of the modern occupation" (1978:17). Secondly, a 2 x 10 ft (.61 x 3.04 m) trench was excavated adjacent to the Wright Earthworks State Memorial on a line that would intersect the projected northeastern wall of the square enclosure. This was done in order to see if subsurface remnants of the wall were preserved beneath the disturbed surface. Hale encountered "stratified zones of light orange clay, dark brown clay, and light brown clay . . . approximately on line with the reconstructed Wright linear mound" (Hale 1978:19). From this evidence Hale concluded that "mound fill was indeed touched upon" (1978:19).

The report of the 1977 investigation was completed in May 1978. Hale concluded that "surface indications of aboriginal occupation in the areas not protected by the state are non-existent" and the earthworks preserved at Moundbuilders and Wright Earthworks State Memorials had been extensively reconstructed with questionable accuracy (1978:20). Nevertheless, he recommended "an extensive sub-surface sampling of the corridor to ascertain whether or not the apparent mound profile in the test trench is: one, cultural and not natural in origin; two, part of a series of mounds and not a unique survival among the Twentieth Century disturbance" (1978:21).

The next phase of field work began in October 1978 and continued in spurts until January 1980. It consisted of apparently haphazard backhoe excavations at scattered locations along the LIC-79 corridor between Raccoon Creek and Moundbuilders State Memorial and a series of 1×1 m test units hand-excavated in the area of a parking lot proposed for Moundbuilders Park. The decision to use a backhoe was based on "the extensive amount of overburden brought in or shoved about during the right-of-way preparation process" (Hale 1980:16).

Based on Hale's 1978 recommendations for subsequent work along the LIC-79 corridor, it may be assumed that the backhoe excavations were concentrated in areas where he expected that remains of earthworks might possibly be found. Indeed, Hale encountered probable remnants of earthworks in three areas: adjacent to the Wright Earthworks where he uncovered the "stratified zones" of different colored clays in line with the restored wall of the square enclosure (1978:19); "in two trenches on opposite sides of Pine Street in the vicinity of Wright Mounds," where Hale described "a compact, fine grained, moisture resistant soil area" that appeared to have "a linear distribution" (1980:42); and "between Wilson Street and Malholm Street," near a concentration of features, where he identified an extensive buried lens of "fire reddened soil and charcoal," which he asserted "was clearly pre-modern" (1980:43).

Nevertheless, Hale ultimately concluded that the excavations "did not locate mound fill or sub-mound structures" (1980:49): "Although some anomalous soils were found, there was *no suggestion* of the presence of earthworks in this part of the project area" (1980:55; emphasis added). Given the documented presence of an intricate series of earthworks in this area (Fig 7.1), it is surprising that these "anomalous soils" (Hale 1980:43) could be so easily dismissed as natural sedimentary structures without detailed soils analysis.

Feature Archaeology

In spite of the fact that in his previous report Hale had concluded that the "original land contours" of the project area were "amazingly well preserved" (1978:17), he asserts in the 1980 report that "the archaeology of Newark is feature archaeology, that is to say archaeology without the benefit of the original land's surface" (1980:53). This is how Hale justified the mechanical stripping of some areas, including at least one site "where the original ground surface has been preserved" (1980:45). When features were encountered, they were usually assigned a number, sometimes mapped and photographed, and then excavated. There was no apparent attempt to investigate the surfaces between the features, presumably because they had already been removed by the backhoe. Several artifacts were recovered outside of features. Usually these were collected from backdirt or from a disturbed surface, and only a single artifact, a projectile point, seems to have been piece plotted (Hale 1980:78). Two general concentrations of features were identified: we have named these Hale's House site (33LI252) and the Meridian Alley site (33LI260) (Figs. 7.1 and 7.2).

Hale's House Site (33LI252)

Hale's House site is a cluster of twenty-three cultural features situated approximately 150 m south of Raccoon Creek and approximately 120 m north and west of the enclosure surrounding the Cherry Valley Cluster of burial mounds (Figs. 7.1, 7.3, 7.4). The features include twelve postmolds, one hearth, one earth oven, one cylindrical pit, four basins, one shallow "hour-glass shaped" basin lined with pebbles and containing mica sheets (Hale 1980:40), one "large refuse pit"

(1980:44), one shallow irregular basin, and one "shallow pit" (1980:46). Patterns of superimposed features, diagnostic artifacts within features, and radiocarbon dates suggest that there were at least four separate occupations of the site including at least one Early Woodland component.

Feature 9a is the remnant of a postmold that was truncated by Feature 9b, the remnants of a hearth (Fig. 7.4). This postmold may be associated with three others (unnumbered) to form "a rough semicircle post pattern" with a shallow basin inside the structure. The hearth was constructed within the "prepared floor" (Hale 1980:45) of an apparently rectangular structure approximately 4.6 m on one side (see also Pacheco 1988:110). Therefore, the semicircular structure, or at least Feature 9a, must predate the rectangular structure.

A large refuse pit (Feature 3) was dug through the floor of the western edge of the rectangular structure apparently obliterating several postmolds. Finally, a postmold (Feature 12) intrudes into Feature 3. Although mica and other artifacts are present within the fill of this postmold, Hale mentions the possibility that this might be a historic postmold (1980:44–45).

Hale collected numerous charcoal samples from the various features and stated that several were "submitted to the laboratory at the University of Georgia" (1980:25). In fact, this never happened.

Lepper obtained the LIC-79 project collections from Hale in 1988 and arranged for three charcoal samples from features at Hale's House site to be processed. Feature 10, a deep earth oven that contained no artifacts other than fire-cracked rock, dates from 2,670 ± 70 B.P. (Beta-27446). Feature 15, a shallow basin that contained mica, Middle Woodland ceramics, a "cache blade" and other lithic artifacts (Hale 1980:28, 34, 38, 40) dates from 1,845 ± 60 B.P. (Beta-28062/ETH-4593). Feature 1, the "hour-glass shaped pit" that was covered with a layer of mica sheets (Hale 1980:40–41) dates from 1,640 ± 90 B.P. (Beta-58450).

Hale recovered numerous sherds of local Scioto Series Middle Woodland ceramics and four others which he classed as exotic "sand tempered" Southeastern Series (1980:38). Recently, James Stoltman (personal communication) determined that these exotic sherds actually were tempered with ground granite from an as-yet-undetermined source in North Carolina.

Hale's House site has been a locus of human occupation since Early Woodland times, but certainly the most intensive use of the site occurred during the Middle Woodland period. The close proximity of the site to the Newark Earthworks is a forceful argument that the activities undertaken here relate, in some way, to the use of this giant complex of geometric earthworks.

The Meridian Alley Site (33LI260)

The Meridian Alley site is a small cluster of four features situated very near, and quite possibly within, what were once, two converging earthen walls (Figs. 7.1 and 7.3). These walls were a part of the network of earthworks that connected the square enclosure and the burial mounds. There are no longer any visible traces of these walls, but Hale did encounter a buried lens of "fire reddened soil and charcoal" in this area (1980:43).

Two of the features are apparently sterile, shallow basins. Feature 17 is a shallow basin containing some mica and the basal fragment of a "cache blade" (1980:40, 34). Finally, Feature 18 is a postmold that contained some mica flakes in the fill (1980:44). Hale noted very few artifacts from this locality, yet five projectile points and one bladelet were collected.

The Meridian Alley site is much smaller than Hale's House site with evidence for only an ephemeral occupation. Its proximity to the walls of the Newark Earthworks suggests a function directly connected with the special activities taking place within the earthworks.

Microwear Analysis

In all, Hale recovered 1,354 lithic artifacts from the LIC-79 sites (Table 7.1); 78 of these, principally from Hale's House site (33LI252), were examined for microwear traces. The focus of this study is on the function of the Middle Woodland artifacts from the sites (particularly the bladelets) and a comparison of the activity patterns at these sites with activity patterns that have been reconstructed at other small Middle Woodland sites in the Upper Ohio River Valley (Yerkes 1990). Although the microwear sample included only 78 (6 percent) of the lithic artifacts (Table 7.1), 95 percent of the formal tools that were available for study (points, bifaces, bladelets, cores, and scrapers) were examined, along with 13 percent of the retouched flakes and 1 percent of the unretouched flakes. Microwear analysis revealed that 14 percent of the examined pieces had been utilized. It should be noted that most of the 1,223 unretouched flakes from the project were small flint chips, whose greatest dimension was less than 2 cm, or blocky, amorphous pieces of chert. Prior studies of chips and chunks like these revealed that they represent flint knapping debris and do not provide much functional information (Yerkes 1987:117; 1990:172). Consequently, only 13 large unretouched flakes were included in the microwear sample; and microwear traces were observed on only one of these objects. As for the three points that were available for study (six cataloged points and some other specimens are missing from the collection), two were bases of points that seem to have been broken in manufacture or during use as projectiles (as indicated by impact fractures).

Hale's House Site (33LI252)

Two putative structures and their associated features were excavated at the Hale's House site. Only a single unretouched flake was recovered from the floor of the rectangular structure, while two unretouched flakes were found in the hearth fill. All of these artifacts were deemed too small for inclusion in the microwear sample. Feature 15, the shallow basin dating from 1,845 ± 60 B.P., contained 59 percent of the lithic and 73 percent of the ceramic artifacts found in the features at the Hale's House site. The large oval refuse pit (Feature 3) accounted for 29 percent of the lithic and 25 percent of the ceramic artifacts from these features. Most of the lithic artifacts (94 percent) from Feature 15 were small unretouched flakes, and none of these was examined for wear traces. However, all three bladelets found in the fill of Feature 15 were included in the microwear sample. In addition, a total of 33 (29 percent) of the 115 lithic artifacts from Feature 3 were included in the microwear sample.

A cylindrical pit (Feature 2) was located northeast of the structures. Three bladelets, representing 14 percent of the 21 artifacts recovered from the pit fill were examined for microwear traces. One retouched flake and 26 unretouched flakes were found in the remaining pits and postmolds of the Hale's House site. The retouched flake was not available for study, and the unretouched flakes were cataloged as recovered from the plowzone above the features at 33LI252. An additional 149 chipped stone pieces were recovered from the excavation backdirt. A total of 163 lithic artifacts were collected from the surface of Parcels 866 and 867, and 9 stone implements were found in an apparent midden deposit that Hale referred to in his notes as the "ash and trash" layer of the site. Two bifaces, one scraper, one core, twenty-four bladelets, two retouched flakes, and two unretouched flakes from these surface, plowzone, and backdirt contexts were included in the 33LI252 microwear sample (Table 7.3).

Meridian Alley Site (33LI260)

Only a single bladelet from the plowzone at the Meridian Alley site was included in the microwear sample. The five points and one biface from the site
were not available for study, and the flakes from the site may have been produced during pre- or post-Hopewell occupations of the site.

Methods of Microwear Analysis

The artifacts were examined under incident light at magnifications of 50x,
100x, 200x and 500x using the "high-power" microwear technique developed
by Keeley (1980). This method involves the examination of microwear pol-
ishes, striations, and edge damage in order to determine the area of a tool that
was used, the method of tool use, and the material that was worked. Functional interpretations are based on comparisons between the wear traces that
form on experimental tools used for specific tasks and wear traces observed
on the artifacts. The method has been evaluated through a series of "blind
tests" (Bamforth 1988; Keeley and Newcomer 1977) and successfully applied in
over one hundred studies of stone tool function in both the Old and New
Worlds (Bamforth 1988; Juel Jensen 1988; Yerkes 1987, 1990; Yerkes and Kardulias
1993).

Results

None of the bifacial tools (points and bifaces) or cores in the microwear sample
showed visible edge-wear traces (Table 7.3). Hale remarked that most of the
points from the site were "abandoned during the process of manufacture or
remanufacture" (1980: 36). From the illustrations in the site report (Hale 1980:
Pls II and III), it appears that some of the points that were not available for
the microwear study may have broken during manufacture or resharpening,
while others seem to exhibit impact fractures that occurred when the points
were used as projectiles. The only point examined in the present study was a
broken corner notched point from Feature 3 at Hale's House site (cat # 375).
This point was snapped at the base and at the tip, possibly reflecting breakage
on impact. One of the lateral edges shows fine retouch above the corner notch;
this seems to be the "original" edge of the point. The other lateral edge has

been removed by what appears to be hard-hammer percussion. This suggests that the point was being reworked, but there is no evidence that it was used as anything other than a projectile point.

Hale classified three bifaces from these sites as "cache blades" (1980:34). One of these was available for study: a broken specimen, both halves of which (cat. #84 and #101) were found in the plowzone at Hale's House site. Microwear analysis revealed only technological traces on the edges of this biface. It may have broken during manufacture as suggested by Hale (1980:34). Two bifaces found in the fill of Feature 3 were examined (#269 and #281); neither had been utilized, nor had a biface from the surface of the Hale's House site (cat. #474). All bifaces examined seem to have been preforms that were broken during manufacture, rather than bifacial knives or other finished tools.

The end scraper found in the "ash and trash" layer at the Hale's House site was a broken piece of black-grey chert (cat. #392, Hale 1980: Pl. VII). The unifacially retouched distal edge displays wear traces indicating that it had been used to scrape fresh hide, but the limited degree of edge rounding and weak edge polish suggests that the tool had not been used extensively. A retouched flake from Feature 3 (cat. #210) also had been used to scrape fresh hide, but the wear traces on this implement were more developed (Fig. 7.5). An unretouched flake from Feature 3 (cat. #280) had been used to cut and scrape fresh hide or meat. All of these implements seem to have been used as expedient tools in butchering and skinning activities at Hale's House site.

Another retouched flake from the fill of Feature 3 (cat. #326) was used to scrape dry hide, but the wear traces on this implement are quite faint. A unifacially retouched flake from the plowzone above Feature 3 (cat. #11) also had weak dry hide polish on one of its lateral edges, while a notch in the opposite lateral edge seems to have served as a spoke shave used on bone or antler (Fig. 7.5). The evidence indicates that hide, bone, and/or antler were being worked at the Hale's House site with expedient and more formal tools.

Hopewell Bladelets

The single bladelet core and all fifty-one of the bladelets available for study were included in the microwear sample (Table 7.4). Analysis revealed that the core was not used for any task other than bladelet production. Metric analysis of the fourteen complete and thirty-seven fragmentary bladelets (including three refitted fragments) was undertaken. Mean length (41.5 mm), width

(12.2 mm), and thickness (3.1 mm) of this sample were very close to the mean values obtained from twelve other Hopewellian localities in Ohio (Table 7.5). The average length of 601 complete bladelets from five of the six domestic sites and all six mound and earthwork locations was 41.0 mm, while the mean width of 2,653 complete and fragmentary bladelets and bladelet fragments was 11.4 mm; the mean thickness of 1,935 bladelets and bladelet fragments from six of these sites was 3.2 mm.[1] There were some slight differences in the dimensions of bladelets from "ceremonial" and "domestic" contexts. The bladelets from the ceremonial localities at mound and earthwork sites were longer (mean length = 45.0 mm), slightly narrower (mean width = 11.2 mm), and thinner (mean thickness = 2.9 mm) than those from domestic contexts, where the mean values for length, width, and thickness were 38.5 mm, 11.5 mm, 3.3 mm, respectively. The mean metric values for the LIC-79 bladelets fall right between the averages for the ceremonial and domestic sites (Fig. 7.6), suggesting that the forty-eight bladelets in the sample may have come from both domestic and ceremonial contexts.

The raw material used to manufacture the bladelets found at the LIC-79 sites consists of Ohio Flint Ridge flint (48 percent), Wyandotte chert ("Indiana Hornstone") (46 percent), and Knife River flint (2 percent). Two bladelets (4 percent) were made of unidentified material. It is quite striking that half of the bladelets in the LIC-79 sample are made of nonlocal, or "exotic," flint or chert varieties. This is especially noteworthy because those tools come from localities that are within 15 km of the renowned Flint Ridge quarry sites. Most of the exotic[2] bladelets were found near the structures at the Hale's House site. The bladelet made of Knife River flint was found in the fill of Feature 3, and seventeen bladelets made of Wyandotte chert (65 percent of the total) were found in plowzone and other feature contexts near this large feature. Bladelets made of Flint Ridge flint were more common in Feature 15 and nearby pits, where seventeen of the twenty-one bladelets in the sample (81 percent) were made of this local raw material. The single bladelet from the Meridian Alley site was made of Wyandotte chert.

1. Metric data on bladelet length was available for five of the six domestic sites and for all six mound or earthwork sites. Data on bladelet width was available for all twelve sites, while data on bladelet thickness was available for four domestic sites and two mound or earthwork sites (Table 7.5).
2. Flint and chert types were identified by macroscopic comparison of the bladelets with samples from the Flint Ridge (Ohio), Knife River (North Dakota), and Wyandotte (Indiana) quarries. In the case of the Knife River flint, examinations under ultraviolet light revealed that the bladelet from the Hale's House site exhibited the same orange fluorescence as the sample of Knife River flint (cf. Hofman et al. 1991).

Only six of the forty-eight (12.5 percent) bladelets in the microwear sample had been utilized (Table 7.1). At the Hale's House site, four bladelets made of Wyandotte chert and two made of Flint Ridge flint had been used. Three of the Wyandotte chert bladelets were found in the fill of Feature 3. One bladelet (cat. #188) was used to incise bone, antler, or shell material; another (cat. #259) was used to cut meat; and the third (cat. #267) had a few very light patches of hide polish on one of its lateral edges. Although twenty-one of the fifty bladelets in the 33LI252 microwear sample exhibited edge damage or abrasions, microwear on the utilized bladelets was neither extensive nor well developed. The implements from Feature 3 appear to have been expediently used for three different tasks: bone, antler, or shell working; butchering; and possibly hide working. There was no clear evidence that any of these bladelets had been hafted.

Two utilized bladelets were recovered from the surface of Parcel 866–867. One of these (cat. #959), made of Flint Ridge flint, was retouched. It had been used to cut soft wood or some other plant material. The other specimen (cat. #964), made of Wyandotte chert had been used to cut meat or fresh hide. Yet another bladelet (cat. #520) made of Flint Ridge flint was found in the backdirt from the excavations at the Hale's House site and may have been used to cut meat. The wear on these implements was not well developed, and they seem to have been expediently used. The bladelet found in the plowzone at the Meridian Alley site was abraded but not utilized.

Conclusions

There has been considerable debate over the nature of Ohio Hopewell settlement patterns. Many scholars believe that large geometric earthwork complexes, like those found at Newark, served as territorial markers or ceremonial centers for dispersed populations (Yerkes 1988). However, it is often assumed that occupations at these sites are restricted to temporary encampments of very small size, "presumably connected with either the construction of the mounds and earthworks or with the holding of momentary ceremonials at these sacred localities" (Prufer 1964:71). The notion that the Ohio Hopewellians lived year-round in small, dispersed "farmsteads" or "hamlets" surrounding essentially "vacant" ceremonial centers has been referred to as the "Prufer model," since Olaf Prufer is credited with developing this settlement model in the 1960s (Dancey 1991; Prufer 1965).

Dancey (1991:39) and Pacheco (1988, chapter 2) claim that Middle Woodland remains in Licking County, Ohio, are organized in the manner proposed
by Prufer. However, there is little convincing evidence that Hopewell "hamlets" like the Murphy site were occupied year-round or that the Newark "ceremonial center" was vacant. The excavations at the Murphy site exposed food
preparation and refuse disposal areas, but neither deep storage features nor
substantial structures were found (Dancey 1991; Yerkes 1990). It should be
noted that structures and storage pits were not exposed at other Hopewell
"hamlets" such as Jennison Guard (Kozarek 1987) and McGraw (Prufer 1965),
although the excavated areas at those sites were much more limited. The available evidence from the Murphy site suggests that it was occupied seasonally
by small groups over a three-hundred-year period. None of the features, artifacts, floral or faunal material from the site demonstrates that it represents a
sedentary "hamlet" (Yerkes 1990).

Limited excavations at the Fort Ancient site by Essenpreis and Connolly
(1989) revealed dense concentrations of Hopewell structures and features
(Connolly, chapter 10). This suggests that permanent habitation areas existed
adjacent to that Hopewell enclosure. This work calls into question the notion
that the Hopewell earthworks were vacant ceremonial centers, but how do the
data from the Newark expressway sites relate to these opposing models of
Hopewell settlement systems?

The Hale's House site (33LI252), located just outside of the major earthen
enclosures at Newark, contains domestic refuse and evidence for repeated
short-term occupations, although artifacts as well as floral and faunal remains
that could serve as precise seasonal indicators are lacking. The presence of
specialized features, such as the "hour-glass shaped" basin and exotic lithic
and ceramic artifacts, suggests that some activities were related to the perfor-
mance of rituals and to the exchange of valued items. However, the site is
neither a specialized mortuary camp, as Prufer's model would suggest, nor a
"factory workshop," as proposed by Hale (1980:52). The likeliest interpretation of the Newark expressway sites is that they represent ordinary domestic
loci occupied for part of the year by Hopewell social groups who came to the
Newark Earthworks for their periodic "rites of passage" and other special events
(cf. Greber, chapter 8; Yerkes 1995). The Hale's House site does not represent a
distinct settlement type, it is the functional equivalent of the Murphy site and
conceivably could have been occupied, at one time or another, by the same
social groups. The low density and scattered nature of the features at sites like
Hale's House and Murphy suggest that they were only occupied briefly. There

is no evidence for substantial structures at these Newark localities that are similar to what was found at Fort Ancient. Nor are there any clear indications that the occupation of a "dispersed hamlet," like the Murphy site, was any more sedentary than the occupations more directly associated with the earthworks at Newark. There is markedly less overlap of features at the Murphy site, but the range in radiocarbon dates (Dancey 1991:50) could indicate that there were multiple reoccupations at this locality as well. It is also likely that the locations favored for habitation adjacent to the earthworks were more limited and easier to relocate from year to year. Therefore, a greater degree of feature overlap could be expected at Newark.

The microwear analysis at both the Murphy and Hale's House sites revealed that expedient tools (including bladelets) were used briefly for a variety of tasks and then discarded. This pattern of tool utilization has been documented at temporary camp sites and seasonally occupied settlements (Yerkes 1987, 1989). Tool assemblages from sedentary farmsteads, hamlets, and villages could be expected to include heavily used, curated implements whose entire uselife was spent at these kinds of permanent habitations. These are just the kinds of tools that are missing from the Murphy and LIC-79 assemblages.

The most important conclusion to be drawn from this reconsideration of Hale's investigation of the Newark expressway corridor is that archaeologically discernible traces of the Newark Earthworks and related occupation loci are preserved, even in developed sections of urban Newark. It is tragic that so much of Newark's ancient greatness has been lost, but it is even more unfortunate that the real and potential archaeological data remaining at Newark and similar sites could be ignored or dismissed by those entrusted with their preservation and study.

Acknowledgments

Radiocarbon dating of the LIC-79 samples was made possible by grants from the Ohio Archaeological Council, the Archaeological Society of Ohio, and a Bloomsburg University Special Initiatives Grant. Special thanks are due to Dee Anne Wymer for her efforts in this regard.

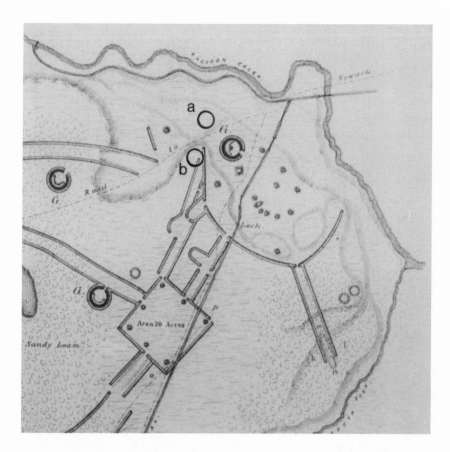

7.1 A portion of the Whittlesey, Squier, and Davis map of the Newark Earthworks with locations of (a) Hale's House (33L1252) and (b) Meridian Alley (33L1250) sites. After Squier and Davis (1848).

7.2 Aerial photograph of Newark, ca. 1980, showing razed LIC-79 project corridor.

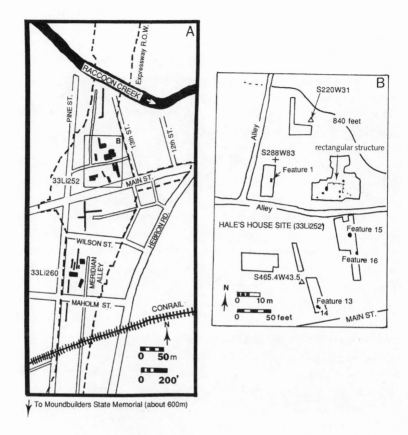

7.3 *A:* Location of the Hale's House (33LI252) and Meridian Alley (33LI260) sites. Excavated areas shown in black. *B:* Enlargement of Hale's House site. Adapted from Hale (1980).

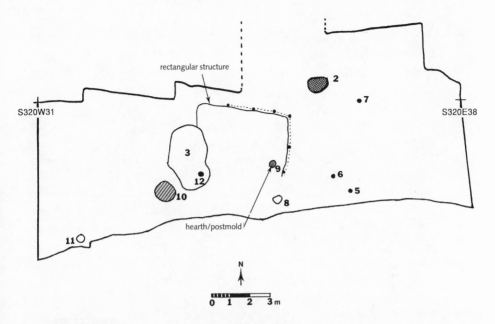

7.4 Features associated with rectangular structure at Hale's House site (33L1252): (2) irregular basin; (3) refuse pit; (8 and 11) basins; (10) earth oven. Other features are postmolds.

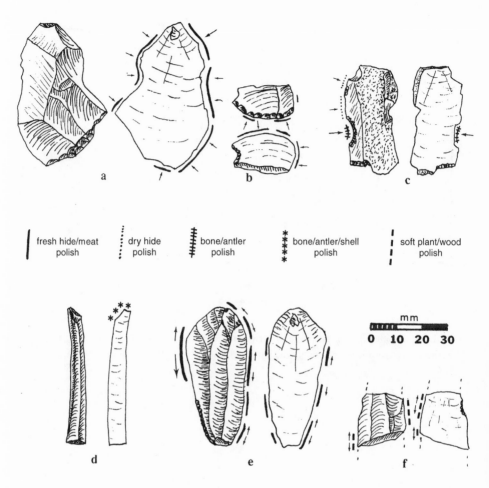

7.5 Microwear examples of utilized tools from 33L1252. Arrows indicate direction of use. Stippled areas represent cortex. (a) retouched FRF flake from Feature 3; (b) broken FRF or UM end scraper from "ash and trash" layer; (c) retouched UM(?) primary flake from plowzone above Feature 3; (d and e) Wyandotte chert bladelets from Feature 3; (f) FRF bladelet from surface of Parcel 866-7.

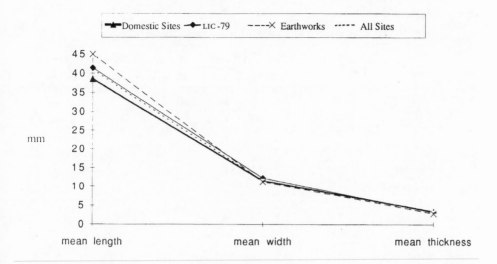

7.6 Metrics of Ohio Hopewell bladelets from six domestic and six mound or earthwork sites compared with mean values for LIC-79 sample. Note that the LIC-79 sample measurements are close to mean values for all twelve sites and fall midway between values for bladelets from "ceremonial" and domestic contexts. Data taken from Table 7.5.

Table 7.1

The 33L1252 and 33L1260 Combined Microwear Sample

Artifact Type	Total in Catalog	Number Available[a]	Number Examined	Percent Examined[b]	Number Utilized	Percent Utilized
Points	9	3	1	33	0	—
Bifaces	7	5	4	80	0	—
Cores	2	1	1	100	0	—
Scrapers	3	1	1	100	1	100
Bladelets	51	51	51	100	6	12
Retouched flakes	59	56	7	13	3	43
Unretouched flakes	1223	1223	13	1	1	8
TOTAL	1354	1339	78	6	11	14

[a]A total of six points, two bifaces, one core, and two scrapers had been removed from the artifact collection to be drawn and were not available for study when the microwear analysis was conducted. In addition, three retouched flakes were missing from the collection. Three of the bladelet fragments could be refitted to other bladelet fragments (see Table 7.4).
[b]Percent of the available artifacts that were examined.

Table 7.2

The Hale's House Site (33LI252) Microwear Sample

Artifact type	Found in Features	Found in Plowzone	Found in Backdirt	Site Total	Available for Study	Number (%) Examined	Number (%) Utilized
Points	2	3	—	5	3	1(33)	0
Bifaces	4	3	—	7	5	4(80)	0
Cores	—	2	—	2	1	1(100)	0
Scrapers	1	1	1	3	1	1(100)	1(100)
Bladelets	25	18	7	50	50	50(100)	6(12)
Retouched flakes	22	29	5	56	56	7(18)	3(43)
Unretouched flakes	351	307	136	794	794	13(2)	1(8)
TOTAL	405	363	149	917	910	77(8.5)	11(14)

Table 7.3

LIC-79 Microwear, Cores, Bifaces, Flakes

Catalog No.	Length	Width	Thickness	Raw Material	Notes	Microwear	Provenience
Bladelet core							
93	43.1	51.4	27.6	Flint Ridge	multiple platform	not used	PZ, S288-32OW 1.0-E20
Bifaces							
84/101	68.9	47.1	10.5	Flint Ridge	refits, broken cache blade	not used	PZ, S288-320W 1.0-E20; S266-240W31-55
269	51.4	28.4	10	Flint Ridge	broken	not used	Fea. 3, Unit 5, Level 1
281	70.3*	28.2	9.3	Flint Ridge	broken	not used	Fea. 3, S320-346, W31-E38
375	48*	27.1*	7.6	Grey Chert	broken corner notch point	not used	Fea. 3, S320-346, W31-E38
474	43.2*	17.5*	9	Upper Mercer	fragment	not used	Parcel 866 Surface
End scrapper							
392	14.6*	24.8	3.2	FRF/UM?	broken, light use	scraping fresh hide	Ash and Trash, 2 feet b.s.
Retouched flakes							
11	43	21.3	7.3	Upper Mercer	notched flake, light use	scraping dry hide, bone/antler	PZ, S320-346, W31-E38-above Fea. 3
210	55.1	37.2	8.6	Flint Ridge	—	scraping fresh hide	Fea. 3, S320-346, W31-E38
261	28	13.6	6	Grey Chert	—	not used	Fea. 3, Level 1, S323-324, W2.4-W18

Table 7.3 Cont'd

#							
279	34	30	—	—	—	abrasion	Fea. 3, S320-346, W31-E38
326	46	35	—	—	light use	scraping dry hide	Fea. 3, S320-346, W31-E38
366	60	24	—	—	—	not used	Fea. 3, S320-346, W31-E38
389	40	34	—	—	—	not used	PZ, S465.5-523.5
Unretouched flakes							
168	30.4	21.1	5	Knife River	cortex	not used	Fea. 3, Level 1&2, S320-346, W31-E38
197	59	30	—	—	cortex, primary flake	not used	Fea. 3, Level 2, S320-346, W31-E38
255	32.4	30.2	11.6	Flint Ridge	—	edge damage	Fea. 3, Level 1, S323-324, W2.4-W18
260	15	13	—	—	cortex, primary flake	not used	Fea. 3, Level 1, S323-324, W2.4-W18
280	50	36	—	—	—	cutting, scrapping fr. hide/meat	Fea. 3, S320-346, W31-E38
301	30	28	—	—	—	not used	Fea. 3, S320-346, W31-E38
302	27	24	—	—	—	not used	Fea. 3, S320-346, W31-E38
364	34.5*	20.3	3.4	Flint Ridge	"blade-like flake"	not used	Fea. 3, S320-346, W31-E38
371	48	26	—	—	—	not used	Fea. 3, S320-346, W31-E38
373	44	24	—	—	—	not used	Fea. 3, S320-346, W31-E38
381	28	25	—	—	—	not used	PZ, S465.5-523.5
386	44	24	—	—	—	not used	PZ, S465.5-523.5
405	19	9	—	—	water rolled?	not used	Fea. 3, S320-346, W31-E38

* broken

Table 7.4

LIC-79 Bladelets

Catalog No.	Platform Scars	Heat Treatment	Raw Materials	Notes	Microwear	Provenience
16/270	—	potlids	Flint Ridge	burned	abrasion edge damage (e.d.)	PZ; Unit 5, Fea. 3, L.1 refit
21	2 short	—	Wyandotte	cortex	—	PZ: S320-346, W31-E38
30	—	—	Wyandotte	—	—	PZ: S320-346, W31-E38
34	—	luster	Flint Ridge	—	abrasion, e.d.	PZ: S320-346, W31-E38
59	—	—	Wyandotte	retouched	edge damage	PZ: S320-346, W31-E38
186	3 short	—	Wyandotte	retouched	abrasion, e.d.	Feature 3, Level 2
188	—	luster	Wyandotte	broken	incising bone/ant./shell	Feature 3, Level 2
190/196	—	—	Wyandotte	retouched	abrasion	Feature 3, Level 2
191	1 short	luster	Wyandotte	—	abrasion, e.d.	Feature 3, Level 2
193	4 short	luster	Wyandotte	—	—	Feature 3, Level 2
194	—	—	Wyandotte	—	—	Feature 3, Level 2
195	—	luster	Knife River	cortex	edge damage	Feature 3, Level 2
237	2 short	luster	Flint Ridge	—	—	Fea. 2, S320-346, W31-E38
249	1 long, 3 short	—	Wyandotte	pointed	—	Fea. 2, S320-346, W31-E38
251	1 long	—	Wyandotte	cortex	—	Fea. 2, S320-346, W31-E38
256	—	luster	Flint Ridge	—	abrasion, e.d.	Unit 5, Fea. 3, Level 1
259	3 long, 1 short	luster	Wyandotte	—	cutting meat, e.d.	Unit 5, Fea. 3, Level 1

Table 7.4 Cont'd

267	—	—	Wyandotte	—	e.d. hide? traces	Unit 5, Fea. 3, Level 1
273	3 short	luster	Wyandotte	—	abrasion, bag damage?	Fea. 3, S328-346, W31-E38
276	—	—	Wyandotte	—	—	Fea. 3, S328-346, W31-E38
277	3 long, 2 short	—	Wyandotte	—	abrasion	Fea. 3, S328-346, W31-E38
303	—	—	?	—	—	Fea. 3, S328-346, W31-E38
312/217	—	—	Wyandotte	—	—	Fea. 3, S328-346, W31-E38
369	—	—	?	—	—	Fea. 3, S328-346, W31-E38
382	—	luster	Flint Ridge	—	abrasion	PZ: S465.5-523.5
399	—	luster	Flint Ridge	—	—	Backdirt: S320-346, W31-E38
421	—	—	Flint Ridge	—	—	Fea. 15 Surface
428	3 short	luster	Flint Ridge	—	red pigment?	Backdirt: S378.5-428, W1.0-E
464	—	luster	Wyandotte	—	abrasion	Surface
471	3 short	luster	Wyandotte	—	edge damage	Surface
477	—	luster	Wyandotte	—	abrasion	Surface
520	—	luster	Flint Ridge	—	cutting meat?	Backdirt: S378.5-428, W1.0-E
565	2 short	—	Flint Ridge	—	—	Backdirt: S378.5-428, W1.0-E
600	—	luster	Flint Ridge	—	edge damage	Backdirt: S378.5-428, W1.0-E
613	—	luster	Flint Ridge	—	—	Backdirt: S378.5-428, W1.0-E
629	—	luster	Flint Ridge	—	—	Backdirt: S378.5-428, W1.0-E
690	1 long, 1 short	—	Flint Ridge	—	abrasion	Fea. 15, S378.5-428, W1.0-E
846	1 long, 2 short	luster	Flint Ridge	polished	—	Fea. 15, S378.5-428, W1.0-E
959	—	luster	Flint Ridge	retouched	cutting soft wood/plants	Parcel 866-867 Surface

Table 7.4 Cont'd.

964	—	—	Wyandotte	light use	cutting meat/fresh hide	Parcel 866-867 Surface
1084	4 short	luster	Flint Ridge	—	edge damage	Parcel 866 Surface
1092	1 long	—	Flint Ridge	—	abrasion	Parcel 866 Surface
1105	3 long, 4 short	luster	Flint Ridge	—	—	Parcel 866 Surface
1121	3 short	luster	Flint Ridge	—	not examined	Parcel 866 Surface
1124	—	—	Flint Ridge	—	—	Parcel 866 Surface
1296	1 long, 2 short	crystals H.T.	Flint Ridge	retouched	abraision, e.d.	Parcel 866 Surface
1343	—	—	Wyandotte	—	abrasion, e.d.	PZ: S1246.5 W165.5

Table 7.5

Bladelet Measurements

Ohio Hopewell Sites	Number of Cases			Maximum Dimension (Mean Value)		
	Length	Width	Thickness	Length	Width	Thickness
Habitation/domestic sites						
Liberty, domestic areas	213	1340	1335	37.6	11.98	3.32
Jennison Guard	—	112	112	—	10.06	2.53
Murphy (feature contents)	58	131	131	38.92	13.51	3.21
Whitacre	26	26	26	43.79	12.89	3.56
McGraw	60	233	—	39.65	9.66	—
Brown's Bottom	13	153	—	35.15	9.37	—
Subtotal/mean	370	1995	1604	38.5	11.5	3.3
Mounds or earthworks						
Capitoleum (mound fill)	15	60	60	34.78	12.31	3.16
Liberty, Location 30	92	266	271	50.59	10.87	2.89
Russell Brown Mound 2	12	12	—	40.25	11.58	—
Russel Brown Surface	5	213	—	44.5	11.53	—
Turner Mounds #1	43	43	—	45.58	11.37	—
Turner Mounds #4 (mound fill)	64	64	—	39.73	10.33	—
Subtotal/mean	231	658	331	45	11.2	2.9
TOTAL/MEAN	601	2653	1935	40.97	11.4	3.2
Test case						
LIC-79	14	48	45	41.45	12.2	3.1

References

Atwater, C.
    1820   Description of the Antiquities Discovered in the State of Ohio and Other Western States. *Archaeologia Americana* 1:105–267.

Bamforth, D. B.
    1988   Investigating Microwear Polishes with Blind Tests: The Institute Results in Context. *Journal of Archaeological Science* 15:11–23.

Belt, B. C.
    1925   A Graphic History of the Extinct Race of the Moundbuilders by One Who Made Their Life a Deep Study. *American Tribune* (Newark, Ohio), October 15.

Dancey, W. S.
    1991   A Middle Woodland Settlement in Central Ohio: A Preliminary Report on the Murphy Site (33LI212). *Pennsylvania Archaeologist* 61:37–72.

Dragoo, D. W., and C. F. Wray
    1964   Hopewell Figurine Rediscovered. *American Antiquity* 30:195–199.

Essenpreis, P. S., and R. Connolly
    1989   Hopewellian Habitation at the Fort Ancient Site, Ohio. Paper presented at the 46th Annual Meeting of the Southeastern Archaeological Conference, Tampa.

Fulton, R.
    1868   Mounds and the Mound Builders. *The American and Wool Grower,* January 3.

Hale, E. E., Jr.
    1978   *Archaeological Survey Report, Transportation Project LIC 79–12.55.* Department of Archaeology, Ohio Historical Society, Columbus.
    1980   *Archaeological Survey Report, Phase III, LIC-79–12–5.* Department of Archaeology, Ohio Historical Society, Columbus.

Hofman, J. L., L. C. Todd, and M. B. Collins
    1991   Identification of Central Texas Edwards Chert at the Folsom and Lindenmeier Sites. *Plains Anthropologist* 37:297–308.

Juel Jensen, H.
    1988   Functional Analysis of Prehistoric Flint Tools by High-Power Microscopy: A Review of West European Research. *Journal of World Prehistory* 2:53–88.

Keeley, L. H.
    1980   *Experimental Determination of Stone Tool Uses: A Microwear Study.* University of Chicago Press, Chicago.

Keeley, L. H., and M. H. Newcomer
    1977   Microwear Analysis of Experimental Flint Tools: A Test Case. *Journal of Archaeological Science* 4:29–62.

Kozarek, S. E.
    1987   *A Hopewellian Homestead in the Ohio River Valley.* Unpublished master's thesis, Department of Anthropology, University of Cincinnati.

Lepper, B. T.

1988   An Historical Review of Archaeological Research at the Newark Earthworks. *Journal of the Steward Anthropological Society* 18:118–140.

1989   A Radiocarbon Date for a Hopewellian Habitation Site Associated with the Newark Earthworks. *Ohio Archaeologist* 39(4):12.

Pacheco, P. J.

1988   Ohio Middle Woodland Settlement Variability in the Upper Licking River Drainage. *Journal of the Steward Anthropological Society* 18:87–117.

Prufer, O. H.

1964   The Hopewell Complex of Ohio. In *Hopewellian Studies*, edited by J. R. Caldwell and R. L. Hall, pp. 35–84. Scientific Papers 12, No. 2. Illinois State Museum, Springfield.

1965   The McGraw Site: A Study in Hopewellian Dynamics. Scientific Papers n.s. 4(1). Cleveland Museum of Natural History.

Squier, E. G., and E. H. Davis

1848   *Ancient Monuments of the Mississippi Valley*. Contributions to Knowledge 1. Smithsonian Institution, Washington, D.C.

Wyrick, D.

1866   Ancient Works Near Newark, Licking County, O. In *Atlas of Licking County, Ohio*, edited by F. W. Beers. Beers, Soule, and Co., New York.

Yerkes, R. W.

1987   *Prehistoric Life on the Mississippi Floodplain*. University of Chicago Press, Chicago.

1988   The Woodland and Mississippian Traditions in the Prehistory of Midwestern North America. *Journal of World Prehistory* 2:307–358.

1989   Lithic Analysis and Activity Patterns at Labras Lake. In *Alternative Approaches to Lithic Analysis*, edited by D. O. Henry and G. H. Odell, pp. 183–212. Archeological Papers 1. American Anthropological Association, Washington, D.C.

1990   Using Microwear Analysis to Investigate Domestic Activities and Craft Specialization at the Murphy Site, a Small Hopewell Settlement in Licking County, Ohio. In *The Interpretative Possibilities of Microwear Studies*, edited by B. Graslund, H. Knutsson, K. Knutsson, and J. Taffinder, pp. 167–177. Societas Archaeologica Upsaliensis and Department of Archaeology, Uppsala University, Uppsala, Sweden.

Yerkes, R. W., and P. N. Kardulias

1993   Recent Developments in the Analysis of Lithic Artifacts. *Journal of Archaeological Research* 1:89–120.

CHAPTER EIGHT

Two Geometric Enclosures in the Paint Creek Valley

An Estimate of Possible Changes in Community Patterns Through Time

N'omi B. Greber

ABSTRACT

A very important part of the settlement pattern of Ohio Hopewell peoples is designated by the remains of extensive earthen and stone walls that apparently mark special areas within the landscape. Patterns of the variations in plan forms, topographic locations, and environmental features found in the areas of the major earthworks are briefly discussed. Within this background, an example of possible changes through time in the use of the earthwork area as part of local and regional Hopewell community patterns in Ross County is presented for the Seip Group.

Large enclosures are a significant element of the ritual, ceremonial, and likely political remains of Ohio Hopewell peoples. Thus, patterning in the design, construction, and/or spatial distribution of such sites tends to reflect factors that helped shape Hopewellian life-styles and settlement strategies. Local through interregional patterns exist. This chapter deals with local and subregional patterns based largely on studies of the Seip Earthworks, a geometric enclosure in the Paint Creek Valley, and its neighbor, the Baum enclosure, as well as three other related sites in the Central Scioto region: the Liberty Works (also called Harness), and Works East (East Banks, Prairie Works) in the Scioto Valley and the Frankfort Works (Old Town) along the North Fork of Paint Creek.

Overview of Seip and Baum

Seip and Baum are situated on opposite sides of Paint Creek, about 5 km apart (Fig. 8.1). The similarities in the plan forms of these enclosures is striking, as is their physical proximity in the landscape. On the basis of archaeological data gathered from the areas within and adjacent to each enclosure, both complexes are multicomponent, although there appear to be differences in the intensity of site use through time. Of particular interest here are the differences seen in the Middle Woodland time period cultural remains. The combined set of similarities and such differences has influenced the interpretations of apparent patterns in domestic settlements and corporate activities that are the focus of this essay.

Archaeological field work at both sites spans nearly two hundred years. At Baum, the two best-known sets of cultural remains are Baum Village, a Fort Ancient–period settlement covering an area approximately the size of the smaller circular enclosure and containing at least forty-nine household structures (Mills 1906), and the great geometric enclosure that is assumed to be of Middle Woodland origin (Atwater 1820; Greber 1986b). Other more spatially limited Middle Woodland components will be discussed in the context of their Seip counterparts.

Overly Mound, a classic Ross County Adena site excavated by William C. Mills, forms part of the archaeological landscape at Seip (Ross County files, Department of Archaeology, Ohio Historical Society). Scattered concentrations of Fort Ancient materials are also recorded (e.g., see Ohio Historical Society cat. nos. 957/246). However, the most intensive use of the Seip area appears to have been during Middle Woodland times. Cultural remains evidencing this use are distributed both within and without the main enclosure. The locations of some representative examples are shown in Fig. 8.2. The survey area contains approximately 160 ha. Data for these localities holding Middle Woodland cultural remains come from nearly two centuries of work. Some of the early work is reported in the classic volume on ancient monuments of the Mississippi Valley by Ephraim Squier and Edwin Davis (1848). Curators from the Ohio Historical Society have directed excavations at Seip through the greater part of this century (Mills 1909; Shetrone and Greenman 1931; *Echoes* 1971; Otto 1972; Baby and Langlois 1979). My own work with materials from Seip began with archival studies (Greber 1976, 1979a) and has continued with field work and analyses conducted under my supervision for the Cleveland Museum of Natural History (Greber 1979b, 1980a, 1980b, 1981, 1983, 1984a,

1984b, 1984c, 1986a, 1993; Greber and D. Griffin 1982). Most of the land involved has been extensively farmed, and large portions are privately owned. Private collections and excavations have contributed to the data base, and the area is still a favorite hunting ground for private collectors.

A fascinating and at times frustrating range of in situ cultural features are documented, as are large quantities of prehistorically redeposited cultural debris. In keeping with the theme of this volume, I will describe these cultural remains in terms consistent with Bruce Smith's synthesis of known Hopewellian habitation sites scattered across eastern North America (Smith 1992: 201–248). I also compare them with the results of Warren DeBoer and John Blitz's archaeological and ethnographic field work among the Chachi of Ecuador (DeBoer and Blitz 1991). Finally, I propose to illustrate one possible interweaving of private domestic and more public corporate Hopewellian activities in a model of a suggested time sequence of events centered on the Seip Earthworks.

Comparing the Scales of Domestic and Ceremonial Remains

Some researchers consider that an incongruity exists between what is known of the domestic and the corporate ceremonial or ritual spheres of Ohio Hopewell life; they describe this situation as a mismatch of scales. That is, massive earthworks, including walls, enclosures, and mounds, and impressive artifact deposits contrast with an apparent lack of large-scale domestic sites. This view appears to me to assume that a well-organized and materially productive ritual sphere requires the constant multiple social interactions that can occur among numerous and densely packed households. This is not a necessary assumption. Also, careful definitions need to be made of the terms "domestic" and "large scale." It is easy to think of an aerial view of Seip today that can still impart the impressive scale of Hopewellian activities, as a snapshot of one instant in time. Theoretical models frequently consider the construction of the more than 3 km of walls, the two large mounds, the more than twenty small mounds, and the various wooden structures, pits, deposits, and other features of the site as coeval. They were not. In determining the true human scale probably represented by such sites, we must consider pace. For any given element of cultural remains, we need to consider both the number of people who were involved in the activities that left the remains and the length of time the activities required. Unfortunately, at Seip, as at all major

Ohio sites, the internal chronology is as much guess as fact. However, an attempt to estimate this chronology may provide some insights for evaluating suggested settlement patterns.

Hints of Internal Chronology

Radiocarbon Assays

Twelve radiocarbon dates are available from three different parts of the site (Greber et al. 1983:90–92). I have discounted the two youngest on technical grounds. The ten remaining dates, even if unquestioned, cannot define the internal chronology of such a complex site. They do suggest a time range in overall site use. Indeed, the range of dates (very approximately A.D. 100–500) comes from a single, relatively bounded, densely occupied area between the Seip-Pricer Mound and the major enclosure wall. Here, variously sized spaces were cleared of topsoil, thus forming a simply prepared but serviceable floor. Activities carried out on these floors include making small fires directly on the floors, and then clearing away the debris and raising large posts, which were ultimately lowered and the postholes refilled. At some point in time, each defined space was covered in a customary Hopewellian manner. The spaces were mantled by a covering of small yellow gravels that are easily obtainable from subsurface deposits of the outwash terrace on which the site was built. Coverings may abut or slightly overlap, but no overlapping structures are known. In Fig. 8.2 the area in question is designated by circles 2 and 3 north of the Seip-Pricer Mound (circle 6). This general location was probably originally chosen because it was a low knoll or elevated area very suitable for the typical simple floor construction technique. Its original extent can only be estimated, since 30 to 70 cm of erosion have truncated the area on the west and a park road abuts its eastern side (Baby and Langlois 1979; Greber 1981; Greber and D. Griffin 1982).

Overlapping radiocarbon dates suggest concurrent use, possibly around A.D. 300, of parts of this ritual area and at least one of the large, multiroomed, elaborately constructed buildings. This structure was eventually covered by the Seip-Pricer Mound (Fig. 8.2, circle 6; Shetrone and Greenman 1931; Greber 1976; Greber 1983:87–92). Radiocarbon dates from two excavated features located immediately west of the major enclosure fall toward the end of Middle Woodland times (Fig. 8.2, circle 3). One of these features was a pit, the other a middenlike deposit of burned rock, mica, colored clays and other materials (Greber 1983:92). In sum, the radiocarbon assays, though few, allow a quite reasonable span of three hundred to four hundred years of site use during Middle Woodland times.

Diagnostic Artifacts

Most areas of the site can only be dated by their artifactual contents. Artifacts have been recovered as in situ remains and from quantities of debris recorded as mound strata, incorporated into wall construction, or found on the surface. Since one of the major questions we are considering contrasts the distribution of "domestic" or household with "ceremonial" or corporate spaces, the assignment of localities yielding redeposited debris to either sphere will affect our conclusions. Unfortunately, due to both Hopewellian earth moving and modern land use, even large-scale excavations, if they were possible, could not answer all our questions as to the primary origins of much of this debris.

In evaluating Hopewellian cultural remains, one cannot use a simple definition that assumes a disjunction between all "ceremonial" and "domestic" artifacts. For example, worked bear canines, figurine fragments, copper tools, fancy sherds, and the ubiquitous cut mica fragments may be made of exotic materials and/or fashioned into exotic forms. They have all been found in clearly ceremonial context, for example, within Great Houses. However, they also occurred in debris at the McGraw site, which has commonly been identified as an archetypical Ohio Hopewell habitation (Prufer 1965). In general, even today such artifacts would not be an unexpected find in a Ross County farm field. A similar situation evidently exists in the Lower Illinois Valley at sites such as Smiling Dan (Stafford and Sant 1985:174–182). As summarized by Struever and Houart, "diagnostic Hopewell artifacts were kept and used in the community, where they were frequently lost. Instead of mortuary items per se, they appear to have been status-specific objects which functioned in various ritual and social contexts (including burials) within community life" (1972:49). Thus, whenever one evaluates the context of this type of diagnostic artifact, it is well to note that some, though not necessarily all, exotic materials or objects were made and used within domestic settings as well as in corporate places that were probably more public than were family homes. The occurrence of a range of such objects in apparent habitation debris affords support for interpreting at least portions of the Hopewellian worldview as pervasive in the lives of the people. Such intensity could encourage and reinforce their commitment to a life-style that required saving resources to support great festivals and putting forth physical effort to construct vast monuments.

Consider the interpretation of a more work-a-day object. Bladelets (prismatic blades) are a widespread Hopewellian lithic tool. Literally thousands of these have been found in contexts ranging from large corporate structures to small lithic scatters located in a variety of topographic settings (e.g., Greber, Davis, and Dufresne 1981). In any particular context, they can be found in various physical conditions, from broken and used to pristine and exquisite. Studies of bladelets from Illinois and Ohio sites have demonstrated that these tools were used for a wide variety of tasks, including cutting, scraping, incising, and engraving relatively soft materials such as bone, antler, hide, and plant materials (see Lepper and Yerkes, chapter 7; Odell 1994). In modern experiments they have been used to cut mica and carve Ohio pipestone. Perhaps they represent the equivalent of a Hopewellian penknife. In comparing Ohio and Illinois, the manufacturing techniques used to make these tools differ, albeit they are intraregionally consistent.

One of the important questions that arises in regard to bladelets is whether surface concentrations of blade cores and other lithic debris associated with the manufacture of bladelets should be called specialized loci of "ceremonial" or "mortuary" craft activities merely because they are located at the edge, or within, great enclosures and mound complexes. Or are these simply secular work areas? Such concentrations exist at Seip and at other major Ohio sites, and all three interpretive labels have been used to classify such activity areas (Smith 1992). As already noted, the nature of the classification affects the conclusions concerning patterns of site distribution.

A careful reading of archaeological field projects, including the earliest, reveals that localities yielding "habitation" debris and/or probable domestic features do occur at sites with large monumental earthworks. The automatic assumption that surface or redeposited remains physically near an obviously corporate monuments are "ceremonial" will, I believe, automatically bias conclusions drawn concerning the uses of the monument sites. Although it may be archaeologically inconvenient to have an overlap between domestic and corporate activities, it is anthropologically more realistic to acknowledge that such overlaps can, do, and did occur. Overlaps may occur in space or in the use of an object in more than one type of cultural setting. Hopewellian bladelets appear to represent the latter situation. These subsistence tools also apparently functioned as an element in a widespread, nonsubsistence "inter-action sphere."

Redeposition and Original Contexts

In reviewing the data, some estimate of the relationship between the in situ and the redeposited remains is needed, particularly because of the quantity of the latter. For example, the debris-filled stratum of the second major phase of the Seip-Pricer Mound was more than four m deep (Shetrone and Greenman: Figs. 8.3 and 8.5). The earlier strata, as is common in Ohio Hopewell mounds, did not contain artifacts. The Seip-Pricer upper fill was identified by the exca-vators as midden containing copper tools, bladelets, utility ware sherds, ani-mal bones, and flint projectile points (Shetrone and Greenman: Figs. 8.43 and 8.48). In 1909 Mills wrote, and I concur, that a major part of this material most likely came from a nearby source located between Seip-Conjoined (Fig. 8.2, circle 5) and the park road. Here, prior to 1900, and most probably during Hopewell times, an extensive area was cleared of topsoil.

Evidence of the initial context represented by the secondary debris found in the enclosure walls is limited. There are, at present, very few places where the embankments can be seen on the ground. During fieldwork conducted by the Ohio Historical Society, a test unit placed in one such section of the large circle revealed reverse stratigraphy consistent with the Squier and Davis (1948) map depicting borrow pits immediately adjacent to the walls. These pits were dug through earlier occupational levels (Baby and Potter 1966 field records, Ohio Historical Society). The depths of the midden fill in the wall are consis-tent with data from areas beyond Ross County and Ohio (e.g., Dancey 1991). Commonly, in situ deposits are relatively shallow, possibly 30–50 cm, and interspersed with occasional pits. Materials recovered in the 1966 Ohio His-torical Society excavations and from separate cuts into two other wall sec-tions include animal bone, charcoal fragments, diagnostic Hopewell ceram-ics, bladelets, and cores. Even where the wall is no longer visible at ground level, the plot of a relatively recent complete pickup of surface finds, mainly small lithic debris, indicates its location. Thus, it appears most likely that this section of the wall also originally contained redeposited cultural remains (Greber 1980b).

No overwhelming numbers of pre-Hopewellian deposits are recorded in the redeposited debris nor seen in private and museum surface collections acquired over many decades (e.g., Ohio Historical Society cat. nos. A3805 and A3931). I am unaware of any diagnostic Fort Ancient artifacts from either wall or mound fill. Based on the recorded volumes, I would estimate that the quantity of midden redeposited in the Seip-Pricer Mound was fifteen to twenty times that of the excavated McGraw site midden. The latter has been interpreted as the debris from domestic use by thirty-five to forty-five individuals (perhaps members of a large extended family) for a generation (Prufer 1965:137). Thus, although I would not, at present, use exact quantitative measures, it appears quite reasonable to conclude that a significant percentage of the redeposited cultural remains at Seip were generated by Hopewellian domestic activities and redeposited in the course of corporate ceremonial, ritual, and/or political events. The amount of such debris combined with in situ remains seems to suggest long periods of moderately intensive activities, shorter periods of more intensive site use, or a combination of both. The last is the scenario I prefer. I readily note that without verifiable quantitative measures of the time represented in redeposited debris, there are and should be error estimates placed upon my hypothetical time sequence interpretations. However, I believe that to ignore this set of cultural remains can easily result in even less satisfactory interpretations.

Suggested Model of Site Use Through Time

For the purposes of illustrating my hypothetical chronology of the domestic and corporate-ceremonial spheres at Seip, I propose to measure Hopewellian time in terms of human generations (Fig. 8.3). In the domestic sphere I assume one household structure for a nuclear family of five and a normal grouping together of four households representing an extended family, possibly parents and three siblings. I prefer to estimate a family compound rather than a single large structure. This nuclear family household size is consistent with the occupant count rule used by Smith (1992). The extended family estimate is consistent with sizes noted by Smith for the larger Scioto corporate structures. However, although one may assume a similar relationship between public space per person and living space per person, it is quite clear that the activities that took place on the floors of the Great Houses are not those of everyday domestic life. Seip domestic activities probably precipitated remains that looked more like those found at the Holding site in Illinois (Fortier et al. 1989).

At the beginning of Hopewellian ceremonial styles, for at least one or two generations, ritual activity was probably centered in areas that were eventually covered by small mounds. A few prepared floors, the raising of posts, special fires, and perhaps isolated burials need not have involved more than one or two extended family units (Fig. 8.3, column 1).

A major increase in the intensity of activities took place with Major Construction Event I (hereafter abbreviated to MCE), the building of a large multiroomed corporate structure (Fig. 8.3, column 2). In a study of the burials placed within this Great House, Lyle Konigsberg estimated the associated living society at 135 individuals (Konigsberg 1985). In the present model I have increased the population count to two hundred. Even this larger estimate, possibly distributed among three lineages, clans, or other social units, gives only ten extended family groupings. Consistent with the situation at other large Ohio sites, during the time that activities were centered in the Great House, rituals and other probably related activities continued to take place in other areas.

At the end of about three generations of this social configuration, the use of the Great House ended. MCE II was the ritual covering of the building with culturally sterile soils and a gravel cap (Fig. 8.3, column 3).

During the following two or three generations the domestic sphere probably shrank to about eight extended families who supported MCE III, the building of another Great House, and MCE IV, the placement of the second stage, also capped with gravel, over the first Great House. This layer contained cultural debris (Fig. 8.3, column 4). I am not comfortable imposing a chronological order upon the next two major constructions. MCE V signaled the end of the use of the second Great House, which was covered and capped in the customary manner, that is, with soils and gravels not containing cultural debris. MCE VI was marked by the construction of the great circular enclosure (Fig. 8.3, columns 5 and 6). I suggest that planning and building the square-shaped enclosure was the final major construction event (Fig. 8.3, column 7). Unlike the circular walls, these relatively low walls contained no midden but were made of carefully chosen soils (Greber 1986a).

The model diagrammed in Fig. 8.3 shows seven major corporate construction events sponsored by possibly twelve to fourteen generations. Given the generation intervals, some individuals of the supporting social groups may not have physically participated in any of these projects. Or, put differently, generations of planning and resource curating may also be represented in each event.

Changes in Land Use: Shifts in Domestic Locations

In addition to the obvious changes in physical activities required by each major construction, I suggest that a significant shift occurred in socially accepted uses of land. As soon as the walls of the large circle were erected, areas were no longer available that could, and I think had, afforded suitable locations for family homes and everyday activities. Just as social customs apparently caused debris to be deposited outside the boundaries of the large prepared floor north of the Seip-Pricer Mound and at other equivalent locations, some types of debris and activities were required to be outside the space defined by embankments. For example, once the major circular wall had been constructed, the elevated areas (old natural levees) along former channels of Paint Creek that fell within the enclosure were no longer used for domestic purposes.

Significant concentrations of debris, probably attributable to the domestic sphere, occur outside the Seip enclosure, even within the 160 ha of arbitrary site bounds. Favored locations appear to have been the levees and beaches along the present channel of Paint Creek and the valley areas north of present-day State Route 50 (e.g., Ohio Historical Society cat. nos. 957/122, 957/331). Many of these places have enough room for groups of structures to house one or even several extended families. One might find three or four neighboring structures. Such a configuration would yield a settlement density above the average noted by Smith (1992). However, most Hopewellian homesteads he discussed occupied only 1 to 7 percent of the defined site area. Such percentages are consistent with my own expectations that, overall, the household densities at Seip are low. It is unlikely that circumstances in the near future will allow stripping of the large areas of those relatively noneroded land surfaces at Seip that would be necessary to confirm the presence of such in situ sites.

Paint Creek Valley: Seip to Baum

Toward the end of the Major Construction Events at Seip—that is, after three conjoined mounds covered the second Great House—disarticulated Hopewellian burials were intruded into these first-phase mounds. These relatively unusual occurrences may indicate a change in corporate and domestic spheres. In particular, I suggest a shift in concentrations of domestic sites from the Seip area toward Baum (Fig. 8.1), about an hour or so downstream (maximum of 9 river km), and a concurrent shift in corporate activities to constructing large enclosures rather than large mounds.

No Hopewell necropolis is known at Baum. Surface finds of Hopewellian artifacts and typical bladelet workshops are still discovered by private collectors today. Hopewellian artifacts are also listed in the Ohio Historical Society catalog from "debris heaps" and pits at Baum Village (e.g., cat. nos. 1/194, 1/189). Although it is possible that these objects had been recycled by the Fort Ancient time period occupants of Baum Village, I consider it more likely that the use of the Middle Woodland features preceded the Fort Ancient village. Scattered, relatively shallow middens seem to resemble the probable Hopewell domestic patterning at Seip. The remarkable design similarities of the enclosures, and the differences in type and number of mounds as well as other Hopewellian constructions at Seip and Baum, suggest to me that these two sites represent a single local society that used the land around and between the two enclosures and considered the entire region to be their social space.

Paint Creek is a major tributary of the Scioto River and was glaciated during the Illinoisan but not during the Wisconsinan ice advance. It shares in the rich variety of ecozones found along the edges of the glacial divide that, as has been noted by several central Ohio Valley researchers, occur in their greatest numbers in Ross County (e.g., Maslowski and Seeman 1992; Greber 1993). The vegetation in Paint Creek at the time of the earliest land surveys was distinct from that of both the broader Scioto and the smaller North Fork of Paint Creek. From the evidence at Seip, we know that the Hopewellian peoples clearly used a range of ecozones—from the forest stands needed to construct their Great Houses to the varied local floral and faunal resources necessary to make the tools they used, the ritual paraphernalia they needed, and the clothing they wore at their ceremonial centers. Many locations in the hills and in the valley near both large enclosures are suitable for households and camps, and I suggest that such areas were used by the several Hopewell generations who lived in this lovely valley.

Ceremonial Centers: Social Uses and Architectural Plans

The Chachi, a native farming people of Ecuador, live in dispersed households of single or extended families, each associated with a corporate center (DeBoer and Blitz 1991:Fig. 2). These centers are used as "calendar, court [as in dispute resolution], church, and necropolis all wrapped up in one" (DeBoer and Blitz

1991:61). The corporate center plan reflects major societal divisions (Fig. 8.4; DeBoer and Blitz 1991:Fig. 9). All groups come to their center twice yearly. In addition, smaller groups come at other times to perform "rites of passage." Some rites take place only when appropriate resources are available. In recent times, modern views are apparently affecting site plans and changing the physical relationship between ancestors and the living. Burial practices that had been carried out for generations are changing, and more burials are now being placed near the church than beneath the floor of traditional corporate houses. DeBoer and Blitz consider that the continued existence of the centers reinforces social ties and serves as a defense against competing land claims for a dispersed population.

I do not think that the Hopewellians living in the Paint Creek Valley had to deal with different ethnic groups competing for their land, but I do think that the Seip and Baum enclosures proclaimed the social existence and social focus of their builders and served the same four practical social functions as do the modern Chachi centers. One can interpret the use of the space within the Great Houses at Seip as reflecting the social organization of the supporting groups, just as the plan of the Chachi center reflects major societal divisions (Greber 1979a). There is less certainty concerning the patterning of sleeping and cooking arrangements in Paint Creek, but such activities obviously did take place. Groups of different sizes did live at Seip for different periods of time and in living quarters whose locations are not yet clear. The knowledge of local astronomical events possibly used in designing the square enclosures suggest that, at least at one point in their cultural history, a segment of the population lived very near these enclosures during much of the solar year (Greber 1986a, 1986b).

DeBoer and Blitz have recorded changes through time in the ground plans, size, number, relative geographic location, and influence of Chachi centers. Similar types of changes occurred in the central Scioto River Valley. The ground plans and apparent uses of the two Great Houses differ in detail though not in general pattern. Changes occurred in burial customs, and I assume the latest of these took place when interments were no longer made in multiroomed corporate structures that were eventually covered by the relatively rare large Middle Woodland mounds. Assuming that the construction of the large mound and large enclosure were not exactly contemporaneous allows a physically reasonable pace for Hopewellian corporate physical labor activities— that is, neither vast armies nor vast food banks would be required to accomplish the constructions. This assumption is consistent with, though not "proven" by, the known physical data. The major wall constructions would then represent a change in corporate expression, possibly concomitant with a change in burial customs. Again, chronological data for ordering the two complex geometric enclosures in the Paint Creek Valley do not exist. Hints of relative Hopewellian chronology are found in the construction of the large Seip-Pricer and Edwin Harness mounds. The strata of each mound can be divided into two major phases. I have previously suggested that the impetus for changing the sources of mound fill seen in the two construction stages may have been related to specific and appropriate occasions in the calendric cycle (Greber 1992). This pattern is repeated in other, smaller local mounds, some of which have pre–Middle Woodland affiliations, as, for example, in a group near the ancient juncture of the Paint Creek and the Scioto River (Greber 1991). The existence of two major construction stages is also documented in recent work (or recently published work) on embankment walls at Newark, Fort Ancient, Fort Hill, and High Banks (e.g., Prufer, chapter 12). As a guess— and I emphasize that this is a guess—the construction of two large, similarly designed enclosures in close proximity to each other, such as those at Seip and Baum, may also reflect corporate activities undertaken in recognition of a two-part calendric cycle.

The Local Region

Seip and Baum are part of a unique set of five enclosures found in the central Scioto drainage. The iconographic details of the circular portions of the walls and the relative location of the square-shaped element with respect to the circular ones suggest groupings of local variations within the set: Seip and Baum in the Paint Creek Valley; the Liberty and Works East in the broad Scioto Valley; and the single Old Town Works at Frankfort, just upstream from the Hopewell site on the North Fork of Paint Creek. The five square enclosures are almost identical in size, construction material, iconographic detail, and their nonrandom orientations on the landscape. This strongly suggests that each was part of one overall architectural design likely to have been built over a relatively short time span. The distribution pattern of large corporate structures and small mounds between the Liberty Works and Works East resembles that seen at Seip and Baum. The repetition of such patterning may lend credence to my interpretation that a single social group claimed the two geometric enclosures in Paint Creek as its corporate cultural expression.

I believe that at a given point in time each pair of sites in some manner functioned as "calendar, court, church, and necropolis all wrapped up in one" for a single corporate group, whose members were strongly committed to their worldview. Precursors of this worldview, which reached a florescence in southern Ohio Hopewell, can be found within the local Central Scioto region expressed in artifacts, structures, and public events marked by the placements of objects and by the initiation and/or completion of various construction projects.

The general patterning seen in the limited data available on the structure covered by one of the three conjoined mounds within the Frankfort enclosure is not greatly different from that seen at the Seip-Conjoined mound, but no estimates can be made of the complete structural pattern (Moorehead 1892:133–143). A square-shaped enclosure was added to the eastern side of the great enclosure wall at the Hopewell site, about 9 km downstream from Frankfort. However, this square differs in size and iconographic details from the five I consider to be a regional unit. The isolated nature of the Frankfort works on the North Fork, contrasted with the duality seen in Paint Creek and Scioto, does not appear as a cultural misfit in terms of my suggested corporate aims for several reasons. First, there is a distinct possibility that the architectural design of the total system required five units and that the Hopewell site square was built at a different time. Also, the Hopewell site itself is unique and stands out in almost any cultural aspect. Finally, local differences undoubtedly existed among the various Hopewellian social and political groups centered in the three valleys. During the many generations involved, the relationships among these groups could, and likely did, change. For example, the size of the local supporting population at Seip probably varied through time. Such changes may have reflected, or may have been directly related to, shifts in the social, political, and/or economic fortunes of the leaders of these groups with respect to their contemporaries. I suggest that the existence of the five remarkably similar complex geometric enclosures records one such set of contemporary interregional relationships. Cultural and social ties among three corporate groups were strong enough to allow or to cause the use of some overarching design principles in the construction of this series of enclosures.

Reflections

An apparent redundancy and fortunate overlap of cultural information exist in the combination of artifactual and structural remains left behind by the

Ohio Hopewellians. The assumption that the fabric of Hopewell society combined facets of both "domestic" and "ceremonial" life offers a viewpoint for interpreting cultural dynamics through generations of site use. The land at Seip and Baum was used by people performing ordinary domestic tasks. Family units also used the sites for their rites of passage or to join with others to celebrate events from their mutual calendars or for purposes we can only surmise. The sizes of the groups living at the sites likely changed through time, as did the patterning of the living spaces. The physical and material expressions of the ceremonial/ritual/political public corporate spheres apparently also changed through time. A considerable amount of the cultural debris found at Seip can reasonably be attributed to Hopewellian activities and also overshadows my estimates of quantity of domestic debris recovered from the relatively densely settled post-Hopewellian Baum Village. The greater length of time represented at Seip contributes to this difference. Yet, available surface and excavated material recovered from within the 160 ha containing the large Seip enclosure does not support the existence of a dense Hopewellian settlement pattern matching Baum Village. Nor does it rule out the existence of a settlement pattern falling between the extremes of a compact grouping of fifty households and an extensive network of geographically isolated single-family residences. Evidence from the Liberty Works appears to reflect a similar possibility (see Coughlin and Seeman, chapter 9).

Much fieldwork and analysis are needed to sort out the intersite and intrasite chronology in Paint Creek, as well as in the other valleys, from the two Miamis to the Muskingum, that were used by Ohio Hopewell peoples. I plan to continue searching, as others are, for the apparently elusive Hopewellian suburbs. Assuming the reality of the Middle Woodland community patterning I am proposing for Seip and Baum, one might find in Paint Creek Valley a group of four to eight contemporaneous Hopewellian household structures. One of my personal goals is to participate in excavating such a settlement.

In conclusion, it is clear that both synchronic as well as diachronic variations formed the mosaic of Ohio Hopewell cultural remains. Even within the central Scioto River Valley, intraregional cultural differences existed, in addition to those discussed above (e.g., Seeman and Greber 1992). Considering a wider area, regional styles reflected in the choice of construction materials and architectural designs of the large enclosures apparently distinguish the central Scioto from the Miami regions. Such differences appear to coincide with other, probably local, styles in ceramics (Hawkins 1993) and ritual/ceremonial practices (Greber 1993). Similar differences distinguish the Muskingum-

Licking region. Other significant interregional differences most likely existed. Thus, I would not, without additional study, project the same type of population and corporate changes, or the same chronological ordering of changes that I have interpreted for a set of sites in the central Scioto region, onto the Turner mounds and earthworks in the Little Miami Valley or onto the Marietta or Newark Works in the Muskingum Valley.

Acknowledgments

Portions of the work discussed were funded by grants to the Cleveland Museum of Natural History from the National Science Foundation; the Explorers Club, New York; and the Pneumo Foundation, Boston. Support also came from the Kirtlandia Society, an associated society of the Cleveland Museum of Natural History. I gratefully acknowledge the continued access to collections and the always-present help from the Ohio Historical Society staff, particularly Curator of Archaeology Martha P. Otto, Archaeology Collections Manager Donald Bier, and former staff members Bradley Baker, Suzanne Langlois, and the late Raymond S. Baby.

This essay began in 1985 while I was a Visiting Scholar at Harvard as the guest of Stephen Williams. The topic was suggested by James B. Griffin, whose encouragement I most value. Jeffrey Brain and Ian Brown discussed first drafts of this paper with me. Alfred Lee and especially Katharine Ruhl have patiently reread current versions. I thank them all and acknowledge that the opinions expressed here are my own, not necessarily theirs, as are any errors.

None of this work could have been done without the continued support of my colleagues and friends who reside in Ross County. I particularly remember and dedicate this essay to the late Mary Ann Schlegel, who spent many summers on the banks of Paint Creek, in the Seip family home, while Henry C. Shetrone directed excavations at the Seip-Pricer Mound; many years later she shared her childhood memories and childhood experiences with me.

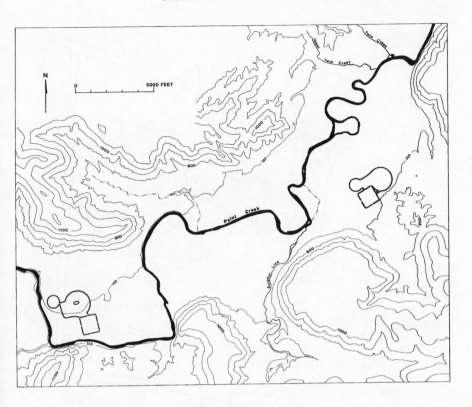

8.1 Topographic setting of the Seip and Baum earthworks in the Paint Creek Valley, Ross County, Ohio.

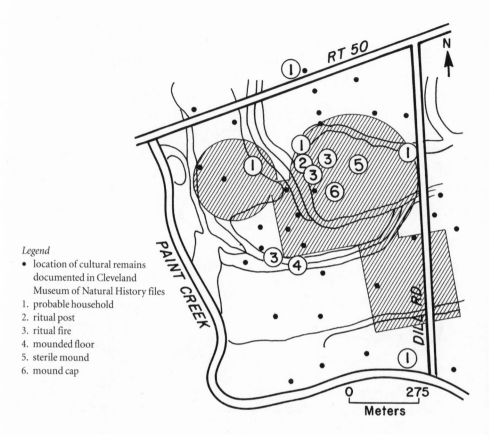

8.2 Cultural remains and old channels of Paint Creek at Seip.

8.3 Model of a suggested time sequence for the Seip Earthworks and environs.

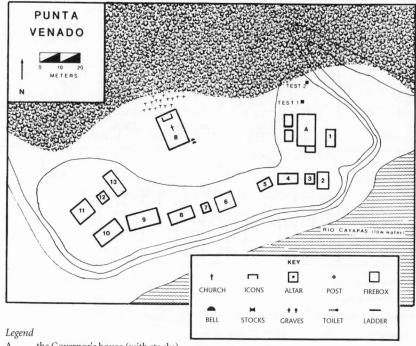

Legend

A. the Governor's house (with stocks)
B. the church (with bells, icons, and associated cemetery)
1–3. guest houses for Pintor (shell middens and graves beneath floors)
4–7. guest houses for Pichiyacu (shell middens and graves beneath floors)
8–9. guest houses for Santa Maria (shell middens and graves beneath floors)
10. guest house for Loma Linda
11. guest house for Pichiyacu (built later than houses 4–7)
12–13. guest houses for chivatillo (shell middens and graves beneath floors)

8.4 Plan of a Chachi ceremonial center reflecting the settlement pattern of its support-
ers and parts of their worldview. (Reprinted with permission from *Expedition* Magazine 33[1]).

References

Atwater, C.
  1820   *Description of the Antiquities Discovered in the State of Ohio and Other Western States.* Transactions and Collections I, Archaeologia Americana. American Antiquarian Society, Worcester, MA.

Baby, R. S., and S. M. Langlois
  1979   Seip Mound State Memorial: Non-Mortuary Aspects of Hopewell. In *Hopewell Archaeology: The Chillicothe Conference,* edited by N'omi Greber and David S. Brose, pp. 16–18. Kent State University Press, Kent, Ohio.

DeBoer, W. R., and J. H. Blitz
  1991   Ceremonial Centers of the Chachi. *Expedition* 33(1):53–62.

Dancey, W. S.
  1991   A Middle Woodland Settlement in Central Ohio: A Preliminary Report on the Murphy Site (33L1212). *Pennsylvania Archaeologist* 61:37–72.

Fortier, A. C., T. O. Maher, J. A. Williams, M. C. Meinkoth, K. E. Parker, and L. S. Kelly
  1989   *The Holding Site: A Hopewell Community in the American Bottom.* FAI-270 Site Reports 19. Center for American Archaeology, Kampsville, Illinois.

Greber, N.
  1976   *Within Ohio Hopewell: Analyses of Burial Patterns from Several Classic Sites.* Unpublished Ph.D. dissertation, Department of Anthropology, Case Western Reserve University, Cleveland.
  1979a Variations in Social Structure Among Classic Ohio Hopewell Peoples. *Midcontinental Journal of Archaeology* 3:35–78.
  1979b A Comparative Study of Site Morphology and Burial Patterns at Edwin Harness Mound and Seip Mounds 1 and 2. In *Hopewell Archaeology: The Chillicothe Conference,* edited by N'omi Greber and David S. Brose, pp. 16–18. Kent State University Press, Kent, Ohio.
  1980a Comparisons of Geophysical Remote Sensing Techniques for Use in Settlement Pattern Survey. Paper presented at the 45th Annual Meeting of the Society for American Archaeology, Philadelphia.
  1980b Field Season Comparisons and Corroboration of Geophysical Remote Sensing Data from Seip Earthworks, Ross County, Ohio. Paper presented at the 25th Annual Meeting of the Midwest Archaeological Conference, Chicago.
  1981   Salvaging Clues to a Prehistoric Culture. *The Gamut* 3:22–45. Cleveland State University.
  1983   *Recent Excavations at the Edwin Harness Mound, Liberty Works, Ross County, Ohio.* Special Paper 5, Midcontinental Journal of Archaeology. Kent State University Press, Kent, Ohio.
  1984a Some Artifacts, Raw Materials, and Styles Found at the Seip Earthworks, Ross County, Ohio with Apparent Origins in the Mid-South. Paper presented at the 5th Mid-South Conference, Pinson, Tennessee.

1984b Geophysical Remote Sensing at Archaeological Sites in Ohio: A Case History. Paper presented at the Annual Meeting of the Society of Exploration Geophysics, Atlanta. Published in volume of proceedings.

1984c Field Results at Seip, 1984. Paper presented the 29th Annual Meeting of the Midwest Archaeological Conference, Chicago.

1986a Astronomy and the Patterns of Five Geometric Earthworks in Ross County, Ohio. Paper presented at the 2nd Oxford Conference on Archaeoastronomy, Merida, Mexico.

1986b Possible Astronomical Alignments Found at Five Hopewell Sites in Ross County, Ohio. Paper presented at the 31st Annual Meeting of the Midwest Archaeological Conference, Columbus.

1991 A Study of Continuity and Contrast Between Central Scioto Adena and Hopewell Sites. *West Virginia Archaeologist* 43(1 & 2):1–26.

1992 Cultural Deposits: Consigned by Hopewellian Custom. Paper presented at the 37th Annual Meeting of the Midwest Archaeological Conference, Grand Rapids.

1993 Considering Some Possible Ecological, Social, and Political Boundaries Among Ohio Hopewell Peoples. Paper presented at the 58th Annual Meeting of the Society for American Archaeology, St. Louis.

Greber, N., R. Davis, and A. DuFresne

1981 The Micro-Component of the Ohio Hopewell Lithic Industry: Bladelets. Conference on the Research Potential of Museum Anthropological Collections, New York Academy of Sciences. *The Annals of the New York Academy of Science* 376:489–528.

Greber, N., and D. Griffin

1982 Comparisons of Excavation and Subsurface Remote Sensing Data from Sections of the Seip Earthwork Complex, Ross County, Ohio. Paper presented at the 39th Annual Meeting of the Southeastern Archaeological Conference, Memphis.

Hawkins, R.

1993 Twin Mound Village and the Hopewell of the Miami Valleys. Paper presented at the 2nd Annual Conference on Ohio Archaeology, Chillicothe, Ohio.

Konigsberg, L. W.

1985 Demography and Mortuary Practice at Seip Mound One. *Midcontinental Journal of Archaeology* 10:123–148.

Maslowski, R. F., and M. F. Seeman

1992 Woodland Archaeology in the Mid-Ohio Valley: Setting Parameters for Ohio Main Stem/Tributary Comparisons. In *Cultural Variability in Context: Woodland Settlements of the Mid-Ohio Valley,* edited by M. F. Seeman, pp. 10–14. Special Paper 7, Midcontinental Journal of Archaeology. Kent State University Press, Kent, Ohio.

Mills, W. C.
    1906   Baum Prehistoric Village. *Ohio Archaeological and Historical Quarterly* 15:45–
            136.
    1909   Explorations of the Seip Mound. *Ohio Archaeological and Historical Quar-
            terly* 18:269–321.
Moorehead, W. K.
    1892   *Primitive Man in Ohio.* AMS Press, New York.
Odell, G. H.
    1994   The Role of Stone Bladelets in Middle Woodland Society. *American Antiquity*
            59:102–120.
Otto, M. P.
    1972   Probing Back 2,000 Years. *Echoes* 11(11):2–3.
Prufer, O. H.
    1965   *The McGraw Site: A Study in Hopewellian Dynamics.* Scientific Publications,
            n.s. 4(1). Cleveland Museum of Natural History.
Petro, J. H., W. Shumate, and M. F. Tabb
    1967   *Soil Survey: Ross County Ohio.* United States Department of Agriculture,
            Washington, D.C.
Seeman, M. F., and N. Greber
    1991   Variations in the Use of Prepared Clay Basins within Ohio Hopewell. Paper
            presented at the 36th Annual Meeting of the Midwest Archaeological Con-
            ference, LaCrosse, Wisconsin.
Smith, B. D.
    1992   *Rivers of Change: Essays on Early Agriculture in Eastern North America.*
            Smithsonian Institution Press, Washington.
Shetrone, H. C., and E. F. Greenman
    1931   Explorations of the Seip Group of Prehistoric Earthworks. *Ohio Archaeo-
            logical and Historical Quarterly* 40:343–509.
Struever, S., and G. L. Houart
    1972   An Analysis of the Hopewell Interaction Sphere. In *Social Exchange and
            Interaction,* edited by E. N. Wilmsen, pp. 47–49. Anthropological Papers 46.
            Museum of Anthropology, University of Michigan, Ann Arbor.
Squier, G. E., and E. H. Davis
    1848   *Ancient Monuments of the Mississippi Valley.* Contributions to Knowledge 1.
            Smithsonian Institution, Washington, D.C.
Stafford, B. D., and M. B. Sant
    1985   *Smiling Dan: Structure and Function at a Middle Woodland Settlement in the
            Lower Illinois Valley.* Research Series 2. Center for American Archaeology,
            Kampsville Archaeological Center, Kampsville, Illinois.

CHAPTER NINE

Hopewell Settlements at the
Liberty Earthworks, Ross County, Ohio

Sean Coughlin and Mark F. Seeman

ABSTRACT

Investigations of settlement patterns often rely on single episode, surface-collected data. In contrast, the present study utilizes the longitudinal data in the Robert Harness surface collection, representing approximately 19,000 artifacts, forty-five sites, and twenty-five years of surface collecting on a 1,500-acre (602 ha) farm in southern Ohio. These data complement those of traditional analyses in the area and are used to document the nature and distribution of thirty-three Middle Woodland period sites as they bear on the Prufer model of Ohio Hopewell settlement. A dispersed pattern of small sites is represented by the Harness settlement data, except that one cluster, the largest recorded in the sample and containing projectile points of a Terminal Middle Woodland age, may constitute a nucleated settlement.

In the 1960s, Olaf Prufer proposed that the long-assumed villages of the Ohio Hopewell moundbuilders did not exist. Despite over a hundred years of archaeological investigations in the area, not a single large village of a scale appropriate for the monumental Hopewell earthwork projects of southern Ohio had been found. As an alternative, he proposed that Hopewell populations lived in dispersed hamlets on the Scioto River floodplain (Prufer 1965). These floodplain soils are among the most productive in Ohio and likely would have been sought out by early farmers. This emphasis on the centrality of farming—explicitly maize farming—set Prufer sharply apart from a developing archaeological perspective that held that the intensive collecting of wild plants, or, at most, a primitive form of horticulture coupled with hunting and gathering, supported the Hopewell social structure (Fowler 1957; Struever 1964). Prufer compared the Hopewell settlement pattern to a lowland Mesoamerican model with a vacant ceremonial center surrounded by dispersed hamlets of maize agriculturalists. In short, Prufer clearly believed that "the general settlement pattern during the Hopewellian period in Ohio seems to have been characterized by a system of semi-permanent shifting agricultural farmsteads or hamlets, clustered around a series of ceremonial centers and burial grounds with which a number of such settlements identified themselves" (1965:137).

In order to test the proposed settlement model, Prufer (1965, 1967; Blank 1965) initiated a program of archaeological survey and excavation along the central Scioto River Valley in the vicinity of present-day Chillicothe, Ohio. In general, the results supported his initial suspicion; habitation sites tended to cluster loosely near the major earthworks, and they certainly were small. Despite a continued focus on Hopewell archaeology in Ohio since Prufer's fieldwork, little has been accomplished to substantiate or clarify his settlement model (see Brown 1982; Dancey 1992; Pacheco 1988). This chapter seeks to evaluate further the usefulness of the Prufer model for the central Scioto Valley using data from the private collection of Robert L. Harness, Jr.

The Harness Farm Collection

Robert L. Harness, Jr., now in his seventies, represents the fifth generation to farm an agriculturally productive section of the Scioto Valley approximately 9.6 km south of the city of Chillicothe. The family farm now consists of approximately 602 ha; over the years, the boundaries have changed only slightly. Today, the farm consists of three main tracts of land separated by two tracts owned by different individuals. The Harness farm is famous for the Liberty or Harness Works, a major Hopewell ceremonial center known since early in the nineteenth century (Greber 1983; Squier and Davis 1848). In addition, the property contains smaller Hopewell ceremonial loci: notably, the Russell Brown mounds (Seeman and Soday 1980), the Ayrshire Mound (Prufer 1967), and a small, unnamed mound at the western end of the Harness-28 site.

Robert L. Harness, Jr., has one of the largest, provenienced collections of prehistoric artifacts in the central Scioto River Valley (Coughlin 1991). In total, it contains over 19,000 artifacts collected from forty-five sites. These materials pertain to all chronological periods and constitute a full array of artifact types. Artifacts were predominantly surface-collected, although a few features discovered while plowing were excavated—including isolated burials, a cache, and several pit features. The Harness collection has been amassed over a twenty-eight-year period from this single south-central Ohio farm.

Mr. Harness provenienced his finds by field and, in some cases, as smaller concentrations within fields. They were given numerical designations on the lower or "home place" portion of the farm (e.g., Site 17) and letter designations on the upstream farms (e.g., Site B). Materials were organized by site, and in the case of most diagnostic artifacts and nearly all Hopewell materials, a site name or number was written on the find for record-keeping purposes. Although most sites were collected several times per year, no effort was made to record the number of visits, duration of collection periods, or completeness of the survey; consequently, the recovery methodology must be characterized as unsystematic. As noted, most sites have been collected several times per year subsequent to their discovery—in some cases, a period of twenty-eight years—and all encountered artifacts, regardless of condition or raw material, were collected. Lithic debitage was also collected, although this sample is biased toward Flint Ridge flint, since Mr. Harness, when he first began to collect, preferentially picked up these brighter, more lustrous flakes. Additionally, it should be noted that although all ground stone tools were collected, only selected examples were provenienced by site and retained due to storage space limitations. Thus, although all categories of ground stone tools known for the area are present in the collection, they probably do not reflect their true frequency of occurrence on site surfaces.

Cumulative data of the sort represented by the Harness collection are rarely available for analysis. The constraints of money and time generally prohibit the calculated development of longitudinal surveys of this magnitude by professionals, nor are many avocational archaeologists as diligent as Mr. Harness in recording their discoveries. The Harness collection represents the complete survey coverage of a limited geographical area with multiple collections over an extended period of time. These multiple collecting episodes allow for a better assessment of the strength of site components than the single collection strategies that typify most professional surface surveys (Lewarch and O'Brien 1981:311; Prufer and Long 1986).

Using the data from the Robert L. Harness, Jr., collection, the present study examines Ohio Hopewell settlements and their distribution. Of particular importance is their association with various landforms and their physical relationship to known Hopewell mounds and earthworks. The distribution and characteristics of these sites provide an opportunity to further evaluate the Prufer model.

Data Framework

The data used in this study consist of artifact, site, and landform categories. There are 5,967 Hopewell artifacts in the Harness collection. Diagnostic Hopewell artifact categories present in the Harness collection include a multitude of lithic, ceramic, metallic, and organic materials. Lithics are dominated by a biface industry leading to the production of distinct styles of projectile points and by a unifacial blade industry. Ohio Hopewell projectile points documented in the Harness collection include 145 Hopewell points (Converse 1973:59), 56 Middle Woodland points (Converse 1973:61), 96 Lowe-Flared Base points of Flint Ridge flint (Justice 1987), and 1 Paint Creek Corner-Notched point (Griffin 1965). The Ohio Hopewell blade industry (see Greber, Davis, and Dufresne 1981) consists of 2,850 blades and 350 blade cores, the vast majority of which consists of heat-treated Flint Ridge flint. Diagnostic Hopewell ceramics are limited to four sherds, two respectively of the Southeastern Series and the Hopewell Series (Prufer 1968); more than anything else, the minimal number of sherds probably reflects the negative effects of modern agriculture on surface materials. Diagnostic Hopewell lithic and mineral materials of an "exotic" nature in the Harness collection include certain obsidian and Knife River flint tools and debitage, crystal quartz fragments, a single mica cutout, and a small copper celt. These materials can be assigned a Hopewell affiliation with confidence despite any ambiguity regarding artifact stylization.

Thirty-three Ohio Hopewell sites or components are recognized on the Harness property (Fig. 9.1). The smallest of these sites produced one diagnostic artifact and the largest 2,470. Artifact quantities and ratios will be used to develop a general categorization of site classes mainly following rank-order principles (Crumley 1976; see also Winters 1969:131). Projectile point frequencies provide the main opportunities for intersite comparisons. Although such an approach cannot separate the effects of reoccupation from occupational intensity, the relative brevity of the Hopewell period in Ohio lends some support to the position that observed differences are more likely to be the effects of actual differences in site function rather than simply reuse. Minimally, superficial artifact differences should differentiate habitation from ceremonial sites; more optimistically, they may allow for the recognition of more refined categories of each.

The Harness property can be divided into three landform categories of presumed cultural significance: the Scioto floodplain, the nonflooding terrace, and the terrace edge. The floodplain is assumed to have been high in resource potential but highly hazardous for subsistence farmers. Historically, it was a swamp forest dominated by elm, sycamore, white oak, and hickory with marshy backwater sloughs and open sections of prairie (Seeman 1980:14). This area was thus proximal to numerous floodplain resources, drinking water, fertile soil, and transport routes via canoe. However, the risk of late spring and summer floods in this area was probably high (Limp 1983:62; Maslowski and Seeman 1992). The floodplain covers 350.3 ha, or 58 percent of the Harness property.

The nonalluviated, Wisconsinan terrace surfaces offered several advantages for prehistoric utilization that the floodplain did not. These surfaces are essentially free from flood hazard, and the sandier soils provide for better drainage than the majority of floodplain contexts. Historically, the vegetation on these landforms was open deciduous forest with white oak and sugar maple as codominants (Seeman 1981:5). Terrace surfaces were much easier to clear than the swamp forest-dominated floodplain for agricultural purposes but were probably somewhat drought prone (Limp 1983:63). Terrace landforms cover 175.6 ha or 29 percent of the Harness property.

Terrace edge locations are defined as those linear environments fringing broader terrace surfaces at the terrace/floodplain boundary. These "edge" locations carry the same advantages and disadvantages for human utilization as the terraces proper. In addition, these surfaces are closer to floodplain resources and offer easily defended, high terrace remnants that extend, finger-like, into the floodplain. Terrace edge situations account for 76.8 ha, or 13 percent of the Harness property.

Using the artifact categories presented above, and given the limitations of the data, two initial questions can be investigated that bear on the Prufer model. First, Hopewell habitation sites, if they are truly small "hamlets" in Prufer's sense, should exhibit a much smaller number of projectile points per site than highly nucleated villages. For example, excavations at the McGraw site, a hamlet, yielded a total of only twelve Middle Woodland corner-notched points,

233 blades, and four exhausted blade cores (Prufer 1965). The Jennison Guard site—another Ohio Hopewell hamlet—produced only six diagnostic projectile points, eighty-seven blades, and one blade core (Blosser 1989). In contrast, Mr. Harness recovered more than six times as many projectile points from the surface of the Harness-28 site (33RO186), a total of seventy-four early Late Woodland Chesser Notched and Chesser Lanceolate points. The main component at Harness-28 is a small early Late Woodland village dating to the period A.D. 600–700 with circular houses, midden development, an earthen fortification, and subsistence evidence for year-round occupation based on excavations by Mark Seeman in 1980 (see also Dancey 1992). It is assumed that the above projectile point totals represent the sort of qualitative differences that characterize homestead/village differences.

A second general question concerns the dispersion of Hopewell sites across the three landforms and around ceremonial constructions. According to the Prufer model, Hopewell hamlets should be concentrated in the floodplain but near the community-orienting earthworks. Correspondingly, sites associated with earthworks can be expected to bear somewhat different artifactual signatures, in this case reflected in projectile point, blade, and blade core frequencies.

Results

A compilation and comparison of Hopewell diagnostics from the Harness collection suggests several patterns. Of the thirty-three identified Hopewell components, six yielded more than three hundred artifacts, five yielded between 100–299 artifacts, four have 40–99 artifacts, eight have 10–39 artifacts, and ten have less than 10 (Fig. 9.2; Table 9.1). Minimally, these differences indicate some degree of functional variability.

Of the large sites, Site 14 and Site A are the most distinctive. Site 14 yielded thirty-seven blades and six blade cores, one Southeastern Series sherd, and no projectile points. More significantly, it also produced a plowed-out cache of 2,427 heavily burned and broken biface fragments of Flint Ridge flint. The lack of success in refitting specimens suggests redeposition from another location (see Seeman and Greber 1991). These materials bespeak a ritual rather than a domestic function for this site.

Site A is a large site that bears a considerably different signature than Site 14. More specifically, it contains by far the largest number of projectile points (n=139) of any of the Hopewell sites on the property (Fig. 9.3; Table 9.1). All other sites produced twenty or less. In addition, Site A produced 184 blades, nineteen blade cores, and the small copper celt. It is the only site that in any way approximates the density of projectile points recovered from the surface of the "control" Late Woodland village on the property. Site A was the focus of considerable Hopewell domestic activity. An inspection of the projectile point styles present suggests that Site A is reasonably late in the Hopewell sequence (Lowe-Flared Base = 82, Hopewell = 28, Middle Woodland = 29); the dominant Lowe-Flared Base points are assumed to be late within the local Hopewell sequence, probably postdating A.D. 200. Other, presumably late, Hopewell sites have produced similar projectile points, notably the Troyer site (Converse 1966).

Of the other "large" sites, Site 25 stands out as a likely special-purpose site for blade production; it yielded no projectile points but an abundance of blades and exhausted cores (n=678, n=58, respectively). This site also yielded the largest number of Knife River flint items (or Knife River look-alikes), all of which are blades. They further emphasize the distinctiveness of the site.

In similar fashion to Site 25, large numbers of blades and blade cores were recovered from Site 28, Site 18, Site 14+, and Site 6 (Table 9.1). Site 18 produced the largest quantity of blade cores on the property (n=73). All of these localities also produced exotic, non-Ohio materials (such as obsidian, Knife River flint, and mica, as well as heavily burned materials). The presence of comparatively large quantities of blades, blade cores, exotics, and other indications of ceremonialism suggests that these sites are special-purpose blade production sites similar to Site 25, small ritual localities, or both.

Of the remaining "large" sites, Sites 13, 15, 27, and 29 all have yielded, in similar ratios, comparable quantities of blades, blade cores, and projectile points. On the basis of these characteristics, and lacking evidence to the contrary, we consider it likely that these sites were large, domestic hamlets. They are here referenced as members of "Domestic Site Category 1."

Of the four smaller localities evidencing between one hundred forty artifacts, three, Sites 1, 11, and 12, are presumed to have been mainly domestic hamlets. This is based on the available lithic evidence, and these sites will be referenced hereafter as members of "Domestic Site Category 2." Site Z, the fourth site of the initial grouping, is better viewed as a likely special-purpose site based on its distinctive blade-to-core ratio.

Of the localities with 10-39 artifacts, Site 5, Site 10, and Site E have high numbers of projectile points and moderate numbers of blades and cores; these are probably domestic habitations, and they are here grouped as "Domestic

Site Category 3." Sites T, 20, 2, C+, and 7 exhibit variable quantities of diagnostics, in many cases without blade cores or projectile points. These small sites are classified as functionally indeterminate. Similarly, sites with less than ten Hopewell artifacts have such ephemeral signatures that we prefer not to speculate on their functions.

An examination of the spatial distribution of various site classes across the landscape reveals several patterns (Fig. 9.4). First, the majority of presumed ceremonial and/or blade-making sites can be convincingly associated with known Hopewell ceremonial centers. Given the location of the Liberty Works, most of these sites are located on interior terrace surfaces. Greber, Davis, and Dufresne (1981) have previously recognized the distinctive character of Site 25 and Site 18 as manufacturing areas associated with the Liberty Works, and the association of specialized blade-making sites—sometimes locally called "core patches"—has been documented at other Ohio Hopewell centers, most notably at the Turner and Baum earthworks. Site 18 and Site 6 also clearly fit this pattern. Site 14+, a terrace edge situation, is on that portion of the terrace edge nearest to the Liberty Works. Site 28 is also located on a terrace edge, in this case relatively far from the major earthworks, but it is directly adjacent to a small, unnamed Hopewell mound. To our knowledge, this type of Hopewell specialized production site has been documented in the Middle Woodland period only in southern Ohio.

Ceremonial Sites 14 and Z also correlate with group-oriented ceremonial constructions located on the terrace interior. Site 14 is located within the earthworks, specifically the large circle, and Site Z is associated with the Ayrshire Mound (Prufer 1967).

In summary, those sites interpreted as pertaining mainly to special-purpose blade production and ceremonialism are all found on the terrace. Of these seven localities, five (71 percent) are terrace interior and two (29 percent) are terrace edge locations. More importantly, all are associated with symbolic, group-orienting constructions.

Turning to those sites interpreted as serving largely a domestic function, it should be noted that sites of Domestic Site Category 1, the larger domestic sites, are divided between the terrace and floodplain locations. Three localities (75 percent) are found on the terrace, specifically the terrace edge, and one (25 percent) is found on the floodplain. Domestic Site Category 2 sites are distributed similarly: two are on the floodplain (67 percent), and one on the terrace edge (33 percent). Domestic Site Category 3 sites reflect a similar "split" distribution, with two sites (67 percent) on the terrace edge and one

(33 percent) on the floodplain. Overall, the locations of presumed domestic hamlets or homesteads are all along the terrace edge (n=6; 60 percent) or on the floodplain (n=4; 40 percent).

Site A is recognized as distinctive. It is the only Hopewell domestic site in the sample that exhibits evidence of domestic aggregation beyond that expected for small-scale, family enclaves of the hamlet or homestead type. This site is situated on a terrace edge location that is somewhat higher and better drained than most other such situations on the Harness farm.

Small sites of "indeterminate" function are found on both the floodplain and terrace interior: four of the five (80 percent) indeterminate locations are on the floodplain; the other site (20 percent) is located on the terrace interior but is far removed from the earthworks.

Ephemeral trace locations are found on all three landforms but with some preference for the floodplain. It should be noted that based on recovered materials and its proximity to the Russell Brown mounds, Site Y is probably a ceremonial or special-purpose location on the terrace interior. The other ephemeral locations are distributed with seven (76 percent) on the floodplain, one (12 percent) on the terrace edge, and one (12 percent) on the terrace interior; none of these bears any direct association with the Liberty Works or other known Hopewell mound or earthwork complexes on the Harness farm. It should perhaps be noted that Site T, located on the floodplain, corresponds to the Browns Bottom site tested in 1963 (Blank 1965).

Conclusions

The distribution of diagnostic surface-collected Hopewell artifacts has been evaluated with regard to their patterned associations with certain landforms and ceremonial centers on the Robert Harness property. In the main, these distributions support the Prufer settlement model. The presence of sites interpreted as ceremonial and/or specialized manufacturing locations does not directly challenge the validity of the model one way or the other, and the correlation of these sites with known mound and earthwork constructions seems clear. Similarly, the many "indeterminate," small sites on the property do not challenge the basic model but do suggest that modification is in order. As Pacheco (1988:99) states: "One principal modification to the Hamlet Hypothesis must be the recognition that logistical sites do not constitute evidence for the rejection of the model. Hunting and nut-collecting, representing seasonal expeditions away from residential bases, are probably also components of the settlement system."

Importantly, the vast majority of sites interpretable as habitation sites on the Harness property are of a size and density to suggest a hamlet or homestead orientation. Many of these are on the floodplain as Prufer originally suggested, but the majority are located on the terrace edge. The presence of sites in both situations represents a pattern meriting further investigation. Based on limited surface survey and the inspection of collections from nearby properties, we believe Prufer was correct in identifying a concentration of small Hopewell domestic sites loosely centering on the Liberty Works (Prufer 1967:Fig. 1 map, 275). More specific interpretations are compromised by the limitations of surface collections of any sort and, in this particular case, by the fact that the majority of land surfaces on this farm have been under cultivation for nearly two hundred years; a 32–35 cm plow-disturbed zone on the terrace surfaces is not unusual here.

Site A differs from the above domestic pattern to a notable degree. Its large size could be explained by the recurrent occupation of a particularly favorable locality; conversely, it could be a site with emergent "village" properties. Regarding the former, it should be noted that this site also has yielded the largest amounts of Middle Archaic, Late Archaic, and Late Prehistoric materials on the entire Harness property and the second largest quantities of Early Archaic and Early Woodland remains (Coughlin 1991). Only in the Late Archaic case, however, is the magnitude of difference between this site and the next largest site as great as it is for the Middle Woodland Ohio Hopewell period. Correspondingly, we interpret Site A as representing an important, and probably late, variation on the predominant Ohio Hopewell settlement layout. In fact, this type of site should be anticipated given the large, "village" character of only slightly later "Newtown" sites in the vicinity, for example, as represented by Bentley (Henderson and Pollack 1985), Hansen (Ahler 1992), or Childers (Shott and Jefferies 1992) with radiocarbon assays dating to the fifth and sixth centuries A.D. Further afield, social processes promoting larger settlements of some sort were clearly at work in the lower Ohio River Valley late in the Middle Woodland period as represented by the Mann phase (Kellar 1979). We suspect that the sociostructural adjustments promoting these trends toward larger habitation sites played out over a period of several centuries may document a shift in central tendency rather than a strict and sudden dichotomous transformation at the Middle Woodland/Late Woodland temporal boundary.

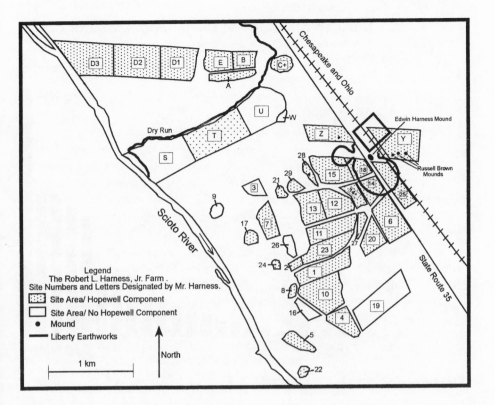

9.1 Map of the Harness Farm collection sites.

Number of Hopewell Diagnostic Artifacts

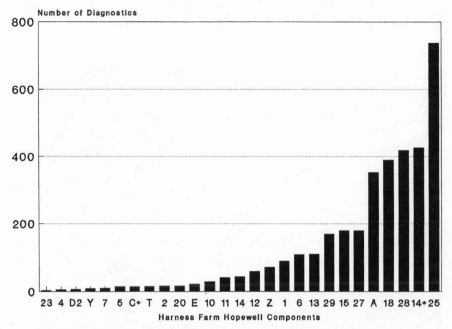

Site 14 (N=2,470), sites N<3 not graphed

9.2 Harness Farm collection. Number of Hopewell diagnostic nonceramic artifacts by component.

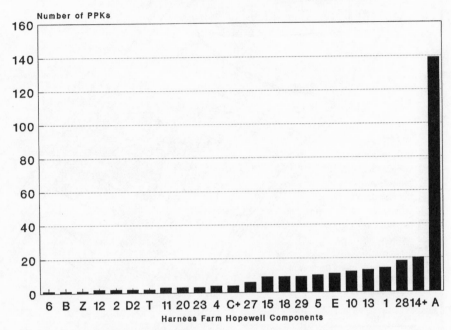

Number of Hopewell Diagnostic PPKs

Components with no PPKs not graphed

9.3 Harness Farm collection. Number of Hopewell diagnostic projectile points/knives by component.

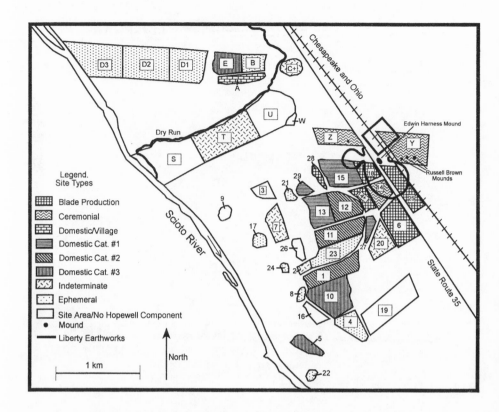

9.4 Map of the Harness Farm site distributions by type.

Table 9.1

Hopewell Diagnostic Artifacts Sorted by Site and Grouped by Site Type

Sites and Landform type[a]	Blades	Blade Cores	Exotic	Hopewell PPK[d]	Middle Woodland PPK	Paint Creek PPK	Lowe Flare PPK	Total PPK	Total Items
Blade Production									
25 (TI)	678	58	2	0	0	0	0	0	738
18 (TI)	308	73	0	8	0	1	0	9	390
14+ (TE)	365	34	8	13	6	0	1	20	427
28 (TE)	368	26	7	9	6	0	3	18	419
6 (TI)	71	32	5	1	0	0	0	1	109
Ceremonial									
14 (TI)	37	6	2427[b]	0	0	0	0	0	2470
Z (TI)	54	16	0	1	0	0	0	1	71
Y (TI)	3	5	0	0	0	0	0	0	8
Domestic/Village									
A (TE)	184	19	10	28	29	0	82	139	352
Domestic Cat. #1									
13 (F)	86	11	0	10	3	0	0	13	110
29 (TE)	143	14	3	8	0	0	1	9	169
27 (TE)	151	20	2	5	0	0	1	6	179

Table 9.1 Cont'd.

15 (TE)	156	13	1	9	0	0	0	9	179
Domestic Cat. #2									
1 (TE)	70	5	0	5	8	0	1	14	89
11 (F)	33	4	1	3	0	0	0	3	41
12 (F)	51	6	0	2	0	0	0	2	59
Domestic Cat. #3									
E (TE)	7	3	1	9	0	0	2	11	22
10 (TE)	15	1	1	11	0	0	1	12	29
5 (F)	4	0	0	10	0	0	0	10	14
Indeterminate									
7 (F)	10	0	0	0	0	0	0	0	10
C+ (TI)	10	0	0	4	0	0	0	4	14
2 (F)	13	1	0	0	1	0	1	2	16
20 (F)	11	1	1	1	2	0	0	3	16
T (F)c	13	0	0	2	0	0	0	2	15
Ephemeral									
17 (F)	0	1	0	0	0	0	0	0	1
21 (F)	1	0	0	0	0	0	0	0	1
22 (F)	1	0	0	0	0	0	0	0	1
23 (F)	0	0	0	1	0	0	2	3	3
24 (F)	1	0	0	0	0	0	0	0	1

Table 9.1 Cont'd.

8 (F)	1	0	0	0	0	0	0	1
B (TI)	1	0	1	1	0	1	0	2
4 (TE)	1	0	2	2	1	1	4	5
D2 (F)	3	1	2	0	0	0	2	6

[a]TI = Terrace Interior; TE = Terrace Exterior; F = Floodplain

[b]This is the burnt cache of bifaces.

[c]This site is the Browns Bottom site, excavated in 1963 (see Blank 1965).

[d]PPK = Projectile Point/Knife

References

Ahler, S. R.

    1992   The Hansen Site (15Gp14): A Middle/Late Woodland Site Near the Confluence of the Ohio and Scioto Rivers. In *Cultural Variability in Context: Woodland Settlements of the Mid-Ohio Valley,* edited by M. Seeman, pp. 30–40. Special Paper No. 7, *Midcontinental Journal of Archaeology.* Kent State University Press, Kent, Ohio.

Blank, J. E.

    1965   The Brown's Bottom Site, Ross County, Ohio. *Ohio Archaeologist* 15(1):16–21.

Blosser, J. K.

    1989   *Mica Working at the Jennison Guard Site: A Middle Woodland Village in Southeastern Indiana.* Unpublished master's thesis, Department of Anthropology, University of Cincinnati.

Brown, J. A.

    1982   Mound City and the Vacant Ceremonial Center. Paper presented at the 47th Annual Meeting of the Society for American Archaeology, Minneapolis.

Converse, R. N.

    1966   The Troyer Site. *Ohio Archaeologist* 16(1):11–15.

    1973   *Ohio Flint Types.* The Archaeological Society of Ohio, Plain City.

Coughlin, S.

    1991   *Prehistoric Population and Land Utilization In the Central Scioto River Valley: An Analysis of the Robert L. Harness Collection.* Unpublished Honors thesis, Department of Anthropology, Kent State University, Kent, Ohio.

Crumley, C. J.

    1976   Toward a Locational Definition of State Systems of Settlement. *American Anthropologist* 78:59–73.

Dancey, W. S.

    1992   Village Origins in Central Ohio: The Results of Recent Middle Woodland and Late Woodland Research. In *Cultural Variability in Context: Woodland Settlements of the Mid-Ohio Valley,* edited by M. Seeman, pp. 24–29. Special Paper No. 7, Midcontinental Journal of Archaeology. Kent State University Press, Kent, Ohio.

Fowler, M. L.

    1957   The Origin of Plant Cultivation in the Central Mississippi Valley: A Hypothesis. Paper presented at the 57th Annual Meeting of the American Anthropological Association, Chicago.

Greber, N.

    1983   *Recent Excavations at the Edwin Harness Mound, Liberty Works, Ross County, Ohio.* Special Paper No. 5, Midcontinental Journal of Archaeology. Kent State University Press, Kent, Ohio.

Greber, N., R. S. Davis, and A. S. Dufresne

1981 The Micro Component of the Ohio Hopewell Lithic Technology: Bladelets. *Annals of the New York Academy of Sciences* 376:489–528

Griffin, J. B.

1965 Hopewell and the Dark Black Glass. *Michigan Archaeologist* 11(3–4):115–155.

Henderson, G. A., and D. Pollack

1985 The Late Woodland Occupation of the Bentley Site. In *Woodland Period Research in Kentucky,* edited by D. Pollack, T. Sanders, and C. Hockensmith, pp. 140–164. Kentucky Heritage Council, Frankfort.

Justice, N. D.

1987 *Stone Age Spear and Arrow Points of the Midcontinental United States.* Indiana University Press, Bloomington.

Kellar, J. H.

1979 The Mann Site and "Hopewell" in the Lower Wabash-Ohio Valley. In *Hopewell Archaeology: The Chillicothe Conference,* edited by D. Brose and N. Greber, pp. 100–107. Kent State University Press, Kent, Ohio.

Lewarch, D. E., and M. J. O'Brien

1981 The Expanding Role of Surface Assemblages in Archaeological Research. In *Advances in Archaeological Method and Theory, Vol. 4,* edited by M. Schiffer, pp. 297–342. Academic Press, New York.

Limp, W. F.

1983 *Rational Location Choice and Prehistoric Settlement Analysis.* Unpublished Ph.D. dissertation, Department of Anthropology, Indiana University, Bloomington.

Maslowski, R. F., and M. F. Seeman

1992 Woodland Archaeology in the Mid-Ohio Valley: Setting Parameters for Ohio Main Stem/Tributary Comparisons. In *Cultural Variability in Context: Woodland Settlements of the Mid-Ohio Valley,* edited by M. Seeman, pp. 10–14. Special Paper No. 7, Midcontinental Journal of Archaeology. Kent State University Press, Kent, Ohio.

Pacheco, P. J.

1988 Ohio Middle Woodland Settlement Variability in the Upper Licking River Drainage. *Journal of the Steward Anthropological Society* 18:87–117.

Prufer, O. H.

1965 *The McGraw Site: A Study in Hopewellian Dynamics.* Scientific Publications, n.s. 4(1). Cleveland Museum of Natural History.

1967 The Scioto Valley Archaeological Survey. In *Studies in Ohio Archaeology,* edited by O. Prufer and D. McKenzie, pp. 267–328. Press of Case Western Reserve University, Cleveland.

1968 *Ohio Hopewell Ceramics: An Analysis of Extant Collections.* Anthropological Papers 33. Museum of Anthropology, University of Michigan, Ann Arbor.

Prufer, O. H., and D. Long
1986   *The Archaic of Northeastern Ohio.* Research Papers in Archaeology 6. Kent State University, Kent, Ohio.
Seeman, M. F.
1980   *An Archaeological and Geomorphological Floodplain Survey of the Scioto River-Paint Creek Confluence.* Kent State University, Kent, Ohio. Report submitted to the Ohio Historic Preservation Office.
1981   *Investigations of the Chillicothe Correctional Institute Chillicothe, Ohio: Phase I (Literature Search) and Phase II (Locational Survey).* Kent State University, Kent, Ohio. Report submitted to the U.S. Department of Justice.
Seeman, M. F., and N. Greber
1991   Flames of Reverence: Variations in the Use of Prepared Clay Basins Within Ohio Hopewell. Paper prepared for the 36th Annual Midwest Archaeological Conference, LaCrosse, Wisconsin.
Seeman, M. F., and F. Soday
1980   The Russell Brown Mounds: Three Hopewell Mounds in Ross County, Ohio. *Midcontinental Journal of Archaeology* 5:73–116.
Shott, M. J., and R. W. Jefferies
1992   Late Woodland Economy and Settlement in the Mid-Ohio Valley: Recent Results from the Childers/Woods Project. In *Cultural Variability in Context: Woodland Settlements of the Mid-Ohio Valley,* edited by M. Seeman, pp. 52–64. Special Paper No. 7, Midcontinental Journal of Archaeology. Kent State University Press, Kent, Ohio.
Squier, E. G., and E. H. Davis
1848   *Ancient Monuments of the Mississippi Valley.* Contributions to Knowledge 1. Smithsonian Institution, Washington, D.C.
Struever, S.
1964   The Hopewell Interaction Sphere in Riverine-Western Great Lakes Culture History. In *Hopewellian Studies,* edited by J. Caldwell and R. Hall, pp. 85–106. Scientific Papers 12, No. 2. Illinois State Museum, Springfield.
Winters, H. D.
1969   *The Riverton Culture: A Second Millennium Occupation in the Central Wabash Valley.* Report of Investigations 13. Illinois State Museum, Springfield.

CHAPTER TEN

The Evidence for Habitation at the Fort Ancient Earthworks, Warren County, Ohio

Robert P. Connolly

ABSTRACT

Recent research has revealed evidence of Hopewell structures adjacent to the Fort Ancient hilltop enclosure in southwestern Ohio. The findings tend to support claims that Ohio Hopewell monuments boasted resident populations. Excavations have identified substantial structures, fire pits, limestone pavements, midden deposits, and several shallow pits on the upland plateau immediately east of the North Enclosure. The excavations are directly north of the area described by Olaf Prufer in 1965 as the "best candidate here for a true (Hopewell) settlement." Distinct scatters of Hopewell artifacts litter the surface of an additional 30+ ha east of the study area.

This paper examines the evidence for Hopewell habitation areas adjacent to the Middle Woodland Fort Ancient earthworks (33WA2) with a focus on lithic artifacts and their contextual associations. I acknowledge that portions of the interpretations included in this paper are based on a synthesis of work initiated by Dr. Patricia Essenpreis in 1982 that she continued until her death in September 1991. I had the good fortune of working with Dr. Essenpreis for half that period and assume full responsibility for any misinterpretations of her research.

The Fort Ancient site rests on a bluff 80 m above the Little Miami River drainage in Warren County, Ohio, 5 km upstream from the Stubbs earthwork reported by Genheimer in this volume. Fort Ancient's 5.7 km of embankment walls encompass approximately 51 ha (Fig. 10.1). The earthwork complex incorporates a multitude of earthen mounds and crescents, stone circles, flagstone pavements and two parallel walls extending .7 km northeast of the enclosure's embankment walls. Although most of the architectural elements at Fort Ancient are intact, the two parallel walls were destroyed by recent historic farming.

Most archaeological investigations conducted at Fort Ancient through 1940 focused on the architectural elements (e.g., Hosea 1874; Moorehead 1890; Mills 1908; Morgan and Ellis 1939, 1940). The restricted focus of these excavations generated interpretations that accentuated the elaborate and minimized the mundane. Beginning in 1982, Essenpreis directed research toward a broader investigation of the entire site. The redirection focused on nonarchitectural components, including the 51 ha of open space within the embankment walls and the plateau extension northeast of the enclosure. Essenpreis continued this work through the 1990 field season[1].

Recent Excavations at Fort Ancient—1982 to 1990

The model of Hopewell settlement proposed in the mid-1960s by Prufer (1964: 70–71) stated that earthworks and mound groups in Ohio were ceremonial centers providing little evidence for domestic activities. He argued that the presence of house structures at earthworks did not necessarily indicate habitation loci but suggested instead, for example, that at the Hopewell and Fort Hill sites their functions were related to ritual activity or to earthwork construction. However, as an exception he noted that "the best candidate here for a true (Hopewell) settlement was found outside the walls encircling the hilltop enclosure at Fort Ancient" (Prufer 1965:126). Prufer contrasts the Fort Ancient evidence with similar deposits recovered near Fort Hill, a Middle Woodland–period hilltop enclosure located in Highland County, Ohio. He questioned whether the Fort Hill material represents a true village "because

1. Excavations conducted between 1985 and 1990 in the area northeast of the Fort Ancient earthworks are summarized by Essenpreis (1985, 1986, 1987, 1988), Connolly (1990, 1991, 1992), and Connolly and Essenpreis (1990).

the materials were excavated from what had obviously been two ceremonial structures contained within circular earthworks" (Prufer 1965:126). Throughout the Middle Woodland period Prufer suggests that there "seem[s] to be elaborate ceremonial centers based upon a mortuary cult and surrounded by very small dependent villages of little permanence" (Prufer 1964:71). Prufer's reference to Fort Ancient suggests the evidence for a settlement at this hilltop enclosure represents a "small dependent village" outside the earthwork, whereas the Fort Hill material is related to ceremonial activity because the materials recovered were associated with structures within an earthwork.

Prufer based his assessment of the Fort Ancient settlement on the presence of pit features and a wide range of utilitarian and Hopewell Interaction Sphere artifacts recorded during salvage operations resulting from Civilian Conservation Corps (CCC) work in the 1930s. The CCC removed the plowzone from a portion of the plateau immediately outside the northeast edge of the earthworks (Pat Essenpreis, personal communication). The location of a part of the disturbance is clearly visible today as a marked depression in the land surface. Fig. 10.2 shows the approximate northern and western boundaries of the CCC operation. Other nonrelated historic period modifications to the plateau extend approximately 200 m south of State Route 350. Fig. 10.2 shows the location of investigations conducted by Essenpreis in 1985. In an area measuring 26 x 21 m Essenpreis detected prior removal of soils ranging in depth from 30 to 120 cm. However, she also noted that immediately east of the study area, the ground surface was "essentially undisturbed" (Essenpreis 1985). Although not stated in her report, the 1985 investigations apparently included a portion of the plateau modified by the CCC in the 1930s. Prufer (1964:126) assumed that the CCC stripping operation destroyed the evidence of habitation activities in the vicinity. Fieldwork conducted from 1986 through 1990 immediately north of the disturbed zone and in adjacent cultivated fields demonstrates this not to be the case and produced evidence on which the present paper is based.

Fig. 10.2 shows the extent of coring and excavation units placed in an attempt to define the boundary of the habitation zone north of State Route 350. Soil cores were placed at 3 m intervals throughout the study area. Besides the evidence of prehistoric activity, discussed in detail below, coring documented the presence of several historic period driveways, two barns, a privy, and a cistern. These historic features either overlay, intrude into, or have destroyed parts of the Middle Woodland habitation zone at the site. In addition, a significant portion of Fig. 10.2 on the north side of S.R. 350 not producing cores with intact prehistoric deposits (i.e., the blank area of the figure) contains subsurface historic features such as driveways or revealed evidence that the upper stratum of soil was modified, thus obliterating the archaeological deposits. While complicating the ability to assess the extent of the domestic activity, this disturbance is superficial when compared to the stripped southern extension of this locality.

The lower portion of Fig. 10.2, labeled "Plow Zone Stripped," defines the approximate location of the "settlement" referred to by Prufer. Coring detected evidence of prehistoric activity immediately south of S.R. 350, between the road and the stripped zone. The single excavation unit in the stripped zone marks the location of a 5 x 5 ft (1.5 x 1.5 m) unit excavated by Essenpreis in 1982. Within the unit Essenpreis excavated a portion of a pit feature containing organic soils and flint debitage. In the same unit, 60 cm east of the pit, she recorded a possible postmold or second pit feature 30 cm in diameter and lined with limestone. Of significance, Essenpreis noted that both features were truncated by plow scars, apparently the result of the CCC stripping operation. The single core sample within the stripped area and located 40 m west of the 1982 unit probably also represents a pit feature. The excavations conducted by Essenpreis along with Morgan's (1970:38–39) brief description of the salvage work suggest that the CCC modification removed the actual prehistoric living floor, leaving only the features that intruded into culturally sterile subsoils to a depth greater than that reached by the scrapping blade.

As represented by the core samples and excavation units, the primary characteristic of the area of intact prehistoric deposits located north of S.R. 350 and immediately east of the Twin Mounds is the accumulation of mottled organic soils containing charcoal and other cultural material in layers ranging in thickness from .5–.75 m below the base of the plowzone. The depth of the deposits is explained by two factors. Fig. 10.2 shows the trajectory of the parallel earthen walls as mapped by Moorehead. The southern wall passes directly over excavation units north of S.R. 350. As discussed in detail below, the habitation area north of S.R. 350 was abandoned or moved before the construction of the parallel walls. Today there is little surface indication of the parallel walls. As early as Locke's 1843 account of Fort Ancient, historic period plowing had nearly obliterated these features (Squier and Davis 1848). The 1 m high and 4 m wide walls are today spread over the habitation area that predated the wall construction. A subtle rise in elevation is present where the walls originally stood.

The depth of prehistoric deposits is also explained by recognizing the accretional development of the Fort Ancient earthwork complex over time. Current research conclusively demonstrates that the Hopewellians significantly modified the natural terrain prior to the construction of architectural features. The modifications minimally include the filling of erosional gullies on the central plateau, the building up and extension of the plateau margins, and the leveling of space enclosed within the North Fort (Connolly 1993; Connolly and Sieg 1993). Also, the construction of embankment walls throughout the enclosure represents at least three distinct construction stages (Essenpreis 1986). In short, the building program at Fort Ancient was not a single event but reflects an evolving architectural program that spatially expanded in both vertical and horizontal directions. This fact is demonstrated below for the habitation area discussed in this paper.

Excavation Data

Excavations conducted north of State Route 350 since 1986 encompass nearly 70 m². The excavated units contained more than 550 probable postmolds, some readily defined as structure walls. Fig. 10.3 is a composite of the postmolds recorded. The overlapping walls, erratic patterns, and varying depths for the origination of postmolds suggest significant rebuilding over the course of the Middle Woodland occupation.

Besides evidence for structures, the excavations exposed pit features, hearths, and earth ovens. To the east of the dense concentration of postmolds shown in Fig. 10.3, coring detected an extensive lithic lens immediately below the plowzone. Excavation revealed that the lens represented the upper level of a three-layered limestone pavement. Coring further delimited a 3 m² zone of charcoal-laden soils within the southeast quarter of the limestone pavement. The east-west dimension of the pavement is about 25 m. The southern portion abuts S.R. 350, and a historic component overlies the northern portion making the pavement's north-south dimensions difficult to determine without additional excavations.

Beginning at E59.98 (Fig. 10.3) and extending east, the pavement consists of a series of three limestone, sand, and gravel lenses that overlay each other. Fig. 10.4 is a schematic representation of the pavements. Interpretation of the pavements, stratigraphy, and function is necessarily tentative, because less than

5 percent of their total surface was exposed. The pavement layers are not completely uniform throughout their 25 m east-west span. The pavement profile shown in Fig. 10.4 represents about 50 percent of total pavement length, but it contains examples of all variations in feature type and stratum thickness found throughout the pavement.

The section in Fig. 10.4 between E77 and E80 contains the most formal or idealized example of the pavement layers. Therefore, this section will serve as a model for discussing the entire pavement. However, the stratigraphic levels of this section, as summarized below, do not include structural variations and nuances that occur in other specific sections of the pavement. A detailed analysis of the pavement trench is beyond the scope of this paper.

(1) Soil A, between the modern surface and Pavement 1, is a 30 cm level of plowzone containing a mixture of historic and prehistoric artifacts. The plowzone level is presumably composed of soils from the parallel walls.

(2) Pavement 1 is a 5 cm level of gravel on top of a 5 cm level of limestone slabs. The limestone slabs range 2–5 cm in thickness and 5–20 cm in length. Gravel is also present within the limestone matrix. Only prehistoric artifacts, in a very low density, were recovered from within the pavement.

(3) Soil B, immediately below Pavement 1, is a very thin and erratic layer of sand followed by a 5–10 cm level of mottled dark-gray to very dark gray silty soils. Postmolds and the illustrated pit feature were defined at this level. The two postmolds, shown in profile, originated at this level; the posts were removed prior to the construction of Pavement 1. Charcoal flecks, burnt clay, red ochre, and flint artifacts were recovered throughout this level. The dark gray soils graded into a brown-yellow silty clay at the interface with Pavement 2. At this interface the artifact densities increased particularly for burned and unburned faunal material. The highest density of artifacts was recovered between E79 and E80 in direct association with Pavement 2. The soil between Pavement 1 and Pavement 2 may, in part, represent deposition over an extended period of time. Alternately, the soils may have been intentionally placed in preparation for the construction of Pavement 1. It is clear however, that the artifacts recovered and postmolds and pit features profiled are temporally related to activities associated with Pavement 2.

(4) The composition of Pavement 2 is similar to Pavement 1 except that the limestone slabs are smaller.

(5) Soil C varies 5–10 cm in thickness between Pavement 2 and Pavement 3. Soil C is similar to Soil B, but with a higher clay content it also yielded increased amounts of cultural material such as mica flakes, flint artifacts in-

cluding bladelets, mussel shells, gastropods, pottery, burned clay, charcoal, and ash. Somewhat surprisingly, the recovered materials were spread evenly throughout the 3 m long section of the pavement and not concentrated in the pit feature. Excavation of the pit revealed a circular-shaped depression approximately 1 m in diameter. The base of the feature contained limestone slabs similar in size to those recovered in Pavement 1. The origin of Soil C is presumed the same as for Soil B.

(6) Pavement 3 varies in thickness 5–10 cm, and its composition is quite different from that of Pavements 1 and 2. Pavement 3 is composed of a mixture of gravel, sand, small pieces of limestone, and clay. An artifact assemblage similar to Soil C but in significantly reduced amounts was recovered.

(7) Soil D consists of highly mottled light to dark yellow-brown silts and clays. A similar but even less dense artifact assemblage than that associated with Pavement 3 was recorded. This level predates all pavement construction. Stratigraphically it is identical to the level containing the postmold patterns (Fig. 10.3) to the west of the pavement.

(8) Soil E is the culturally sterile subsoil.

The E77–E80 profile is generally representative of the stratigraphy of the entire pavement complex investigated to date. Additional comments regarding other specific aspects of the pavements are necessary.

(1) The thickness of the three pavements and associated soils, as well as their differential presence or absence, varies across the length of the trench. For example, Pavement 3 is virtually nonexistent between E81 and E84 (Fig. 10.4). Similarly, between E66 and E67 Pavement 2 rests directly on Pavement 3 with no intervening Soil C, and Pavement 1 is not present (but it is exposed in the South Wall Profile). Although such inconsistencies and breaks in stratigraphic continuity occur, all three pavements and soil strata discussed can be traced across the 25 m extent of the excavated trench. In addition, the southern portion of the pavement was tested at the isolated unit within the pavement boundary (see Fig. 10.2). At this location, the same three pavement layers and intervening soil strata could be documented. Rebuilding of the pavement and underlying structures, features intruding into lower levels of the pavement, and the limited amount of the pavement area exposed to date, complicate interpretation of this complex stratigraphy.

(2) The greater depth of Soil A between E58 and E61 when compared with E84 reflects the proximity to the original location of the parallel walls. That is, when the walls were plowed out in historic times, those areas closest to the walls received the greatest amount of overburden.

(3) Although postmolds were recorded throughout the extent of the pavement, they cluster between E60 and E79, or the west end of the pavement. The same spatial density of postmolds is noted in Soil D, the stratum that corresponds to the level of structures shown in Fig. 10.3 west of the limestone pavements.

(4) Without exception, all classes of artifacts recovered were found to increase in density from west to east across the three pavements. Similarly, soils between and below the pavements increased in organic content from west to east. This distribution suggests that the space within and on the periphery of the structures was kept clean of debris.

(5) There is virtually no possibility that the limestone pavements discussed above represent the pavements described by Atwater (1820) and Moorehead (1890) for the area between the parallel walls. In 1820 they were partially visible on the ground surface, whereas no early reference is made to the three limestone pavements that form the subject for the present discussion. In addition, Moorehead describes the pavement between the parallel walls as a single layer with a spongy underlying clay. A pavement and underlying clay identical to that described by Moorehead is recorded in the isolated excavation unit 30 m northeast of Site Datum AB (see Fig. 10.2). Stratigraphically, this pavement is nearly 40 cm above the series of three limestone pavements located further to the east.

(6) All diagnostic artifacts recovered from the present excavations, including ceramics, projectile points, and bladelets, as well as raw materials such as mica and Ohio Flint Ridge chert, indicate a Middle Woodland occupation. The flint assemblage will be discussed below.

At least two and possibly three discrete Middle Woodland period occupational episodes occurred at the area shown in Fig. 10.2. The separate occupations also demonstrate a functional shift in the locality's use through time. The initial occupation includes the area shown in Fig. 10.3 consisting of a Hopewell habitation site resting on a well-defined "A" horizon (Essenpreis and Connolly 1989). The spatial extent of this habitation zone is unknown. The portions of Fig. 10.2 labeled "Soil Cores with Intact Prehistoric Deposits" represent the absolute minimum extent of the initial occupation. The 4 x 4 ft (1.2 x 1.2 m) excavation unit located 35 m due east of Site Datum AB (Fig. 10.2) contained twelve postmolds. Six of these contained chinking stones and formed an east-west line through the center of the unit suggesting the presence of a structure at this location (Connolly and Essenpreis 1990). It should be noted that already Mills (1908) recorded pit features north of the area shown in Fig. 10.2.

Further, it can be reasonably conjectured that the habitation zone on the north side of State Route 350 was contemporaneous with that on the south side of the road discussed by Prufer (1964) and reported by Morgan (1970). In summary, as noted by Prufer thirty years ago, extensive evidence for Middle Woodland habitation is present immediately outside the northeast embankment walls of the Fort Ancient enclosure. Whether the habitation zone predates the construction of the so-called North Fort of the site is not clear. However, evidence for pre-embankment activities by Middle Woodland populations is documented in the Middle Fort portion of the site (Connolly 1993).

Postdating, or possibly in part coeval with, this habitation activity was the construction of the three limestone pavements. The portion of the pavement trench profile between E58 and E66 clearly indicates that the Soil D postmolds predate the construction of the pavement. Many postmolds originating in the Soil D level contained gravel and soil of low organic content, suggesting the removal of the posts in conjunction with the building of Pavement 3. Although the pavement does not extend as far west as the postmold patterns shown in Fig. 10.3, stratigraphically all the postmolds shown in this figure originate at a level lower than Pavement 3, therefore predating the onset of pavement construction.

It is clear, then, that the series of pavements overlay a portion of the original habitation zone. The Soil A deposits above the habitation zone west of E60, the western-most extent of the pavements, contain homogenous soil to a depth of 70 cm. The upper half of this stratum contained historic artifacts, while the lower half yielded only prehistoric materials. No intact prehistoric features were encountered in Soil A. This suggests the possibility that a portion of the habitation zone was not abandoned but continued to function after the pavement was constructed. If this scenario is correct then the subsequent addition of the three pavements would have formed a raised platform next to the structures.

The final construction episode was the addition of the parallel walls. The parallel walls as reported by Atwater (1820) were 1 m high and 4 m wide with a 40 m space between them. The walls extended .7 km to the northeast along the trajectory, as reported by Moorehead (1890) and shown in Fig. 10.2. The first 150 m between the two walls was lined with limestone slab. The southern wall runs directly through the habitation zone north of S.R. 350; it minimally abuts and most likely covers at least portions of the limestone pavements. Therefore, although the pavements possibly functioned in association with the parallel walls, the habitation zone was definitely terminated or moved elsewhere upon wall construction. The evolution of more formal architectural elements through time (i.e., pavements and parallel walls) represents a shift from unspecified habitation to corporate public space. This architectural development is in line with the assertion by Essenpreis (1986) that Fort Ancient was constructed in multiple stages, with the earliest stage occurring in the South Fort and organized by independent social groupings, and the last stage in the North Fort carried out through some sort of centralized organization.

In summary, the lack of radiocarbon determinations and limited excavations conducted to date provide the basis for proposing only tentative interpretations of the construction and occupation episodes discussed thus far. The temporal depth of the Middle Woodland occupation at this portion of Fort Ancient is also unclear. Given the amount of rebuilding evident in the habitation zone north of State Route 350, at least several generations are suggested for this first occupation. The limestone pavements that postdate the original occupation may also have evolved over several generations. This argument is based on the accumulation of soils between the pavements and the limited evidence from postmold patterns suggesting multiple structures through time on the pavement proper. The parallel walls postdate the habitation zone and the initiation of the pavement construction. They mark the final building phase at this portion of the site.

Analysis of Flint Artifacts

Following an initial assessment of the quantity and contexts of the materials recovered from the excavations north of State Route 350, the flint artifact assemblage was separated into three samples. The first sample of flint is from Soil D and includes the portion of the excavations that provide significant evidence of structures and features associated with domestic activity in the stratum below the limestone pavement. For present purposes, this sample is referred to as the "Habitation Sample." The second sample is composed of flint artifacts from Pavements 1, 2, and 3 along with those from the intervening Soils B and C. This sample includes materials from the excavations above the habitation area but within the limestone pavements. This sample is referred to as the "Pavement Sample." It was treated as a single unit because of the nearly identical composition of flint artifacts recovered from the individual limestone pavement layers. The number of artifact types, the incidence of use-wear, amount of cortex, and the number of flint raw material varieties associated with each layer are remarkably similar. The third sample is composed of flint artifacts from Soil A. It includes material from the excavations of the plowzone and parallel wall deposits above the limestone pavements habitation area. It is here assumed that the artifacts in this sample represent secondary deposits from the historic plow disturbance of the parallel walls as well as some of the artifacts from activities associated with Pavement 1. This sample is referred to as the "Plowzone Sample."

The summary flint analysis[2] presented below is based on the assumption that no single attribute such as raw material, striking platform, use-wear, or artifact morphology is sufficient for generating meaningful interpretations of a flint artifact assemblage. Instead, it is hoped that the consideration of some combined multiple, mutually exclusive measures will result in the generation of patterns of significant artifact use and contextual distribution. It should, however, be noted that a full and exhaustive consideration of all measures for the Fort Ancient site assemblage is beyond the scope of this chapter. Thus, for present purposes only, selected attributes are considered in some detail. These data are summarized on Tables 10.1 and 10.2 and in Figs. 10.5 and 10.6. The following is a brief discussion of the attributes here under consideration.

Flint Artifact Attributes

Relative Flake Thickness

The relative thickness of a complete flake is defined as the sum of the flake's length and width divided by the flake's thickness. This variable describes flake morphology for generating broad interpretations of reduction stages. However, relative thickness cannot stand alone as a reliable and valid measure, because flakes with different metric values and different morphologies may yield the same relative thickness. Therefore another flake attribute should be factored into the equation; this factor is weight.

Weight

Factoring in weight allows for the different metrics and morphologies of two flakes to be recognized, thus providing a more robust description of artifact

---

2. See Connolly 1991 for a detailed discussion of lithic analysis methodology. Primary sources for the analysis include Pi-Sunyer (1965) for bladelets, Sullivan and Rozen (1985) for flake material, and Vickery (1983) and Kozarek (1987) for flint raw materials.

form. The utility of the median value of a sample's relative thickness in combination with the sample's median weight of complete flakes is useful in providing a general measure of the reduction stage represented. This assertion is based on a large-to-small, primary-to-tertiary reduction continuum.

Cortex

The presence of cortex on flint artifacts is used as an attribute to gauge the stage of reduction in a flint debitage assemblage. For the material under consideration, cortex was present only on a very small number of artifacts in all samples examined (< 1 percent). Beyond noting the absence of cortex, the ability of this variable to add significant meaning to the current study is considered small. However, the rarity of cortical surface on flakes indicates that only very limited primary reduction of raw flints occurred in the study area.

Flint Varieties

Middle Woodland period sites are noted for producing a wide range of exotic flint varieties. At Fort Ancient, Wyandotte (Harrison County) and Ohio Flint Ridge flints are the primary exotic types; they comprise more than 15 percent of virtually all samples examined. For the purpose of this paper, all other exotic chert varieties are grouped together except as warranted by special consideration.

Bladelets

Bladelets are not only formal tools, but they are also obvious Middle Woodland Hopewell diagnostic artifacts. Bladelets are present throughout the Fort Ancient site samples, whereas other formal tools such as bifaces and drills are absent from the assemblages. Genheimer (1993) argues that bladelets functioned as multipurpose tools during the Middle Woodland period. His assertion is supported by the abundance of bladelets and bladelet fragments in the Fort Ancient site assemblage especially when compared to the scarcity of other tool types.

Use-wear

Traces of use-wear were recorded on all flint artifacts with 10-power magnification. In addition, types of use-wear trace (e.g., microflaking, dulling, sheen, striation) and intensity of use (percentage of total edge) were recorded. Table 10.3 presents summary use-wear data.

Flint Artifacts from Excavated Samples

The Plowzone Sample contained the greatest quantity of lithic debitage in the entire Fort Ancient site assemblage excavated to date (see Connolly 1991 for additional samples not considered in this paper). Presumably as a function of primary reduction activities, the Pavement and Plowzone Samples contained a slightly greater percentage of complete flakes than the Habitation Sample (Fig. 10.5). The difference is small and does not constitute more than a minimal amount of primary reduction. None of the three samples provides significant evidence for the manufacturing of chipped stone tools. Use-wear rates (Table 10.3) for the excavated sample are considerably greater than that reported at other habitation sites. For example use-wear rates at the following habitation sites are significantly lower than those given in Table 10.3 for Fort Ancient site data: Jennison Guard, 3.2 percent (Kozarek 1987:88–92); Massey, 1.5 percent (Farnsworth and Koski 1985:92); Smiling Dan, 12.03 percent (Stafford 1985:281). However, the rate at Fort Ancient is comparable to that reported by Genheimer (1984) for flint assemblages collected near the Stubbs Earthwork located 5 km downstream from Fort Ancient. The lack of evidence for tool manufacture and the relatively high use-wear rates from the excavated samples suggest that the habitation zone and overlying pavements were primarily used for the processing of diverse materials.

The variation in Wyandotte (Harrison County) and Ohio Flint Ridge chert varieties throughout the samples are partially functions of sample size, the low number of bladelets in the Pavement Sample, and the high rate of local chert in the Pavement Sample (Table 10.3). Ohio Flint Ridge is the chert variety that comprises approximately 40 percent of all bladelets in the excavated samples. Only 9 bladelets or bladelet fragments were recovered from the Pavement Sample; 30 and 101 bladelets and fragments were recovered from the Habitation and the Plowzone Samples, respectively. Therefore, the lower Ohio Flint Ridge percentage for the Pavement Sample is a function of the variation in number of bladelets. Of greater significance is the 49 percent local chert contained in the Pavement Sample that is directly accounted for by a rate of debris (shatter) more than double that of any other Fort Ancient sample. The most likely explanation for this is that the pavement provided an excellent surface for bipolar percussion of local pebble cherts to test their suitability for further reduction. With the exception of this single anomaly, all lithic attributes of the three excavated samples are virtually identical.

The general assemblage characteristics of the Northeast excavations are those expected of a multipurpose activity area. These expectations include a diverse range of chert varieties, a broad range of lithic artifact types, and a moderate amount of use-wear on both flake implements and formal tools. Because of the stratigraphic control and feature associations of the Northeast excavations, a discussion of the specific recovery contexts of lithic artifacts is possible.

Soil D in the pavement trench (Fig. 10.4) between E61 and E85 contained scattered postmolds not readily associated with structures. Excavations in these units also yielded several poorly defined pit features and some amorphous staining of the living floors. This section of Soil D contained heavily mottled soils with high organic content, flint artifacts, mica flakes, charcoal, animal bone, and shell distributed throughout the strata.

In the section of Soil D with readily defined structure walls and cooking features (Fig. 10.3) artifact densities are very low. The Middle Woodland residents regularly maintained clean living floors within the structure(s). This pattern of segregated and clearly defined living, cooking, and refuse areas can be duplicated at other excavated Middle Woodland habitation sites (e.g., Stafford 1985; Kozarek 1987; Fischer 1971). Excavations in Soil D east of the structure(s) and cooking features (Fig. 10.4) yielded up to thirty times more flint artifacts than the area characterized by the structure(s). With few exceptions, the percentages of individual lithic artifact types and raw materials were equally distributed throughout the individual strata. The density and distribution patterns of other materials, such as ceramics and faunal remains, were similar to that of the flint artifacts.

The segment of the pavement trench between E61 and E64 contained a line of posts running along the northern area of the unit, as well as random posts in the remainder of the unit originating in Soil D. The northern line of posts was not evenly spaced or readily interpretable as a single structure wall. Two pit features, also originating in Soil D, and the heavily mottled living floor produced a substantial quantity of flint flakes, faunal material, mica, and charcoal. The flint flakes are of an unknown exotic variety, similar in appearance to Ohio Flint Ridge flint. The flakes are thin and small and contain no cortex or evidence of edge damage through use, thus representing a tertiary reduction process. This translucent blue-green flint with opaque white splotches is similar to that described by Genheimer (1984) from excavations near the Stubbs Earthworks.

The distribution of lithic artifacts in the Pavement Sample is the same as that of the Habitation Sample but with increasing densities from west to east. A Snyders Cluster biface was recovered directly beneath Pavement 1 at E79. Snyders Cluster points are reported as diagnostic of the early Middle Woodland period (Justice 1987:201).

The lithic artifacts recovered from the Pavement Sample do not provide evidence of activities different from those associated with the Habitation Sample. This suggests that the pavement functioned as a nonspecific, multipurpose activity area. Although clear evidence of postmolds existed on the periphery and within the pavement, the limited excavations conducted to date do not permit a reliable interpretation of the associated structures. The data available for assessing the function of the limestone pavement are admittedly meager. Excavations exposed less than 5 percent of the entire pavement area. The interpretations proposed here assume that the exposed portions of the feature can be generalized to the entire pavement. Only fuller fieldwork can prove the accuracy of those interpretations.

Surface Collections

Over the past several years, surface collections from cultivated fields east of Fort Ancient have produced substantial quantities of lithic artifacts (n=>15,000). Fig. 10.1 shows the locations of the collections discussed below. Samples 518 and 519 were uncontrolled, while Sample 1146 was a controlled collection. Sample 588 consisted of a 10 m^2 area near a cache of obsidian, quartz, Wyandotte (Harrison County), and Ohio Flint Ridge artifacts recovered by a local collector (Essenpreis and Moseley 1984:26). From Sample 1146 (Fig. 10.1), Sample 518 was collected 350 m to the east, Sample 519 was collected 350 m to the east, and Sample 588 was collected 405 m to the northeast. (Distances are approximate measurements from center to center of the noted collections.)

As far as flint artifacts are concerned, significant sampling bias must be expected for all surface collections in the study area. Plowed fields near the Fort Ancient site have been extensively and systematically exploited by adventurers, collectors, and pot hunters since the 1800s. Moorehead (1890) noted that landowners surrounding the enclosure maintained individual collections with thousands of whole artifacts each. This practice continues to the present day, resulting in an underrepresentation in the number of whole artifacts (e.g., bladelets, bifaces) that can still be recovered. This is true not only for the Fort Ancient site proper but also for other surface-collected sites nearby (Genheimer 1984). Therefore, the uncritical comparison of excavated and surface-collected samples is problematic.

Figure 10.6 shows the distinct clustering of all flint artifact types for Sample 1146. Distributions of total flake densities, tools, and cores further support the clusters noted. The cluster in the north-central area of Fig. 10.6 yielded limited evidence of primary core reduction in the form of a small number of complete flakes exhibiting exterior cortex. The north-central cluster and the cluster immediately south produced nineteen of twenty-one bladelets recovered from this collection unit. Sixteen of the bladelets exhibit traces of use-wear, indicative of the processing activities. Local/unknown flint varieties dominate the sample while exotic varieties account for over 30 percent of the sample; 90 percent of the use-wear has been noted for the exotic flint varieties. This suggests the use of local flint for shaped tool production and exotic flint for expedient flake tools.

Sample 1146 exhibits no predominant technological or functional activity and appears to represent the multipurpose and nonspecialized activities expected in household areas. The lower incidence of use-wear compares favorably with flint assemblages from other Middle Woodland habitation sites. If the patterning in the distribution of flint artifacts from Sample 1146 minimally reflects actual manufacturing and discard areas, then the collection unit as a whole is likely to represent a single household. Portions of the collection unit with very low artifact densities may be indicative of a household structure kept free of debris. The concentration of fire-cracked rock in the central area of the unit may be indicative of a cooking location.

No clustered areas were recorded in the distribution of artifacts for Sample 518. The collection is notable in that it has a significantly lower incidence of specimens with use-wear than the total assemblage norm; it also is characterized by an exceptionally large quantity of Wyandotte (Harrison County) chert and other exotic flint varieties. The sample contains the thinnest and lightest complete flakes and flake fragments in the entire lithic assemblage from the site (Fig. 10.5). In addition, the sample contains fourteen multidirectional cores and core fragments, nine of exotic chert varieties. Analysis of the recovered artifacts suggests that Sample 518 represents a lithic manufacturing or debitage disposal area.

Sample 519, collected immediately north of Sample 518, yielded a considerably different set of flint artifacts. Greater quantities of use-wear and larger flake artifacts characterize this material. The raw material content is more consistent with that of other areas of the site. Except for an increased incidence of use-wear, Sample 518 is similar in composition to Sample 1146. The proximity of Samples 518 and 519 and their differing sample characteristics suggest that the two collection units may have been part of a household unit similar to that proposed for Collection 1146. Unfortunately, neither the 518 nor 519 collection units were controlled for the detection of artifact clusters.

Sample 588 is a random collection of flint artifacts within a 5 m radius in the immediate vicinity of the Powell Cache. The collection was biased toward the recovery of large and exotic flint artifacts (Patricia S. Essenpreis, personal communication). The Powell Cache was discovered and removed by a local collector during the spring of 1984. It consisted of seventeen spear points and curved knives of obsidian, eleven 20 cm long blades of Wyandotte (Harrison County) chert and five quartz blades, each approximately 7 cm in length (Essenpreis and Moseley 1984:26). The artifacts were deposited horizontally and arranged by raw material in the base of a shallow pit less than 50 cm in diameter (Eugene Powell, 1992, personal communication). Apart from these formal tools, the cache contained approximately twenty large flakes and blocky chunks of obsidian. However, no evidence for tertiary reduction of the obsidian tools was recovered. Virtually all the tools and most of the obsidian flakes and blocky chunks contain traces of use-wear. The intensity of use-wear varies from 10 to 90 percent of the usable tool edges. Traces of use-wear include distinct microflaking, battering, dulled edges, as well as impact fractures.

Because of the intentional bias in collecting Sample 588, the material is not included in the present data tables or figures. The sample collected contains a large proportion of Wyandotte (Harrison County), Ohio Flint Ridge, and Paoli flint varieties. An unknown exotic flint type comprised most of the remaining flint objects in the sample and also occurs in minute quantities at other localities throughout the Fort Ancient site. The unknown flint is tan to orange in color and grades from fine-grained to a pitted coarse-grained texture.

The high incidence of cortical flakes and cores in Sample 588 indicates primary lithic reduction activities. The sample also contains a large quantity of Ohio Flint Ridge tertiary flakes. This is in contrast to other Middle Woodland period contexts at Fort Ancient, where bladelets and their production debris account for nearly all Ohio Flint Ridge chert recovered.

The specific interpretation of Sample 588 is not without ambiguity. A 25 x 40 m controlled surface collection of the same location in the summer of 1992 yielded up to one thousand flakes per 5 m^2 collection unit. Although not completely analyzed, an initial examination of this collection shows that tertiary-stage reduction of Ohio Flint Ridge, Wyandotte (Harrison County), and Paoli chert varieties dominates the sample. Sample 588 is isolated from any apparent multifunction lithic clusters such as noted for Sample 1146. Determining the time frame of the cache deposit and lithic reduction activities represented in the collected sample also confounds attempts at interpretation. If the Powell Cache and Sample 588 predate the construction of the parallel walls and are directly associated with households adjacent to the Fort Ancient earthworks, then the artifacts may represent the deposit of a single individual or family. However, if the artifacts postdate the construction of the parallel walls, consideration of a more public or corporate character of the material may be warranted.

Summary

The excavations and surface collections conducted at the Fort Ancient site over the past ten years do not adequately test Prufer's dispersed hamlet hypothesis. Pacheco (1988:92) has argued that households of Hopewellian communities were small, structurally redundant, contained similar assemblages, and were spatially dispersed. The collections in plowed fields near the Fort Ancient enclosure only minimally test Pacheco's criteria. Discrete and varying activity areas were noted. Sample 1146 and combined Samples 518–519, consisting solely of lithic materials, conform to expectations of a single hamlet. Sample 588 appears to represent a specialized activity not related to a household unit.

The excavations conducted immediately adjacent to the enclosure produced residential debris and structures. The diversified artifact assemblage, discrete midden area, and the hearth and pit features clustered outside the Fort Ancient embankment walls contain the full complement of features and artifact assemblages researchers use to characterize domestic sites during the Middle Woodland period (e.g., Dancey 1991; Kozarek 1987; Stafford 1985; Wiant and McGimsey 1986; Fischer 1971). The maze of overlapping wall sections indicates continued occupation over an extended period of time. However, the structures and associated artifacts excavated northeast of the Twin Mounds do not completely conform to the expected habitation model. Habitation debris is low when compared with data from other Middle Woodland domestic sites such as Jennison Guard (Kozarek 1987) and Murphy (Dancey 1991). Postmolds are large and deep, and the primary structure encloses more floor space than expected of a household unit (Smith 1992).

Little doubt can exist that the area immediately to the northeast of the Fort Ancient hilltop enclosure functioned in part as a habitation zone. Questions related to the occupation (such as seasonal or year-round residence), the social position of occupants, the sacred and secular activities of the residents, and the relationship of habitation sites on the periphery of an earthwork to those more distant from the centers remain unresolved.

Research in Ohio that evaluates the areas surrounding Middle Woodland monumental architecture has been conducted near the Newark (Pacheco 1990), High Banks (Shane 1971:145), and Stubbs Earthworks (Genheimer 1984) as well as at Seip Mound (Baby and Langlois 1979:18), among others. Although some of this research has relied solely on surface collections, the authors propose a diverse range of prehistoric activities, similar to those suggested at Fort Ancient. Data from the Fort Ancient site and other noted Ohio Valley earthworks, indicate that the complexes and their immediate environs were loci of activity for Hopewell populations, including residential households. Future research that focuses more intensely on earthwork peripheries should provide much-needed information as to the nature of the residential components of Middle Woodland earthwork complexes.

Acknowledgments

I wish to thank William S. Dancey, Kent D. Vickery, David C. Grove, Sue E. Kozarek, and Allan P. Sullivan III for their comments, criticism, and assistance in preparing this report. Susan Baldry assisted in the production of all figures. Errors contained in this paper are, of course, my own responsibility.

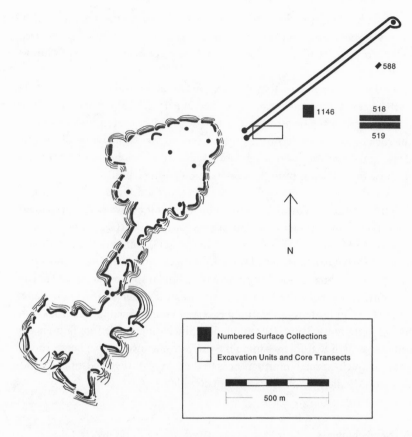

10.1 Map of the Fort Ancient site showing the location of investigation units referred to in the text.

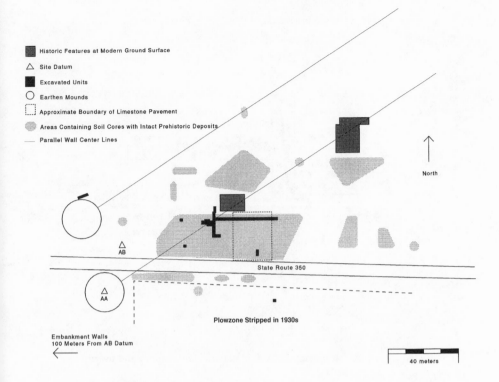

10.2 Fort Ancient Site (33WA2). Soil cores, excavations, and historic disturbances east of Twin Mounds.

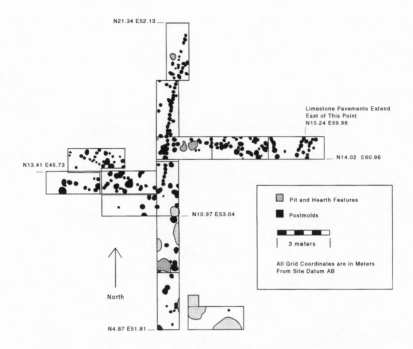

10.3 Northeast habitation zone postmold patterns, pit features, and hearths.

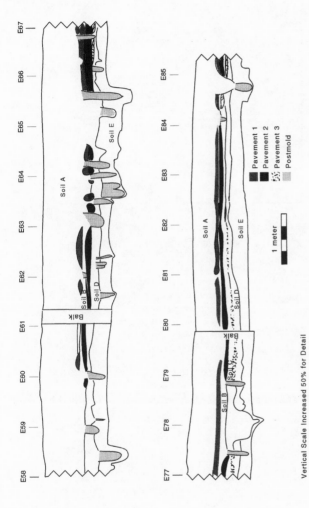

10.4 Fort Ancient State Memorial (33WA2). Schematic of limestone pavements east of Twin Mounds—partial north profile.

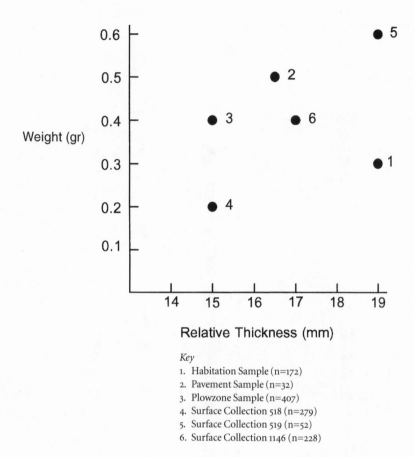

Key
1. Habitation Sample (n=172)
2. Pavement Sample (n=32)
3. Plowzone Sample (n=407)
4. Surface Collection 518 (n=279)
5. Surface Collection 519 (n=52)
6. Surface Collection 1146 (n=228)

10.5 33WA2 lithic samples: Complete flake median weight, median relative thickness.

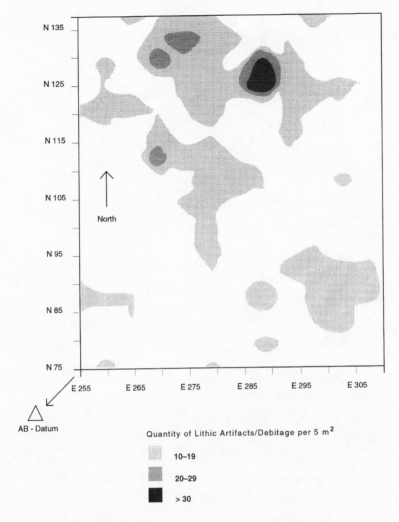

10.6 1039/1146 surface collection sample distribution of flint artifacts.

Table 10.1

Percentage of Artifact Types in 33wa2 Samples

	Complete Flake	Proximal Flake	Flake Fragment	Debris	Core Material	Complete Bladelet	Partial Bladelet	Biface	Biface Fragment	TOTAL
Habitation Sample	28	20	37	8	2	1	4	0	1	100
Pavement Sample	23	10	32	30	1	1	4	0	1	100
Plowzone Sample	24	19	36	13	1	1	5	0	0	99
Sample 1146	15	27	44	7	2	0	3	0	0	98
Sample 518	31	22	39	5	2	0	1	0	0	100
Sample 519	17	25	48	6	2	0	1	0	0	99

Table 10.2

Percentage of Raw Material Types in 33WA2 Samples

	Local Chert	Exotic Chert	Wyandotte- Harrison Co.	Ohio Flint Ridge	Total Number of Artifacts
Habitation Sample	36	39	5	20	605
Pavement Sample	49	32	10	9	167
Plowzone Sample	37	35	12	17	1694
Sample 1146	51	34	10	5	1701
Sample 518	12	50	29	9	928
Sample 519	40	32	20	7	351

Table 10.3

Percentage of Use-Wear in 33WA2 Samples

	Quantity of Bladelets	Number of Bladelets with Use-Wear	Percentage of Bladelets with Use-Wear	Number of All Artifacts with Use-Wear	Percentage of Artifacts with Use-Wear
Habitation Sample	27	23	87	80	17.5
Pavement & Plowzone	110	73	66	406	21.2
Sample 1146	58	47	81	248	14.5
Sample 518	10	10	100	81	8
Sample 519	0	0	0	72	20.1

References

Atwater, C.

1820 *Description of the Antiquities Discovered in the State of Ohio and other Western States.* Transactions and Collections of the American Antiquarian Society 1. *Archaeologica Americana* 1:105–267.

Baby, R. S., and S. M. Langlois

1979 Seip Mound State Memorial: Nonmortuary Aspects of Hopewell. In *Hopewell Archaeology: The Chillicothe Conference,* edited by D. S. Brose and N. Greber, pp. 16–18. Kent State University Press, Kent, Ohio.

Connolly, R. P.

1990 *Revised Preliminary Report of 1988 Excavations at the Fort Ancient State Memorial.* Ms. on file, Ohio Historical Society, Columbus.

1991 *Prehistoric Site Structure at the Fort Ancient State Memorial: New Evidence from Lithic Analysis.* Unpublished master's thesis, Department of Anthropology, University of Cincinnati.

1992 The Fort Ancient Site (33Wa2) Warren County, Ohio: Activity Areas Examined, 1982–1990. *Florida State Journal of Anthropology* 17:7–15.

1993 Prehistoric Land Modification at the Fort Ancient Hilltop Enclosure—A Model of Formal and Accretive Development. Paper presented at the 2nd Annual Conference on Ohio Archaeology, Chillicothe.

Connolly, R. P., and P. S. Essenpreis

1990 *Preliminary Report of 1989 Excavations at the Fort Ancient State Memorial.* Ms. on file, Ohio Historical Society, Columbus.

Connolly, R. P., and L. E. Sieg

1993 Prehistoric Architecture and the Development of Public Space at the Fort Ancient Hilltop Enclosure. Paper presented at the 5th International and Interdisciplinary Forum on Built Form and Culture Research, 2nd CSPA Symposium on Architectural Practice, Cincinnati.

Dancey, W. S.

1991 A Middle Woodland Settlement in Central Ohio: A Preliminary Report on the Murphy Site (33LI212). *Pennsylvania Archaeologist* 61:37–72.

Essenpreis, P. S.

1982 Excavation forms from 1982 field work at the Fort Ancient State Memorial (33Wa2). Ms. on file, Ohio Historical Society, Columbus.

1985 Archaeological Investigations at the Fort Ancient State Memorial: Borrow Area and Gateway 44. Ms. on file, Ohio Historical Society, Columbus.

1986 An Architectural Examination of Fort Ancient. Paper presented at the 51st Annual Meeting of the Society for American Archaeology, New Orleans.

1987 Preliminary Report of Investigations Conducted at the Fort Ancient State Memorial, 33WA2, From June 19–August 7, 1986. Ms on file, Ohio Historical Society, Columbus.

1988   Preliminary Report of Investigations Conducted at the Fort Ancient State Memorial Between June and August of 1987. Ms. on file, Ohio Historical Society, Columbus.

Essenpreis, P. S., and R. P. Connolly

1989   Hopewellian Habitation at the Fort Ancient Site, Ohio. Paper presented at the Annual Meeting of the Southeastern Archaeological Conference, Tampa.

Essenpreis, P. S. and M. E. Moseley

1984   Fort Ancient: Citadel or Coliseum? *Field Museum of Natural History Bulletin* 55(6):5–10, 20–26.

Farnsworth, K. B., and A. L. Koski

1985   *Massey and Archie: A Study of Two Hopewellian Homesteads in the Western Illinois Uplands.* Research Series 3. Center for American Archeology, Kampsville Archaeological Center, Kampsville, Illinois.

Fischer, F. W.

1971   *Preliminary Report of University of Cincinnati Archeological Investigations, 1970.* Ms. on file, Department of Anthropology, University of Cincinnati.

Genheimer, R. A.

1984   A Systematic Examination of Middle Woodland Settlements in Warren County, Ohio. Ms. on file, Ohio Historic Preservation Office, Cincinnati.

1993   Bladelets are Tools Too: The Predominance of Bladelets Among Formal Tools at Ohio Hopewell Sites. Paper presented at the 2nd Annual Conference on Ohio Archaeology, Chillicothe.

Hosea, L. M.

1874   Some Facts and Considerations About Fort Ancient, Warren County, Ohio. *Cincinnati Quarterly Journal of Science* 1(4):289–302.

Justice, N. D.

1987   *Stone Age Spears and Arrow Points of the Midcontinental and Eastern United States.* Indiana University Press, Bloomington.

Kozarek, S. E.

1987   *A Hopewellian Homestead in the Ohio River Valley.* Unpublished master's thesis, Department of Anthropology, University of Cincinnati.

Mills, W. C.

1908   Field Notes from the 1908 Excavations at the Fort Ancient State Memorial (33Wa2). Ms. on file, Ohio Historical Society, Columbus.

Moorehead, W. K.

1890   *Fort Ancient: The Great Prehistoric Earthwork of Warren County, Ohio.* Robert Clarke, Cincinnati.

Morgan, R.

1970   *Fort Ancient.* Ohio Historical Society, Columbus.

Morgan, R., and H. H. Ellis

1939   Field Notes from 1939 Excavations at the Fort Ancient State Memorial. Ms. on file, Ohio Historical Society, Columbus.

1940   Field Notes from 1940 Excavations at the Fort Ancient State Memorial. Ms. on file, Ohio Historical Society, Columbus.

Pacheco, P. J.

1988   Ohio Middle Woodland Settlement Variability in the Upper Licking River Drainage. *Journal of the Steward Anthropological Society* 18:87–117.

1990   The Hopewell Settlement Pattern as Revealed by Siteless Survey. Paper presented at the 57th Annual Meeting of the Eastern States Archaeology Federation, Columbus, Ohio.

Pi-Sunyer, O.

1965   The Flint Industry. In *The McGraw Site: A Study in Hopewellian Dynamics*, edited by O. H. Prufer, pp. 60–89. Scientific Publications n.s. 4(1). Cleveland Museum of Natural History. Cleveland, Ohio.

Prufer, O. H.

1964   The Hopewell Complex of Ohio. In *Hopewellian Studies*, edited by J. R. Caldwell and R. L. Hall, pp. 37–83. Scientific Papers 12, No. 2. Illinois State Museum, Springfield.

1965   *The McGraw Site: A Study in Hopewellian Dynamics*. Scientific Publications, n.s. 4(1). Cleveland Museum of Natural History.

Shane, O. C., III

1971   The Scioto Hopewell. In *Adena: The Seeking of an Identity*, edited by B. K. Swartz, pp. 142–158. Ball State University Press, Muncie, Indiana.

Smith, B. D.

1992   *Rivers of Change: Essays on Early Agriculture in Eastern North America*. Smithsonian Institution Press, Washington, D.C.

Squier, E.G., and E. H. Davis

1848   *Ancient Monuments of the Mississippi Valley*. Contributions to Knowledge 1. Smithsonian Institution, Washington, D.C.

Stafford, B. D.

1985   Lithic Analysis. In *Smiling Dan: Structure and Function at a Middle Woodland Settlement in the Lower Illinois Valley*, edited by B. D. Stafford and M. B. Sant, pp. 258–297. Research Series 2. Center for American Archeology, Kampsville Archaeological Center, Kampsville, Illinois.

Sullivan, A. P., and K. C. Rozen

1985   Debitage Analysis and Archaeological Interpretation. *American Antiquity* 50:755–779.

Vickery, K. D.

1983   The Flint Sources. In *Recent Excavations at the Edwin Harness Mound, Liberty Works, Ross County, Ohio*, edited by N. Greber, pp. 73–85. Special Papers 5, Midcontinental Journal of Archaeology. Kent State University Press, Kent, Ohio.

Wiant, M. D., and C. R. McGimsey

1986   *Woodland Period Occupations of the Napoleon Hollow Site in the Lower Illinois Valley*. Research Series 6. Center for American Archeology, Kampsville Archaeological Center, Kampsville, Illinois.

CHAPTER ELEVEN

Stubbs Cluster

Hopewellian Site Dynamics at a Forgotten Little Miami River Valley Settlement

Robert A. Genheimer

ABSTRACT

Although Whittlesey recorded Stubbs Earthwork in 1839, systematic archaeological investigations in the vicinity of the geometric earthwork were not conducted until the late 1970s and early 1980s. During the latter period, more than two dozen Middle Woodland sites were recorded both north and south of the Little Miami River. Surface scatters were identified adjacent to the former earthwork complex on elevated terraces above the earthwork landform and on the opposite bank of the river. Debris recovery was high, and a large number of bladelets and exotic materials were collected. Systematic controlled collection was undertaken at three site locations in 1983 in an effort to obtain more precise settlement data. Both blade and nonblade debris were suggestive of domestic activities and not specialized craft tasks. Debris distribution was diffuse at the largest of the sites, but some evidence of debris clustering was noted at two of the sites removed from the earthwork location. It is possible that these latter clusters represent household locations, although it is difficult to assess in the absence of excavation data.

This paper presents data gathered during the last decade at the Stubbs Cluster, a set of Hopewellian communities along the middle reaches of the Little

Miami River in southwest Ohio. Located only 7 km downstream from Fort Ancient State Memorial and 30 to 35 km from the Turner and Milford earthworks, the Stubbs Cluster represents a major corporate center of the Middle Woodland period (Fig. 11.1). Both Fort Ancient and Turner have received considerably more attention in the literature, in part because of the spectacular architecture at the former and because of the exotic artifact assemblages at the latter. Stubbs Cluster, on the other hand, has received little archaeological attention. The earthwork nucleus (Fig. 11.2) had been destroyed by the end of the nineteenth century, and the site's numerous debris scatters have only recently been discovered by the professional community.

From 1979 to 1980, the Stubbs Cluster area was subjected to intensive archaeological survey, in the course of which more than two dozen Middle Woodland sites were recorded (Fig. 11.3). This study resulted in the collection of nearly 9,700 artifacts and artifact fragments, including more than 1,400 Hopewellian bladelets, one of the largest surface collections of blades in Ohio. In an attempt to more clearly define settlement patterns at the Stubbs Cluster, systematic controlled collections were undertaken in the summer of 1983 at three site locations. These sites produced a wide range of Hopewellian diagnostics, including exotic materials, and each locality was representative of a discrete topographical zone. This paper summarizes the results of the controlled collection and an evaluation of the possible settlement types they represent.

The Stubbs Cluster

Although it is likely that the Stubbs Earthwork was known to locals since the initial settlement of Warren County in the first decade of the nineteenth century, the earthen embankments were not documented until December 1839, when Charles Whittlesey sketch-mapped a series of mounds and earthworks in the area (Whittlesey 1851). Included in Whittlesey's rendering is the Stubbs Earthwork, a large rectangular enclosure with an adjoining semicircle, and what has come to be referred to as the Warren County Serpent Mound. This latter series of connected embankments was thought by many to represent a serpent effigy. Unfortunately, Whittlesey surveyed the earthworks during a period of adverse weather (Whittlesey 1851:8), and it is likely that those conditions had a detrimental impact on the accuracy of his survey and the resultant final maps. We may never know the true morphology of the geometric earthwork because subsequent investigators were unable to relocate it. The so-called Serpent Mound was reinvestigated during the late nineteenth century and became the subject of much controversy then and during the early years of the twentieth century (Kientz and McPherson 1954).

The Stubbs Cluster is located along the valley of the Little Miami River between the communities of Morrow and South Lebanon in Warren County, Ohio. The cluster area extends along both banks of the Little Miami River for approximately 6 km and exceeds 1 km in width south of the mouth of Halls Creek. The area is best viewed as a riverine valley zone exhibiting a series of elevated glacial formations that contain a high number of clustered, but discrete, Middle Woodland surface scatters.

1979–1980 and 1983 Investigations

1979–1980 and the 1983 archaeological investigations located twenty-eight discrete Middle Woodland surface scatters between South Lebanon and Morrow, Ohio (Genheimer 1984, 1992). Although these sites display variable debris densities (Table 11.1), areal expanses, and topographical settings, they all attest to the significant utilization of this valley segment by Middle Woodland populations. Eleven of the Middle Woodland sites are located north of the river and east of South Lebanon in what is referred to as the north subcluster. However, more than 84 percent of all diagnostic Middle Woodland artifacts were recovered from seventeen sites in the south subcluster, approximately 1.2 km west of Morrow. Of the 142 diagnostic Middle Woodland artifacts recovered north of the river, 111 (>78 percent) are contained within one assemblage—33WA317. In all, 9,684 fragments of cultural debris including 1,730 fragments (17.9 percent) of diagnostic Middle Woodland debris were recovered.

Middle Woodland sites frequently yield exotic materials, and the Stubbs Cluster sites are no exception (Table 11.2). The use of nonlocal materials is noticeable in the lithic assemblage, including projectile points, bifaces, and various cutting and scraping tools; it is most pronounced in the selection of exotic raw materials for the production of the blade industry. Nearly all complete and fragmented bladelets, exhausted blade cores, and blade core trimming/waste flakes were manufactured from Wyandotte chert, Ohio Flint Ridge chalcedony, Knox, or other unidentified and probably exotic flints. Wyandotte, Ohio Flint Ridge, and Knox flints are also present in the debitage and nonblade assemblages at most of the sites. Additional nonlocal lithic materials include crystalline quartz, Knife River chalcedony, and obsidian; copper and mica have also been recovered from these sites.

Although Middle Woodland grit-tempered ceramics are present at the Stubbs Cluster localities, they are only noted at ten locations and in limited quantities. Prior to the 1983 controlled collection at several site locations, only 132 Middle Woodland sherds had been recovered. They comprise only 1.4 percent of the recovered debris and approximately 7.6 percent of the total diagnostic Middle Woodland assemblage. Only at two sites, 33WA317 and 362, do ceramics constitute a significant proportion of the diagnostic artifacts.

On the basis of glacial and fluvial data, site locations recorded during the 1979–1983 investigations could be segregated into several topographical zones (Fig. 11.4). In general, Middle Woodland sites are located either on the flood plain or in terrace zones bordering the Little Miami River channel. Clearly, most sites (N=22, or 78.6 percent) are on the Wisconsinan outwash terraces. In order of ascending mean elevation, thirteen (46.4 percent) occur on Fox terraces, five (17.9 percent) on Ockley terraces, and four (14.3 percent) on Williamsburg terraces, all of Wisconsinan age. Preference for the choice of Fox terrace location is not surprising in light of the broad, flat quality of this landform. Six (21.4 percent) Middle Woodland sites were recorded along the floodplain of the Little Miami River, all within the north subcluster. The size of identified sites varies substantially, ranging from 465 m² at 33WA302 to nearly 48,000 m² at 33WA256. The overall mean site area is 13,281 m², although the standard deviation (s=10,495) suggests much dispersion about that mean.

Fox terrace sites also dominate debris density figures and account for approximately 82 percent of all recovered debris as well as for more than 95 percent of all Middle Woodland diagnostics. Nearly 1,400 Middle Woodland diagnostics were recovered at 33WA256 (n=458), 33WA257 (n=418), 33WA258 (n=380), and 33WA260 (n=142), all in the vicinity of the geometric earthwork. Conversely, floodplain sites produced only negligible quantities of Middle Woodland debris (n=13), amounting to less than 1 percent of total Hopewellian diagnostics. Ockley and Williamsburg terraces produced a combined total of seventy-two Hopewellian diagnostics, or only slightly more than 4 percent of the total.

The most significant aspect of the identified Middle Woodland sites is the large number of blade industry elements. Prior to the 1983 systematic controlled collection, a total of 1,526 such items were identified. These include 1,411 bladelets and bladelet fragments, 33 blade cores, and 82 blade core trimming/waste flakes. Such large a number of blades has been reported for only a handful of other Hopewell centers in the Midwest. This alone suggests that the Stubbs Cluster is an important source of data on the Hopewell complex.

Systematic Controlled Collections

It was clear that a thorough analysis of local and regional settlement data would not be possible on the mere basis of data gathered during the 1979–1980 and early 1983 Miami Purchase Association for Historic Preservation investigations. Collection had not been controlled, site features were not plotted, and fire-cracked rock was neither collected nor recorded. Therefore, a process utilizing nonweighted criteria was formulated in order to select sites that were both viewed as representative of potential settlement types and that exhibited ideal criteria for addressing a variety of research questions. After careful consideration of the selection criteria (i.e., debris density, presence of manufacturing/ processing debris, evidence of midden or features, and physical relationship to the geometric earthwork), three sites, 33WA256, 317, and 362, were selected for systematic controlled collection.

33WA256

The topography at 33WA256, also known as the Stubbs Mill Blade Site, is characterized by a relatively level outwash terrace truncated to the west by Bigfoot Run, a small perennial stream. The southern boundary of the site is formed by a shallow drainage swale that feeds Bigfoot Run. Several low, but perceptible, rises are present near the west-central portion of the eastern terrace segment, each separated by broad and extremely shallow depressions. In planview, the site is an elongated oval with maximum dimensions of 300 m (N-S) by 250 m (E-W). The western segment encompasses 2.35 ha, while the eastern portion contains approximately 2.43 ha. Only the eastern portion was examined during systematic controlled collection.

The surface assemblage encountered during systematic collection consists overwhelmingly (99.8 percent) of lithic items (Table 11.3). Most of these are either unmodified flint debitage or utilized flakes. Ceramic density is extremely low, with only eleven badly weathered sherds located in a diffuse pattern across the site. A minimum of eight sheet mica fragments was recovered, bringing the total assemblage of mica at 33WA256 to approximately twenty-five sheets. Mica fragments range in size from small scraps to several exceeding 125 mm in length. Although many are likely fragments of mica cutouts, continual plow disturbance has rendered their outlines ambiguous. Only two bone fragments were recovered.

Approximately 392 Middle Woodland diagnostics (14.9 percent of all prehistoric debris) were identified. These include 315 bladelets, 3 blade cores, 2 Middle Woodland projectile points, 6 obsidian flakes, 2 Knife River chalcedony flakes, 11 grit-tempered ceramic sherds, 20 crystalline quartz fragments, >8 mica fragments, and 25 blade core trimming/waste flakes.

33WA317

The Hayner #3 site, the name by which this locality is also known, occurs in an isolated location near the center of a broad Fox outwash terrace in the north subcluster. The topography is generally flat, although a gentle (2 percent slope gradient) NE to SW slope is apparent. This contour relief is amplified by a shallow swale along the western periphery of the site. The Little Miami River is presently entrenched against steep bluffs approximately 425 m south of 33WA317, but an examination of alluvial soils indicates that the stream may have been as close as 130 m south of the site during its occupation. 33WA317 is much longer than wide, measuring 210 m in length (E-W) by a maximum of 70 m (N-S) in width. Total site area is 1.35 ha, although the Middle Woodland concentration constitutes only .125 ha.

A total of 1,424 fragments of prehistoric cultural debris was encountered during the controlled collection of 33WA317 (Table 11.4). Recorded-only debris, comprised solely of fire-cracked rock, dominates the assemblage accounting for 1,307 items or 91.8 percent of all prehistoric cultural objects. Only 117 artifacts or artifact fragments were collected.

In general, debris densities at 33WA317 were significantly lower than those encountered at either of the other collected sites. During the systematic controlled collection, only seventeen Middle Woodland diagnostics were encountered. These include seven bladelet segments, four mica fragments, three grit-tempered ceramic sherds, two crystalline quartz fragments, and one Middle Woodland expanding base/corner-notched projectile point. The yield of bladelets and ceramics was considerably below that of previous investigations. This was particularly unfortunate because 33WA317 had produced the largest ceramic assemblage among the Stubbs Cluster Middle Woodland sites.

33WA362

This locality, also known as the Smith site, lies at the toe of an extensive upland slope comprised at its northern limits of sandy Williamsburg silt loam. The site perimeter is defined by sharp contours to the west, north, and east, resulting in an elliptical site configuration. Unlike 33WA256 and 317, contour relief at 33WA362 is substantial. For example, the northwest sector of the site is 6.4 m higher in elevation than the southern sector. The slope gradient (>12 percent) is substantial on both the eastern and western slopes. Much of the southern portion of the site is relatively level, except for a central sandy ridge or plateau.

The Smith site exhibits a maximum width of 60 m near site center and only 30 m at its northwest terminus. Its maximum length is 120 m (NW-SE). The total site covers approximately .745 ha.

Examination of debris frequencies reveals that more than 94 percent of all recovered debris consists of lithic elements (Table 11.5). Of the lithic total, 81.9 percent consist of flakes, both waste (debitage) and utilized. Flint bladelets account for an additional 10.1 percent, while the remainder includes bipolar debris, projectile points, cores, bifaces, and a few stone tools. The quantity of unmodified reduction waste suggests significant manufacturing and maintenance activities, although identified tool types are noticeably meager. Grit-tempered ceramics comprise only 5.1 percent of total recovered prehistoric debris, but they occur in much greater frequency than at either 33WA256 or 33WA317.

Blade industry debris constitutes the majority of the diagnostic Middle Woodland artifact sample at the Smith site. Fifty-two bladelets, one of which is a complete specimen, and one blade core trimming/waste flake were recovered. No blade cores were collected. A total of thirty-six other diagnostic Middle Woodland artifacts were recorded, bringing the total diagnostic count to ninety-two (16.8 percent of the recovered debris assemblage). Nonblade industry diagnostics included twenty-eight grit-tempered ceramic sherds, five crystalline quartz fragments, two Knife River chalcedony flakes, one expanded-base projectile point, one obsidian flake, one copper fragment, and one mica fragment.

Settlement Data

The following settlement data are based on the analysis of blade and non-blade debris, spatial patterning, and comparisons with other more thoroughly investigated Middle Woodland sites.

33WA256

With the exception of the now destroyed geometric enclosure, the Stubbs Mill Blade site appears to be the primary site within the Stubbs Cluster. It is the largest of the sites on the broad Fox outwash plain and was clearly associated with the nearby earthwork. Precise data on the limits of the rectangular earthwork are not available, but it is likely that 33WA256 was adjacent to the enclosure's southern wall.

From 1979 to 1983, more than 4,800 fragments of cultural debris, including 850 diagnostic Middle Woodland artifacts, were collected from the 4.8 ha surface scatter. Blade manufacturing debris, represented by 722 bladelets and 9 blade cores, dominates both the Middle Woodland diagnostic and formal tool assemblages. Near-universal bladelet use was noted. Usewear analyses of bladelets at other Middle Woodland sites (Odell 1985; Yerkes 1990) illustrate that blade tools served as general-purpose, utilitarian cutting and scraping implements, although some craft specialization uses, involving engraving or incising (see Odell 1994), may also have occurred. Domestic activities are further suggested by the recovery of other formal tools and debris, such as bifaces, projectile points, bipolar objects, scrapers, gravers/perforators, and drills. Only twenty-nine ceramic sherds were recovered over the years, but this represents more than one-fifth of the entire Stubbs Cluster pottery collection.

In general, both bladelets and nonblade debris occur in a diffuse distribution across the site. Some isolated "hot spots" were noted, but such concentrations may be due as much to contour anomalies as to the intensity of archaeological activity (Fig. 11.5). There is some evidence that fire-cracked rock and perhaps burned limestone were removed from the northern and central portions of the site and deposited along its southern margin. The purpose of this "clearing" is not known, but it may represent periodic attempts to free the site of large thermal by-products. The only site in which features were identified is 33WA256. Small, circular areas of midden, each containing crumbly ceramic sherds, burned bone, and carbonized floral remains, were noted near the south-central portion of the site. Eight small test units were placed at the site in 1983, but only one, Test Unit #4 in the central area of the site, produced remains below the plowzone. A band of artifact-yielding midden was noted between .28 and .90 m below surface.

There is considerable doubt as to how meaningful current site boundaries are. Our determination of site limits was based on a noticeable decrease in surface debris and upon the abrupt boundaries of the terrace landform. It is certainly possible that numerous discrete debris clusters, activity areas, or even household units may be contained within the defined boundaries. It is not likely that cultivation has completely "masked" the location of internal concentrations; and hence, the general diffuse nature of debris patterning suggests multiple short-term, or perhaps cyclical, seasonal occupations.

Pacheco (1988:92) has established a series of four correlates that supposedly enable the Hamlet Hypothesis, or Prufer's (1965) theory of dispersed agricultural communities, to be tested. Those correlates are that hamlets (1) will be small in size, (2) will have functionally redundant assemblages, (3) will be structurally redundant, and (4) will be spatially dispersed but clustered around earthwork or burial mound complexes.

Correspondence with the Hamlet Hypothesis is difficult to assess considering the questionable nature of site boundaries. The Stubbs Mill Blade site is by no means small, and it certainly does not represent the location of a single, or even several, household. It may, however, form the general location of a number of short-term or seasonal encampments over a protracted period of time. Such a history of site use may explain the diffuse or "blurred" nature of cultural debris. There is little evidence to support the second correlate, although one could argue that the limited formal tool collection is typical of other Middle Woodland surface assemblages. The third correlate is not met because there is no bull's-eye clustering of debris; rather, a pattern of diffuse material discard is represented. There are no current data to address the spatial dispersion of Little Miami Valley Middle Woodland sites specified in the fourth correlate, although there is a clear pattern of clustering of debris scatters around the corporate elements at Stubbs.

In summary, surface data at 33WA256 delineate a large but diffuse area of domestic activity at a location that was undoubtedly associated with the corporate nucleus of the Stubbs Cluster. It is possible that the apparent domestic debris is associated with "craft production" or "corporate earthwork maintenance," but more systematic studies are required to verify these determinations.

33WA317

In contrast to 33WA256, the Hayner #3 site is one of the smallest Middle Woodland debris scatters identified within the cluster boundaries. Although originally recorded as 1.35 ha, systematic controlled collection revealed that the Middle Woodland concentration was no more than 30 to 40 m in diameter. A liberal estimate of site area would thus be approximately .125 ha. The site is also isolated—both from the geometric earthwork and other Middle Woodland debris clusters. Additional Hopewell sites were identified in the north subcluster, but 33WA317 alone produced significant quantities of debris.

During two episodes of surface collection, only 467 fragments of cultural material were recovered, but more than one-quarter of these consisted of diagnostic Middle Woodland artifacts and debris. A total of fifty-eight bladelets are included, but of particular importance is the subassemblage of sixty-eight grit-tempered ceramic sherds, the largest such collection from any of the sites accompanying the Stubbs Cluster localities. Debris recovery during systematic collection was disappointingly low. Only a small number of tools was collected, but bifaces, endscrapers, gravers/perforators, and stone tool fragments are suggestive of a domestic occupation. Quartz and mica fragments indicate that the inhabitants most likely participated in a regional trade network. Limited testing (eight small test units) at the site revealed no subplowzone context, although the excavations were not designed to adequately sample subgrade portions of the site.

Spatial data indicate a bull's-eye pattern (Fig. 11.6) of Middle Woodland domestic debris in a roughly circular area encompassing .125 ha. The site corresponds closely to Smith's (1992:240) "spatially discrete and dispersed single household settlement," and it compares favorably with areal estimates of several other purported single household sites. The single rectangular structure at Twin Mounds Village in Hamilton County (Fischer 1971) is the only documented domestic Middle Woodland house in the Little and Great Miami River Valleys. The house occupied less than 100 m², and the Western Habitation Area debris scatter encompassed approximately .5 ha of the ridgetop (Bennett 1986:xxii, 36). Because only a part of the site was excavated, it is not known whether additional structures were present. Dancey (1991:42) reports that the Murphy site is 1.0 ha in extent and the central feature area, interpreted as a structure location, is .2 hectares in extent. The McGraw site, the type site of the Hamlet Hypothesis, is nearly identical in size to 33wa317, measuring .12 ha (Prufer 1965:10). Site 33wa317 is also similar in size to a pair of Middle Woodland sites from southern Illinois. The Truck 7 site in the American Bottoms encompasses .16 ha and has been interpreted as a single household, perhaps for an extended or multifamily unit (Fortier 1985:276; Smith 1992:237). Only one structure was located. In the Lower Illinois Valley, excavations within a .2 ha Middle Woodland surface scatter at the Massey site revealed an oval structure with a series of storage and food processing pits (Farnsworth and Koski 1985).

The Hayner #3 site closely corresponds to the archaeological correlates of the Hamlet Hypothesis (Pacheco 1988). The site is small and undoubtedly represents the locus of a single structure or household unit. As noted at other

Stubbs Cluster sites, the formal tool assemblage is meager but again suggestive of a small range of domestic activities rather than specialized tasks. The most obvious spatial feature is the concentration of the majority of Middle Woodland specimens within a tightly defined area. The association of 33WA317 with the corporate nucleus in the south subcluster is probably not as direct as the presumed relationship between 33WA256 and the earthwork, but assuming contemporaneity, the close proximity of 33WA317 is certainly suggestive of a strong affiliation.

33WA362

The most prominent feature of 33WA362 is its location on an elevated and restricted terrace overlooking the "serpent" embankments, the large geometric earthwork, and surrounding debris scatters. The debris scatter conforms to the relatively level and gently sloping portions of the landform, although cultivation has resulted in some downslope movement. The size of the site is approximately .745 ha. Although situated in what appears to be an upland setting, the site rests on glacial deposits that have left rich soils of silt, loam, and sand.

Densities of recovered prehistoric debris at 33WA362 (.074 fragments/m^2) are significantly greater than those encountered at 33WA317 (.018 fragments/m^2) but less than those at 33WA256 (.121 fragments/m^2) on the nearby Fox terrace. Approximately 745 items were recovered during two collection episodes. Diagnostic Middle Woodland artifacts and debris number 120 specimens, or one-sixth of the total assemblage. Only one blade core was found, but sixty-nine bladelets have been identified. Much of the remaining diagnostic material consists of grit-tempered ceramic sherds. Forty sherds, roughly 29 percent of the total Stubbs Cluster assemblage, were recovered during the collection episodes. Once again, nonblade formal tools were recovered in small numbers. They include bifaces, bipolar objects, a few projectile points, drills, and several stone tool fragments. A stone smoking pipe stem (circular) fragment from the central cluster represents the only artifact of that type found within Stubbs Cluster boundaries.

Recovered debris is present in a generally diffuse distribution across the site, although three subtle debris clusters (central, north-central, and northeast) have been identified for specific debris categories (Fig. 11.7). Each of the clusters is similar in content; it is not known, however, whether they represent discrete household units or are terrain-based anomalies. Contours at the site suggest the former. There is no surface evidence of midden or features, but testing did reveal an isolated subplowzone, low-density debris horizon in a single test unit at the northeast cluster. Average distance between clusters is approximately 30 to 40 meters.

Site 33WA362 is similar in most respects to 33WA317, although multiple concentrations of debris are present at the former. As a result, there is a general concordance with the correlates of Pacheco's Hamlet Hypothesis (1988). The site is small in size, and site boundaries are believed to be accurately represented because of topographic restrictions. Site 33WA362 shares the same limited tool assemblage found at other systematically examined sites in the cluster. Bifacial tools are rare, but they suggest general rather than specialized activities. Spatial patterning of the clusters making up the site suggests that each cluster marks the approximate location of a household. No analysis has been done to determine whether or not they were occupied contemporaneously. Close proximity to the Stubbs Earthwork indicates a clear association with the corporate nucleus of this mid–Little Miami Valley Middle Woodland community.

Areal comparisons with other Middle Woodland sites indicate that 33WA362 corresponds closely with multiple household clusters. At the Smiling Dan site in the Lower Illinois River Valley, three to four subrectangular structures were exposed with intervals of 15 to 30 m between them. There was some question as to whether the structures were contemporaneously occupied, and it is possible that they represent a sequence of farming settlements rather than a single household group (Stafford and Sant 1985). Between four and seven structures were also exposed at the Holding site in the American Bottoms. These structures and intervening spaces encompassed an area of .6 ha. Of particular interest is the fact that the structure fill boundaries were often diffuse with only slightly higher debris densities noted within structure areas (Fortier et al. 1989:58). And finally, Smith (1992:229) notes that the vast majority of Middle Woodland habitation sites in the lower Illinois Valley are less than 2 ha in size. He equates these small sites with one to three household farming settlements. No multihousehold settlements have been excavated in Ohio.

Summary

Recent investigations at the Stubbs Cluster sites have produced large quantities of settlement and other debris and promise to provide invaluable data on Middle

Woodland settlement in this previously underinvestigated segment of the Little Miami River Valley. The pattern at Stubbs Cluster is one that has been noted elsewhere: a nucleus of a large geometric earthwork surrounded by apparent domestic debris scatters. These concentrations of domestic debris occur both on the same terrace as the earthwork and on adjacent and more elevated terrace situations. Given the surface nature of the evidence, it is not possible to assess fully how these data fit with the Hamlet Hypothesis, but there is some suggestion that at some of the sites, particularly 33WA317 and 362, household clusters may be present. At 33WA256, there is no immediate evidence of household clusters; indeed, the diffuse nature of debris patterning is more suggestive of a sequence of short-term or seasonal occupations related to the nearby enclosure. What is known is that further work, specifically excavations at suspected household sites, is necessary to answer the questions raised by the currently available surface data.

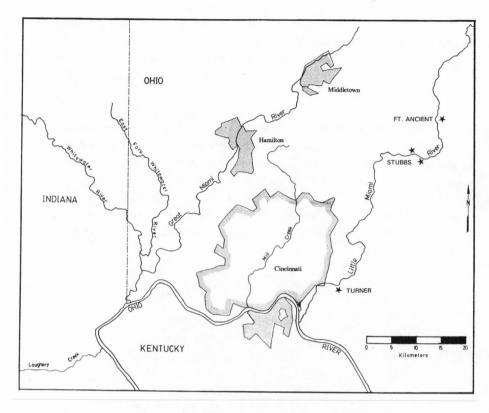

11.1 Stubbs Cluster (north and south subclusters) in relation to other major Little Miami River Valley Hopewell sites.

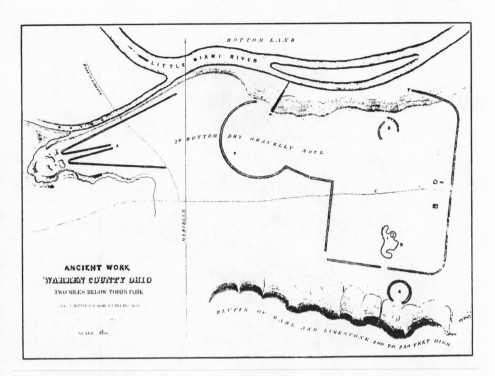

11.2 Stubbs Earthwork and nearby "Warren County Serpent Mound" as mapped by
Whittlesey in 1839 (Whittlesey 1851:Plate II).

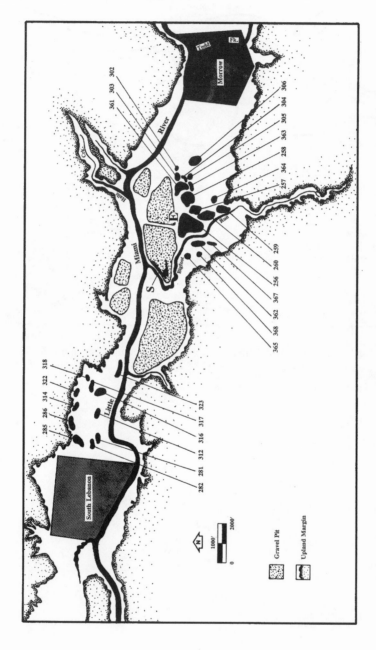

11.3 Middle Woodland sites between South Lebanon and Morrow, Ohio. All site designations are Warren County numbers (S, location of controversial Warren County Serpent Mound; E, general location of the geometric Stubbs Earthwork).

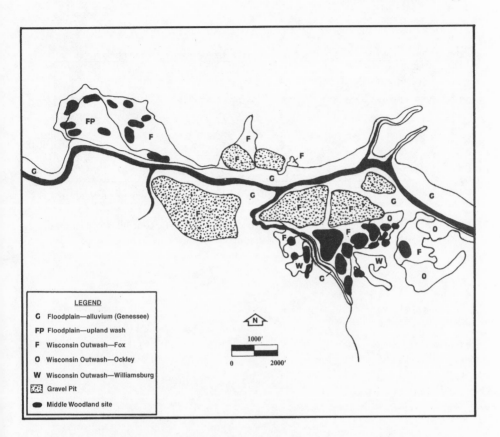

11.4 Landform associations of Middle Woodland sites.

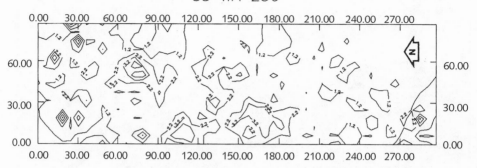

11.5   33WA256: Isopleth map of recovered debris density, systematic controlled collection of 1983. Scale in meters east and south of datum.

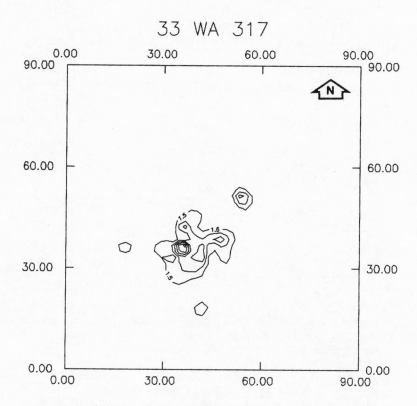

11.6 33WA317: Isopleth map of recovered debris density, systematic controlled collection of 1983 (scale in meters east and north of datum).

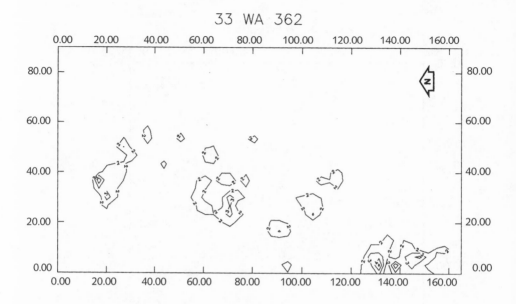

11.7 33WA362: Isopleth map of recovered debris density, systematic controlled collection of 1983 (scale in meters east and south of datum).

Table 11.1

Debris Totals and Densities for Stubbs Cluster Sites (1983 Systematic Controlled Collection Not Included)

	TD^a	MW^b	$B^c/B^d/B^e$	NMW^f	Percentage of MW^g	Percentage of NMW^h	DSM^i	$MWSM^j$
WA 256	2000	458	407/6/8	12	20.8	0.5	0.046	0.010
WA 257	1785	418	329/7/25	6	23.4	0.3	0.092	0.022
WA 258	1863	380	356/7/11	6	20.4	0.3	0.093	0.019
WA 259	81	8	6/0/0	1	9.9	1.2	0.003	0.001
WA 260	838	142	120/7/4	6	16.9	0.7	0.035	0.006
WA 281	46	3	1/0/0	1	6.5	2.2	0.004	0.001
WA 282	73	4	3/0/0	0	5.5	n/a	0.019	0.001
WA 285	99	1	1/0/0	2	1.0	2.0	0.008	0.001
WA 286	114	2	2/0/0	7	1.8	6.1	0.005	0.001
WA 302	455	13	6/0/3	1	2.9	0.2	0.978	0.028
WA 303	58	2	1/0/1	0	3.4	n/a	0.004	0.001
WA 304	27	3	2/1/0	1	11.1	3.7	0.003	0.001
WA 305	36	2	0/0/1	0	5.6	n/a	0.003	0.001
WA 306	9	1	0/0/1	1	11.1	11.1	0.001	0.001
WA 312	143	2	0/0/1	3	1.4	2.1	0.029	0.001
WA 314	33	8	3/0/0	1	24.2	3.0	0.007	0.002
WA 316	299	6	4/0/0	4	2.0	1.3	0.010	0.001
WA 317	350	111	51/0/2	3	31.7	1.4	0.034	0.010
WA 318	8	3	3/0/0	0	37.5	n/a	0.003	0.001
WA 322	20	1	0/0/0	0	5.0	n/a	0.005	0.001
WA 323	341	1	1/0/0	4	0.3	1.2	0.051	0.001
WA 361	208	50	38/1/11	1	24.0	0.5	0.016	0.014
WA 362	196	28	17/1/0	0	14.3	n/a	0.100	0.016
WA 363	287	59	41/2/12	2	20.6	0.7	0.023	0.005
WA 364	17	2	1/0/0	0	11.8	n/a	0.002	0.001
WA 365	29	17	15/1/1	0	20.2	n/a	0.016	0.003
WA 367	29	3	2/0/1	0	10.3	n/a	0.006	0.001
WA 368	40	2	1/0/0	1	5.0	2.5	0.021	0.001

[a]total recovered debris
[b]total recovered Middle Woodland artifacts and debris
[c]bladelets
[d]blade cores
[e]blade core trimming/waste flakes
[f]total recovered non–Middle Woodland diagnostic artifacts
[g]percentage of Middle Woodland debris
[h]percentage of non–Middle Woodland debris
[i]total recovered debris per square meter
[j]total recovered Middle Woodland debris per square meter

Table 11.2

Distribution of Middle Woodland Diagnostics in Stubbs Cluster Sites (1983 Systematic Controlled Collection Not Included)

	B^a	B^b	B^c	Q^d	O^e	KR^f	CO^g	M^h	PO^i	PP^j	TOTAL
WA 256	X	X	X	X	X	X	X	X	X	X	10
WA 257	X	X	X	X	X	X	—	X	X	X	9
WA 258	X	X	X	X	—	—	—	X	X	X	7
WA 259	X	—	—	X	—	—	—	—	—	—	2
WA 260	X	X	X	X	X	—	—	X	X	X	8
WA 281	X	—	—	—	—	—	—	—	X	X	3
WA 282	X	—	—	—	—	—	—	—	X	—	2
WA 285	X	—	—	—	—	—	—	—	—	—	1
WA 286	X	—	—	—	—	—	—	—	—	—	1
WA 302	X	—	X	X	X	—	—	—	—	X	5
WA 303	X	—	X	—	—	—	—	—	—	—	2
WA 304	X	X	—	—	—	—	—	—	—	—	2
WA 305	—	—	X	X	—	—	—	—	—	—	2
WA 306	—	—	X	—	—	—	—	—	—	—	1
WA 312	—	—	X	—	—	—	—	—	—	X	2
WA 314	X	—	—	—	—	—	—	X	X	—	3
WA 316	X	—	—	—	—	—	—	—	X	X	3
WA 317	X	—	X	X	—	—	—	X	X	X	6
WA 318	X	—	—	—	—	—	—	—	—	—	1
WA 322	—	—	—	—	—	—	—	—	—	X	1
WA 323	X	—	—	—	—	—	—	—	—	—	1
WA 361	X	X	X	—	—	—	—	—	—	—	3
WA 362	X	X	X	X	X	X	X	X	X	X	10
WA 363	X	X	X	X	X	—	—	—	—	X	6
WA 364	X	—	—	—	—	—	—	—	—	—	1
WA 365	X	X	X	—	—	—	—	—	—	—	3
WA 367	X	—	X	—	—	—	—	—	—	—	2
WA 368	X	—	—	—	—	—	—	—	—	X	2

ᵃbladelets
ᵇbladelet cores
ᶜblade core trimming/waste flakes
ᵈcrystalline quartz
ᵉobsidian

ᶠKnife River chalcedony
ᵍcopper
ʰmica
ⁱpottery (grit-tempered)
ʲprojectile points (Middle Woodland)

Table 11.3

33WA256: Systematic Controlled Collection,* Debris Densities

Artifact Category	Number	Percentage of Observed Debris	Percentage of Recovered Debris	Percentage of Recovered Lithics
Lithic Artifacts				
Flint debitage	1291	12.2	49.2	49.6
Utilized flint flakes	785	7.4	29.2	30.2
Flint bladelets	315	3.0	12.0	12.1
Flint flake cores	41	0.4	1.6	1.6
Bipolar flint artifacts	37	0.3	1.4	1.4
Flint biface fragments	33	0.3	1.3	1.3
Blocky flint flakes	20	0.2	0.8	0.8
Crystalline quartz fragments	20	0.2	0.8	0.8
Projectile points/fragments	15	0.1	0.6	0.6
Stone tools/fragments	13	0.1	0.5	0.5
Steep-edged flint scrapers	10	<0.1	0.4	0.4
Obsidian flakes	6	<0.1	0.2	0.2
Flint gravers/perforators	5	<0.1	0.2	0.2
Flint bladelet cores	3	<0.1	0.1	0.1
Flint endscrapers	2	<0.1	<0.1	<0.1
Flint spokeshaves	2	<0.1	<0.1	<0.1
Knife River chalcedony	2	<0.1	<0.1	<0.1
Flint drills	1	<0.1	<0.1	<0.1
Subtotal	2601	24.6	99.1	100.00
Other Artifacts				
Middle Woodland sherds	11	0.1	0.4	—
Mica fragments	8	<0.1	0.3	—
Bone (unburned)	2	<0.1	<0.1	—
Burned clay	2	<0.1	<0.1	—
Subtotal	23	0.2	0.9	—
TOTAL	2624	24.8	100.0	100.00

*Sample Statistics
2694 (9m²) units → 24,246 m² collected
Total cultural debris: 10,664
Total prehistoric cultural debris: 10,591

Total fire-cracked rock: 7,967 (75.2 percent)
Total recovered prehistoric cultural debris: 2,624
(24.8 percent)

Table 11.4

33WA317: Systematic Controlled Collection,* Debris Densities

Artifact Category	Number	Percentage of Observed Debris	Percentage of Recovered Debris	Percentage of Recovered Lithics
Lithic Artifacts				
Flint debitage	50	3.5	42.7	45.9
Utilized flint flakes	28	1.9	23.9	25.7
Flint bladelets	7	0.5	6.5	6.4
Flint biface fragments	6	0.4	5.1	5.5
Flint projectile points	4	0.2	3.4	3.7
Bipolar flint debris	4	0.2	3.4	3.7
Flint flake cores	3	0.2	2.6	2.8
Flint endscrapers	2	0.1	1.7	1.8
Stone tools/fragments	2	0.1	1.7	1.8
Crystalline quartz fragments	2	0.1	1.7	1.8
Flint spokeshaves	1	<0.1	0.9	0.9
Subtotal	109	7.7	93.2	100.0
Other Artifacts				
Mica fragments	4	0.3	3.4	—
Middle Woodland sherds	3	0.2	2.6	—
Bone (burned)	1	<0.1	0.9	—
Subtotal	8	0.6	6.8	—
TOTAL	117	8.2	100.0	100.0

*Sample Statistics
700 (9m²) units → 6,300 m² collected
Total cultural debris: 1,425
Total prehistoric cultural debris: 1,424
Total fire-cracked rock: 1,307 (91.8 percent)
Total recovered prehistoric cultural debris: 117 (8.2 percent)

Table 11.5

33WA362: Systematic Controlled Collection,* Debris Densities

Artifact Category	Number	Percentage of Observed Debris	Percentage of Recovered Debris	Percentage of Recovered Lithics
Lithic Artifacts				
Flint debitage	302	7.2	55.0	58.2
Utilized flint flakes	119	2.8	21.9	22.9
Flint bladelets	52	1.2	9.5	10.0
Bipolar flint artifacts	12	0.2	2.2	2.3
Flint flake cores	8	0.1	1.5	1.5
Flint biface fragments	7	0.1	1.3	1.3
Flint projectile points	6	0.1	1.1	1.2
Crystalline quartz fragments	5	0.1	0.9	1.0
Stone tools/fragments	2	<0.1	0.4	0.4
Flint drill fragments	2	<0.1	0.4	0.4
Knife River chalcedony flakes	2	<0.1	0.4	0.4
Obsidian flakes	1	<0.1	0.2	0.2
Stone pipe fragment	1	<0.1	0.2	0.2
Subtotal	519	12.4	94.5	100.0
Other Artifacts				
Middle Woodland sherds	28	0.6	5.1	—
Mica fragment	1	<0.1	0.2	—
Copper fragment	1	<0.1	0.2	—
Subtotal	30	0.7	5.5	100.0
TOTAL	549	13.2	100	100.0

*Sample Statistics
828 (9m²) units → 7,452 m² collected
Total prehistoric cultural debris: 4,172
Total fire-cracked rock: 3,622 (86.8 percent)
Total recovered prehistoric cultural debris: 549 (13.2 percent)

References

Bennett, R. A. H.

1986 *The Twin Mounds Village and Hopewell in Southwestern Ohio: A Ceramic Identity Crisis.* Unpublished master's thesis, Department of Anthropology, University of Cincinnati.

Dancey, W. S.

1991 A Middle Woodland Settlement in Central Ohio: A Preliminary Report on the Murphy Site (33LI212). *Pennsylvania Archaeologist* 61:37–72.

Farnsworth, K. B., and A. Koski

1985 *Massey and Archie: A Study of Two Hopewellian Homesteads in the Western Illinois Uplands.* Research Series 3. Center for American Archeology, Kampsville Archaeological Center, Kampsville, Illinois.

Fischer, F. W.

1971 Preliminary Report on the University of Cincinnati Archaeological Investigations, 1970. Ms. on file, Department of Anthropology, University of Cincinnati.

Fortier, A. C.

1985 Middle Woodland Occupations at the Truck #7 and Go-Kart South Sites. In *Selected Sites in the Hill Lake Locality,* edited by Andrew Fortier, pp. 163–281. FAI-270 Site Report 13. American Bottom Archaeology. University of Illinois Press, Urbana.

Fortier, A. C., T. O. Maher, J. A. Williams, M. C. Meinkoth, K. E. Parker, and L. S. Kelly

1989 *The Holding Site: A Hopewell Community in the American Bottom.* FAI-270 Site Report 19. American Bottom Archaeology, University of Illinois Press, Urbana.

Genheimer, R. A.

1984 *A Systematic Examination of Middle Woodland Settlements in Warren County, Ohio.* Ms. on file, Ohio Historic Preservation Office, Columbus.

1992 *Bladelets at the Stubbs Earthwork Cluster: An Examination of Middle Woodland Settlement in the Little Miami River Valley.* Unpublished master's thesis, Department of Anthropology, University of Cincinnati.

Kientz, P., and H. R. McPherson

1954 The Warren County Serpent Mound. Ohio Indian Relic Collectors Society, *Ohio Archaeologist* Special Number.

Odell, G. H.

1985 Microwear Analysis of Middle Woodland Lithics. In *Smiling Dan: Structure and Function at a Middle Woodland Settlement in the Illinois Valley,* edited by Barbara D. Stafford and Mark B. Sant, pp. 298–326. Research Series 2. Center for American Archeology, Kampsville Archeological Center, Kampsville, Illinois.

1994   The Role of Stone Bladelets in Middle Woodland Society. *American Antiquity*
        59:102–120.

Pacheco, P. J.
1988   Ohio Middle Woodland Settlement Variability in the Upper Licking River
        Drainage. *Journal of the Steward Anthropological Society* 18:87–117.

Prufer, O. H.
1965   *The McGraw Site: A Study in Hopewellian Dynamics.* Scientific Publications,
        n.s. 4(1). Cleveland Museum of Natural History.

Smith, B. D.
1992   Hopewellian Farmers of Eastern North America. In *Rivers of Change: Essays
        on Early Agriculture in Eastern North America,* edited by B. D. Smith, pp.
        201–248. Smithsonian Institution Press, Washington, D.C.

Stafford, B., and M. B. Sant (editors)
1985   *Smiling Dan: Structure and Function at a Middle Woodland Settlement in
        the Lower Illinois Valley.* Research Series 2. Center for American Archeology,
        Kampsville Archeological Center, Kampsville, Illinois.

Whittlesey, C.
1851   *Descriptions of Ancient Works in Ohio.* Contributions to Knowledge 3(7).
        Smithsonian Institution, Washington, D.C.

Yerkes, R. W.
1990   Using Microwear Analysis to Investigate Domestic Activities and Craft Spe-
        cialization at the Murphy Site, a Small Hopewell Settlement in Licking
        County, Ohio. In *The Interpretative Possibilities of Microwear Studies,* edited
        by B. Graslund, H. Knutsson, K. Knutsson, and J. Taffinder, pp. 167–176.
        Societas Archaeologica Upsaliensis and Department of Archaeology, Uppsala
        University, Uppsala, Sweden.

CHAPTER TWELVE

Fort Hill 1964

New Data and Reflections on
Hopewell Hilltop Enclosures in Southern Ohio

Olaf H. Prufer

ABSTRACT

This paper describes the stratigraphic profile of a trench excavated through
a portion of the Fort Hill enclosure in 1964. As has been found at other
such monumental public works tested systematically in Ohio, this portion
of Fort Hill exhibits at least two stages of construction. A review of previous literature of this type of enclosure reveals that despite accumulating
knowledge regarding their construction, little new has been learned about
the function(s) of these places.

In the late spring of 1964, from June 10 to June 16, I directed test excavations at
the presumed Hopewellian hilltop enclosure of Fort Hill, Highland County,
Ohio. This operation was carried out in the context of a major National Science Foundation–sponsored project (Grant Gs-8) dedicated to the investigation of Hopewellian phenomena in Ohio which, after decades of neglect, were
in urgent need of reassessment and renewed exploration. At the time, my
major concern was with questions pertaining to Hopewell settlements, subsistence and internal chronology. The hilltop enclosures of southern Ohio,
such as Fort Ancient, Fort Hill, Spruce Hill, Fort Miami—to mention but a
few—were of only tangential concern to these endeavors. Nevertheless, these

structures were an integral part of Hopewell and deserved, at least, a passing glance, especially since so little was known about them. I picked Fort Hill for examination partly because it was located near the central area of my investigations (the southern Scioto Valley), partly because it appeared to be associated with clear-cut Hopewellian debris immediately outside and below the circumvallation (Baby 1954), and partly because, after some extended negotiations, Raymond S. Baby, the late curator of archaeology at the Ohio Historical Society, was willing to grant permission to excavate at this state monument. The results of this operation were never published. In view of a recent upsurge in Ohio Hopewellian studies, they should be made available to both professionals and the public. My own base of operations at the time was Case Institute of Technology in Cleveland.

In the early 1960s our knowledge of southern Ohio's hilltop enclosures, the so-called "forts," was not much better than it had been in the late nineteenth century when Moorehead (1890) and Overman (1887–88) had carried out more or less extensive investigations at Fort Ancient and Fort Hill in Warren and Highland Counties, respectively. I might add that on the whole, the present status of our knowledge, as far as understanding the function(s) of the enclosures is concerned, is only marginally better than it was when I was testing Fort Hill in 1964. The following is a brief summary of what, in a general way, is known of these enclosures and what I perceive to be the major archaeological problems they presented then and now.

The hilltop enclosures are predicated on the presence of the suitable, mesalike hills characteristic of the dissected southern and east-central Appalachian regions of Ohio. The often impressive enclosure walls usually encircle the entire hilltop periphery. Thus, the shape and size of these structures are not determined by any preconceived architectural design but by the topographic configurations of the terrain. Many of the walls are characterized by interior ditches that no doubt furnished much of their building material. They are variously interrupted by gaps that in some instances are clearly entrances and in others are probably erosional features. Other such openings, again, may have served functions that cannot be determined at this time. In some cases, such as Fortified Hill in Butler County, gateways were furnished with parapets, suggesting some sort of protective structures, and some contain apparently man-made depressions that have variously been interpreted as ponds or reservoirs for the collection of water or burrow pits from which the building material for the enclosures had been quarried.

With some notable exceptions, the interior spaces of the enclosures seem to be devoid of occupational debris. Whenever such debris occurs, it does not appear to be commensurate with the dimensions of the enclosures. In the main, the latter appear to have been "vacant," although some of the older as well as current investigations at Fort Ancient have produced some clearly Hopewellian artifacts from within (and without) this immense enclosure (Connolly 1992; letter to Prufer, June 18, 1993). Regarding the apparent vacancy of the "forts," a caveat is perhaps in order. Given the huge dimensions of these structures, and given the fact that Hopewellian settlements in southern Ohio seem to have been characteristically small, perhaps in the nature of tiny farmsteads or hamlets (Prufer 1965), the absence of occupational debris may be, at least to some extent, a matter of sampling error, especially in light of the fact that virtually all hilltop enclosures are unplowed; they are covered by vegetation, which masks all evidence that might otherwise be gathered by standard survey procedures.

The major problems associated with the enclosures were, and still are, their cultural and, within that context, chronological affiliation(s) and function(s). Over the years, and beginning as early as the first half of the last century, two schools of thought have attempted to explain these structures, largely on the basis of logic and speculation, as either defensive or ceremonial in nature.

The truth may lie somewhere in the middle ground between these two extremes, but with primary emphasis on the military interpretation. The various positions have been summarized at some length by Prufer (1964a, 1964b, 1965), Faulkner (1971), Fischer (1974), and Essenpreis and Moseley (1984). I have always favored the notion that the primary function of the enclosures was defensive, although it is clear, and not especially surprising, that some ceremonial functions were also carried out in the context of these edifices. I have seen no reason to revise my judgment, which is based upon numerous considerations, including analogies with similar Old World prehistoric and historic structures. Thus, I largely concur with Fowke's statement that their "method of construction and their position relative to the surrounding country, make it obvious that they were intended as a place of refuge in time of danger from foes" (1902:238).

While the apparently obvious need not necessarily be true, it should not be rejected for the sake of what is often little more than ideologically inspired argument. In all such cases one would do well to apply William of Ockham's (A.D. 1280–1349) famous "razor," which states, in essence, that complex explanations should never be invoked unless there are compelling reasons to do so. On the evidence, I see no such compelling reasons. In any event, and given the current state of our knowledge, the question of whether the hilltop enclosures served military and/or ceremonial functions is largely a matter of (hopefully) educated opinion. Good evidence can be adduced for both positions; similarly, some of the evidence does not fit either particularly well.

The cultural and, by implication, chronological affiliations of all the hilltop enclosures or "forts," are difficult to determine because of the scarcity of directly and unambiguously associated cultural debris. However, the consensus is that these structures belong in the Hopewell complex of Middle Woodland times, dated conservatively in Ohio from about 100 B.C. to A.D. 350. The evidence rests on the discovery of Hopewellian artifacts in direct association with the circumvallation at Fort Ancient and on the presence of Hopewellian structures and other cultural remains, including some ceremonial ones, in the immediate vicinity of this and several other such "forts," including Fort Hill and Fort Miami in Hamilton County (Morgan 1965; Prufer 1961, 1964a; Fischer 1974). Nevertheless, although most likely, it is not entirely certain that all Ohio hilltop enclosures are of Hopewellian affiliation.

It is probably fair to say that, at the time of my work on Hopewellian problems in the early 1960s, the tacit assumption was that most, if not all, of the hilltop enclosures represent a single constructional event, the implication being that they were erected for a single and temporally specific type of function. In my own interpretive scheme of Hopewellian culture history (Prufer 1961, 1964a, 1964b, 1965), this implied that toward the end of the Hopewellian episode of the Woodland period, there arose a time of troubles that led to a retreat of the Hopewellians from their great valley-based southern Ohio centers onto easily defensible hilltop positions in the Appalachian hinterland of the region. It is with this in mind that I decided to probe the problem of the hilltop enclosures by trenching through the walls at Fort Hill.

In 1964 structural information regarding hilltop enclosure walls was woefully inadequate. It is fairly clear that the various operations carried out successively by Moorehead, Mills, and Morgan and Ellis at Fort Ancient between the late nineteenth century and 1940 indicate a complex architectural history, both for the "fort" as a whole and as far as construction stages of the component walls are concerned. These construction stages are not uniform in nature. They involve, in one test area excavated by Moorehead in 1891, wall segments containing a massive core of stone blocks covered with earth and ultimately "paved" with small limestone slabs. Subsequent operations by Morgan in

1940 in another wall segment revealed an earthen embankment with clear evidence of basket loading and some horizontal erosional surfaces that appear to betoken periods of exposure to weathering. Most of this information is derived from the excavators' more-or-less cryptic and unpublished original field notes, which are maintained in the archives of the Ohio Historical Society. For purposes of handy reference, the present summary is based on a paper by Essenpreis and Moseley (1984). Moorehead's published conclusions, if they can be trusted, given his well-known appalling excavation procedures, suggest that in the construction of the embankments "some time must have elapsed, after the completion of the lower layer, before the upper layer of stones and earth was placed upon it. Some vegetable matter has accumulated between the two layers. It seems quite evident that grass and small sprouts grew upon the lower stratum before the higher one was placed upon it" (1890:31).

These early data for Fort Ancient do not permit more precise statements as to the construction sequence at the "fort." At the time of my own operations, information for other hilltop enclosures was even less comprehensive and precise. Thus Putnam notes that the enclosure at Foster's Crossing in Warren County was "made up of a carefully laid wall of flat stones, both large and small, making nearly half the structure; and behind and over these stones a mass of clay burnt to all degrees of hardness, in places forming a vitreous surface. . . . At every part of the work through which a trench was dug the same story was told" (quoted by Fowke 1902:256).

As far as Fort Miami in Hamilton County is concerned, Fowke merely noted that there "is very little stone in the wall, it being composed almost entirely of earth obtained from a ditch along the bottom of the inner side. . . . At one place in the north wall, at the largest ravine, there are some stones which seem to have been piled on one another into a rough wall, as a revetment" (1902:254).

The only structural information in the older literature regarding Fort Hill is provided by Overman, who notes that the enclosure wall was "evidently constructed by an excavation of earth and stones around the brink of the hill thus raising a wall, which, at the present time, has a base averaging twenty-five feet and a height averaging from six to ten feet" (1887–88:260).

Thus, prior to my own operations in 1964, as far as multistage construction of the numerous hilltop enclosures is concerned, only the various excavations at Fort Ancient seem to suggest such a possibility with any degree of reliability. Since 1964, increasingly reliable evidence indicates that at least some of the hilltop enclosures represent more than one phase of construction. Consequently, the notion of a single "period of troubles," presumably toward the end of the Hopewellian period, that caused the erection of the geographically remote "forts" may have to be modified.

Fischer's 1965 investigations at Fort Miami in Hamilton County clearly demonstrate that the walls here were constructed of earth, stone, and wood. Fischer interprets this structure as essentially military in nature. He notes that (at least) the north wall of the enclosure appears to have been rebuilt after the superstructure of an earlier wall, perhaps a wooden palisade, had been destroyed by fire (Fischer 1965:7). A radiocarbon date obtained from a sample of charred wood from the original subembankment surface yielded a date of A.D. 270 ± 130, which places Fort Miami squarely into the Hopewellian period (Crane and Griffin 1968:84).

Somewhat similar evidence for at least two construction periods at a hilltop enclosure comes from the Pollock earthworks in Greene County. Here Riordan (1993) found evidence of a wooden stockade that, immediately upon destruction by fire, was replaced by the construction of an earthen embankment. A series of six radiocarbon dates with a range from A.D. 132 to 236 affiliates the stockade unambiguously with the Hopewellian Middle Woodland period. Finally, ongoing investigations at Fort Ancient, by far the largest and most complex of the Ohio hilltop enclosures, seem to confirm that this structure is indeed Hopewellian and that it represents several construction phases. Apart from diagnostic artifacts such as Hopewellian bladelets, pottery, and mica, which were discovered in direct association with the embankments, the structure proper (as opposed to features external to the "fort") yielded three radiocarbon dates (Connolly, letter to Prufer, June 18, 1993). Two of these gave values, calibrated to 1 s.d., of 100 B.C.–A.D. 120 (uncorrected: 1990 ± 130 B.P.; Beta 56270) and 105 B.C.–A.D. 88 (uncorrected: 1990 ± 90 B.P.; Beta 56271). Although these dates fall squarely within the Hopewellian period, in my estimation they may be somewhat early. A third date from the structure proper, with a value calibrated to 1 s.d. of 757–252 B.C. (uncorrected: 2340 ± 130 B.P.; Beta 56269), should date events unrelated to the Hopewellian occupation of the site.

As noted, my own excavations at Fort Hill were prompted by several considerations, not the least of which was that the site appeared to be, if only indirectly, associated with an excavated Hopewellian component located some 400 ft (122 m) below the mesa top of Fort Hill. Here, to the south of the "fort," two circular earthworks and a debris-strewn "village area" were tested by the Ohio Historical Society in 1952, 1953, and 1954. These operations were never adequately published. They produced evidence of complex wooden structures and numerous typical Hopewellian artifacts, including ceramics, bladelets, and mica fragments. My analysis of the ceramics from these excavations suggested that this locality, and by implication the "fort," represent a late phase in the Hopewell continuum (Prufer 1968:90–92).

The Fort Hill enclosure (Fig. 12.1), which follows the contours of the mesa top, at an elevation of 1,283 ft (391 m) above sea level, covers an area of about 40 acres (16.2 ha) (Morgan and Thomas 1948:31; 48 acres [19.4 ha] according to Squier and Davis 1848: Pl. V). The walls, in their present condition, vary in height from 6 to 15 ft (1.9 m to 4.6 m), with an average basal width of about 40 ft (12.2 m). The enclosure wall is somewhat more than 1.5 miles (2.5 km) in length, and has thirty-three openings or gates. It is characterized in places by a true interior ditch from which much of the building material for the wall was derived. In other places, the interior ditch is not a real ditch but the result of the positioning of much of the wall on a ledge below the summit of the mesa. This ledge was modified by the quarrying of raw material for the construction of the wall. Although they don't quite say so, already Squier and Davis (1848:15) were aware of this, as is shown on their Plate V, transect a–b (Fig. 12.1). Finally, the interior of the structure contains three depressions that may or may not be artificial; if they were, they may have been additional sources of building material for the walls (Morgan and Thomas 1948).

I decided to cut a trench through the wall of the "fort" at a point directly north of, and as close as possible to, the circular enclosure and the so-called village area at the bottom of the mesa. This trench, 5 ft (1.5 m) in width, was laid out in sections of 5 ft (1.5 m) cutting through the wall from the apex into and through the interior of the pseudo-ditch at 22 degrees east of north from the north-south baseline.

The stratigraphy of the wall is fairly complex. Since the natural floor upon which the wall was constructed (the ledge) is not level, but slopes toward the outer edge of the mesa, precise depth measurements are not particularly meaningful; the reader is thus referred to the scale on Figs. 12.2 and 12.3 in order to get a picture of the wall's dimensions.

The earliest construction phase is represented by a primary core wall consisting of a colluvium of weathered and unweathered dark humus with inclusions of large blocks of local Berea sandstone and intermingled with tiny flecks of charcoal. This wall was erected on a rather soft, natural surface of mixed small rocky debris and clay (erroneously referred to as "till" in the field documents) that could be distinguished clearly from the soils composing the primary core wall. The surface of this base was characterized by numerous tiny specks of charcoal. In places, basket loading of buff-colored earth could be distinguished in the structure of the wall. Berea sandstone of the paleozoic Mississippian period forms the capping deposit of the Fort Hill mesa. Originally, this inner core wall was covered by a single layer of large, more-or-less dressed, flat sandstone slabs. Some of these were found in situ. Elsewhere, due to erosion and/or modifications prior to the subsequent (second) construction phase, these slabs appear to have been dislocated. The largest slab encountered measured approximately 2.8 ft (.853 m) square, with a thickness of .8 ft (20.3 cm). The field notes record that the "majority of these [slabs] were so large that they could not be moved without being broken into manageable sizes. This made for slow progress and for low spirits among . . . the crew" (field notes, June 12, 1964). It is during this construction phase that the first version of the interior ditch must have come into being as a result of quarrying soil and rocks for the building of the wall.

After this primary core wall had apparently fallen into disuse, an inner retaining wall, or "ring," entirely "composed of large slabs that were well fitted and having between their junctions a deposit of a highly gumbotil material . . . much harder and of a[n] entirely different character than any of the soils in the area" was encountered (field notes, June 11, 1964). This retaining wall rested directly on the natural surface of the mesa and was partly leaning against the interior edge of the primary core wall that had been laterally truncated in order to accommodate the retaining wall. The latter also partly impinged on (and thus modified) the profile of the original interior ditch.

The construction of this retaining wall marks the first stage in the erection of the second and final embankment, which consists of a buff-colored, weathered colluvium that includes occasional, irregular blocks of Berea sandstone. As the field notes indicate (June 11, 1964), there was evidence for basket loading, because the soil "gives the impression of being a molded deposit for one could detect a sequence of deposition for each individual load. The loads differed in . . . texture" and specks of charcoal were noted throughout. This buff-colored colluvium covers both the inner stone ring and the primary core wall. In the form of a thin layer, it also extends into the interior ditch. None of the tiny and very dispersed specks of charcoal was collected for radiocarbon dating. At the time, given the state of the art, such samples were deemed far too small for meaningful assays. Furthermore, being contained in the wall fill, there was no gainsaying what such samples may actually have dated.

The field notes for June 11, 1964, note that after having been piled up to the builders' satisfaction, this final enclosure wall was neatly covered by "a ballast of large sandstone slabs which followed the contour of the surface. . . . These slabs ranged from 0.1–2.6 ft in maximum dimension. From the arrangement of these slabs and the way that they were cut . . . they were purposely fitted to form a ballast or pavement. The ballast was layered and formed a covering from 3 to 4 slabs thick." This pavement in turn was covered by a layer of recent humus. This basic stratigraphy was verified by two test holes placed at 100 ft (30.5 m) intervals on either side of the main trench.

In addition to testing the enclosure wall at Fort Hill, a casual attempt was made to ascertain whether the interior of the "fort" might yield some cultural debris. To that end, several 3 x 3 ft (.9 x .9 m) squares were dug into the two southern depressions and at various locations in the central and northern sections of the enclosure. All of these units proved to be culturally sterile.

The structure of the enclosure at Fort Hill, at least in the area investigated in 1964, consists of two basic construction stages involving an inner, primary core wall and a much more extensive and complex final wall, the erection of which entailed the simultaneous construction of an interior retaining wall. Both walls had been carefully covered by flat Berea sandstone slabs. There is no evidence of any kind of a wooden palisade. Furthermore, at least in the area of excavation, there was no real interior ditch. The walls were constructed on an exterior ledge below the summit of the mesa. Material quarried from the recessed ledge of the hilltop was incorporated into the wall structure. Thus a spurious, ditchlike depression between the apex of the embankment and the natural top of the mesa was created in this segment of the wall.

In conclusion, it should be noted that all southern Ohio hilltop enclosures that have been tested and reported on are characterized by at least two chronologically distinct construction phases. In addition, all the sites were tested either on the grounds of direct and/or indirect diagnostic artifact association or on the basis of radiometric assays, clearly affiliated with the Hopewellian complex of the Middle Woodland period. Since the Fort Hill tests in 1964, none of the renewed efforts at the hilltop enclosures has added anything definitive to resolving the debate as to the military and/or ceremonial function of these structures.

Within a week of these excavations, on June 22, 1964, I discussed my conclusions in a letter to Elisabeth Baldwin (Garland), now Professor Emerita of Anthropology at Western Michigan University, who in 1963 had been my field supervisor at the excavations of the Hopewellian McGraw site (Prufer 1965). Since these conclusions were drawn immediately after the event rather than in hindsight and based upon data analysis, they might be worth quoting; the relevant sections of this letter also convey an idea of the conditions under which we were operating:

Fieldwork: We have already one session for 1964 under our belt. With J. Blank et al. we spent about ten days at Fort Hill, digging under appalling conditions. The field-house is an old converted barn at the bottom of the hill with a "straight" [i.e., common] outhouse inhabited at day-time by wasps and at night by mosquitos. The whole locality is strictly in the hinterland, even by today's standards. The nearest town (no motel) is Bainbridge; the nearest "settlement" a place called Sinking Springs (it gives you a sinking feeling merely to contemplate this place . . .). The Fort itself is densely covered with forest. Some of it seems primary forest to boot: the trees are some 7–8 feet in diameter which should make them older than the odd 180 years of White occupation of the area. Inside the fort, [rational] selection of a locale for digging is impossible; the forest cover is too dense (ibid. poison ivy & mosquitos plus other assorted creepy-crawley). We laid out a trench through the enclosure into the interior ditch. Not a single artifact was found. Yet the structure of the wall was a great, if laborwise, painful surprise. It turned out to be built of dry masonry. At the point of the trench [i.e., apex] the wall from top to base measured 7 1/2 feet—this is by no means the highest section of this enclosure . . . Here, then, is the picture: The interior base consisted of a retaining wall of sandstone blocks, roughly similar to the "stone rings" frequently found at the base of many Hopewell mounds. Above this and stretching outward is the primary core of the wall consisting of earth and large blocks of sandstone. There are, in this deposit—as throughout the structure—specks of charcoal, but not in sufficient quantity to permit dating. Above this primary core we found a secondary core consisting [almost] entirely of earth. The whole structure was capped with several layers of carefully laid flat sandstones. . . . At present, I would interpret the hill top enclosures not so much as fortifications *sensu strictu* but as refuges in times of trouble similar to the European Fliehburg structures of the Bronze and Iron Ages and, again, during the Hungarian invasions. That is to say, these things are defensive alright, but not in the modern sense of the word. They serve as highly temporary occupation areas in times of trouble, when the going was bad. Normally—but as Hopewell [is] already in retreat from the old River Valleys—the mob was down at the foot of the hill farming, etc., as usual. During raids or whatever, kids, women, etc. may have been shunted up to the top of the structure. This situation may explain also, by the way, the notorious lack of culture trash in these hill top enclosures.

At present, all documents pertaining to the Fort Hill excavations reported upon here are curated at Kent State University. A word is in order regarding the profiles illustrated in Figs. 12.2–12.4. Fig. 12.2 is the precise profile, pencil-drawn by me and R. S. Baby, as it presented itself after excavation. It is shown without any attempt at reconstruction of the wall (i.e., replacing slipped sandstone slabs within the trench into their original positions prior to erosion and artificial modification). Fig. 12.3, drawn by John Blank on June 16, 1964, is a schematic reconstruction of the profile to what the original wall structure seems to have been. It takes into consideration the original position of many of the displaced and slipped sandstone slabs actually found in the excavation. Fig. 12.4 (pencil-drawn by me and Baby) illustrates the outward extension of the wall in relation to the original land surface at the edge of the mesa top after intensive probing along the steep outer slope and drop aimed at locating the interface between the wall and the natural surface of the mesa.

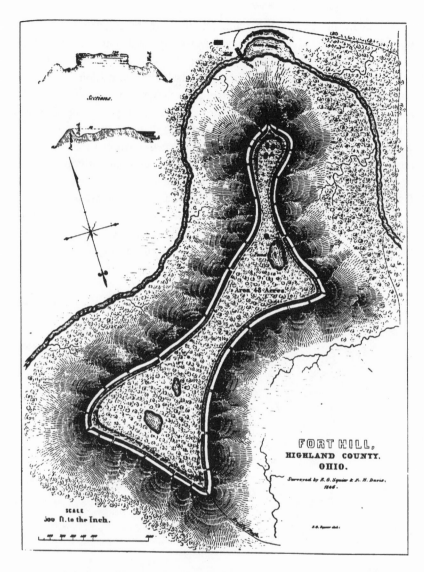

12.1 Map of Fort Hill by Squier and Davis (1848).

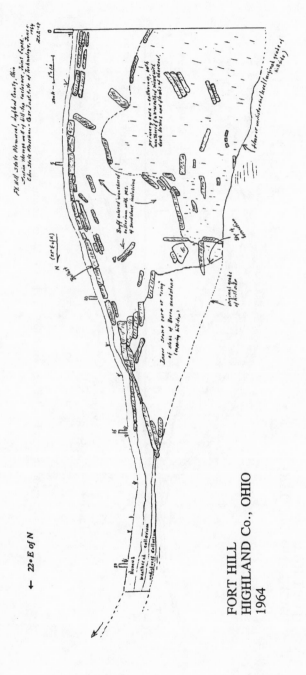

12.2 Partial field profile of 1964 section through circumvallation at Fort Hill. Reduction of pencil drawing by O. H. Prufer and R. S. Baby.

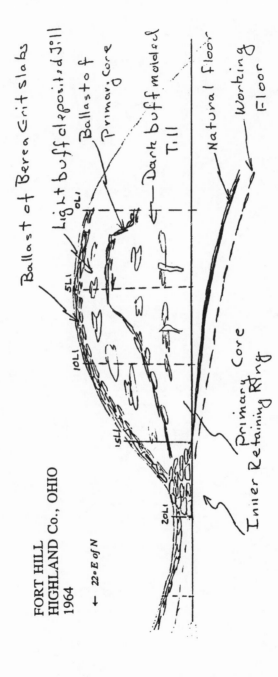

FORT HILL
HIGHLAND Co., OHIO
1964

← 22° E of N

Ballast of Berea Grit slabs

Light buff deposited Jill

Ballast of Primary core

Dark buff molded Till

Natural Floor

Working Floor

Primary Core

Inner Retaining Ring

12.3 Reconstruction of circumvallation at Fort Hill, drawn in the field by J. E. Blank on June 16, 1964.

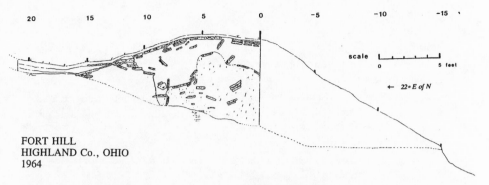

FORT HILL
HIGHLAND Co., OHIO
1964

12.4 Complete field profile of 1964 section through circumvallation at Fort Hill, illustrating outward extension of wall in relation to original land surface at the edge of the mesa top. Reduction of pencil drawing by O. H. Prufer and R. S. Baby.

References

Baby, R. S.

    1954   Archaeological Explorations at Fort Hill. *Museum Echoes* 27(11):86–87.

Connolly, R. P.

    1992   Prehistoric Land Modification at the Fort Ancient Hilltop Enclosure, Warren County, Ohio. Paper presented at the 37th Midwest Archaeological Conference, Grand Rapids, Michigan.

Crane, H. R., and J. B. Griffin

    1968   University of Michigan Radiocarbon Dates XII. *Radiocarbon* 10(1):61–114.

Essenpreis, P. S., and M. E. Moseley

    1984   Fort Ancient: Citadel or Coliseum? *Field Museum of Natural History, Bulletin* 55(6):5–10, 20–26.

Faulkner, C. H.

    1971   *The Old Stone Fort: Exploring an Archaeological Mystery*. University of Tennessee Press, Knoxville.

Fischer, F. W.

    1965   Preliminary Report of 1965 Archaeological Investigations at Miami Fort. Ms. on file, Department of Anthropology, University of Cincinnati.

    1974   *Early and Middle Woodland Settlement, Subsistence and Population in the Central Ohio Valley*. Unpublished Ph.D. dissertation, Department of Anthropology, Washington University, St. Louis.

Fowke, G.

    1902   *Archaeological History of Ohio: The Mound Builders and Later Indians*. Ohio State Archaeological and Historical Society, Columbus.

Morgan, R. G.

    1965   *Fort Ancient*. Ohio Historical Society, Columbus.

Morgan, R. G., and E. S. Thomas

    1948   *Fort Hill*. Ohio State Archaeological and Historical Society, Columbus.

Moorehead, W. K.

    1890   *Fort Ancient*. Robert Clarke, Cincinnati.

Overman, H. W.

    1887–8   Fort Hill, Ohio. *Ohio State Archaeological and Historical Quarterly* 1:260–264.

Prufer, O. H.

    1961   *The Hopewell Complex of Ohio*. Unpublished Ph.D. dissertation, Department of Anthropology, Harvard University. Cambridge, Massachusetts.

    1964a   The Hopewell Complex of Ohio. In *Hopewellian Studies*, edited by J. R. Caldwell and R. L. Hall, pp. 35–84. Scientific Papers 12. Illinois State Museum, Springfield.

    1964b   The Hopewell Cult. *Scientific American* 211(6):90–102.

1965 *The McGraw Site: A Study in Hopewellian Dynamics*. Scientific Publications, n.s. 4(1). Cleveland Museum of Natural History.

1968 *Ohio Hopewell Ceramics: An Analysis of the Extant Collections*. Anthropological Papers 33. Museum of Anthropology, University of Michigan, Ann Arbor.

Riordan, R. V.

1993 A Timber Stockade at the Pollock Works. Paper presented at the Biannual Meeting of the Ohio Archaeological Council, Columbus.

Squier, E. G., and E. H. Davis

1848 *Ancient Monuments of the Mississippi Valley*. Contributions to Knowledge 1. Smithsonian Institution, Washington, D.C.

PART FOUR

Middle Woodland Habitations in the Ohio Hopewell Periphery

CHAPTER THIRTEEN

Beyond the Scioto Valley

Middle Woodland Occupations in the

Salt Creek Drainage

Flora Church and Annette G. Ericksen

ABSTRACT

The record of Ohio Middle Woodland occupations is not limited to major
river valleys like that of the Scioto. Peripheral drainages have also provided
substantial evidence for occupations throughout the Early and Middle
Woodland periods. An examination of the Salt Creek drainage based upon
recent excavations at the Wade site (33VI315) in Vinton County, Ohio, inte-
grates data on subsistence, community structure, and relationships to burial
mounds and ceremonial centers in order to test Prufer's Hopewell settlement model. This model of dispersed, sedentary agricultural settlements
around earthworks is partially validated in the Salt Creek data.

The purpose of this study is to examine a number of models for Hopewell
settlement patterns presented by Prufer (1965, 1967), Pacheco (1988), and Smith
(1987) on the basis of data from the Salt Creek Valley in southern Ross and
northern Vinton Counties, Ohio. Testing of these models is based on the excavation of a portion of the Wade site (33VI315) and on survey data from other
sites in the valley (Prufer 1967, Appendix to chapter 13; Blank 1972, 1977).

The fundamental way of life of the Ohio Hopewellians eluded us until well
into the twentieth century, when Prufer (1965) excavated the McGraw midden

just north of the confluence of the Paint Creek and the Scioto River in Ross County, Ohio. Based on his excavation and on the results of the Scioto Valley Archaeological Survey (hereafter SVAS), in which a number of other sites with Middle Woodland components were recorded (Prufer 1967), Prufer hypothesized that the Middle Woodland settlement pattern in the region consisted of a series of semipermanent shifting agricultural farmsteads, or hamlets, clustered around ceremonial centers and burial grounds (Prufer 1965:137).

This hypothesis remained untested by further data until the 1980s when Cowan et al. (1981) and Dancey (1991) surveyed and excavated the Murphy site (33LI212) on the Raccoon Creek in Licking County, Ohio. Dancey interpreted this early Middle Woodland site (ca. 100 B.C.–A.D. 200) as a sedentary hamlet, or one segment of a dispersed community. Pacheco (1988) has tested Prufer's hypothesis through data collected during more recent survey and test excavations in the Raccoon Creek Valley. Dubbing this the Hamlet Hypothesis, Pacheco has developed four archaeological correlates in order to test the hypothesis. He predicted that hamlets, if traces of them existed in the archaeological record, would be characterized by (1) small size, (2) functionally redundant assemblages, (3) structural redundancy, and (4) clustering around earthwork or mound complexes.

Further, he has proposed that neither seasonal use nor brevity of occupation should affect the status of a site as a hamlet or the settlement system as sedentary (1988:96). In addition, he postulated that irregularly spaced logistical camps for special-purpose activities (e.g., hunting, nut collecting, mortuary activities, or quarrying) may also be part of the Middle Woodland settlement system (1988:94). He concluded that the hypothesis cannot be rejected as long as seasonal movements maintained the hamlet residence pattern (1988:88).

Smith (1987), in his paper on Hopewell farmers of eastern North America, summed up three models of Hopewell habitation settlement systems using data from Tennessee, the lower Illinois River Valley, the American Bottom, and, in part, Ohio (Prufer 1964, 1965). The first of these models postulates that the Hopewellians occupied permanent, year-round villages from which small groups periodically moved throughout the annual seasonal cycle in order to establish short-term resource procurement camps elsewhere (Smith 1987:24). The second model is the equivalent of the Hamlet Hypothesis; it predicts a pattern of dispersed year-round farmsteads augmented by short-term seasonal camps. The third model is based on a three-tier habitation pattern of (1) farming hamlets occupied during the growing season, (2) cold-season homesteads, and (3) logistical short-term camps set up for the procurement of special resources such as nuts, berries, deer, fish, and specific raw materials. Smith suggests that clusters of such sites, in the main river valleys, would have been located in the general vicinity of corporate-ceremonial centers (1987:64). He further concludes that "Hopewellian farming settlements were small, dispersed, apparently independent, and redundantly egalitarian in appearance" (Smith 1987:65). In this chapter, a number of sites from the Salt Creek Valley, a tributary of the Scioto River, will be discussed in the context of Middle Woodland settlements beyond the Scioto, the major river in central Ohio well known for its Hopewellian corporate-ceremonial centers.

The Salt Creek Valley Data Base

Information on the Salt Creek Valley is largely based on information derived from the Wade site (33VI315), which was partially excavated in 1988 in the course of a cultural resource management project (Church 1989). Data on other sites in the Salt Creek Valley are based on earlier surveys and excavations published by Prufer (1967) and Blank (1972, 1977, 1985). In addition, we have added to this study a contribution by Prufer (Prufer, personal communication to Church; Appendix to chapter 13) in which he presents his analysis of unpublished materials recovered by him and his associates at the Ilif Riddle sites near Londonderry in Ross County. The detailed description of the Wade site, combined with the information from these other localities, constitutes the basis of the present study.

The Wade Site (33VI315)

The Wade site is located on a rise in the floodplain of the Salt Creek just east of its confluence with Pike Run (Fig. 13.1). Elevations across the landform range from 177 to 213 m. Minimal elevation differentials of up to 18 cm were noted across the top of the rise. Limited testing during the cultural resource survey suggested site dimensions of 45 m EW x 20 m NS, or roughly .16 ha (Norris and Skinner 1988). However, a more extensive survey by Blank (1972) identified a lithic scatter covering .9 ha.

The Salt Creek Valley lies within the Unglaciated Allegheny Plateau portion of the Appalachian Plateau Province of eastern North America (Fenneman 1938), a region marked by long, deeply entrenched stream valleys; elevations range from 183 to 610 m above mean sea level. The recent topography of the valley is the result of varying resistance to erosion of the underlying series of bedrock shales and sandstones. Accompanying these deposits, Zaleski flint, a high-quality black mineral, commonly occurs in Vinton County in the form of outcrops and stream cobbles (Stout and Schoenlaub 1947). This material is often hard to distinguish from Upper Mercer flint, which also outcrops in the region and, in case of doubt, has here been noted as Upper Mercer/Zaleski or Upper Mercer flint, depending on how reliably specific identifications could be determined.

Situated on the floodplain between the Salt Creek and Pike Run, the Wade site is located on a Pope loam soil, which follows Pike Run and expands into the confluence area. A finger of Chenango silt loam borders the Pope soil to the north, while a thin band of Huntington loam parallels the Salt Creek to the east and south (Paschall et al. 1938). These soils are derived from upland slope wash. The Salt Creek Valley has a continental climate marked by warm, humid summers and cold winters (Pierce 1959). Oak-chestnut is the principal upland forest association, while oak-pine forests predominate locally in Eagle township (Braun 1941; Beatley 1959). A mixed mesophytic forest association characterizes the lower northern and eastern ridge exposures, especially in Eagle township, while an oak-chestnut-tulip tree forest association dominates in ravines, coves, and other moist upland areas. The presence of pine in Eagle township is suggestive of differing water availability and temperature ranges between the floodplain and ridgetops. The floodplain supports beech-maple and elm-ash swamp forests, with a beech-maple climax evident on terraces. Blank (1972) points out that prairie wetland grasses may have existed on those portions of the floodplain that were subject to annual flooding. Such areas are known to have existed at the confluence of the Salt Creek and the Scioto River. These forest associations did, and still do, support many faunal resources. At the time of the first Euro-American settlements, thirty-four mammalian species were common in Ohio (Blank 1972). Together with diverse wild plant food resources, many of these animals would have been readily available, while the soils suggest a reasonable potential for the cultivation of domesticated annuals.

Features

During excavation of that portion of the site to be affected by modern construction activities, a total of twelve features was documented within the project right-of-way (Fig. 13.2). Three wood charcoal samples from feature contexts were submitted for radiocarbon dating; 690 artifacts were recovered; and microwear as well as archaeobotanical analyses were performed. Six feature types could be identified (Table 13.1), including small shallow basins, hearths, earth ovens, a random postmold, fire-cracked rock concentrations, and features of unknown function. Small shallow basins of variable plan and cross-section (Fig. 13.2) were found to contain unstratified, charcoal-flecked fill with little or no rocks in the matrix. Feature 2 is an example of a hearth (Fig. 13.2); a circular, sloping basin with fire-reddened sides, it is filled with fire-cracked rock and charcoal. Two radiocarbon samples from this feature were submitted for analysis (Table 13.2).

Earth ovens are represented by two features (Fig. 13.2); they are large deep pits lined with fire-cracked rocks. One of these, Feature 3, yielded large amounts of charcoal, potsherds, lithics (including a bladelet), and mica fragments. One radiocarbon date was obtained for this feature. Two other pits may have functioned as smaller earth ovens or, possibly, as other food processing/storage facilities before ending up as refuse pits (Fig. 13.2). These two features also yielded charcoal, potsherds, lithics, mica fragments, and nutshell. Feature 9 is a small deep basin of unknown function; it has an oval plan and sloping profile (Fig. 13.2). In addition to these formal structures, small fire-cracked rock concentrations were identified at the site. They may represent discards from stone-boiling episodes (Seeman and Soday 1980) or hearth cleaning; or they may be the bases of severely truncated, no longer identifiable features. Finally, the site yielded a single circular postmold with a sloping profile. In general, the Wade site features are indicative of a diversity of activities carried out at this locality. As will be shown below, lithic microwear and archaeobotanical analyses further underscore such diversity.

Based on their clustering (Fig. 13.3), lack of general stratification, judicious consideration of the radiocarbon dates (Table 13.2), and the homogeneity of artifact types discussed below, the Wade site features have been interpreted as representing a single cultural component dating from the period between ca. B.C. 200 and A.D. 200. This places the site somewhere between the Early/Middle Woodland transition and the mature Middle Woodland period.

Ceramics

A total of 434 ceramic sherds was recovered, including 14 rim sherds; 33 (8 percent) of these came from features. The assemblage is 99 percent grit-tempered; 53 percent of the sherds have plain surfaces, and 26 percent are characterized by Z-twist cordmarking. All rims are plain and grit-tempered, with a thickness range of 5–9 mm (mean=5.9 mm); body sherd thickness ranges from 4–11 mm (mean=6.1 mm). The average thickness of cordmarked body sherds is 5.2 mm, while that of the plain surfaced sherds amounts to 6.5 mm.

The variables of rim shape, tempering material, relative temper particle size and density, and sherd thickness derived from the Wade site ceramic assemblage were compared to a number of Early and Middle Woodland ceramic assemblages. The Early Woodland samples involved were taken from Adena mounds, while the Middle Woodland samples came from habitation sites in Licking County. The Wade site assemblage shares color, temper type, and temper particle size and density with the late Adena ceramics, although the paste of the former is more linear and less crumbly in texture than that of the latter. However, the Wade assemblage is most similar to a series of black, feldspar-tempered, thin sherds from the Murphy site in Licking County (Dancey 1991). In addition, it generally agrees with the type descriptions published for the Middle Woodland Scioto Series (Prufer 1965). It should, however, be noted that plain/cordmarked ratios at McGraw differ from those of the Wade site, with 23 percent plain and 71 percent cordmarked. Since the percentages of cordmarked over plain wares during the Middle Woodland period appear to increase through time (Prufer 1968:148–149), those exhibited at the Wade site would seem to support a chronological placement of this site as earlier in Middle Woodland than McGraw.

Features 2, 3, 6, and 8 yielded pottery; the remaining sherds were clustered in the vicinity of Features 1 and 8, corresponding to a small, shallow dip in the rise. This area may have been a midden, or, alternatively, the artifacts may have been part of a secondary deposit. Finally, a small group of sherds was recovered from the area of the site's eastern feature cluster.

Chipped Stone

Chipped stone represents 97 percent of all lithics. Locally available Upper Mercer/Zaleski flint accounts for 58 percent of all chipped stone material, whereas Vanport flint accounts for an additional 20 percent. Fifteen whole and fragmentary projectile points were recovered (Table 13.3), including two Robbins points, one possible early Middle Adena point (recovered from the plowzone), and four Snyders points (Justice 1987; Converse 1973). These types suggest a temporal range of occupation compatible with that derived from the ceramic analysis and radiocarbon assays. The Middle Woodland points are distributed across the entire excavated area of the site.

Six Hopewellian bladelets were identified; one of these was reconstructed from two fragments. Three were made of Vanport flint, and three of Upper Mercer/Zaleski flint. Four were recovered from the eastern third of the project area (one within Feature 3), and two were recovered from the western third of the excavated area. Other lithic tools include a Vanport biface, an Upper Mercer scraper, and eleven cores, three of which are made of Upper Mercer, two of Vanport, and six of local raw material. The remainder of the lithic assemblage consists of debitage. Ninety-one percent (n=77) of the Upper Mercer/Zaleski flakes, 100 percent of the Vanport flakes (n=37), and 76 percent (n=19) of those made from local flint varieties represent advanced stages of tool manufacture. Most of this material was clustered around the eastern group of features; some was recovered from the small dip in the rise that also produced some ceramics. The predominance of diagnostic Middle Woodland tools in the overall assemblage supports a Middle Woodland interpretation of the Wade site. The presence of late Early Woodland points may indicate an additional earlier occupation or secondary curation of such earlier materials in a Middle Woodland household.

Lithic microwear analysis was conducted by John P. Nass, Jr., on twenty-one whole flakes from both feature and nonfeature, subplowzone contexts. The actual rate of tool use (52 percent) was, given the small sample size, relatively high. Documented activities include butchering, hide scraping, and wood and bone/antler working.

Archaeobotanical Summary

Twenty-seven flotation samples from ten features and ten from nonfeature contexts were analyzed by Annette G. Ericksen. A localized and nonselective strategy of firewood procurement, with identified taxa such as elm, black walnut, persimmon, maple, and hickory, appears to have been the norm. These trees were readily available in the surrounding valley and uplands. Hickory and walnut nutshells, in this order of frequency, were also recovered.

Carbonized seeds were retrieved in low densities (n=39). At least three of the identified species can be considered economically important: goosefoot (*Chenopodium* sp., n=3), maygrass (Phalaris sp., n=4), and blueberry (*Vaccinium* sp., n=1). Bedstraw (*Galium* sp., n=16) may also have been economically useful. Goosefoot was recovered from Feature 2 and maygrass from Features 2 and 3 as well as from the small dip in the rise, some 50–60 cm be-low surface. The single blueberry seed was recovered from Feature 3, while bed- straw came from Features 2 and 3. Goosefoot and maygrass are considered to be members of the Eastern Agricultural Complex. The *Chenopodium* seeds could not be identified as to species, but they do not appear to represent *C. bushi-anum* or any other cultivated variety of goosefoot. The genus *Galium* includes some species that produce a red dye (Steyermark 1963). Like other plants of the Eastern Agricultural Complex, bedstraw grows in open fields, waste places, and disturbed forest areas; it flowers in midsummer. Maygrass becomes available for harvesting by early May and lasts through early June (Cowan 1985). Wild forms of goosefoot can be eaten green during the summer, or they can be taken from the stalk through late fall and even early winter, depending on whether or how long the seeds remain attached to the plant. Other weedy, non-economic seed species identified in the floral assemblage include hawthorn, carpetweed, spurry, and vervain. All are representative of disturbed areas.

Although the observed frequencies of economically important floral remains at the Wade site are low, such low frequencies are not uncommon in the archaeological record. They may be related to cultural factors such as the nature of resource storage, manner of food processing, modes of consumption, and waste disposal. Also, natural factors such as soil acidity may be responsible for the scarcity of such botanical remains at many sites, not to mention techniques of recovery.

Settlement Plan

The absence of a controlled excavated sample across the entire site and the identification of only one postmold make it impossible to suggest the location and size of such structures as may have been present. However, the quantity and diversity of features and artifact types suggest concentrated zones of household activities. Earth ovens, hearths, and various basins form redundant feature groups. Lithics and ceramics cluster around the features. The character of the lithic assemblage indicates the procurement and use of locally available flints for expedient tool use. It was possible to document such activities as meat cutting, hide scraping, wood working, and bone/antler working. Formal tools were made of high-quality Upper Mercer and Vanport flints.

A small, natural depression or dip in the rise of the site also contained subplowzone deposits of lithics and features. On first consideration, it seemed possible that these represented a small, thin midden deposit that had buried Features 1 and 8, the latter marking an earlier occupational episode. However, soil profiles across this portion of the site do not show any evidence of such a deposit. Instead, pottery sherds and lithics were oriented vertically, suggesting that a single depositional event, such as flooding or wash, had redeposited materials from other parts of the site into this depression. Analysis of feature contents and artifacts, as well as radiocarbon dates, support the interpretation of the site as a single occupation. Additional occupational debris probably accumulated in other, unexcavated areas of the site.

The examination of subsistence data suggests that the site may have been occupied from late spring/early summer to mid-to-late fall. Economically important plant resources such as goosefoot and maygrass were present in low densities in several features. While no obvious agricultural implements were recovered, this does not rule out horticultural activities aimed at encouraging the growth of cultigens or locally available stands of wild resources. Simple garden chores such as planting, tilling, and weeding could have been accomplished by means of digging sticks or other wooden tools. The presence of ceramic containers clearly allows for both short-term storage and cooking activities, and the location of the site on a disturbed floodplain habitat would have been ideal for horticultural purposes.

Further evidence for plant utilization at the Wade site can be inferred from the nonselective use of locally available trees for firewood, and by the presence of hickory nuts and walnuts. The latter were not present in any quantities suggestive of intensive harvesting or storage of foodstuffs, nor were there any deep storage pits. Thus, it does not appear that the occupation was geared toward either selective or intensive procurement of nuts. Nonsubsistence activities may be inferred from the mica fragments present in several features. The use of bladelets for cutting mica has been documented in a microwear study of such tools from the Murphy site (Yerkes 1990); bladelets were recovered at Wade from the same features that also produced mica.

Thus, the Wade site appears to date from the early Middle Woodland period, circa 200 B.C.–A.D. 200. One or more households appear to have occupied the Salt Creek floodplain for periods of time that seem to have encompassed late spring/early summer through mid-to-late fall. The archaeobotanical assemblage shows that food resources were varied and occurred in low frequencies, and use-wear analysis of flint tools indicates a diversity of processing and other activities. All this suggests a mixed resource procurement strategy that included the harvesting of naturally available nuts, berries, and seeds; the low-level cultivation of other seedplants such as maygrass; and hunting. In short, the occupants of the Wade site were not intensively utilizing any particular resource. Such a mixed economic strategy is consistent with the concept of the development of agriculture as a continuum of behaviors, wherein a pattern of broad-spectrum, generalized resource utilization is characteristic of the initial stages of this continuum toward greater differentiation (Cowan 1985; Flannery 1973; Rindos 1984). The Hopewell inhabitants of the Wade site were not concentrating on the production of Eastern Agricultural Complex cultigens; this was only part of their repertoire of subsistence practices. In addition, a variety of other domestic and economic activities typified the daily lives of these people.

Comparative Sites in the Salt Creek Valley

Other Middle Woodland occupations are known from the Salt Creek Valley in Vinton and Ross Counties (Table 13.4). Those with diagnostic Middle Woodland lithics and/or ceramics were included in the present analysis, as were relevant mound sites that are listed in the Ohio Archaeological Inventory files (Table 13.5). All locations were plotted on the 7.5 USGS topographic map for the area (Fig. 13.4) or highlighted on Prufer's modified Scioto River Valley survey map of 1967 (Fig. 13.5) to illustrate the broader archaeological context of the Wade site.

Almost all of the sites are multicomponent (Table 13.5). Only the Newton Farm site, located south of the Scioto River/Salt Creek confluence in Ross County, was interpreted by Prufer as a single-component Middle Woodland occupation. This site yielded Middle Woodland diagnostics, and pit features were evident in the plowed bottom after rain. Also, the major occupation of the Lynch-4 site was considered Middle Woodland. Prufer viewed this site as another small farmstead similar to the McGraw site (1967:311). Excluding mounds, twelve (63 percent) of these sites are distributed along terraces; the remaining seven sites (37 percent) are located on floodplains. No upland sites have been recorded.

Average site size is 1.5 ha (Table 13.5); this figure is undoubtedly inflated by the multicomponent nature of most of these sites. No data on site size are available for the two Drake sites and the single-component Newton Farm.

The actual Hopewellian loci on the Caldwell's Bottom, Morrison Farm, and Higby sites are quite small, but their Middle Woodland artifact scatters have never been plotted for area; thus their dimensions, as given, are probably excessive (Prufer, personal communication). The dimensions of Lynch-4, the major component of which is a clearly defined Hopewellian locus, and of the two Ilif Riddle sites have been estimated at .8, .6, and .3 ha, respectively (Prufer personal communication). Among those sites in closest proximity to Wade, size averages .5 ha. As the crow flies, all sites are less than 13 km from the Liberty earthworks (Fig. 13.5).

Surface collections from six sites yielded Middle Woodland ceramics. Of these Caldwell's Bluff, Caldwell's Bottom, Lynch-4, and Newton Farm are located at the Scioto River/Salt Creek confluence. Ilif Riddle 1 and 2 are located on the Salt Creek, some 8 km upstream from the Scioto/Salt confluence and about midway between that point and the Wade site. The remaining sites are multicomponent lithic scatters.

Evaluation of the Hamlet Hypothesis

With an estimated dimension of .9 ha, the Wade site conforms to the first of Pacheco's archaeological correlates—small size. This is also the upper limit for the size range of published Middle Woodland habitations in the upper Licking River drainage. The majority of the Salt Creek drainage sites also fall within this range (Fig. 13.6); the exceptions are those large, multicomponent sites for which the loci of Hopewellian occupation are not specified.

In terms of the second correlate—functionally redundant assemblages— the Wade site produced ceramics and chipped stone tools such as projectile points, bifaces, cores, bladelets, and expedient flake tools identified by microwear analysis with butchering, hide working, and other activities. Furthermore, five fragments of mica recovered from three different features, assorted botanical remains, and possibly three ground stone celt fragments found by Blank in the initial site survey (Blank 1972:112) all fall within the domain of Pacheco's second archaeological correlate. The Wade site assemblage compares well with that from the Murphy site. This would also seem to hold true for the Ilif Riddle-1 site (see Appendix), especially in the light of the fact that Prufer and his associates made no attempt to recover botanical remains at the time of their limited excavations. All things considered, the diversity of tools and other remains recovered, and the presumed activities they represent, support the notion that the Wade site served as a habitation rather than a special purpose site.

On the basis of surface collections, Middle Woodland sites that have yielded projectile points, cores, bladelets, and ceramics have been defined as habitations. Assemblages from Morrison Farm, Ilif Riddle-2, and Lynch-4 produced projectile points, cores, bladelets, and ceramics; three additional sites, Caldwell's Bluff, Newton Farm, and Ilif Riddle-1 (the latter in considerable quantities) yielded bladelets, ceramics, and projectile points. On this basis, at least six sites in addition to Wade can be classified as habitations. This list may, however, be too restricted, because it should be recalled that the original surface collection from Wade did not include ceramics. Thus, it is entirely possible that the remaining sites in the sample lack pottery merely due to sampling error. On the other hand, the single Middle Woodland points recovered from such sites as Drake's Lower Terrace and Drake's Corn Crib, as well as the three bladelets from Mae Brown-1, may represent traces of special-purpose sites rather than habitations. As it stands, for the Salt Creek Valley Pacheco's second correlate is currently supported by seven sites. These sites suggest the presence of dispersed Hopewell habitations in this drainage system.

Pacheco's third correlate, structural redundancy, is impossible to evaluate in the Salt Creek Valley for any but the Wade and Ilif Riddle-1 sites. Wade revealed a total of twelve features in the excavated area of the site. Feature types documented include earth ovens, hearths, refuse pits, postmolds, and small basins. Once more, the diversity of feature types represented at this site is comparable to that documented at the Murphy site in Licking County (Dancey 1991) and at Hopewell habitation sites elsewhere in the Eastern Woodlands (Smith 1987). While the Wade site excavations were limited in extent, the overall dimensions of the site, and the distribution of features suggest that the community plan was not equivalent to that of a nucleated village, such as the early Late Woodland Water Plant site (Church 1987; Dancey 1988). Clear cut functional areas with feature clusters, deliberately maintained open spaces and, possibly, refuse areas were apparent, although no house patterns could be defined. Numerous pits reported at Newton Farm and midden remnants documented through test excavations at Lynch-4 indicate that these sites, too, were habitations (Prufer 1967:310–311). Similarly, Ilif Riddle-1 produced feature clusters, at least one postmold, a dense artifact scatter from a plow-disturbed midden, and concentrated masses of fire-cracked rocks (see Appendix). The third correlate is thus supported as well.

Pacheco's fourth and final correlate predicts that hamlets will cluster around earthworks and mound complexes. No precise data are available on expected hamlet-to-hamlet distances nor on the expected distances from hamlet clusters to specific ceremonial complexes. Based on the mapping of Middle Woodland sites in the Scioto River Valley survey by Prufer (1967), the site cluster at the Scioto River/Salt Creek confluence is approximately 4 km in diameter (Fig. 13.4). Within this cluster, six sites occur in three pairs, each separated by approximately 400 m. This is similar to Blank's (1985) data on two Middle Woodland sites in Licking County that he described as being 300 m apart. These sites may represent dispersed hamlets.

Further upstream, the second group of sites, located near Londonderry/ Vigo, has a diameter of 5 km (Fig. 13.5). Within this cluster, and with the exception of Bolte, sites are found in pairs: the two Riddle sites are located within 500 m of each other; the distance between the two Mae Brown sites is even less. The closest site to Wade is the Mae Brown-1 locality, at 800 m. Given the known sample of sites, all limited to the terraces and floodplain, it would appear that small Middle Woodland sites tend to cluster together as might be expected of the segments of a dispersed community.

When the proximity of these sites to ceremonial centers is considered, a distinction should be made between major earthworks centers such as Liberty and isolated single mounds or small mound groups. There are no great ceremonial centers in the Salt Creek Valley, but there are a number of mounds that are either known or suspected to be of Hopewellian affiliation.

It should be noted that all the Salt Creek valley sites so far considered are within less than 2–3 km from a known mound. In the case of the northern site cluster, to which Wade belongs, the closest mounds are the Brown mounds 1 and 2. Their cultural affiliation is not certain; because of their proximity to a known Early Woodland site, they have been tentatively assigned to that period. The same may be true of certain other mounds in the area, especially because their immediate environs have produced no Hopewellian materials (Blank 1972). In actual fact, however, their cultural affiliation is unknown. The same holds true of the cluster of sites near Londonderry/Vigo. Here the Riddle sites and Bolte are in close proximity to the Bethel mound, again of uncertain affiliation (Fig. 13.4). Although only excavation will resolve the question, Prufer argues that the Brown mounds and the Bethel mound are not accidentally located within reach of the Hopewellian habitation site clusters under discussion in this paper. He feels that this is especially true in light of the situation near the Scioto/Salt confluence. The habitation sites in this cluster are located in the immediate vicinity of two mounds, one of which is clearly Hopewellian, the other, on the basis of its structural characteristics as an elongated, lobed mound, almost certainly so. The former is the Caldwell mound associated with the Caldwell's Bluff and Caldwell's Bottom sites. It produced a classic Ross Barbed Spear, mica, a copper headdress, and copper bracelets (Kramer 1951). The latter is an unexcavated mound located in the modern cemetery of Richmondale (Prufer, personal communications). In sum, then, the Salt Creek Middle Woodland site clusters here under consideration are all within short distances from actual, presumed, or possible Hopewell mounds. This appears to be a pattern. As far as relationships of the site clusters to major Hopewellian ceremonial centers are concerned, the fact is that no earthworks have been documented along the Salt Creek drainage.

Yet, the Wade site and the northern site cluster lie within 12.8 km from the Harness or Liberty earthworks on the Scioto River. The group of sites at the Scioto/Salt confluence is located at less than 10 km south of this ceremonial center. Whether the Salt Creek Valley sites are in some way related to this complex cannot be determined at this time. In any event, beyond some correlation between the Salt Creek clusters with isolated mounds, the correspondence of the Salt Creek clusters to Pacheco's fourth correlate cannot be directly confirmed by the data at hand. This may be so because (1) the distance to, and implied relationships with, major corporate ceremonial centers has not been quantified in any testable fashion, or because (2) local participation in the major ceremonial aspects of Hopewell lifeways may not have been contingent on physical proximity to a specific center; perhaps it was based on kinship ties within a particular social group dispersed among several different local communities. As Prufer suggests, it is also conceivable that (3) participation in the ceremonial Hopewell sphere may have been local in nature rather than tied to a major center (Prufer, personal communications).

While it is not clear whether the Wade (and Ilif Riddle-1) sites were directly tied to any particular ceremonial complex, it is apparent that its inhabitants participated in a level of socioreligious relationships that transcended the immediate local community. This seems implicit in the fact that typical Interaction Sphere materials such as mica were recovered from sites.

To summarize, three of Pacheco's four correlates defining the Hamlet Hypothesis are directly supported by the Salt Creek Valley data. Pacheco (chapter 2) suggests the possibility that such sites as Wade may have functioned in concert with corporate-ceremonial centers, thus supporting the fourth correlate as well. Does this mean that the Hamlet Hypothesis is essentially correct?

Does the Wade site represent a "semi-permanent shifting agricultural farm-stead" (Prufer 1965:137) or, perhaps, a sedentary hamlet such as has been sug-gested for the Murphy site? In order to address these questions, it is impor-tant to understand what Prufer meant by semipermanent. He suggested an occupation of a single generation or thirty years for McGraw, which corre-lates well with many ethnographic models of temperate swidden-based vil-lage agricultural or horticultural communities.

Other Hopewellian settlement models also address this point. Smith (1987) describes one such model which suggests that permanent year-round villages were present in parts of the Eastern Woodlands. The problem is that this pat-tern does not explain the data from Ohio, where Hopewellian habitations were not nucleated villages. Smith's second model proposes that hamlets were year-round farmsteads; this is based in part on Prufer's Ohio data, and, at bottom, is the equivalent of Pacheco's Hamlet Hypothesis. This raises the question as to how one can establish archaeologically the sedentariness of a prehistoric community. Sedentary, as defined by Rafferty (1985), refers to any settlement occupied year-round by at least part of its population. Tradition-ally, this is done by documenting the seasons represented in the archaeologi-cal debris of a given site. Ideally this involves the identification of seasonal indicators among the botanical and faunal remains as well as functional con-siderations pertaining to the nature of processing and extracting tools and of associated features.

The Wade site produced no faunal remains. Most likely this was a function of preservation conditions in the acidic soils of the floodplain. No bone tools were recovered either, although stone tools indicate the processing of bone and antler. Seasonal food resources identified include maygrass, goosefoot, blueberry, hickory, and walnut, which are available from late spring through late fall. No house patterns were identified, possibly because of the limited scope of the excavations. Thus, it is not possible to determine whether such dwellings may have contained interior hearths suggestive of cold-weather oc-cupations. Likewise, no storage features that might imply the caching of food-stuffs for winter consumption could be identified (Hart 1992). A similar situ-ation has been observed at the Murphy site, which also produced neither faunal material nor bone tools but which yielded wear patterns on stone tools in-dicative of the processing of such materials. The Murphy botanical evidence was similar to that from the Wade site. Again, at neither site was there evi-dence for dwelling structures. In the case of the Murphy site, Dancey (1988:66) has argued for a sedentary settlement based, in part, on Kozarek (1987:127), who, having examined the relationship between mobility and maintained spaces in settlements, concluded that the latter are more likely to be representative of sedentary occupations. Deliberately maintained spaces appear to be present at the Wade site, but no year-round seasonal indicators could be identified, and no structures were defined in the excavated portion of the site. Thus, the available evidence does not allow a clear-cut resolution of the problem.

Smith's (1987) third model describes a settlement system in which growing-season farming hamlets alternate with cold-season homesteads, both being supplemented by short-term resource procurement camps. Pacheco's interpretation of the Hamlet Hypothesis is similar to this model, for he states that the hypothesis cannot be invalidated on the basis of seasonal occupation alone as long as the pattern of seasonal movement also maintained the hamlet pattern. In this third model, Wade would be interpreted as a growing-season farmstead, with cold-season habitation sites, presumably away from the open valley floor, being predicted at other environmentally suitable locations. However, all surveys in the Salt Creek Valley have been limited to the valley proper; no upland sites have been recorded to date, let alone investigated and analyzed. Middle Woodland components are known from some rockshelters in southeastern and south-central Ohio, but the nature and intensity of such occupations is not clear.

Originally, the Wade site was thought to fit Smith's third model (Church 1989), but further intensive analysis of all the evidence suggests a revised interpretation. Based on the nonselective, broad-spectrum pattern of resource utilization that was spread over a range of seasons, and based on the presumed chronological position of Wade early within the Middle Woodland sequence, this site may perhaps better be viewed as a seasonal homestead (as opposed to farmstead) that was part of a dispersed community. This terminology is intended to emphasize the fact that horticultural activities were not the focus, but rather a minor aspect, of the site's subsistence economy. In any event, year-round occupancy of the site cannot be determined on the basis of present evidence.

Summary

Based on the information obtained by the Wade site excavations, and taking into consideration the evidence from other Hopewell sites in the Salt Creek Valley, the presumed early Middle Woodland settlement pattern in this area is believed to have been characterized by a number of small homesteads in dispersed communities situated along terraces and floodplains of this stream. These communities are thought to have been tied into a wider social and/or religious network that centered around mound and earthwork complexes situated in the major river valleys and some of their tributaries. While this evidence does not support Prufer's model of year-round hamlets occupied for a generation (1965:137), it does support a pattern of seasonal, dispersed hamlets.

Acknowledgments

This research grew out of the mitigation of the Wade site for Archaeological Services Consultants, Inc., It was further supported by grants from ASC, Inc., and the Ohio Archaeological Council. Access to comparative collections was arranged by Martha Potter Otto, curator of Archaeology at the Ohio Historical Museum, and by William S. Dancey, Department of Anthropology, The Ohio State University. For their advice, support, and helpful comments, thanks are offered to our colleagues John P. Nass, Jr., William S. Dancey, Paul W. Sciulli, and Olaf H. Prufer. Responsibility for the format and content of this paper rests, as always, with the authors.

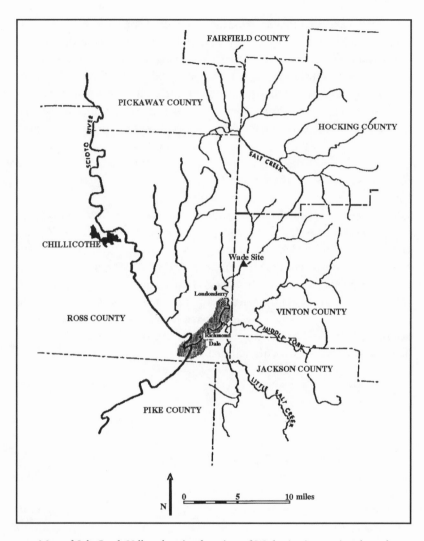

13.1 Map of Salt Creek Valley showing location of Wade site (33v1315). Adapted from Blank (1977:Fig. 1).

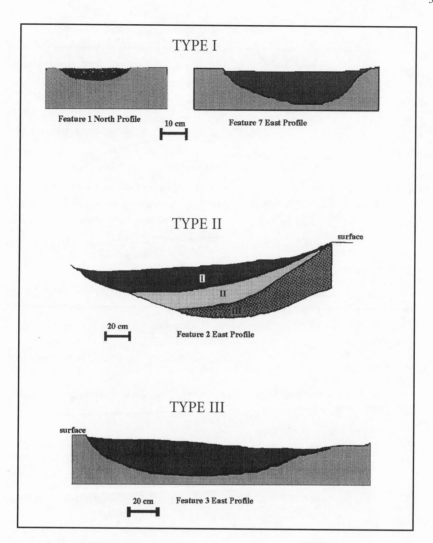

TYPE I

Feature 1 North Profile

10 cm

Feature 7 East Profile

TYPE II

surface

I

II

20 cm

Feature 2 East Profile

TYPE III

surface

20 cm   Feature 3 East Profile

13.2 Example of major feature types from the Wade site. (I) small basins, (II) hearth, (III) earth oven.

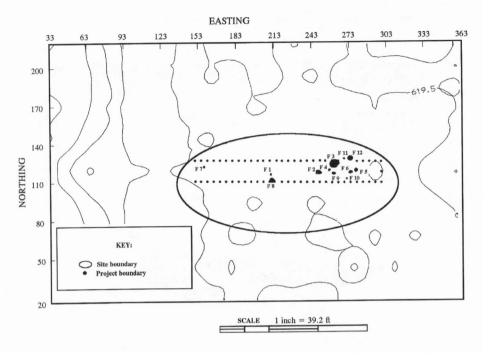

13.3 Feature distribution at the Wade site.

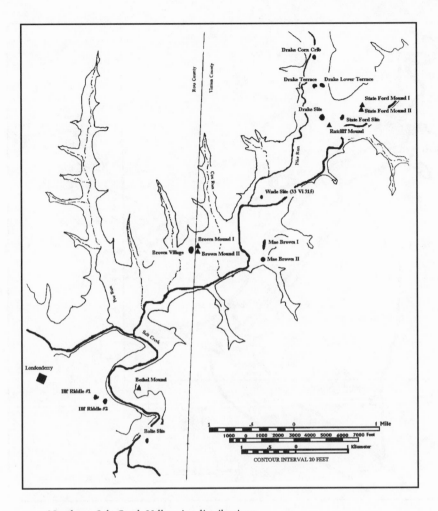

13.4 Northern Salt Creek Valley site distributions.

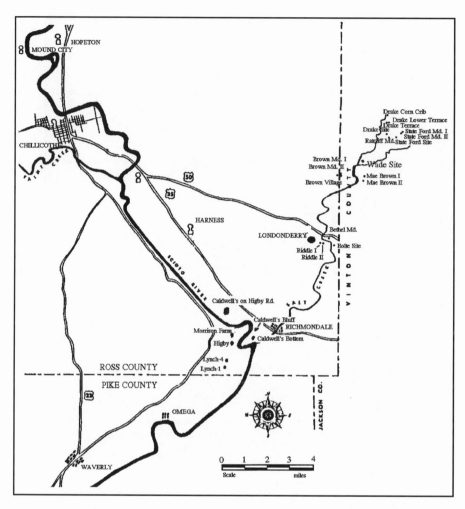

13.5 Southern Salt Creek Valley sites at the Scioto River confluence. Adapted from Prufer (1967:Fig. 1).

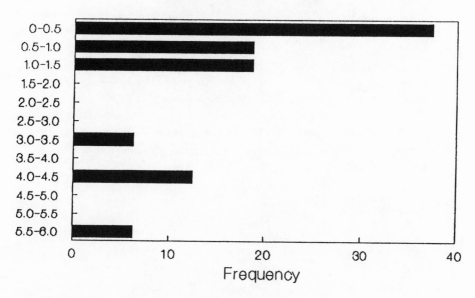

13.6 Size distribution of Middle Woodland sites in the Salt Creek Valley.

Table 13.1

Wade Site Feature Characteristics

Feature	Length (mm)	Width (mm)	Depth (mm)	Volume (l)	Profile	Contents
1	30	25	5	0.15	Basin	Charcoal, rock
7	44	55	15	1.54	Basin	1 rock
2	123	105	30	15.96	Basin	Charcoal, FCR
5	100	64	22	5.84	Basin	Charcoal, FCR, mica, nutshell
8	65	140	40	36.44	Cone	Charcoal, FCR, mica sherds, lithics
3	145	178	26	26.18	Basin	Charcoal, FCR, mica sherds, lithics
9	31	25	24	1.81	Cone	Charcoal
10	14	15	11	0.15	Basin	Charcoal
11	—	—	—	—	—	FCR
12	—	—	—	—	—	FCR

Table 13.2

Wade Site Radiocarbon Dates

Sample Number	Context	C-14 Date/ yrs. B.P.	Calibrated Date[a]
Beta-29446	Feature 3	1800±100	A.D. 80–377
Beta-29447	Feature 2/II	2050±170	B.C. 356–A.D. 127
Beta-29448	Feature 2/III	2170±120	B.C. 390–72

[a]Stuiver and Becker (1986), Method A, 2 "delta".

Table 13.3

Typed Projectile Points from the Wade Site

Provenience	Point Type	Length (mm)	Width (mm)	Thickness (mm)	Reference
Unit 17/L2	Middle Woodland	43	33	7	Converse (1973:61)
Unit 40/L2	Robbins	n/a	28	7	Justice (1987:186)
Unit 44/L2	Snyders	—	—	—	Justice (1987:202)
Unit 53/L3	Snyders	—	—	—	Justice (1987:202)
Unit 57/L3	Robbins	57	24	9	Converse (1973:56)
Unit 60/L1	Early/Middle Adena	50	25	10	Converse (1973:56)
Feature 8	Snyders	55	39	9	Justice (1987:202)

Table 13.4

Characteristics of the Salt Creek Valley Sites

Site	Size (ha)	Landform	Components	Reference
Wade	0.9	Floodplain	Single	this chapter
Riddle I	0.6	2-Terrace	Multiple	this chapter
Riddle II	0.3	2-Terrace	Multiple	Blank 1972
Bolte	1.0	2-Terrace	Multiple	Blank 1972
Drake	0.4	Terrace	Multiple	Blank 1972
State Ford	1.0	Terrace	Multiple	Blank 1972
Drake Lower Terrace	n/a	Terrace	Multiple	Blank 1972
Drake Corn Crib	0.2	Terrace	Multiple	Blank 1972
Mae Brown I	0.7	1-Terrace	Multiple	Blank 1972
Mae Brown II	0.2	Terrace	Multiple	Blank 1972
Brown Village	0.7	2-Terrace	Multiple	Blank 1972
Drake Terrace	n/a	Terrace	Multiple	Blank 1972
Caldwell/Higby Road	1.2	Floodplain rise	Multiple	Prufer 1967
Caldwell's Bluff	3.2	Terrace bluff	Multiple	Prufer 1967
Caldwell's Bottom	6.0	Floodplain	Multiple	Prufer 1967
Morrison Farm	4.0	Floodplain rise	Multiple	Prufer 1967
Higby	4.0	Floodplain	Multiple	Prufer 1967
Lynch-1	0.4	Floodplain	Multiple	Prufer 1967
Lynch-4	0.8	Floodplain rise	Multiple	Prufer 1967
Newton Farm	n/a	Floodplain	Single	Prufer 1967
Bethel Mound	n/a	Terrace	—	Blank 1972
Ratcliff Mound	n/a	Terrace	—	Blank 1972
State Ford Mound I	n/a	1-Terrace	—	Blank 1972
State Ford Mound II	n/a	1-Terrace	—	Blank 1972
Brown Mound I	n/a	Terrace	—	Blank 1972
Brown Mound II	n/a	Terrace	—	Blank 1972

Table 13.5

Diagnostic Middle Woodland Artifacts from Sample Sites

Site	Projectile Points	Bladelets	Cores	McGraw Ceramics	TOTAL
Wade	4	6	—	434	—
Riddle I	7	340	—	325	672
Riddle II	1	7	1	1	10
Bolte	19	16	—	—	35
Drake	10	10	—	—	20
Brown Village	18	4	—	—	22
Drake Lower Terrace	1	—	—	—	1
Drake Corn Crib	1	—	—	—	1
Mae Brown I	—	3	—	—	3
Mae Brown II	1	—	—	—	1
Drake Terrace	15	2	—	—	17
Caldwell/Higby Road	1	—	—	—	1
Caldwell's Bluff	1	1	—	1	3
Caldwell's Bottom	1	1	—	—	2
Morrison Farm	3	16	1	17	37
Higby	—	1	—	—	1
Lynch-1	1	1	—	—	2
Lynch-4	2	9	2	40	53
Newton Farm	1	4	—	9	14

References

Beatley, J. C.
1959 The Primeval Forests of a Periglacial Area in the Allegheny Plateau (Vinton and Jackson Counties, Ohio). *Ohio Biological Survey Bulletin* 1(1):1–182.

Blank, J. E.
1965 The Brown's Bottom Site, Ross County, Ohio. *Ohio Archaeologist* 15(1):16–21.
1972 *Archaeological Investigations in the Salt Creek Reservoir, Ohio: Season I, the Drake Terrace Site (33VI11)*. Report of Investigations, National Park Service Research Contract No. 14-10-950-39.
1977 *Archaeological Investigations in the Salt Creek Reservoir, Ohio: Season II, the Drake Site (33VI6) and the Brown Village Site (33VI107)*. Cleveland State University.
1985 *Results of a Phase I and Phase II Archaeological Survey of the Newark Wastewater Treatment Plant Project Area, Licking County, Ohio*. Report to Licking County Commissioners, Newark, Ohio.

Braun, E. L.
1941 The Differentiation of the Deciduous Forests in Ohio. *Ohio Journal of Science* 41:235–241.

Church, F.
1987 *An Inquiry into the Transition from Late Woodland to Late Prehistoric Cultures in the Central Scioto Valley, Ohio circa AD 500 to AD 1250*. Unpublished Ph.D. dissertation, Department of Anthropology, The Ohio State University, Columbus.
1989 *Phase IV Excavation at 33VI315, Vinton County, Ohio: Construction Mitigation for the Parkersburg-Hopetown Segment of the AT&T Fiber Optics Cable*. Archaeological Services Consultants, Columbus, Ohio. Report submitted to Buker, Willis and Ratliff, Chillicothe, Ohio.

Converse, R. N.
1973 *Ohio Flint Types*. Archaeological Society of Ohio, Plain City.

Cowan, C. W.
1985 Understanding the Evolution of Plant Husbandry in Eastern North America: Lessons from Botany, Ethnography and Archaeology. In *Prehistoric Food Production in North America*, edited by R. I. Ford, pp. 205–244. Anthropological Papers 75. University of Michigan, Museum of Anthropology, Ann Arbor.

Cowan, C. W., B. Aument, L. Klempay, and L. Piotrowsky
1981 Variation in Hopewell Settlement Patterns and Lithic Industries in the Vicinity of the Newark Earthworks: Some Preliminary Observations. Paper presented at the 26th Midwestern Archaeological Conference, Madison, Wisconsin.

Dancey, W. S.

    1988   The Community Plan of an Early Late Woodland Village in the Middle
            Scioto River Valley. *Midcontinental Journal of Archaeology* 13:223–258.

    1991   A Middle Woodland Settlement in Central Ohio: A Preliminary Report on
            the Murphy Site (33LI212). *Pennsylvania Archaeologist* 61:37–72.

Fenneman, N. M.

    1938   *Physiography of the Eastern United States.* McGraw-Hill, New York.

Flannery, K. V.

    1973   The Origins of Agriculture. *Annual Review of Anthropology* 2:271–310.

Hart, J. P.

    1992   *Storage and Monongahela Subsistence-Settlement Change.* Paper presented
            at the Eastern States Archaeological Federation Annual Meeting, Pittsburgh.

Justice, N. D.

    1987   *Stone Age Spear and Arrow Points of the Midcontinental and Eastern United
            States.* Indiana University Press, Bloomington.

Kozarek, S. E.

    1987   *A Hopewellian Homestead in the Ohio River Valley.* Unpublished master's
            thesis, Department of Anthropology, University of Cincinnati.

Kramer, L. G.

    1951   Ohio Ceremonial Spears. *Ohio Archaeologist* 1(3):7–16.

Norris, R., and S. Skinner

    1988   *Phase II Addendum and Phase III Eligibility Assessment for the Parkersburg-
            Hopetown Section of the AT&T Fiber Optics Cable.* Archaeological Services
            Consultants, Columbus, Ohio. Report to Bucher, Willis and Ratliff,
            Chillicothe, Ohio.

Pacheco, P. J.

    1988   Ohio Middle Woodland Settlement Variability in the Upper Licking River
            Drainage. *Journal of the Steward Anthropological Society* 18:87–117.

Paschall, A. H., et al.

    1938   *Soil Survey of Vinton County, Ohio.* Bureau of Chemistry and Soils, Series
            1933, No. 21. United States Department of Agriculture, Washington, D.C.

Pierce, L. T.

    1959   Climate of Ohio. United States Department of Commerce, Weather Bu-
            reau, *Climatography of Ohio* Nos. 60–33, pp. 1–19.

Pi-Sunyer, O.

    1965   The Flint Industry. In *The McGraw Site: A Study in Hopewellian Dynamics,*
            edited by O. H. Prufer, pp. 60–89. Scientific Publications, n.s. 4(1). Cleve-
            land Museum of Natural History.

Prufer, O. H.

    1964   The Hopewell Complex of Ohio. In *Hopewellian Studies,* edited by Joseph

R. Caldwell and Robert L. Hall, pp. 35–84. Scientific Papers 12. Illinois State Museum, Springfield.

1965   *The McGraw Site: A Study in Hopewellian Dynamics.* Scientific Publications, n.s. 4(1). Cleveland Museum of Natural History.

1967   The Scioto Valley Archaeological Survey. In *Studies in Ohio Archaeology,* edited by O. H. Prufer and D. H. McKenzie, pp. 267–328. Western Reserve University Press, Cleveland.

1968   *Ohio Hopewell Ceramics: An Analysis of the Extant Collections.* Anthropological Papers 33. Museum of Anthropology, University of Michigan, Ann Arbor.

Rafferty, J. E.

1985   The Archaeological Record of Sedentariness: Recognition, Development and Implications. In *Advances in Archaeological Method and Theory, Vol. 8,* edited by M. B. Schiffer, pp. 113–156. Academic Press, New York.

Rindos, D.

1984   *The Origins of Agriculture: An Evolutionary Perspective.* Academic Press, New York.

Seeman, M. F., and F. Soday

1980   The Russell Brown Mounds: Three Hopewell Mounds in Ross County, Ohio. *Midcontinental Journal of Archaeology* 5:73–116.

Smith, B. D.

1985   *Chenopodium Berlandieri* ssp *Jonesianum:* Evidence for Hopewellian Domesticate from Ash Cave, Ohio. *Southeastern Archaeology* 4(2):107–133.

1992   Hopewellian Farmers of Eastern North America. In *Rivers of Change: Essays on Early Agriculture in Eastern North America,* edited by B. D. Smith, pp. 201–248. Smithsonian Institution Press, Washington, D.C.

Steyermark, J. A.

1963   *Flora of Missouri.* Iowa State University Press, Iowa City.

Stout, W., and R. A. Schoenlaub

1947   *The Occurrence of Flint in Ohio.* Bulletin 46. Ohio Department of Natural Resources, Division of Geological Survey, Columbus.

Stuiver, M., and B. Becker

1986   *Radiocarbon* 28:86–90.

Yerkes, R. W.

1990   Using Microwear Analysis to Investigate Domestic Activities and Craft Specialization at the Murphy Site, a Small Hopewell Settlement in Licking County, Ohio. In *The Interpretive Possibilities of Microwear Studies,* edited by B. Graslund, H. Knutson, K. Knutson, and J. Taffinder, pp. 167–177. Societas Archaeologica Upsaliensis, Department of Archaeology, Uppsala University, Uppsala, Sweden.

The Ilif Riddle Sites

Olaf H. Prufer

Because of the significance of the Riddle material to the subject of this chapter, I wish to add the following information and analytical data. There are actually two Riddle sites, Ilif Riddle 1 and Ilif Riddle 2. Both are located on terraces close to and above the meandering Salt Creek southeast of Londonderry in Ross County, Ohio. Both sites are multicomponent and have yielded Hopewellian materials. All artifact counts are based on material presently curated at Kent State University. I repeatedly surveyed these localities between 1964 and 1972, as did Orrin C. Shane in 1968. In 1964 I excavated a small pitlike feature at Ilif Riddle 1, and in 1967 Robert Riddle, a kinsman of the owner, opened seven contiguous 5 x 5 ft squares at the same locality. The only published information on these sites is a passing reference in Smith (1985:112). The following is a brief account of what was found at these sites.

Ilif Riddle 1

The Hopewellian component is embedded in a large, very productive, essentially Archaic occupation. Except for a triangular point, there is no post-Hopewellian material. The densely artifact-strewn center of the Hopewellian area measures some 10 x 10 m. Beyond that, the Hopewell scatter encompasses an area of circa 50 x 50 m. My own and Riddle's tests revealed the presence, beneath the thick plowzone, of a combined total of eight decapitated, poorly delineated, shallow, circular features arranged in no discernible pattern. One of these appears to have been a small postmold; none exceeds 36 cm in diameter, and only one reaches a depth of 42 cm. They contained ashy-sandy fill. A few Hopewellian bladelets and McGraw sherdlets in some of these features demonstrate their cultural affiliation. Their function is uncertain. Surface and plowzone finds in the well-defined center of the site include Hopewellian lithic artifacts, Middle Woodland ceramics, mica, and numerous (presumably associated) fire-cracked rocks. The following are some relevant details.

Bladelets: The site produced 340, mostly fragmentary, bladelets. In the present sample, all but twenty-seven bladelets are made of Flint Ridge chalcedony; twenty-five fall within the range of Upper Mercer flint, and two specimens seem to be made of Wyandotte chert. All are uniformly small, narrow, and almost dainty. Virtually none exhibits deliberate retouch. Thirty-one specimens had been accidentally exposed to fire. There are no typical Hopewellian blade cores in the assemblage. Note that at McGraw (Pi-Sunyer 1965) and Brown's Bottom (Blank 1965) sites, which also yielded large bladelet assemblages, bladelet cores are, if not absent, at least very uncommon. The bladelet/core ratios for these sites are McGraw 233/4 and Brown's Bottom 153/1.

Projectile points: Among the numerous specimens found, I would accept seven to fall within the range of Middle Woodland types. They are akin to the Snyders-related and other corner-notched and expanded-base varieties. For what it is worth, among the large amounts of debitage from this multicomponent site, I would guess that at most 1 percent consists of Flint Ridge chalcedony.

Ceramics: The site yielded 325 plain and cord-marked sherds, including two small rims. All but one sand-tempered fragment are grit-tempered, and most are quite small and badly eroded. About 25 percent are McGraw Cordmarked and 75 percent McGraw Plain, although their eroded condition and small size leave much room for error.

All in all, the Ilif Riddle 1 site is very similar to the Brown's Bottom site in the Scioto Valley described by Blank (1965). In my view it fits the pattern of a Hopewellian hamlet or farmstead.

Minimal faunal remains from features included small bone fragments of turtle and deer, as well as riverine pelecypods. No attempts were made to recover botanical specimens.

Ilif Riddle 2

This is a small multicomponent site. The Hopewellian material consists of a thin, dispersed scatter of material embedded in a Late Archaic context. The total dimensions of the site do not exceed 75 x 75 m. The definable Hopewell component consists of seven Hopewell bladelets, including one burnt specimen, one exhausted blade core, and one typical Middle Woodland expanded-base point, all made of Flint Ridge chalcedony. In addition, one grit-tempered McGraw Plain sherd was found. Being less productive than the Ilif Riddle 1 site, this locality was not as extensively surveyed as the former. It is my impression that, on the basis of present evidence, this site should not be ranked as a small hamlet or farmstead.

CHAPTER FOURTEEN

Living on the Edge

A Comparison of Adena and Hopewell Communities in the Central Muskingum Valley of Eastern Ohio

Jeff Carskadden and James Morton

ABSTRACT

Information from recent survey work in the central Muskingum Valley of eastern Ohio suggests that certain elements of the local Hopewellian settlement pattern, particularly dispersed clusters of river-bottom hamlets, can be found rooted in the preceding local Adena communities. There was no major shift of peoples from the hinterlands to the river valleys from early Adena to Hopewell; the economies of early and late Adena populations were already focused on the river bottoms. Most of the riverine hamlet clusters or communities appear to have been continuously occupied from early Adena into Hopewell times. Hinterland Adena communities have been documented as well within the survey area, and they also appear to have been continuously occupied into Hopewell times. Ceramics and lithic artifacts, coupled with an array of radiocarbon dates, suggest that some of these local communities, both river bottom and hinterland, maintained an Adena "flavor" well into the first century A.D. The ritual/mortuary focus of both the Adena and Hopewell residents of these communities were nearby mounds, sometimes accompanied by a circular earthwork.

From 1971 through 1991 the authors undertook a survey of prehistoric sites in Muskingum County, eastern Ohio. Muskingum County is the third largest county in the state, covering an area of approximately 1,717 km². The area encompassed by the county boundaries includes portions or all of several natural physiographic areas, including 67 km of bottoms along the central Muskingum River Valley and another 26 km of bottoms along the lower Licking River, a major tributary of the Muskingum, and all or portions of several lesser drainage basins and hinterland areas extending for as much as 24 km on each side of the Muskingum River. Prominent dividing ridges between tributary drainage basins and other interesting topographical features can be found in the survey area, including the eastern portion of the well-known Flint Ridge (Vanport) flint deposits. Muskingum County also lies on the periphery of the "Licking Polity" (Pacheco 1992a), an area intensively occupied by Adena and Hopewell populations centering on the Newark earthwork, the largest Hopewellian earthwork complex in the state.

During this twenty-year period, a total of 866 prehistoric sites was recorded or verified. This figure includes 684 open sites, 28 rockshelters, 3 clusters of flint quarry pits, 1 petroglyph, 135 mounds, and 15 earthworks. A total of 181 of the open sites (26 percent) and 7 of the shelters (25 percent) contain Adena and/ or Hopewell components, which are the topic of this chapter. In addition, most of the mounds (116) and earthworks (11) probably fall within the period under study (Fig. 14.1), and their relationships to the nonmound sites will also be discussed. The remaining mounds and earthworks are early Late Woodland.

Information on Adena and Hopewell site distribution gleaned from the Muskingum County survey will be compared with similar surveys of Woodland period sites recently conducted in the upper Licking River and Jonathan Creek Valleys of neighboring Licking and Perry Counties (Bowen 1990; Pacheco 1988, 1992a, n.d.) and elsewhere in eastern and southeastern Ohio, particularly the Hocking Valley (Black 1979; Skinner and Norris 1982; Abrams 1989, 1992b) and generally the central and upper Ohio Valley (Fischer 1974; Maslowski 1985; Niquette and Boedy 1986; Clay and Niquette 1989; Railey 1991). Although there do appear to be some general similarities between the local Adena and Hopewell settlement patterns and those noted in these other areas, there are some differences. While these differences may be the result of uniquely local patterns in the Muskingum Valley, such patterns may simply have gone unreported in these other areas due to a paucity of information on hinterland site distribution. We have also used a different approach to studying the data— site density per km² surveyed rather than raw numbers of sites or percentages.

We believe this presents a more accurate picture of the Adena and Hopewell settlement distribution in the area.

Natural Setting

The Muskingum River

Muskingum County lies entirely within the Muskingum River drainage basin, the largest watershed in the state. At Coshocton, the Muskingum forms at the juncture of the Tuscarawas and Walhonding Rivers. The river then follows a somewhat circuitous course southward for 178 km through four counties (Coshocton, Muskingum, Morgan, and Washington), finally entering the Ohio River at Marietta. The river cuts Muskingum County roughly in half.

Squier and Davis provide the following description of the Muskingum Valley in their *Ancient Monuments of the Mississippi Valley* (1848:77): "The valley of the Muskingum is for the most part narrow, affording few of those broad, level, and fertile terraces, which appear to have been the especial favorites of the race of moundbuilders, and upon which most of their monuments are found. As a consequence, we find few remains of magnitude in that valley." Squier and Davis are of course referring to the lack of any extensive Hope-wellian geometric earthworks along the Muskingum above Marietta like those seen along other southern Ohio rivers, and their description aptly fits the central and lower portions of the river valley. Through much of Muskingum, Morgan, and Washington Counties the river bottoms rarely reach more than .8 km in width, with steep hills and occasionally cliffs bordering the bottoms along much of the river's course. At some locations the hills rise abruptly from the riverbank to elevations as high as 90 m above the valley floor.

Squier and Davis apparently never saw the Muskingum above Dresden in northern Muskingum and southern Coshocton Counties. Here the river follows the abandoned channel of the pre-lllinoisan Deep Stage Newark River, and the bottoms can reach as much as 3.2 km in width. It is probably not a coincidence that the greatest concentration of Hopewell habitation sites along the Muskingum River north of Marietta can be found along this portion of river bottoms, as well as two possibly early Hopewellian circular earthworks (Fig. 14.2). These bottoms are still much narrower than the 5 to 7 km wide bottoms in the vicinity of Hopewell centers along the Scioto River in southern Ohio. Various researchers have pointed out the correlation between wide bottoms and the occurrence of Hopewellian earthwork/mound complexes along the Scioto (Seeman 1979) and elsewhere (Struever 1964).

The Licking River

The Licking River, the largest tributary of the Muskingum below Coshocton, is an Illinoisan outwash stream that flows from the confluence of the North and South forks at Newark in Licking County 47 km in an easterly and southeasterly direction to Zanesville, where it enters the Muskingum River. The bottoms along the lower 16 km of the Licking from Zanesville to Irville are quite constricted, averaging less than .6 km in width. From Irville to the Licking County line, however, the bottoms widen to more than 1.6 km in width. This is especially true where presently underfed valleys of pre-lllinoisan streams, once northwestward flowing tributaries to the Deep Stage Newark River, intersect the present valley of the Licking. The Licking River is especially significant to this present study for several reasons, not the least of which are the presence of Flint Ridge quarry pits less than 4 km from the river and of the Hopewellian Newark earthworks complex at the head of the valley, 21 km upriver from the Muskingum-Licking county line.

Hinterlands

Although Muskingum County lies for the most part within the Unglaciated Allegheny Plateau physiographic province, the diversity of topography, soils, and vegetation, resulting in part from Pleistocene drainage reversals and stream capture, provides a high degree of ecological variability within the survey area. The topography of the hinterland portions of the county ranges from low, well-rounded hills and wide, gently sloping, underfed, basinlike valleys to rugged, narrow ridges and V-shaped gorges. The lesser-order stream valleys (Fischer's [1974] "hinterland aquatic habitat"), with occasional stretches of bottomland and low terraces, as well as the bordering uplands, provided a number of seasonal resources that might have attracted Woodland populations. Although there were some prairielike openings along the Muskingum River and elsewhere, vegetation over most of the county at the time of the first township/range surveys (ca. 1803; Gordon 1966) consisted primarily of a closed deciduous forest.

Two hinterland areas of the county are of special interest to any study of Adena and Hopewell—the Jonathan Creek Valley and the Rix Mills divide.

The valleys of Jonathan Creek and its tributaries in the southwestern part of the county may have been an area in which flint was a special attraction. Kent Run, a tributary of Jonathan Creek, drains a 57 km² area starting at the southern flank of Flint Ridge. The headwaters area of Jonathan Creek proper in Licking and Perry Counties contain a high density of mounds, enclosures, and other pre-historic sites (Bowen 1990; Pacheco n.d.), and this area of intense Adena and Hopewell activity spills over into southwestern Muskingum County along the lower reaches of Jonathan Creek and even further east into the Brush Creek Valley. The increased density of mounds in this area can be plainly seen in Fig. 14.1. In addition to the proximity of Flint Ridge, numerous small rockshelters, formed in Maxville limestone, can also be found along the Jonathan Creek tributaries that flow south from the Ridge. At least four of these shelters are noted for having Hopewell material (Pickenpaugh 1974; Felumlee 1983).

The Salt Creek/Wills Creek drainage divide (known locally as the Rix Mills divide) is a particularly interesting area in terms of Adena and Hopewell settle-ments, especially since at first glance there is no obvious reason for the high density of sites that occur along this divide. There are no flint deposits, for example, although the divide does roughly mark the boundary between two major forest zones (mixed oak and mixed mesophytic [Gordon 1966]) and could have served as an easement into a wide range of drainages and ecological zones. This narrow, moderately steep ridge line, which averages 1,100–1,200 ft in elevation (335–365 m amsl), runs for about 16 km along the Muskingum-Guernsey county line. Although the Muskingum River lies only 10 km to the west, the elevation at the mouth of the Salt Creek at Duncan Falls is only 684 ft (208 m amsl), or 602 ft (183 m) below the summit of Gibeaut Hill, the highest point on the divide. The streams that drain the western flanks of the Rix Mills dividing ridge drop more than 300 ft in just the first mile (91 m/1.6 km). Jeff Brown's survey work (1985) along this dividing ridge found evidence of paleoindian through Late Prehistoric occupation, with a site density of almost ten sites per linear km surveyed along the crest of this ridge. A concentration of Adena and Hopewell sites along one particular area of the ridge is discussed later in this paper.

The Site Survey

In the early 1970s when we began our survey, only 21 percent of the total area of Muskingum County was in what is known as "harvested cropland"—that is, plowed fields (360 km²). The rest of the county consisted of pasture (26 percent), forests (35 percent), surface mines (10 percent), urban areas and miscellaneous (8 percent). During the course of this twenty-year project, all of the cultivated bottomland along the major rivers in the county were surveyed (Muskingum, Licking, and Wills Creek—39.7 km²), and an additional 5.3 km² in the Dillon Reservoir area were examined for sites during periods of low water. Of the 320 km² of cultivated area in the hinterland portions of the county, a total of 209 km² or 65 percent have been surveyed to date. This figure includes acreage personally covered by the authors as well as 23 km² in Monroe and Highland Townships surveyed by William Buker (information on file, Carnegie Museum) and another 26 km² in Union Township surveyed by Jeff Brown (1985). The amount of acreage varied with each township because of the topography and varying amounts of cultivation, although all areas of the county are represented to varying degrees. This hinterland figure, combined with the surveyed river bottoms, represents 68 percent of the total acreage available for surface survey within Muskingum County. Although this figure represents only 14 percent of the total area of the county, much of the remaining 86 percent consists of uninhabitable slope land. Not included in the above figures are the numerous wooded or otherwise uncultivated ridges and hilltops that were examined for mounds.

In addition to the mounds and earthworks shown in Fig. 14.1, a total of 126 Adena nonmound sites have been identified in Muskingum County. Fifteen of these sites had to be omitted from this present study because we could not determine if they were early or late Adena. These sites, seven of which were simply point find spots, were characterized by a generalized stemmed point that typologically did not fit neatly into any of the previously defined early or late Adena point styles. Considering that some of the remaining 111 Adena sites had both early as well as late Adena occupations, a total of 136 individual Adena components are available for study in the survey area. A total of 102 Hopewellian nonmound components were also found, although this represents only an additional 55 sites, since 47 also had Adena components.

Hopewell Occupation

According to current conventional wisdom, Adena and Hopewell are simply stages in a continuous developmental sequence (Greber 1991), and there are obviously sites in the survey area that span the "transitional" period between what would be called late Adena and classic Hopewell. These sites produced projectile points that appear intermediate between the late Adena Robbins type and the later Hopewellian corner-notched forms, as well as plain-surfaced pottery with characteristics of Adena Plain and McGraw Plain/Murphy Plain. For purposes of this report, however, sites with parallel-sided bladelets and blade cores are considered Hopewell. This tool type appears rather abruptly on the scene throughout much of southern Ohio and has long been considered a horizon marker for Hopewell (Pi-Sunyer 1965; Greber et al. 1981; Pacheco and Pickard 1992).

Bladelets and other Hopewell artifacts were associated with calibrated radiocarbon dates of 105 B.C. at the Kohl Mound on the Tuscarawas River (Whitman 1977) and 92 B.C. at the Cox C site on the Muskingum (Morton and Carskadden 1987), dates that correspond nicely to the 100 B.C. date often cited as the beginning of Hopewell in southern Ohio. However, there is a confusing array of later radiocarbon dates for sites in the Muskingum Valley (mostly below Zanesville) that have late Adena traits (Robbins points, Adena Plain/McGraw Plain pottery), and lack bladelets altogether (Table 14.1). Similarly late dates have been reported from Adena sites in the Hocking Valley (Skinner and Norris 1984; Norris and Skinner 1985; Abrams 1992a), suggesting that at least in certain areas of eastern and southeastern Ohio, including portions of the Muskingum Valley, what we call "late Adena" may have lasted well into the first century A.D. Equally plausible is the imprecise nature of radiocarbon dating, although the sheer number of Adena dates falling after A.D. 1 would suggest the former idea.

We would also add that the 92 B.C. date from Cox C, while a good date for Hopewell generally, is probably too early for this particular site if one interprets this calibrated mean date literally, because the ceramic assemblage at Cox C is characterized exclusively by McGraw Cordmarked pottery. Early Hopewell sites would be expected to have at least some plain-surface pottery, as at the Hopewellian Murphy site along Raccoon Creek west of Newark where cord-marked pottery comprised only 7 percent of the ceramics. Radiocarbon dates were obtained between ca. 100 B.C. and A.D. 200. We would suggest that the calibrated date of A.D. 77 from the nearby Cox B site, associated with plain, cord-marked, as well as rocker-stamped pottery, probably comes closer to dating the beginning of the Hopewellian component of the Cox site cluster, and the beginning of cord-marked pottery in the central Muskingum Valley.

In spite of Squier and Davis's comment cited earlier, at least three possible rudimentary Hopewellian geometric earthwork complexes are known for the Muskingum Valley above Marietta. Two of these (the Dresden Circle and the Lichtenau Circle) are located in the 3.2 km wide bottoms of the upper

Muskingum between Dresden and Coshocton, and the third is located in a narrower portion of the valley at Gilbert, about midway between Dresden and Zanesville. The earthwork just above Dresden, situated near the Hopewellian Cox sites (Fig. 14.2), was a circle about 174 m in diameter, surrounding an area of a little less than 2.4 ha. The Lichtenau earthwork, located about 4 km below Coshocton, consisted of a circle of a similar size (Carskadden and Morton 1986).

Although late Adena as well as Hopewell habitation sites can be found in the immediate vicinity of both of these circles, the diameters of these earthworks are nearly 30 m larger than the largest of the known Adena "sacred circles" listed by Clay (1987:48). In fact, the known Adena circles within the survey area range in diameter from only a little over 12 m to around 40 m, the latter size being more typical of Adena circular earthworks throughout the Ohio Valley. We believe, therefore, that the Dresden and Lichtenau earthworks were probably constructed in early Hopewell times. Following Byers (1987), we would further suggest that the Dresden and Lichtenau circles, as well as the Fairgrounds Circle at Newark, are examples of local Hopewellian ceremonial centers that were developing simultaneously out of late Adena at various locations in the upper Licking and upper Muskingum Valleys.

As to why other (and presumably later) geometric earthwork forms (e.g., squares and octagons), such as those also found at Newark, are lacking at Dresden and Lichtenau is not known, although following the reasoning of Struever and Houart (1972), one could argue that the Newark earthwork expanded and became more complex because of its proximity to Flint Ridge and its possible role as a "regional transaction center," channeling Flint Ridge flint into the Hopewell Interaction Sphere. For whatever reason, the populations in these local Hopewellian communities along the Muskingum appear to have been small, and there simply may not have been the work force or inclination to construct large earthworks. Other small Hopewellian communities in the survey area lacked earthworks altogether, although in several cases Hopewell mounds have been identified nearby. To what degree Newark became the focal point of ritual and ceremonial life in the upper Muskingum area is not known, although the ceramic assemblage at Cox C and at other Hopewell sites in the Dresden area (i.e., cord-marked pottery), suggests that some Hopewell hamlets near the Dresden Circle were still inhabited fairly late (post ca. A.D. 200), and presumably the ritual space within the circle continued to be utilized.

The other possible candidate for a Hopewellian earthwork complex along the Muskingum River in the survey area is the set of parallel walls and the D-shaped enclosure on the T-4 terrace at Gilbert, 16 km north of Zanesville

(Carskadden and Morton 1986). The parallel walls were reportedly "several feet" high, over 300 m long, and about 30 m apart, and are reminiscent of various "sacred ways" at other Hopewell geometric earthwork complexes (including Newark). The enclosure was situated near one end of the parallel walls. These earthworks have been destroyed by cultivation and no further information is available, other than the fact that at least two Hopewell habitation sites were situated on the floodplain and T-1 terrace below the D-shaped enclosure. Just where these earthworks fit into the above scenario is not known.

By the beginning of the early Late Woodland period in the central Muskingum Valley (ca. A.D. 400), local mortuary centers in the form of ridgetop mound groups (two to five mounds) were springing up all along the Muskingum. In Muskingum County these included the Philo Mound Group, Henderson Mounds, and Krebbs/Little Group (Carskadden and Morton 1989, n.d.; Carskadden and Edmister 1992). Single ridgetop mounds such as the Black Dog Mound are also known to occur, although these are usually in the vicinity of the mound groups. The regional trend toward nucleated villages in this period (Dancey 1992) can also be seen in the Muskingum Valley. While ceremonial earthworks were no longer constructed, the mound groups are often associated with typical earth-walled villages. (Carskadden and Morton n.d.). Not only the relatively large number of mounds within these groups, but also changing modes of burial and mound construction, suggest long-term usage of some of these centers, possibly going back into late Hopewell times (e.g., Philo Mound Group).

About the only vestiges of the now mostly defunct Hopewellian Interaction Sphere, however, are a few mica sheets (found in four out of nine of these late mounds excavated by the authors). In fact, it was the presence of mica at the Philo Mound Group that led the original investigators to suggest that these mounds were Hopewell (Foraker 1975; Morton 1977). Mica was a rather ubiquitous trade item on Hopewell sites throughout southern Ohio, and Greber and Ruhl (1989) have suggested that mica, along with copper, was probably the earliest exotic material in Hopewell. We would add that evidence from the various early Late Woodland mounds along the Muskingum suggest that mica may have also been the last exotic material available, at least in eastern Ohio. It is also interesting to note that the mica sheets found in what we believe to be the latest of these early Late Woodland mounds (Black Dog and Henderson 2) are much smaller and thinner than those found in the earliest of these sites (Philo Mound Group). It is almost as if whoever was responsible for curating this item (the "Keepers of the Mica") were doling out smaller and thinner pieces as this material became harder and harder to obtain in the Muskingum Valley.

Habitations

Hopewell settlements in the upper Licking Valley–Raccoon Creek area and elsewhere in southern Ohio have been characterized generally as clusters of dispersed sedentary farmsteads or hamlets occurring in the general vicinity of earthwork complexes (e.g., Smith 1987; Pacheco 1988). Similar, if not identical, patterns of dispersed Hopewell habitation sites can be seen along the lower Licking and in the central and upper Muskingum Valley, where a number of clusters of up to six households or hamlets each are known (Figs. 14.2, 14.3, and 14.4). Isolated Hopewell hamlets occur only rarely in the survey area, and this is usually where there is a limited area exposed by plowing. Only at Dresden and presumably Gilbert (and Lichtenau in Coshocton County), however, are these hamlet clusters associated directly with an earthwork. Cox B and Cox C are the only Hopewell hamlets along the Muskingum that have been tested.

There seems to be some justification for dividing Hopewell open-air habitation sites found during the course of our survey into at least two categories, which we have designated "long-term" and "short-term" habitations. The so-called long-term sites, which from all indications fit the definition of farming hamlets set forth by Pacheco (1988), are often characterized by hundreds of bladelets, dozens of projectile points, and an abundance of lithic debris, whereas short-term localities are characterized by two or three bladelets, one or two projectile points, and a smattering of chippage. Pottery sherds and pit features are usually, but not always, restricted to the long-term sites; single pit features have been plowed out at several of these short-term sites. Although some of the short-term localities might be "upgraded" to long-term with additional surface survey or excavations, we feel that the designations we have made are, for the most part, fairly accurate.

Pacheco (1992a) has also identified these smaller Hopewell sites in the Newark area, which he designates as "small artifact clusters." His small clusters average .14 ha in size and have artifact densities of $<.2$ per m^2, whereas the hamlets average .45 ha and have artifact densities $>.2$ per m^2. Pacheco also suggests that these small, or low-density, clusters are short-duration specialized camps or activity areas.

Fifty-six percent of these short-term sites found in our survey occur in the bottomlands of the Muskingum or Licking River Valleys, usually in the general vicinity of the hamlet clusters. The remaining 43 percent, however, occur in the hinterlands, mostly in the valleys of small streams (Table 14.2). This contrasts with the occurrence of only 20 percent of the long-term hamlets in the hinterlands and suggests perhaps that residents of the river-bottom hamlets may have been making seasonal forays into these small valleys. None of these sites has been excavated, and we hesitate to guess their function.

The "Workshop" Problem

There may also be a third type of Hopewell site in the study area represented by the so-called ridgetop "workshops" located mostly in the Jonathan Creek drainage south of Flint Ridge. These workshop sites are generally characterized by their close proximity to the flint quarries (although some are at least 6 km away) and by the abundance of lithic debris, particularly bladelet cores and triangular bifaces or "blanks" in various stages of manufacture. These sites are presumed, for the most part, to lack pit features, since few have been plowed out or discovered by excavation on these localities. At the Dodson "Village" near Flint Ridge State Park, for example, a site long regarded by old-time artifact collectors as the most prolific Hopewell site in the Ridge area, excavations in 1932 revealed only two "fire pots" or cooking features, a smattering of animal bone, and some pot sherds. After a recent analysis of this material, Murphy and Morton (1984:24) concluded that the site "represents very short term occupations over a long period of time by comparatively small groups of people intent upon procuring Flint Ridge flint." Bernhardt (1976:45) has also suggested that these sites represent specialized briefly occupied lithic processing camps, arguing that the poor soil conditions on the Ridge would have prohibited the "growing of crops," although he was writing at a time when maize agriculture was thought to be the mainstay of the Hopewell economy. He also points out that earlier investigators on the Ridge, such as William C. Mills, came to the same conclusion, namely that "the ridge was not permanently settled but rather was the scene of cyclical forays to select quarry and workshop sites by parties of laborers who transferred the raw materials and finished products to their settlements in the valley and later into the interaction network."

The recent excavations at the Murphy sites have also produced as much in the way of lithic debris as many of the so-called workshop sites on the ridge (Dancey 1991; Pacheco 1992a), which suggests that the abundance of such debris does not preclude a site being a farming hamlet. The accumulation of a large quantity of lithic debris may simply be the result of a long duration of occupation. Pacheco has also characterized the high density of Hopewell sites, traditionally considered workshop sites, in the upper Jonathan Creek drainage just west of this present survey (.44 sites per km²), coupled with a number of known or possible Hopewellian mounds and earthworks, as evidence of "intense occupation by a substantial permanent population" (Pacheco n.d.:21). However, the question as to whether these sites are temporary flint procurement camps, specialized craft centers, or permanent farming hamlets (or a combination) will remain unresolved until these sites are examined systematically. There are, however, ridgetop Hopewell sites elsewhere in Muskingum County, distant from any flint outcrops, that appear to fit the definition of hamlets. These are discussed below.

Adena Antecedents and Settlement Continuity

To better understand the dynamics of Hopewellian communities in the central Muskingum Valley, we must take a brief look at local Adena. Previous studies of Adena and Hopewell settlement patterns in the lower Scioto Valley (Shane 1971), Hocking Valley (Black 1979), and the southern Ohio area in general (Fischer 1974) suggest the following scenario: early Adena sites were located in diverse topographic settings due to seasonal movement from one primary resource zone to another. These settings included not only river bottoms but also hilltops and small stream valleys often many miles from major rivers. A shift is seen in late Adena toward greater use of river bottoms, and Hopewell sites tended to be located primarily in the bottoms of the major rivers. This shift from uplands to bottomlands is thought to be the result of a shift from a generalized subsistence strategy toward an increased dependence on a variety of bottomland resources (Ford 1979; Smith 1987; Wymer 1987). These would include riverine fauna, supplemented by the exploitation of cultigens in and around bottomland clearings (natural or artificial).

Although a study of the Hocking Valley found late Adena sites evenly distributed between river bottomlands and hinterlands (Skinner and Norris 1982), the most recent work suggests that most of the latest of the late Adena sites in the Hocking drainage (dating after A.D. 1) will be found in the bottoms of the Hocking River proper (Abrams 1992b). All of these researchers have commented, however, on the lack of comparative information from hinterland areas. Evidence from the Muskingum County survey, where 209 km² of hinterland have been surveyed, indicates that during all three periods (early Adena, late Adena, and Hopewell) the bottoms of the Muskingum and Licking Rivers were exploited to a much greater degree than the hinterlands, if site density is any indication. In comparing the density of all types of open sites per km² surveyed along the riverbottoms to the density of sites in the surveyed hinterland areas (Table 14.3), we find that the density of river bottom sites is 5.9 times greater than the average hinterland density for early Adena sites, more than 4.8 times for late Adena, and 6.3 times for Hopewell. In looking just at hamlets (not findspots, workshops, or short-term habitations), we find an even greater disparity: 6.6 times for early Adena, 6.3 times for late Adena, and 18.3 times for Hopewell, although when the so-called workshop sites are included, the ratio of river-bottom to hinterland Hopewell sites drops back to 8.6.

We suspect that the disparity between the density of river-bottom sites versus hinterland sites is even greater than the figures indicate, considering that the Adena and Hopewell sites found on the terraces and in the floodplains may represent but a few of the sites that were actually once situated in these low-lying localities (Table 14.4). Excavations undertaken by the authors at a number of localities along the Muskingum River have revealed evidence of extensive silting, including as much as 1.5 m of flood-deposited sand and silt over a recently excavated protohistoric site. Although to date no deeply buried Adena or Hopewell sites have been found along the Muskingum or Licking Rivers within the survey area, undoubtedly such sites exist, especially considering that late Adena and Hopewell may have "farmed" these floodplain localities. There are also probably a number of Woodland period sites along the lower Licking that are permanently underwater behind Dillon Dam.

Early and late Adena sites have their greatest density along the Muskingum River, whereas the greatest density of Hopewell sites can be found along the Licking, possibly due to the proximity of Flint Ridge and the Newark earthworks. In fact, there may have been a slight depopulation of the Muskingum River bottoms in favor of the Licking Valley if one considers the density of hamlet localities (Table 14.5), and it appears that at least one new Hopewellian community was established along the Licking (Table 14.6).

The dispersed nature of Adena habitation sites (hamlets) has long been recognized. In the 1940s, for example, Webb (1942:363) observed that "individual house groups perhaps were several hundred feet apart, each group a small unit in itself, yet scores of such house groups might have been within an area of a few square miles."

This pattern is dramatically apparent for the late Adena sites near Dresden (Fig. 14.2) and at other locations along the Muskingum, although it also holds true for early Adena in the area as well. Abrams (1989, 1992b) has recently described the Adena occupation along Sunday Creek, a tributary of the Hocking River near Athens, as consisting of dispersed clusters of one or two mounds associated with two or more habitation sites. In Muskingum County, at locations where large enough contiguous areas have been cultivated, these Adena site clusters can consist of as many as six to eight households/hamlets. At Philo, six late Adena hamlets have been located in the river bottoms below a single ridgetop burial mound (Fig. 14.3), although it is not known how many, if any, of these hamlets may have been contemporaneous. The mounds are usually situated on ridgetops or high terraces overlooking the habitations (Table 14.4) and are thought to have been constructed in these prominent locations to serve as territorial boundary markers or "territorial displays," visible from the valley floor for all to see (Charles and Buikstra 1983; Clay 1992; Pacheco 1992b). The idea that mounds could have served as territorial displays may be demonstrated in the distribution of mounds around one of the Adena-Hopewell hamlet clusters on the Rix Mills divide (Fig. 14.4). It can be seen in the figure that the outlying mounds appear to have been placed along various approaches to the hamlets.

It is apparent from the examples that the local Hopewell settlements take on the same dispersed pattern as seen in earlier Adena. We believe that this pattern seen in Hopewell was simply the culmination of a long tradition of dispersed riverine hamlets, going back locally as far as early Adena. Not only does there appear to be a general continuity of settlement patterns within the river valleys of the survey area, but there also appears to be a propensity for repeatedly selecting the exact same site location, or nearly so, throughout Adena and Hopewell. Of the early Adena river-bottom habitation sites, 52 percent were reoccupied during late Adena (or were continuously occupied into late Adena). A total of 34 percent of all late Adena sites in the river bottoms were also occupied in Hopewell (about half of them long-term and half short-term). Twenty percent of the river bottom sites were occupied during all three time periods. At the very least, this continuity in site selection presumably reflects a continuity in subsistence strategies. We would suggest that these hamlet clusters represent continuously occupied communities whose individuals were tied to a particular area by lineage or descent. At least one of these communities or hamlet clusters along the lower Licking River contains only Hopewell hamlets, and we suspect that this represents an actual movement of peoples into the Licking Valley sometime after the Newark earthwork became the corporate center for the area (Table 14.6).

Adena hamlets in the survey area are more ephemeral than Hopewell hamlets; there is less in the way of diagnostic artifacts, chippage, and pottery. These characteristics of Adena habitations have been noted elsewhere in the Ohio Valley (Clay and Niquette 1989; Railey 1991). Excavated late Adena hamlets in or near the survey area (Carskadden and Gregg 1974; Bush 1975; Carskadden n.d.a), indicate that Adena hamlets covered areas ranging from .28 to .32 ha, with a scattering of postmolds, usually in no readily identifiable pattern, in the immediate vicinity of a cluster of cooking/thermal features. Although some possible storage pits and a midden were identified at one site (Duncan Falls), there is no real indication that these sites were occupied for great lengths of time. Hopewell hamlets, on the other hand, are thought to have been occupied year-round (Dancey 1991). It is not known if the internal arrangement of Adena hamlets will be similar to the redundant pattern seen in Hopewell sites such as Murphy (i.e., refuse zones, food processing zones, and structure zones); thus far they have not been, as can be seen in Fig. 14.5. The varying layouts of these sites may reflect different functions and/or seasonality.

Lacking in the central Muskingum Valley are the large (2 ha) late Adena sites that are known to occur along the Hocking River proper by the first century A.D. (Abrams 1989; 1992b). These large sites, which Abrams suggests may represent "population growth as well as hamlet unification," occur especially in the vicinity of the Plains, where a large concentration of late Adena mounds and earthworks can be found (fourteen mounds and ten earthworks). Similar concentrations of Adena mounds and earthworks are also absent in the central Muskingum Valley. Although seven Adena "sacred circles" are known for the county (Fig. 14.1), these are scattered at various distances along the Muskingum (n=5) and Licking (n=1) Rivers or in the hinterlands (n=1). This is unlike the pattern generally noted for the occurrence of these circles elsewhere in the Ohio Valley (usually clusters of two or more [Clay 1987]) and obviously contrasts with the situation in the Hocking Valley. While radiocarbon dates suggest that very late Adena in the central Muskingum Valley was contemporaneous with very late Adena in the Hocking (i.e., post A.D. 1), it is apparent that what was going on in the Hocking Valley at this time was quite different from what was occurring in the central Muskingum Valley.

Hinterland Communities

Although the focus of Adena and Hopewell settlement was the river bottoms, evidence from the Rix Mills area, as well as from the Jonathan Creek drainage, indicates that certain late Adena and Hopewell groups were still living in, or at least making use of, certain hinterland areas within the survey area. Whereas the density of early Adena hinterland sites is about the same throughout much of the county, in the Jonathan Creek drainage we already see twice the density of habitation sites (Fig. 14.6). Since little use was made of Flint Ridge flint during early Adena times, there must have been other factors that attracted early Adena populations to this area. By late Adena, the density of sites in the Jonathan Creek drainage is nearly triple that seen in other hinterland portions of the county, with the exception of the Rix Mills drainage divide, where a similar increase is beginning to occur. A similarly high density of Hopewell sites can also be found in these two hinterland areas.

Although Flint Ridge flint appears to have played a role in the Hopewell trading network, it became apparent from our survey that Flint Ridge was an important source for flint during late Adena, at least locally. Over 84 percent of the late Adena (Robbins) projectile points found throughout the survey area were fashioned from Flint Ridge flint. This contrasts with only 22 percent use of Flint Ridge in early Adena and 74 percent in Hopewell times. Apparently the channeling of Flint Ridge artifacts into the Hopewell Interaction Sphere had its beginnings in late Adena, when artifacts of this material were being channeled into the "Adena Interaction Sphere" possibly by the residents of these local hamlets in the Jonathan Creek drainage (c.f. Thomas 1970; McConaughy 1990).

Most of the ridgetop and small-stream valley hinterland habitation sites (Adena and Hopewell) in these two areas also have all the characteristics of typical bottomland hamlets, at least from surface indications, and where enough area is exposed by cultivation, these sites always occur in clusters, just like the communities in the river bottoms. Hinterland Hopewell clusters always seem to occur in the general vicinity of, if not on the exact site of, late Adena hamlet clusters (Fig. 14.4). This continuity of site selection, similar to that seen in the river-bottom communities, goes back into early Adena; 65 percent of early Adena hinterland habitation sites also had late Adena components, and 25 percent of the hinterland late Adena habitation sites also had either long-term or short-term Hopewell components (about half and half). About a fourth (23 percent) of all these hinterland sites were occupied at some point during all three periods.

While it is possible that these hinterland locations may represent special resource areas that were continually exploited on a seasonal basis throughout Adena and Hopewell by groups coming from the river bottoms, revisiting the same old clearings generation after generation, we would argue that these hinterland enclaves represent continuously occupied Adena-Hopewell communities. We would suggest that sometime toward the end of early Adena there was a "settling in" of the local populations. Whereas most of the local communities were already well established in river bottoms, there were a few groups that had become established in the hinterlands and, for whatever reason, remained there into Hopewell; there was no apparent movement of these late Adena populations from the hinterlands into the river valleys, at least such a movement does not appear in the archaeological record. In the case of the Rix Mills area, the resident Adena-Hopewell communities may have remained there into early Late Woodland. It is probably not a coincidence that a fortified (earth-walled), nucleated early Late Woodland village can be found in a stream valley just below the concentration of Adena and Hopewell sites. This is the only village of its kind not located immediately along the Muskingum River in the survey area.

The presence of numerous burial mounds in these two hinterland areas also suggests a degree of permanence (see Fig. 14.1), especially for late Adena. In addition to the twenty-seven mounds and one enclosure in the lower Jonathan Creek drainage, for example, another thirty-one mounds and five earthworks (mostly Adena) can be found in a 96 km^2 area along Jonathan Creek immediately west of the survey area (Pacheco n.d.). At least one Hopewell mound is known for the Rix Mills divide (Carskadden and Slater 1969), although none of the mounds in the immediate vicinity of the hamlet cluster shown in Fig. 14.4 has been identified as Hopewell. Another Hopewell mound is known for the lower Jonathan Creek Valley (Baby 1962), and at least one possible Hopewell earthwork has been reported in the upper Jonathan Creek drainage (Pacheco n.d.)

Summary

Information from recent survey work and excavations in the central Muskingum Valley/Muskingum County area suggests that the pattern of dispersed river-bottom Hopewell hamlet clusters can be found rooted in the preceding local Adena communities. There was no major shift of people from the hinterlands to the river bottoms from early Adena to Hopewell. If site density is any indication, the economies of early and late Adena populations were already focused on the river bottoms. Most of these riverine hamlet clusters or communities appear to have been continuously occupied from early Adena into Hopewell. Although hinterland Adena communities did occur infrequently in the survey area, the evidence indicates that these communities were also continuously occupied into Hopewell. Ceramics and lithic artifacts, coupled with an array of radiocarbon dates, suggest that some of these local communities, both river bottom and hinterland, maintained an Adena "flavor" well into the first century A.D.

The ritual and mortuary focus of both the Adena and Hopewell residents of these various communities were nearby mounds, sometimes accompanied by a circular earthwork. The earthworks are more commonly associated with the river-bottom communities, however, where there may have been larger populations and a larger work force. The relationship of these local communities to the Newark Earthwork complex at the head of the Licking Valley is not known, although there may have been a shift of focus toward Newark at some point. This may be indicated by a marked increase in the density of Hopewell hamlets along the Licking River and a corresponding decrease along the Muskingum within the survey area. On the other hand, ceramic evidence from the various Hopewell hamlets in the vicinity of the Dresden Circle suggests that the Hopewell occupation there had a long duration.

Acknowledgments

The authors would like to thank Christopher Carr, Arizona State University, and Herbert Hass, Southern Methodist University, for allowing us to include the Locust site dates in Table 14.1. Funds for these dates were provided by grants awarded to Carr by the National Science Foundation (BSN-8604544) and the Arizona State University College of Liberal Arts and Sciences Summer Research Award Program.

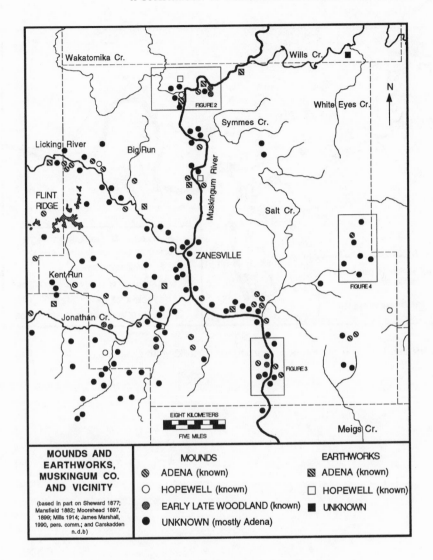

14.1 Mounds and earthworks in Muskingum County and vicinity.

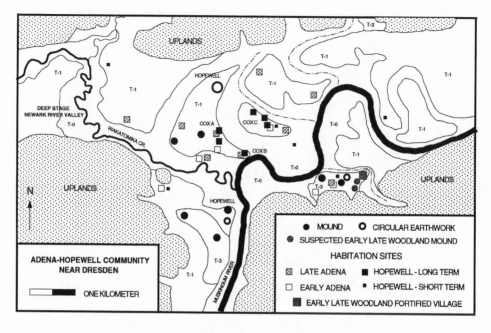

14.2 Adena and Hopewell communities near Dresden, Muskingum County.

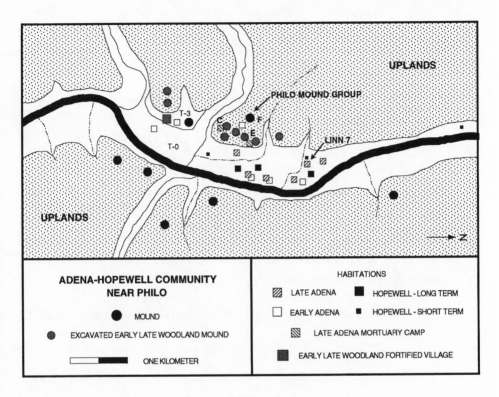

14.3 Adena and Hopewell communities near Philo, Muskingum County.

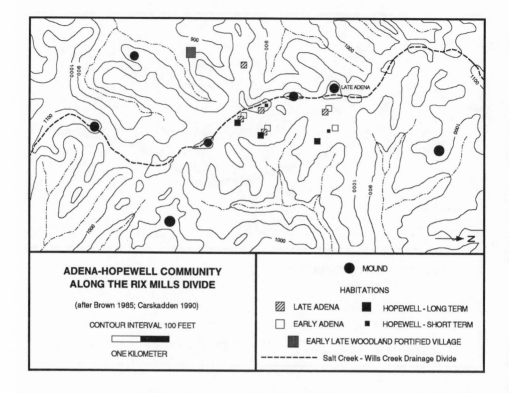

14.4 Adena and Hopewell communities along the Rix Mills divide, Muskingum County.

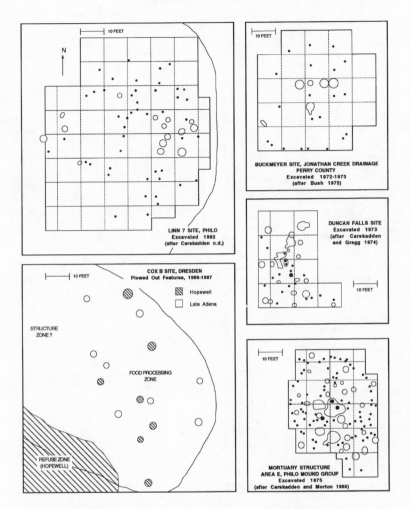

14.5 Examples of Late Adena habitations in the central Muskingum Valley.

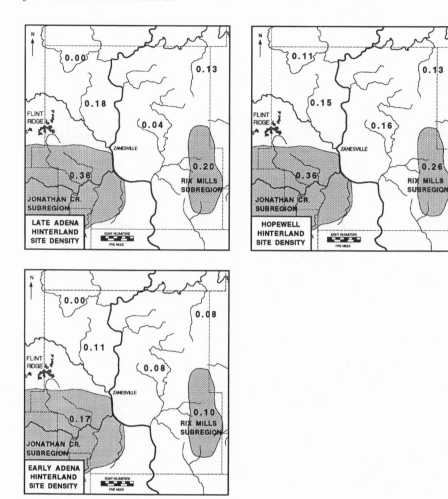

14.6 Adena and Hopewell site densities per km² of hinterlands surveyed (all open-air sites from Table 14.3).

Table 14.1
Radiocarbon Dates from Adena, Hopewell, and Early Late Woodland Sites in the Muskingum Valley

Site	Location (County)	Component	Raw Date	Corrected Date	Reference
Black Dog Mound	Muskingum	E. Late Woodland	A.D. 430±80	A.D. 548	Carskadden & Edmister 1992
Henderson Mound 2	Muskingum	E. Late Woodland	A.D. 350±80	A.D. 429	Carskadden & Edmister 1992
Philo Mound B	Muskingum	E. Late Woodland	A.D. 300±60	A.D. 405	Morton 1977
Linn 7 Site	Muskingum	Late Adena	A.D. 170±80	A.D. 239	unpublished
Locust Site	Muskingum	Late Adena/Hopewell	A.D. 151±118	A.D. 216	Carr & Haas*
Locust Site	Muskingum	Late Adena/Hopewell	A.D. 115±80	A.D. 172	Carr & Haas*
Linn 7 Site	Muskingum	Late Adena	A.D. 100±80	A.D. 134	unpublished
Miskimens Mound	Coshocton	Hopewell	A.D. 90±60	A.D. 128	Mortine & Randles 1981
Philo Mound Group Mound F,	Muskingum	Late Adena	A.D. 40±80	A.D. 82	unpublished
Cox B Site	Muskingum	Hopewell	A.D. 30±80	A.D. 77	unpublished
Locust Site	Muskingum	Late Adena/Hopewell	A.D. 20±100	A.D. 60	Carr & Haas*
Philo Mound Group Area C,	Muskingum	Late Adena	A.D. 1±80	A.D. 58	unpublished
Gerlack Mound	Morgan	Late Adena	A.D. 1±115	A.D. 58	Prufer & McKenzie 1975
Gerlack Mound	Morgan	Late Adena	B.C. 10±180	A.D. 28, 45, 51	Prufer & McKenzie 1975
Philo Mound Group Area E,	Muskingum	Late Adena	B.C. 10±180	A.D. 28, 45, 51	unpublished

Table 14.1 Cont'd.

Site	County	Culture	Date	Corrected date	Reference
Buckmeyer Site	Perry	Late Adena	B.C. 25±200	A.D. 18	Bush 1975
Nashport Mound	Muskingum	Late Adena	B.C. 80±55	B.C. 43	Greber 1977
Cox C Site	Muskingum	Hopewell	B.C. 100±80	B.C. 92	Morton & Carskadden 1987
Kohl Mound	Tuscarawas	Hopewell	B.C. 130±70	B.C. 105	Whitman 1977
Nashport Mound	Muskingum	Late Adena	B.C. 170±85	B.C. 168	Greber 1977
Area E, Philo Mound Group	Muskingum	Late Adena	B.C. 210±60	B.C. 196	Carskadden & Morton 1989
Buckmeyer Site	Perry	Late Adena	B.C. 235±200	B.C. 344, 319, 205	Bush 1975
Nashport Mound	Muskingum	Late Adena	B.C. 340±80	B.C. 391	Greber 1977
Merry's Cave	Muskingum	Early/Late Adena	B.C. 340±50	B.C. 391	unpublished
Nashport Mound	Muskingum	Late Adena	B.C. 400±115	B.C. 400	Greber 1977
Area D, Philo Mound Group	Muskingum	E. Woodland	B.C. 1040±80	B.C. 1261	Carskadden 1989

*Date provided by Christopher Carr, Arizona State University, and Herbert Haas, Southern Methodist University.
Note: Corrections based on Stuiver and Reimer 1986.

Table 14.2

Physiographic Setting for Adena and Hopewell Nonmound Sites

Site Type by Period	N	River Orientation			Hinterlands[a]	
		R-AB[b]	R-SV[c]	R-UP[d]	H-SV[e]	H-UP[f]
Hopewell (all)	102	54	2	2	29	15
Long-term open	25	20	—	—	1	4
Short-term open	30	17	—	—	11	2
Workshops	7	1	—	—	1	5
Shelters	6	—	—	1	4	1
Point find spots	34	16	2	1	12	3
Late Adena (all)	83	37	3	5	17	21
Open habitations	47	25	1	3	6	12
Workshops	2	—	—	—	—	2
Shelters	2	—	—	—	2	—
Point find spots	32	12	2	2	9	7
Early Adena (all)	53	24	2	3	12	12
Open habitations	22	17	1	3	5	7
Workshops	1	—	—	—	—	1
Shelters	2	—	—	—	1	1
Point find spots	17	7	1	—	6	3

[a]Hinterlands = more than 1.6 km (1 mile) from Muskingum or Licking Rivers
[b]R-AB = alluvial bottoms along Muskingum or Licking Rivers
[c]R-SV = small stream valley, within 1.6 km (1 mile) of Muskingum or Licking Rivers
[d]R-UP = ridgetops (uplands) immediately bordering Muskingum or Licking Rivers
[e]H-SV = hinterland small stream valleys
[f]H-UP = hinterland ridgetops (uplands)

Table 14.3
Density of Adena and Hopewell Open Site per km² Surveyed by Natural Areas

Area	km² Surveyed	Sites of All Periods	Per km²	Early Adena	Per km²	Late Adena	Per km²	Hopewell	Per km²
Big Run–Stump Run subregion	45	121	2.68	5	0.11	8	0.18	7	0.15
Jonathan Creek subregion	42	86	2.04	7	0.17	15	0.36	15	0.36
Rix Mills subregion	30	48	1.60	3	0.10	6	0.20	8	0.26
Salt Creek subregion	24	46	1.91	2	0.08	1	0.04	4	0.16
White Eyes Creek subregion	23	48	2.08	2	0.08	3	0.13	3	0.13
Wakatomika Creek subregion	9	17	1.88	0	0.00	0	0.00	1	0.11
All other hinterlands	36	87	2.41	3	0.08	3	0.08	1	0.02
TOTAL HINTERLANDS[a]	209	453	2.16	22	0.09	36	0.17	39	0.19
River Bottom Open Sites									
Muskingum River	32	131	4.09	19	0.59	29	0.90	38	1.18
Licking River	13	64	4.92	5	0.38	8	0.62	16	1.23
TOTAL RIVER BOTTOM	45	195	4.33	24	0.53	37	0.82	54	1.20

[a]Hinterland = more than 1.6 km (1 mile) from the Muskingum or Licking Rivers.

Table 14.4

Specific Locations of River-Oriented Sites

Site Type by Period	Floodplain (T-0)	Cut Terrace (T-1)	Late Wisconsinan (T-2)	Late Wisconsinan (T-3)	Illinoian (T-4)	Ridgetop
Hopewell						
Long-term open	2	14	3	1	—	—
Short-term open	1	10	5	1	—	—
Workshop	—	—	1	—	—	—
Point find spots	5	8	1	2	—	1
Late Adena						
Open habitations	4	13	4	4	—	3
Point find spots	3	4	5	—	—	2
Early Adena						
Open habitations	2	10	1	4	—	3
Point find spots	—	4	3	—	—	—
Mounds and earthworks						
Hopewell mounds	—	1	1	—	—	—
Hopewell enclosures	—	1	—	—	1	—
Adena mounds	—	—	1	1	2	12
Adena enclosures	—	2	1	1	—	2

Table 14.5

Hamlet Density per km^2 Surveyed (Includes "Workshops")

	Early Adena	Late Adena	Hopewell
Muskingum River	0.47	0.59	0.34
Licking River	0.15	0.46	0.77
Both rivers	0.38	0.55	0.46
Jonathan Creek	0.07	0.19	0.19
Rix Mills	0.13	0.16	0.10
All hinterlands	0.06	0.09	0.05

Table 14.6

Number of Individual Hamlets/Households for Selected Adena-Hopewell Communities (Includes "Workshops")

	Early Adena	Late Adena	Hopewell
Dresden (Fig. 2)[a]	4	8	6
Philo (Fig. 3)[a]	6	6	3
Rix Mills (Fig. 4)[a]	4	5	3
New Nashport (Licking Valley)[a]	—	1	6
Kent Run (Jonathan Creek)[b]	—	3	6[b]

[a]Indicates enough cultivated area for complete coverage
[b]Includes one site in Perry County

References

Abrams, E. M.

    1989   Early Woodland Settlement Patterns in the Hocking River Valley, South-eastern Ohio. Paper presented at the 54th Annual Meeting of the Society for American Archaeology, Atlanta.

    1992a Archaeological Investigation of the Armitage Mound (33-At-434), The Plains, Ohio. *Midcontinental Journal of Archaeology* 17:80–110.

    1992b Woodland Settlement Patterns in the Southern Hocking River Valley, South-eastern Ohio. In *Cultural Variability in Context: Woodland Settlements of the Mid-Ohio Valley,* edited by M. F. Seeman, pp. 19–23. Special Paper No. 7, Midcontinental Journal of Archaeology. Kent State University Press, Kent, Ohio.

Baby, R. S.

    1962   Prehistoric Hand Prints. *Echoes* 1(2):1. The Ohio Historical Society, Columbus.

Bernhardt, J. E.

    1976   A Preliminary Report of Middle Woodland Prehistory in Licking County, Ohio. *Pennsylvania Archaeologist* 46:39–54.

Black, D. B.

    1979   Adena and Hopewell Relations in the Lower Hocking Valley. In *Hopewell Archaeology, the Chillicothe Conference,* edited by D. S. Brose and N. Greber, pp. 19–26. Kent State University Press, Kent, Ohio.

Bowen, J. E.

    1990   Hopewell Middle Woodland Components in the Western Flint Ridge Area, Ohio. Paper presented at the 35th Midwest Archaeological Conference, Evanston, Illinois.

Brown, J. D.

    1982   *Archaeological Reconnaissance of Corps of Engineers Dams in the Muskingum River Basin.* Report prepared for the Huntington District Corps of Engineers in fulfillment of contract DACW69-82-C-0006.

    1985   *Archaeological Sites and Surface Mining in Southeast Ohio.* Ms. on file, Ohio Historic Preservation Office, Ohio Historical Society, Columbus.

Bush, D. E.

    1975   A Ceramic Analysis of the Late Adena Buckmeyer Site, Perry County, Ohio. *The Michigan Archaeologist* 21(1):9–23.

Byers, A. M.

    1987   *The Earthwork Enclosures of the Central Ohio Valley: A Temporal and Structural Analysis of Woodland Society and Culture.* Unpublished Ph.D. dissertation, Department of Anthropology, State University of New York, Albany.

Carskadden, J.

1989   Excavation of Mound D at the Philo Mound Group, Muskingum County, Ohio. *Ohio Archaeologist* 39(1):4–8.

1990   Bradley Atchinson and the High Hill Mounds. *Ohio Archaeologist* 40(1): 4–7.

n.d.a   Excavation of Linn 7: A Late Adena Habitation Site in Muskingum County, Ohio. Ms. on file, Muskingum Valley Archaeological Survey, Zanesville.

n.d.b   A Catalogue of Prehistoric Works in Muskingum County, Ohio. Ms. on file, Muskingum Valley Archaeological Survey, Zanesville.

Carskadden, J., and L. Edmister

1992   Excavation of Henderson Mound 1, Muskingum County, Ohio. *Ohio Archaeologist* 42(1):6–9.

Carskadden, J., and T. Gregg

1974   Excavation of an Adena Open Site, Duncan Falls, Ohio. *Ohio Archaeologist* 24(2):4–7.

Carskadden, J., and J. Morton

1983   A Hopewell Mound, Dresden, Ohio. *Ohio Archaeologist* 33(1):44–47.

1986   "Sacred Circles" Along the Muskingum: A Preliminary Survey. *Ohio Archaeologist* 36(4):4–8.

1989   Excavations of Mound E at the Philo Mound Group, Muskingum County, Ohio. *West Virginia Archaeologist* 41(1):42–53.

n.d.   Early Late Woodland Mound Building and other Activities in the Muskingum Valley of Eastern Ohio. Ms. on file, Muskingum Valley Archaeological Survey, Zanesville.

Carskadden, J., and L. Slater

1969   The Brown Mound—A Hopewellian Site in Muskingum County, Ohio. *Ohio Archaeologist* 19(4):119–120.

Charles, D. K., and J. E. Buikstra

1983   Archaic Mortuary Sites in the Central Mississippi Drainage: Distribution, Structure, and Behavioral Implications. In *Archaic Hunters and Gatherers in the American Midwest,* edited by J. L. Phillips and J. A. Brown, pp. 117–145. Academic Press, New York.

Clay, R. B.

1987   Circles and Ovals: Two Types of Adena Space. *Southeastern Archaeology* 6:46–56.

1992   Chiefs, Big Men, or What? Economy, Settlement Patterns, and Their Bearing on Adena Political Models. In *Cultural Variability in Context: Woodland Settlements of the Mid-Ohio Valley,* edited by M. F. Seeman, pp. 77–80. Special Paper No. 7, Midcontinental Journal of Archaeology. Kent State University Press, Kent, Ohio.

Clay, R. B., and C. M. Niquette

1989   *Phase III Excavations at the Niebert Site (46MS103) in the Gallipolis Locks and*

Dam Replacement Project, Mason County, West Virginia. Contract Publication Series 89-06, Cultural Resource Analysts, Lexington, Kentucky.

Dancey, W. S.

1991 A Middle Woodland Settlement in Central Ohio: A Preliminary Report on the Murphy Site (33LI212). *Pennsylvania Archaeologist* 61:37–72.

1992 Village Origins in Central Ohio: The Results and Implications of Recent Middle and Late Woodland Research. In *Cultural Variability in Context: Woodland Settlements of the Mid-Ohio Valley,* edited by M. F. Seeman, pp. 24–29. Special Paper No. 7, Midcontinental Journal of Archaeology. Kent State University Press, Kent, Ohio.

Felumlee, G.

1983 Report on the Knight Hollow Rock Shelter. *Ohio Archaeologist* 33(4):22–28.

Fischer, F. W.

1974 *Early and Middle Woodland Settlement, Subsistence and Population in the Central Ohio Valley.* Unpublished Ph.D. dissertation, Department of Anthropology, Washington University, St. Louis.

Foraker, L.

1975 Excavation of a Hopewell Mound in the Muskingum Valley. *Ohio Archaeologist* 25(1):10–14.

Ford, R. I.

1979 Gathering and Gardening: Trends and Consequences of Hopewell Subsistence Strategies. In *Hopewell Archaeology: The Chillicothe Conference,* edited by D. S. Brose and N. Greber, pp. 234–238. Kent State University Press, Kent, Ohio.

Gordon, R. B.

1966 Natural Vegetation of Ohio at the Time of the Earliest Land Surveys (map). Ohio Biological Survey, Columbus.

Grantz, D. L.

1986 Archaeological Investigation of the Crawford-Grist Site #2 (36FA262): An Early Woodland Hamlet. *Pennsylvania Archaeologist* 56:1–21.

Greber, N. B.

1977 *Report on the 1975 Excavation at the Nashport Mound (33–MU-15), Dillon Lake, Ohio.* Report submitted to the National Park Service in Compliance with Contracts CX-6000-5-0186 and CX-5000-6-0301.

1991 A Study of Continuity and Contrast Between Central Scioto Adena and Hopewell Sites. *West Virginia Archeologist* 43:1–26.

Greber, N. B., R. S. Davis, and A. S. DuFresne

1981 The Micro Component of the Ohio Hopewell Lithic Technology: Bladelets. *Annals of the New York Academy of Sciences* 376:489–528.

Greber, N. B., and K. C. Ruhl

1989 *The Hopewell Site.* Westview Press, Boulder, Colorado.

Hemmings, T. E.

1978 *Exploration of an Early Adena Mound at Willow Island, West Virginia.* West Virginia Geological and Economic Survey, Morgantown.

Holmes, W. H.

1919 Introductory, the Lithic Industries. In *Handbook of Aboriginal American Antiquities, Part 1.* Bulletin 60. Bureau of American Ethnology, Washington, D.C.

Mansfield, M.W.

1882 Muskingum County (map). In *J. F. Everhart's History of Muskingum County, Ohio.* A. A. Graham, Columbus.

Maslowski, R. F.

1985 Woodland Settlement Patterns in the Mid and Upper Ohio Valley. *West Virginia Archeologist* 37:23–24.

McConaughy, M. A.

1990 Early Woodland Mortuary Practices in Western Pennsylvania. *West Virginia Archeologist* 42:1–10.

Mills, W. C.

1914 *Archaeological Atlas of Ohio.* The Ohio State Archaeological and Historical Society, Fred J. Heer Printing Co., Columbus.

1921 Flint Ridge. Ohio State Archaeological and Historical Quarterly 30:90–161. (Reprinted as *Certain Mounds and Village Sites in Ohio* 3[3]. Fred J. Heer Printing Co., Columbus.)

Moorehead, W. K.

1897 Report of Field Work, Carried on in the Muskingum, Scioto and Ohio Valleys During the Season of 1896. *Ohio Archaeological and Historical Publications* 5:165–274.

1899 Report of Field Work in Various Portions of Ohio. *Ohio Archaeological and Historical Publications* 7:110–203.

Morgan, R.

1929 *Geological Aspects of Ohio Archaeology.* Unpublished master's thesis, The Ohio State University, Columbus.

Mortine, W. A., and D. Randles

1978 *The Martin Mound: An Extension of the Hopewell Interaction Sphere into the Walhonding Valley of Eastern Ohio.* Occasional Papers in Muskingum Valley Archaeology 10. Muskingum Valley Archaeological Survey, Zanesville.

1981 *Excavations of Two Adena Mounds in Coshocton County, Ohio.* Occasional Papers in Muskingum Valley Archaeology 12. Muskingum Valley Archaeological Survey, Zanesville.

Morton, J., and J. Carskadden

1987 Test Excavations at an Early Hopewellian Site Near Dresden, Ohio. *Ohio Archaeologist* 37(1):8–12.

Morton, J.
  1977   Excavations of Mound B, a Hopewellian Site in the Muskingum Valley. *Ohio Archaeologist* 27(1):22–24.
Murphy, J. L., and J. Morton
  1984   Dodson "Village": A Flint Ridge Habitation Site. *Ohio Archaeologist* 34(3):23–26.
Niquette, C. M., and R. D. Boedy
  1986   *The Calloway Site (15MT8): A Transitional Early to Middle Woodland Camp in Martin County, Kentucky.* Contract Publication Series 86-12. Cultural Resource Analysts, Lexington, Kentucky.
Norris, R., and S. M. Skinner
  1985   Excavation of Connett Mound 3, the Wolf Plains National Register District, the Plains, Ohio. *Ohio Archaeologist* 35(1):21–26.
Pacheco, P. J.
  1988   Ohio Middle Woodland Settlement Variability in the Upper Licking River Drainage. *Journal of the Steward Anthropological Society* 18:87–117.
  1992a   Ohio Middle Woodland Intracommunity Settlement Variability: A Case Study from the Licking Valley. Paper presented at the 57th Annual Meeting of the Society for American Archaeology, Pittsburgh.
  1992b   The Legacy of the Licking River Basin Mound Builders. In *Vanishing Heritage: Notes and Queries about the Archaeology and Culture History of Licking County, Ohio,* edited by P. E. Hooge and B. T. Lepper, pp. 12–31. Licking County Archaeology and Landmarks Society, Newark.
  n.d.   Prehistoric Settlement Patterns in East Central Ohio: Evidence from the Robert L. Sterling Collection of Upper Jonathan Creek Valley. Ms. on file, Department of Anthropology, The Ohio State University, Columbus.
Pacheco, P. J., and W. H. Pickard
  1992   A Laterally Halfed Ohio Hopewell Bladelet from Dow Chemical #2 (33Li302). *Ohio Archaeologist* 42(2):12–15.
Pickenpaugh, M. E.
  1974   The Fred Gutridge Cave. *The Redskin* 9(2):60–65.
Pi-Sunyer, O.
  1965   The Flint Industry. In *The McGraw Site: A Study in Hopewellian Dynamics,* edited by O. Prufer. Scientific Publications 4(1):60–90. Cleveland Museum of Natural History.
Prufer, O. H., and D. H. McKenzie
  1975   *Studies in Ohio Archaeology.* Kent State University Press, Kent, Ohio.
Railey, J. A.
  1991   Woodland Settlement Trends and Symbolic Architecture in the Kentucky Bluegrass. In *The Human Landscape in Kentucky's Past,* edited by C. Stout and C. K. Hensley, pp. 56–77. Kentucky Heritage Council, Frankfort.

Seeman, M. F.

1979 *The Hopewell Interaction Sphere: The Evidence for Interregional Trade and Structural Complexity.* Prehistory Research Series 5(2). Indiana Historical Society, Indianapolis.

1985 *The Locust Site (33Mu160): The 1983 Test Excavation of a Multicomponent Workshop in East Central Ohio.* Kent State Research Papers in Archaeology 7. Kent State University, Kent, Ohio.

Shane, O. C. III

1971 The Scioto Hopewell. In *Adena: The Seeking of an Identity,* edited by B. K. Swartz, Jr., pp. 142–145. Ball State University, Muncie, Indiana.

Sheward, J. H.

1877 The Mound Builders. *Zanesville Daily Courier,* November 5.

Skinner, S. M., and R. Norris

1982 Settlement/Subsistence Patterns within the Hocking Drainage: An Examination of Late Archaic through Early Fort Ancient Site Distribution. Paper presented at Annual Meeting of the Ohio Academy of Science, Columbus.

1984 Excavation of the Connett Mound 4, the Wolf Plains National Register District, the Plains, Ohio. *Ohio Archaeologist* 34(4):23–26.

Smith, B. D.

1987 Hopewellian Farmers of Eastern North America. Paper presented at the Plenary Session, Eleventh Congress, International Union of Prehistoric and Protohistoric Sciences, Mainz, Germany.

Smith, C. M.

1885 A Sketch of Flint Ridge, Licking County, Ohio. In *Smithsonian Institution Annual Report for 1884,* pp. 851–873. Washington, D.C.

Squier, E. G., and E. H. Davis

1848 *Ancient Monuments of the Mississippi Valley.* Contributions to Knowledge 1. Smithsonian Institution, Washington, D.C.

Struever, S.

1964 The Hopewell Interaction Sphere in Riverine–Western Great Lakes Culture History. In *Hopewellian Studies,* edited by J. R. Caldwell and R. L. Hall, pp. 85–106. Scientific Papers 12. Illinois State Museum, Springfield.

Struever, S., and G. Houart

1972 An Analysis of the Hopewell Interaction Sphere. In *Social Exchange and Interaction,* edited by E. N. Wilmsen, pp. 47–49. Anthropological Papers 46. Museum of Anthropology, University of Michigan, Ann Arbor.

Stuiver, M., and P. J. Reimer

1986 A Computer Program for Radiocarbon Age Calibration. *Radiocarbon* 28:1022–1030.

Thomas, R. A.

1970 Adena Influences in the Middle Atlantic Coast. In *Adena, the Seeking of an*

Identity, edited by B. K. Swartz, Jr., pp. 56–87. Ball State University, Muncie, Indiana.

Webb, W. S.

1942   *The C & O Mounds at Paintsville.* Reports in Anthropology and Archaeology 5(4). University of Kentucky, Lexington.

Whitman, J. K.

1977   Kohl Mound, a Hopewellian Mound in Tuscarawas County. *Ohio Archaeologist* 27(3):4–8.

Wymer, D. A.

1987   *The Paleoethnobotanical Record of Central Ohio—100 B.C. to A.D. 800: Subsistence Continuity Amid Cultural Change.* Unpublished Ph.D. dissertation, Department of Anthropology, The Ohio State University, Columbus.

PART FIVE

Afterword

Interpretations of Ohio Hopewell 1845–1984 and the Recent Emphasis on the Study of Dispersed Hamlets

James B. Griffin

ABSTRACT

Over the course of the last century and a half, American archaeologists have gradually improved our understanding of the people who built the enclosures and mounds of the Mississippi Valley. One of the most important contributions was the recognition that these works were the product of prehistoric Native Americans. In Ohio it became apparent that the mounds and earthworks were the product of more than one cultural group, possibly representing an extended cultural sequence. The remains identified as the product of the Ohio Hopewell people represent the finest cultural examples of this grandiose tradition. The papers in this volume are a welcome contribution to the long-ignored domestic problem fostered by the artifact-rich Ohio Hopewell mounds. The emphasis in the volume on a settlement pattern composed entirely of dispersed hamlets is perhaps somewhat overdrawn. Based on the observations of earlier archaeologists of village debris near earthworks, it is suggested that Ohio Hopewell settlement systems included permanent settlements, perhaps of great size, near the Hopewell centers.

In the late 1840s the observations of Squier and Davis concerning the societal organization and motivation of people who built the mounds of the Mississippi

406 · JAMES B. GRIFFIN

Valley were derived both from earlier interpretations and their own labor. In contemporary terminology they viewed their mound and earthwork builders as having advanced from savagery and barbarism to civilization because of their knowledge and practice of maize agriculture. They ascribed a religious origin to most of the earthworks and argued that the geometric form of many of them had a symbolic meaning. The large complex earthworks in Ohio were indeed identified as "Sacred Enclosures." They viewed the population as large and as having interarea connections from the Great Lakes to the Gulf and the Mexican mountains, where obsidian was obtained, and from the Alleghenies on the east to the Plains. Their estimate of the age of the mound builder occupation of over a thousand years was based on the count of the annular rings of large second-growth trees growing on and within the earthworks and the decaying evidence of earlier forest giants and also on the evidence of location of the earthworks on earlier river terrace formations and not on the modern terraces. They unfortunately regarded all of the enclosures and mounds throughout the greater Mississippi Valley as constituting "a single system of works" (Squier and Davis 1848:7) even though subdivisions of form and function could be recognized. They also viewed the builders of the earthworks as an ancient vanished population, and that was certainly true.

There were other authors before Squier and Davis who believed that the mound builders were a different, more accomplished "race" than the Indians known to Europeans. A recent publication by Huddleston (1967) is a review of varied interpretations of Europeans from the Columbus landfall in 1492 up to the 1730s, on the origins of the American Indians. The major influence on almost all of the writers of the 250-year record was the Judeo-Christian historical-theological tradition, which presented a Near Eastern interpretation of the origin of the world and of man (people) that was inadequate to the task and also inaccurate. Huddleston states one of two major themes (1967:viii):

> The Acostan Tradition, characterized by a moderate skepticism with respect to the comparative and exegetical methodology of the day, by an adherence to geographical and faunal considerations in theorizing, and by a reluctance to produce finished origin theories is named for Joseph de Acosta, who gave the tradition its earliest extended example in the *Historia natural y moral de las Indias* in 1589/90. The Garcian Tradition, named for the author of the Origin de las Indias (1607/1729), is marked by an uncritical acceptance of the comparative ethnological technique of determining origins and a tendency to accept trans-Atlantic migrations.

Even in the sixteenth century various authors identify the mythical Atlantis, the Carthaginians, Greeks, Hebrews, Egyptians, Africans, Ethiopians, French, Irish, Welsh, Norwegians, and/or Danes. The most popular ancestors for American Indians and their civilizations in this century was Atlantis. During the early seventeenth century, as knowledge of the short distance between Asia and America across the Bering Strait became better known, the idea that Indians were descended from Asiatic "Tartars" became increasingly popular, and some writers realized that there never were Ten Lost Tribes of Israel. The controversy over the origin(s) of the Indians continued into the nineteenth and twentieth centuries. One of the strongest surviving myths was that the Indians were descended from the Jews. James Adair, whose book on the history of the American Indians was published in 1775, strongly supported this derivation. However, by the first half of the nineteenth century the better-informed and rational writers on American Indian origins and the relationship of the Indians to the Mississippi Valley mounds took the position that— because of the distinction of the one hundred or more Indian languages, not only between Indian tribes and areas but also with Old World languages, and because of their physical appearance, which was most similar to Mongoloids, and their distinctive New World cultural developments and absence of many of those traits characteristic of the Old World—the Indians had come from northeast Asia and that in the Ohio Valley the Indians were the descendants of the builders of the earthworks.

One of the early writers of the nineteenth century, Constantine S. Rafinesque, was a Swiss naturalist who was somewhat erratic in his scientific works, but he did do some adequate surveys of Adena earthworks in Kentucky, and some of these were incorporated into Squier and Davis's *Ancient Monuments of the Mississippi Valley*. Rafinesque taught at Transylvania University in Lexington, and in his *Ancient History or Annals of Kentucky* (1824) he discussed four early migrations from the Old World to account for the varieties of peoples and cultures that were encountered by Europeans. One of those was essentially that of the migration legend of the Delaware informants recorded by the missionary John Heckewelder. This path to the Mid-Atlantic states from the West recorded encounters with advanced peoples who were interpreted as the "Cherokee," or a nonidentifiable and non-Indian group. He also adopted the idea of transoceanic movements from Europe and Asia. These oceanic movements were described in considerable detail as to their contribution to the North, Middle, and South American Indians. To be brief, Rafinesque's abilities to propose nonexistent contributions to the Western Hemisphere

populations and cultures far outdoes modern authors engaged in the same
endeavor. A fair evaluation of his works was made by Samuel F. Haven: "Mr.
Rafinesque was a laborious student in almost every conceivable department
of knowledge, and only wanted the faculty of judicious discrimination to
secure him a distinguished name among men of science" (Haven 1855:41).
The Walum Olum is now known to be a fraud by Rafinesque.

A considerable number of writers adopted and believed a bewildering
amount of misinformation, copied from others, and this mishmash was readily
available in print for an interpretation claimed to be a supernatural revelation
but which is as equally erroneous as those more secular statements based
only on human mistakes. One of the early-nineteenth-century scholars published the results of his research, after at least fifteen years of study, and referred particularly to the identification of the builders of the Ohio and Mississippi Valley mounds and earthworks. "From all the facts I have been able to
collect upon the history of these antiquities, I am decidedly of opinion, that
they were erected by Indian tribes of North America" (McCulloh 1829:519).
Lewis Cass, the first governor of Michigan, Henry Schoolcraft, and others believed that the Ohio monumental earthworks and the artifacts found in them
were constructed at some indefinite period of the past by the ancestors of the
Indians. In the latter half of the nineteenth century, an increasing number of
competent students adopted this position, beginning with Samuel F. Haven,
Librarian of the American Antiquarian Society, whose scholarly review of the
Archaeology of the United States was published by the Smithsonian Institution
in 1856. The increasing but still small number of individuals attached to but a
few academic institutions began to devote a considerable amount of time to
archaeological pursuits. Gradually it was recognized that, for example, in southern Ohio, there were a number of different prehistoric (obviously Indian)
cultures and the early recognition of temporal succession was proposed in
the latter half of the nineteenth century by Putnam and Mills.

Putnam, and probably some of his associates working in southwest Ohio as
well, knew that there was a small amount of historic trade goods at the Madison-
ville site in Hamilton County. Since Euro-American manufactured materials
did not appear at the Turner site, then Turner should be an older prehistoric
Indian manifestation. Putnam also emphasized the distinctiveness of what is
now called "Hopewell" from Fort Ancient by the mid 1880s (Putnam 1886:500).
Mills, while recognizing the difference between the Scioto Valley Fort Ancient
sites and the large Hopewell mounds and earthworks, interpreted the Robert
Harness mound as a Fort Ancient construction with a Hopewell burial intru-

sive in its upper levels. The mound is best regarded as an Adena monument (Griffin 1943). He viewed Hopewell as a higher cultural development that was later than Fort Ancient. He did not seem to make the connection between the Scioto Valley Fort Ancient sites and those of southwestern Ohio (Mills 1906:135–136). After further investigations of Hopewell and Fort Ancient sites, Mills decided that Fort Ancient and Hopewell cultures were contemporaneous. He interpreted the Hopewell cache just east of the eastern wall of Fort Ancient as the result of Fort Ancient conquest of a Hopewell population and destruction of their artifacts and that similar evidence of contemporaneity was found at the Feurt village site. Mills also viewed the Westenhaver mound he dug, along with the Adena mound, as a cultural progression toward Hopewell.

W. K. Moorehead, in the last decade of this century, accepted the separate identities of Fort Ancient and Hopewell and proposed a third complex, which he called the "Glacial Kame Culture" (Moorehead 1909:127–150). He felt that the Hopewell culture had a southern origin, moving north before some of the distinctive characteristics of Etowah and other Mississippian sites made their appearance. The first real description of Ohio Hopewell, and other Ohio cultures, as the word "culture" was then used, was by H. C. Shetrone in 1920. He included an Adena subgroup of Hopewell following Mills's suggestion that Adena was an early form of Hopewell and also that they were an Algonquian group. He placed the Serpent Mound and the Fort Ancient site in the Fort Ancient group because there were Fort Ancient village sites on both locations. Shetrone did not approve of the placement of Ohio Hopewell as a minor northern complex marginal to the Tennessee area or of the theory that Hopewell was a former cultural expression of the Cherokee before they moved south. He thought that Hopewell "appears to be a definite and distinctive variety, with but little apparent relationship to any known group of the native race or to any observed archaeological area, and that scant evidence has been adduced that can be taken as indicative of its origin or earlier habitat" (Shetrone 1926:158–159). He identified the area of Hopewell occupation as being from the mouth of the Muskingum to the Cincinnati area with the Ross County, Scioto Valley, locale as the main center. He also recognized a northwestward extension across Indiana to Iowa. Adena he regarded as sharing some number of characteristics with Hopewell but was quite distinctive and, in the absence of sound stratigraphic or evolutionary evidence, hesitated to call Adena early Hopewell. He continued to follow Mills's view that Hopewell and Fort Ancient cultures were contemporaneous, although which one appeared first and which one was the last to disappear had not been determined.

Some ten years later Shetrone's *The Mound Builders* (1930) included sites regarding similar cultural complexes to Ohio Hopewell in states to the west and south as well as discussions of effigy mounds in the upper Mississippi Valley and Mississippian sites in the Southeast. While Shetrone was no doubt the prime contributor of the presentation of the Ohio material, Emerson Greenman, Curator of Archaeology who aided in the compilation, probably had a substantial role in writing the text on the non-Ohio materials. The term "Hopewell" is used for sites now regarded as Havana Hopewellian in Michigan, Illinois, Iowa, and Wisconsin.

Following the first relief labor program at the Marksville site in Louisiana by Frank M. Setzler, assisted by James A. Ford, a major disagreement arose to explain whether the Marksville material with its clay platform pipes and zoned stamped "Hopewell" style pottery was earlier and a donor to the northern cultural units or vice versa. Setzler presented reasons to believe either view but clearly favored the Marksville priority (Setzler 1933:1–21). Ford, however, strongly supported Marksville as the source for the northern Hopewell materials (Ford and Willey 1941:141–142).

While excavations by the Peabody Museum by F. W. Putnam began in 1886 at the Turner site, with intermittent exploration until 1905, a final report was not issued until 1922 (Willoughby and Hooton 1922). Willoughby presented the excavation data and description of the archaeological materials while Hooton described the skeletal materials. In this monograph the term Hopewell culture is not used by Willoughby, for he preferred to call them the Great Earthwork Builders. He correctly stated that the builders of Fort Ancient were not the population of the culture called by that name and that the Fort Ancient culture followed that of the Great Earthwork Builders. He viewed the Serpent Mound as a shrine of the Great Earthwork Builders.

In the late 1930s, Griffin (1943, 1946) prepared two statements on Ohio Hopewell in which it was stated that Adena-Hopewell were central Ohio Valley representations of Woodland culture and that there was not a single origin of Hopewell but that it had many donors from earlier and contemporary societies in the eastern United States. Local regional expressions with interchange of ideas, materials, and finished products were recognized as resulting from contemporaneity with Ohio Hopewell and not the result of conquest or colonization from the Ohio center. Evidence was produced for the development of Ohio Hopewell primarily from an Adena base (Griffin 1946:57).

The phrase Hopewellian Interaction Sphere was presented by Joseph Caldwell (1964) in a paper that he had originally given at an American Anthropological Association meeting in 1961, along with four other papers from the same symposium and one by James A. Brown. He recognized that there were regional variations in the Midwest and Southeast with their own developmental background as most archaeologists had agreed for many years. It was stated that "nothing is clearer to the archaeologists than that over broad geographical regions various societies tend to change in concert" (Caldwell 1964:135). It was the "interaction" between societies that produced innovation. At the time of the several Hopewellian societies, "the interactions and hence the connections among the several societies are in mortuary-religious matters, but not, primarily, at least, in other departments of culture" (Caldwell 1964:137). Caldwell tended to overemphasize the similarities of burial procedures among the different societies and spoke of exact similarities of mortuary artifacts throughout the Midwest and Southeast. He believed that the burial practices had originated in the north in Adena societies in the central Ohio Valley or in Havana societies in the Illinois Valley. Other mortuary items originated in various southeastern societies. "That various separate societies were interacting within and beyond the boundaries of their respective regional traditions is perhaps the one thing about the Hopewellian situations we can be sure of" (Caldwell 1964:138). In an earlier paper he had used the term "diffusion sphere" to refer to the Southeast area interchange of goods and ideas between regional societies. He explained "the climactic features of the Hopewellian interaction sphere" as resulting from the introduction of diverse forms into societies resulting in innovations and inventions. He did not identify what those were in the several societies. In the early 1960s the term "diffusion" had become a bad word, for it was claimed that it did not "explain" why concepts or behavior were adopted by regional societies once they were introduced. However, the Hopewellian Interaction Sphere of Caldwell was adopted even though it appears to be a narrow form of diffusion.

On the other hand, in the same series of papers, Stuart Struever referred to the Hopewell Interaction Sphere as having developed in the Havana societies of Illinois, Michigan, and Wisconsin as the result of changes in the food procurement and societal systems particularly in the Illinois Valley and of the sharing of distinctive artifact styles between the several regional localities. He did not accept Caldwell's concept that the sharing of similar mortuary behavior and burial goods meant that they were strictly religious-ceremonial in nature. His view was that raw materials and stylistic ideas were diffused in a logistic network. In this paper Struever did not deal with Ohio Hopewell but left that area to be discussed when he presented his views of the logistic network.

This appeared early in the 1970s as "An Analysis of the Hopewell Inter-action Sphere" by Stuart Struever and Gail L. Houart (1972). They presented their view of a graded system of the acquisition and distribution of raw mate-rials and manufactured goods in Hopewellian sites, primarily in the Ohio Valley and the Illinois Havana societies. They proposed that there was a hier-archy of Regional Transaction Centers, Local Transaction Centers, and Talus Slope Settlements in the lower Illinois River Valley and their associated Bluff Crest Centers. They identified the major Ohio centers, emphasizing the Hopewell site as a major manufacturing center. In their paper many valid observations appear. However, one of their major points was that earlier stu-dents had regarded Hopewell as a unitary culture from New York to Kan-sas and from Michigan to Florida. This was simply not the case, for anyone who had worked with Ohio Hopewell and the data from contemporary re-gional Hopewellian societies was well aware of the marked differences, and even that Ohio Hopewell was not a unitary cultural expression. A reading of their study gives the impression of a highly organized, controlled acquisition of raw materials from great distances manufactured and distributed on a regu-lar schedule of trade and exchange. This imaginative and regimented model received wide acceptance but has been criticized in archaeological meetings, published reports, and in a substantial monograph by Mark Seeman (1979). Seeman's interpretation of Ohio Hopewell and its trade and exchange activi-ties is fairly close to those adopted in this paper but were not derived from his study.

Another interpretation of Ohio Hopewell is by Olaf Prufer, whose thesis was a presentation of the salient characteristics garnered from the literature and an examination of museum collections. In two papers (Prufer 1964a, 1964b) he gave his views on the origins and nature of Ohio Hopewell. He presented a chronological sequence of early, middle, and late sites, which was followed by "Latest Hopewell," identified as the building of the hilltop en-closures. This was done rather suddenly by the Hopewell people as a defensive measure, which might have been against the arrival of the Fort Ancient people. He viewed Ohio Hopewell as having a strong component of Late Adena, plus the arrival of Havana populations from Illinois. He viewed the elaborate ma-jor earthworks and burial mounds as each having been constructed in a short period of time by rather large numbers of people who lived not at the center but in small independent villages. The villages were shifted from time to time, and the Hopewell people were in an early agricultural stage with maize as the major cultivated crop. Hopewell trade was seen as a mechanism that both acquired exotic raw materials and introduced items manufactured in Ohio, along with Ohio ideas and concepts.

In the more popular of these articles, Prufer (1964b) refers to the burial ceremonialism as the Hopewell cult, which was brought into southern Ohio from Illinois by an elite group. They were responsible for the earthwork and burial mound construction and were the individuals buried in the mounds. As such they were a small segment of the total population in the area. The occupants of the small scattered villages were Adena or Adena-descended peoples dominated by the high-status elite. The latter people comprised the group that controlled the trade and exchange that introduced the Hopewell cult in many areas of eastern United States and fueled the extraordinary Ohio development. With the breakup of the trade and exchange network, the cult activities died out between A.D. 550 and 750, leaving the regional traditions to continue without the religious-ceremonial superstructure. Prufer agreed with Willoughby that Hopewell was probably a prehistoric Algonquian society or societies. Prufer was wrong then in almost every point—and is still wrong.

The preceding pages of selected contributions to Ohio Hopewell studies is a prologue to recent subsequent efforts to understand the Hopewell phenomenon. It should be emphasized that, with rare exceptions, the term Hopewell should be restricted to those Indian remains in southern Ohio of about A.D. 1 to 350. The large number of contemporary societies in the United States and south-central Canada can be recognized as regional expressions that indicate relationships to Ohio Hopewell in varying degrees but that had their own developmental histories. For example, in the Illinois River Valley and the western Great Lakes and upper Mississippi Valley contemporary Indian societies are known as Havana Hopewellian named after the town of Havana on the east banks of the Illinois River in Mason County. Early Havana culture is about 150 years earlier than Ohio Hopewell and the late Havana expressions are almost over by A.D. 300. At one time in the mid-1900s a number of archaeologists felt that Ohio Hopewell was initiated by a movement of Havana populations into Ohio. Fortunately this idea has had a relatively short life span because of the absence in Ohio of artifacts and behavior that are specifically Havana. Before radiocarbon dating it was more common to think Hopewellian expressions to the west and south were derived from Ohio. However, it is doubtful if in the Havana sites there is a significant amount of imported artifacts made in Ohio.

I used to be confident that some number of platform pipes in Illinois were imports from Ohio. Quite recently archaeological survey work by Kenneth Farnsworth in the Sterling area along the Rock River of northwest Illinois found on sites in that vicinity a considerable amount of worked clay stone. This was also present in the collections of local people and was identified as coming from local deposits. Laboratory work, I believe by Kenneth Tankersley, further identified the Sterling area material as distinctly different from Ohio pipestone in the Lower Scioto River area. The majority of Illinois platform pipes is clearly of local Illinois deposits, which, in turn, are from different geological deposits from the strata in Ohio.

The lesson here is that identifying objects with the "naked" eye is not good enough; wherever it has been checked by chemical-physical studies, the results have been somewhat surprising. Such studies should be continued to obtain accurate source identifications regarding the trade networks of materials brought into Ohio and those of objects made in Ohio Hopewell times and exported. On the basis of what we know now, it seems that trade, or Ohio personnel, brought large amounts of raw material to Ohio that went to artisans at the major Hopewell sites and then may have been traded locally, although actual export was quite small.

In 1979 the volume *Hopewell Archaeology: The Chillicothe Conference* appeared. The compendium was organized by David H. Brose and edited by N'omi Greber. Brose managed to obtain papers on Hopewellian activity in ten states and Ontario by some fifty-four contributors. The volume may be regarded as a tribute to the people who have provided information over the two hundred-year period between 1794–1978 on the prehistoric Indian occupation of most of the eastern United States. I do not believe that there is any significant information that was obtained from the historic Indian occupants of Ohio on the origin of the Hopewell mounds and earthworks. The individuals to whom the volume was dedicated produced data on the remarkable development of Indian cultures from the earliest hunter-gatherers of some ten thousand years prior to Ohio Hopewell.

Many of the contributors emphasized regional diversity; the trade relationships were recognized over most of the east but the actual amount was not, by any means, overwhelming. The amount of trade goods from Ohio into the Illinois Valley would have been a canoe load if moved at one time. Most of the contributors recognized that the Ohio populations traveled down the west side of the Appalachians into North Carolina for mica and into East Tennessee and Georgia for some copper and probably for the few gold fragments at the Turner site. Their trading activities took them to the headwaters of the Chattahoochee and then to the west coast of Florida, where they obtained some of the marine shells they valued.

The several contributors did not seriously attempt population assessments; but in the Lower Illinois Valley, which witnessed an increase from Early Woodland times, it is estimated at one person per square mile. A number of authors reported on the identification of native plants that were domesticated in the Late Archaic societies. This domestication has been recognized as providing a substantial dietary component in Early Woodland and Hopewell times (Smith 1985 to 1992). Others were also working on this problem, and it is quite clear that the eastern Indian societies had produced an agriculture base of "gardening" independently. Their familiarity with seed crop nurture helped them to successfully grow maize when it was introduced into the midcontinent around A.D. 1, probably from the Southwest. A number of authors in the 1978 meeting in Chillicothe discussed settlement patterns in Illinois and Missouri, but there was little emphasis on this in other papers. Robert Hall introduced a study of Adena and Hopewell concepts that might have survived into the early historic period. This interest in trying to understand the ideology of Indian societies of the past has rarely been attempted. A last comment that may be made is that the Chillicothe conference produced papers by regional specialists whose ideas about the independent development of cultures in their areas into those of the Hopewellian period sounded the death knell for attempts to attribute Ohio or the lower Mississippi Valley as the stimulators for the appearance of the multiple Middle Woodland Hopewellian societies. The conference has been called "The Revolt of the South" against a prehistoric Indian northern intruder.

The papers presented on "Ohio Hopewell Community Organization" at the 57th meeting of the Society for American Archaeology in Pittsburgh in 1992, organized by William Dancey and Paul Pacheco, represent a significant change of emphasis in Ohio Hopewell studies. The various authors present some of the data recently gathered from some of the more than ninety locations with Hopewell period occupational debris. The theme was to test the accuracy of Olaf Prufer's Vacant Ceremonial Center model of Hopewell settlements, which was patterned after an incorrect interpretation of the Maya area and which has now been largely abandoned. As Dancey and Pacheco say in their summary of Prufer's model (chapter 1), Prufer regarded Hopewell as an immigrant group. This interpretation, I believe, is also wrong, as I would regard Hopewell as primarily a development from Adena societies in southern Ohio. In Prufer's chapter in this volume, a remarkable mini-autobiography, he prefers to still believe that Adena people were growing maize on the basis of its presence in Daines Mound 2 in Athens. I still prefer to be suspicious on

416 · JAMES B. GRIFFIN

the grounds that, with all the Adena mounds that have been excavated in five states without any evidence of corn, a burrowing "beastie" is a more likely answer, and also for the McGraw corn. I also do not know why Richard Ford did not publish the Daines or McGraw site dates that have aggravated Olaf. The only Hopewellian site that has produced corn recently is the Holding site (Fortier et al. 1989) in the American Bottom. The maize fragments were preserved and shipped to the University of Illinois. They were not run before the report was finished because of the suspicion that they were from modern crops on the site. Within the last few years Tom Riley of the Department of Anthropology at the University of Illinois sent some of it for accelerator dating to the University of Arizona. There it was dated as having grown in the first century of our era, which is what the corn should have dated at the Holding site (Riley et al. 1994). There is also corn from a Middle Woodland site in Tennessee that has been dated in the early years after A.D. 1. It is true, I think, that if there were maize kernels, they grew on a cob, which grew on a corn stalk, which had to be planted by people. While maize came to the eastern United States from Mexico, the route by which it was introduced is not known for certain. The most likely scenario is that maize moved up the western part of Mexico to the Southwest by at least 1000 B.C. and was then carried east in Basket Maker II–Middle Woodland Times. It would appear that the presence of maize might best be determined by identification of its occurrence in human skeletal material by stable isotope analysis.

In her paper in this volume, Wymer does not include maize as a significant food source in Hopewell times, and this view is shared by other active workers in eastern palaeobotany. Maize as a significant part of the food supply appears, as far as we know now, in the American Bottom in Late Woodland sites between A.D. 700–850 and is an important addition that helped produce the emergent and early Mississippian societies in the central Mississippi Valley. A major point in the Wymer paper is that the plants nurtured and consumed imply forest clearance by the Hopewell people and subsequent maintaining of an environment favorable for early horticultural gardening.

The resuscitation of Prufer's fieldwork at Fort Hill some thirty years ago can now be integrated into the recent excavation at Fort Ancient by Connolly and the late Patricia Essenpreis. The hill or "mesa" top enclosures in southern Ohio would seem to represent multiple building periods and perhaps for multiple purposes. I would propose that their use as a defensive barrier against attack by invaders was the least likely. The size of the enclosed area would have required a sizable number of defenders to defend against "Mississippian" invaders. The latter were not alive and not available for some six hundred years. Such invaders were in Prufer's original interpretation, and he seems to be less enthusiastic on the basis of further excavations by others.

Sue Ellen Kozarek's chapter on the Jennison Guard site in Dearborn County, Indiana, near the confluence of the Great Miami River with the Ohio, supports the interpretation that it was the result of a residentially sedentary occupation with travel for specific raw materials or for hunting trips. Her chapter is, I believe, solid evidence for a different settlement type than that presented in most of the other chapters in this volume.

The Newark earthworks contribution by Lepper and Yerkes is a critical examination of the report on salvage excavations by E. E. Hale, and edge-wear analysis of stone tools to determine their function. The authors take the position that evidence obtained from the occupational discards from the Newark expressway sites are not specialized occupational remnants but ordinary domestic debris from short-term occupations. The lithic analysis favors this interpretation and is bolstered by the absence of heavily curated large stone tools that would be expected at a sedentary location. One of the radiocarbon dates is clearly too early, but the other two are within the ranges of Hopewell occupation. I hope that Lepper will have the time to run down the evidence from early newspaper accounts and small papers such as those by Isaac Smucker, a mid–nineteenth century collector of evidence of the prehistoric Indians around and in Newark.

When I first began work in the Museum of Anthropology at the University of Michigan in February 1933, among other pottery collections that Carl Guthe had obtained for the Ceramic Repository of the Eastern United States, there were a few Hopewell sherds from the Seip-Pricer mound, which is discussed by Greber along with the Hopewell material from the Baum earthworks. Some years later when Richard G. Morgan visited me, he was surprised to see them, and at his request I sent them back to Columbus. They are the Seip sherds that were cataloged in Ann Arbor with red paint. The sherds were presumably from the mound excavation. On one of my visits in the 1930s to the Ohio State Museum, I talked with Robert Goslin, who participated in many of Shetrone's excavations. He assured me that there was habitation debris in the big Seip mound, under it, and under and in the earthworks that surrounded it. It is fair to say that habitational debris was not a compelling interest of the responsible excavator.

I am pleased that Dr. Greber has embarked on the difficult task of separating domestic products from "ceremonial" ones, when the Hopewell people apparently did not in some instances. She seems to accept the possibility that the house structures excavated within the enclosure were not necessarily constructed for occupation while the people were producing "ceremonial" objects to place with the dead. She also points out that the upper fill of the Seip-Pricer mound contained habitational debris. Greber estimates that the fill was between fifteen to twenty times that of the McGraw site midden. I find it difficult however to believe that Mills in 1909 agreed that the debris came from a specific location when the fill was not identified until some twenty years later. Perhaps this is an example of psychic archaeology. In her evaluation of Seip-Pricer from data in the Ohio Historical Society catalog she says that it "appears quite reasonable to conclude that a significant percentage of the redeposited cultural remains at Seip were generated by Hopewellian domestic activities and redeposited in the course of corporate ceremonial, ritual, and/or political events. The amount of such debris combined with in situ remains suggest long periods of moderately intensive activities, shorter periods of more intensive site use, or a combination of both." The last is the scenario I prefer.

Greber also attempts an interpretation of the length of occupations of Seip and Baum from her analysis of discrete activity areas largely based on the construction stages of the Seip-Pricer mound. She proposes the length of occupation at about twelve to forty-four generations. If the generation figure is thirty years, then Seip would have lasted roughly 350 to 400 years. If the generation figure is twenty, then occupation span would be roughly 250 to nearly 300. Her interpretation is that one local Hopewell group expanded down Paint Creek, because of the strong similarity of the earthworks at Seip and Baum. Greber compares the settlement pattern of a modern Ecuadorian society to help explain the pattern of the Ross County Hopewell people. The interpretation of two construction phases at Seip, she believes, is also present at least in three other Ohio Hopewell sites. She also emphasizes that there are important differences in the constructions in southwest Ohio and in southeast Ohio and that it is improbable that the settlement pattern of the central Scioto is present in those areas.

It is a special pleasure to have experienced archaeologists study and report on the remarkable collection of Robert Harness from the Liberty-Harness site. It is to be hoped that the authors of this contribution can provide a larger version that will be illustrated in the future. The uniqueness of the collection is not only its size but, even more significantly, that it is documented according to locality. While there have been earlier views of some of the collection, a large illustrated publication should be possible. Coughlin and Seeman recognize some thirty-three Ohio Hopewell components found on the Scioto flood-plain, the alluviated terrace, and the terrace edge. The authors believe that their analyses support the Prufer model, "in the main," and also that the presence of an early Late Woodland habitation site bolsters, with other areas, the notion that there was a gradual transition from Middle Woodland into Late Woodland. This certainly parallels the situation in the Havana Hopewellian area. The Hopewell people in Ohio did not move away; their cultural products gradually changed. There was no invasion from Mississippian peoples to produce Fort Ancient culture. The Late Woodland populations gradually, over an occupation of about six hundred years, with the addition of maize to their diet and some interaction with Mississippian societies to the south and east, produced Fort Ancient societies.

The paper by Connolly on Fort Ancient is a fine statement of prehistoric activities at one of the most remarkable locations of Hopewell people. As he states, Prufer refers to the sites as one of the places where habitational debris was present. This resulted from Prufer's association with Richard G. Morgan, Curator of Archaeology at the Ohio Historical Society, and I think also from some of many discussions with me. I do not know the exact extent of the CCC excavations east of the Fort Ancient eastern wall, but there were excavations to a depth of at least 2 ft extending at least 100 yds south of the state road. I first saw the work in the summer of 1934 while studying Clifford C. Anderson's collection from the Fort Ancient village. He told me that the earth that was excavated was moved a short distance east to fill a low area on which the house of the Superintendent of Fort Ancient was to be built. My observation of this deplorable activity eventually added additional witnesses to the burned areas, the bottom of refuse pits, and scattered lithic debris. In the fall of 1937, I drove from Ann Arbor to Columbus, picked up Morgan and Shetrone, and met Moorehead, Eli Lilly, and Glenn Black. By that time vegetation had grown in the area, but shovel testing convinced them of the Hopewell habitation area at that locality. A snapshot of the group at Fort Ancient can be seen in the biography of Lilly by James Madison (1989:125).

The recent fieldwork at Fort Ancient demonstrated that it was built over a fairly long time period, beginning with dirt removal to fashion a surface, which included habitational debris, on which the earthworks would be built. More evidence was found north of the state road in the same area where Mills (1908) found his cache of Hopewell artifacts and which, along with his misinterpretation of the Fort Ancient site, caused him to assert that Hopewell and Fort Ancient populations were contemporary. I am pleased that Connolly reports on the objects removed from the remarkable cache by Eugene Powell. Pat Essenpreis sent me kodachrome slides of those materials that were clearly Ohio Hopewell specimens. I hope Connolly's fieldwork can continue, and I think it will demonstrate that while there do not seem to be deep midden refuse deposits, the evidence will suggest concurrent occupation by the builders of the fort of greater magnitude than short-term hamlets. Connolly refers to some flint projectiles as belonging to the Snyders cluster. This may be so, but I have not seen any good Snyders points from Ohio. They are early in the Havana Hopewellian point styles in Illinois.

Genheimer's paper on the Stubbs Cluster in the Little Miami Valley provides information on the several sites located within a short distance south of Fort Ancient and it is tempting to suggest that its populations were closely involved with the builders of that dominant site in the Little Miami Valley. The sites he discusses are not well known, and his evidence is based on collection from the surface, in most cases, and, as he insists, excavations should provide more satisfactory evidence on whether they support the Hamlet Hypothesis of Dancey and Pacheco. At present most of the several sites represent relatively small scatters of indubitable Hopewell affiliation, including several that have both Knife River flint from South Dakota and obsidian from the Yellowstone River area. If you find one of these in Hopewellian sites, you are likely to find the other. Indeed the results of many excavations have documented a wider distribution of these exotic raw materials than was known at the time of my summaries (Griffin 1965; Braun and Griffin 1982) of obsidian and Knife River flint distribution in the Midwest. Most of the field areas are quite small, but a few are of larger size, approaching some of the smaller habitation areas that have been excavated in Illinois. The Stubbs habitation locales should be excavated before they too are obliterated by contemporary population expansion.

The chapter on the mounds and habitation sites in the Salt Creek drainage, which flows into the Scioto River a short distance north of Waverly, Ohio, in southeast Ross County, is by Flora Church and Annette Ericksen. Their discussion of settlement pattern suggests that it was one of seasonal dispersed hamlets. I am puzzled by the interpretation of the Wade site as representing a single component in existence between 200 B.C. and A.D. 200 and, further, that the occupation was probably near the transition between Early and Middle Woodland. I am not certain the Wade site in the Salt Creek Valley, or the Murphy site, represent a single component. The radiocarbon dates from Feature 2 at the Wade site came from a hearth filled with fire-cracked rock and charcoal. The two dates can reasonably be regarded as essentially the same and dating from about 375 B.C. This would surely be in Early Woodland or Adena times, while the third date from Feature 3, which had Hopewell artifacts, was dated well within Hopewell time range.

The paper provides a fine assessment of distribution and nature of the Middle Woodland sites in the Salt Creek locality. It joins the other papers in this volume in expanding knowledge of the Hopewell settlement pattern, which does not seem to correspond to what might be expected from true farming communities carefully nurturing the so-called Eastern Agricultural Complex.

The relatively unknown eastern margin of Ohio Hopewell is effectively covered by Carskadden and Morton in "Living on the Edge." In addition to concentrating on the nature of the Hopewell settlement, this chapter emphasizes a continuity of pattern from Adena times into Hopewell, and the authors suggest that some of the Adena communities were occupied into early Hopewell times. Over twenty years ago the authors embarked on a twenty-year survey of Woodland occupations of Muskingum County, which has changed that area from one of little usable information to one characterized by abundant information. In addition, the authors encompass in their comparative analyses the work done by others. The physiographic limitations of their area were not favorable for large settlements in prehistoric days, or for large-scale earthworks, but at the mouth of the Muskingum are, or rather were, the magnificent Marietta Earthworks and in the northern area the Flint Ridge formation and at Newark the largest Hopewell earthwork in the state, if not the country. One result of their survey, which I regard as remarkable, is the identification of well over a hundred habitation sites attributed to Adena. While some of the authors' Adena areas may have had only minimal remains, I can recall a time when Adena was said not to have habitation sites either in Ohio or Kentucky. The authors clearly identify these earthworks associated with Adena, and with Hopewell as a continuity into Late Woodland times of what appear to be fortified habitations. Indeed their opinion is that there is overlap in the specifics of the three major cultural periods that would imply population continuities from Adena into Late Woodland times. They also comment on the evidence for occupation in the river-bottom land and refer to their excavations at sites, some of them covered with over 1.5 m of flood deposits. The two authors have submitted a comprehensive and insightful resume of the area with which they are familiar. Their assessment of the nature of the prehistoric habitants from about 500 B.C. to A.D. 500 is one of the best I have seen.

The editors, as well as the authors of these chapters, have provided an unusual volume for Ohio—or for most studies of prehistoric occupations. While they recognize a considerable number of habitation areas, I am left to assume that the people during Hopewell times lived an ethereal existence, for I do not see a single example from hundreds of identified sites of the products of their industries. The volume will not sell to the considerable number of individuals who are interested in a pictorial presentation, especially in color, but may be tempted to purchase the book for its excellent identification of site locations. Dancey has a tendency to dismiss the evidence of any of the earliest observers of Hopewell habitation at Marietta, Hopewell, Hopeton, Fort Ancient, and that I am not prepared to do. While I did not know Hildreth, Atwater, or even Squier and Davis, I did know Moorehead, Cliff Anderson, Shetrone, and Morgan, and I have reasonable confidence in their observations during fieldwork. In my pursuit of an understanding of the nature of prehistoric sites, I have noticed that it is extremely difficult to assert that such an understanding is the result of continual occupation by the same people over a short period of a few hundred years, or of the reoccupation of a desirable location by the same or different culturally similar people. I noticed that most of the examples of periodic activity came from locations adjacent to, or within, Hopewell mound groups or earthworks. Perhaps the laborers paused to spread out into hamlets, nucleated villages, or whatever in order to get something to eat. The number of known mini-sites near the large burial mounds and earthworks may not have satisfied the nutritional needs of the hard-working builders.

Pacheco's chapter is a detailed analysis of lithic scatter in the upper Licking drainage, north and west of the Newark Earthworks. The evidence for occupations that he recovered is entirely that of small hamlets, apparently occupied over a short period of time during the Middle Woodland period. He hopes for a future emphasis on the study of local communities and their regional integration. He believes that stability in community organization was a major feature of the Hopewell settlement system and that during the period of the construction of the earthworks, straw bosses blew a pan pipe at quitting time so that the weary workers could trudge to their dispersed hamlets. This devotion to a single interpretation is, perhaps, a bit too much for the major interpretation of Hopewell existence. I cannot help but wonder what would have happened if a large-scale archaeological attack could have been launched ten years or even a hundred after completion of Newark. I suspect it would have been quite different.

Madsen has presented an admirable statement on the methodologies that should be applied to the study of dispersed communities. Many new measurement techniques as discussed might be applied not only to the study of dispersed hamlets but to any other data from the Hopewell occupation whenever applicable. I am reminded of an earlier "How To" book by Walter Taylor (1948) which he formulated while a student and which he believed should profoundly alter archaeological field and laboratory work. His criticisms of past practitioners were severe and without apparent understanding of how differing times and differing circumstances shape archaeological work. As one reviewer stated, Taylor's approach would require considerable financial support to accomplish. Taylor himself, in spite of his spartan life-style, was signally unable to apply his conjunctive approach to his own case site. I suspect that large-scale analysis of quite a few of the approaches to understanding Hopewell settlement systems would be quite time consuming and therefore expensive. I doubt that any such studies could have generated the funds to build a large museum on The Ohio State University, Columbus, campus, at least not with the help of the legislature.

I applaud the concerted effort by Dancey, Pacheco, and the other authors of this volume for their identification of a considerable number of new habitation locations. What I deplore is the long time from 1964 to 1997 that has passed for the corrective data in this volume to appear. What I regard as my noble effort to call attention to papers by many archaeologists of past generations in regard to the location of Hopewell habitational debris is regarded as irrelevant. That evidence was largely ignored by archaeologists in the 1920s and 1930s. For example, Emerson F. Greenman thought the habitational sites of the Hopewell people were the Fort Ancient villages. If Squier and Davis had been able to exploit many of the analytical approaches to a study of their work, how long would it have taken? And would it have been published by the Smithsonian Institution? My paper in the 1993 Chillicothe Conference (soon to be published by the Ohio Archaeological Council), entitled "A View from the Core: A Conference Synthesizing Ohio Hopewell Archaeology," was not an attempt to be a worm at the core but simply to provide more wheels for the runaway wagon of hamlet horses. Madsen mistakes my effort as a denial of the evidence for small habitational units. I still think culture history within archaeology is a valid pursuit, and I understand that Madsen's several approaches to analyzing Hopewell data are intended to provide better interpretations of what happened through time. When contemporary students with newly developed approaches get good results, I believe those will be a part of cultural history. I approve of all of them when they are done by a reliable person.

References

Adair, J.

1775   *The History of the American Indians.* N.p. London.

Atwater, C.

1820   Description of the Antiquities Found in the State of Ohio and Other Western States. *Archaeologia Americana* 1:105–267.

Braun, D. P., J. B. Griffin, and P. F. Titterington

1982   *The Snyders Mounds and Five Other Mound Groups in Calhoun County, Illinois.* Technical Papers 13. Museum of Anthropology, University of Michigan, Ann Arbor.

Brose, D. S.

1976   *A Historical and Archaeological Evaluation of the Hopeton Works, Ross County, Ohio.* Report submitted to the National Park Service in fulfillment of Contract PX-6115-6-0141.

Brose, D. S., and N. Greber (editors)

1979   *Hopewell Archaeology: The Chillicothe Conference.* Kent State University Press, Kent, Ohio.

Caldwell, J. A.

1964   Interaction Spheres in the Prehistory of the Eastern United States. In *Hopewellian Studies,* edited by J. C. Caldwell and R. L. Hall, pp. 133–143. Scientific Papers 12. Illinois State Museum, Springfield.

Essenpreis, P. S., and M. E. Moseley

1984   Fort Ancient: Citadel or Coliseum. *Field Museum of Natural History Bulletin* 55(6):5–10, 20, 26.

Ford, J. A., and G. Willey

1941   An Interpretation of the Prehistory of the Eastern United States. *American Anthropologist* 43(3):325–363.

Fortier, A. C., T. O. Mahler, J. A. Williams, M. C. Meinkoth, K. E. Parker, and L. S. Kelly

1989   *The Holding Site: A Hopewell Community in the American Bottom.* Site Report 21. American Bottom Archaeology FA1-270 Project. University of Illinois Press, Urbana.

Greber, N.

1983   *Recent Excavation at the Edwin Harness Mound, Liberty Works, Ross County, Ohio.* Special Paper No. 5, Midcontinental Journal of Archaeology. Kent State University Press, Kent, Ohio.

Griffin, J. B.

1943   *The Fort Ancient Aspect: Its Cultural and Chronological Position in Mississippi Valley Archaeology.* University of Michigan Press, Ann Arbor.

1946   Cultural Change and Continuity in Eastern United States Archaeology.

In *Man in Northeastern North America,* edited by F. Johnson, pp. 37–95. Paper No. 3. R. S. Peabody Foundation for Archaeology, Andover, Massachusetts.

1965   Hopewell and the Dark Black Glass. *Michigan Archaeology* 11(3–4):115–155.

Haven, S. F.

1865   *Archaeology of the United States.* Contributions to Knowledge 8(2). Smithsonian Institution, Washington, D.C.

Hildreth, S. P.

1843   Pyramids at Marietta. *American Pioneer II* 1:243–248.

Huddleston, L.

1967   *Origins of the American Indian.* University of Texas Press, Austin.

Madison, J. H.

1989   *Eli Lilly: A Life 1885–1977.* Indiana Historical Society, Indianapolis.

McCulloh, J. H., Jr.

1829   *Researches Philosophical and Antiquarian Concerning the Aboriginal History of America.* Fielding Lucas, Jr., Baltimore.

Mills, W. C.

1906   Exploration of the Baum Prehistoric Village Site. *Ohio Archaeological and Historical Quarterly* 15(1):45–136.

Moorehead, W. K.

1890   *Fort Ancient.* Robert Clarke, Cincinnati.

1922   *The Hopewell Mound Group of Ohio.* Anthropological Series 6(5). Field Museum of Natural History, Chicago.

Morgan, R. G.

1946   *Fort Ancient.* Ohio State Archaeological and Historical Society, Columbus.

Potter, M. A., and E. S. Thomas

1970   *Fort Hill.* Ohio Historical Society, Columbus.

Prufer, O. H.

1964a   The Hopewell Complex of Ohio. In *Hopewellian Studies,* edited by J. C. Caldwell and R. L. Hall, pp. 35–48. Scientific Papers 12. Illinois State Museum, Springfield.

1964b   The Hopewell Cult. *Scientific American* 211(6):90–102.

Putnam, F. W.

1886   Report of the Curator. Eighteenth Annual Report. *Peabody Museum* 401–419, 477–502.

Rafinesque, C. S.

1824   *Ancient History or Annals of Kentucky.* N.p. Frankfort.

Riley, T. J., G. R. Walz, C. J. Bareis, A. C. Fortier, and K. E. Parker

1994   Accelerator Mass Spectrometry (AMS) Dates Confirm Early *Zea mays* in the Mississippi River Valley. *American Antiquity* 59:490–498.

Seeman, M. F.

    1978 *The Hopewell Interaction Sphere, the Evidence for Interregional Trade and Structural Complexity*. Prehistory Research Series 5(2). Indiana Historical Society, Indianapolis.

Setzler, F. M.

    1933 Pottery of the Hopewell Type from Louisiana. *Proceedings of the U.S. National Museum* 82:2.

Shetrone, H. C.

    1920 The Culture Problem in Ohio Archaeology. *American Anthropologists* 22(2):142–172.

    1926 Explorations of the Hopewell Group of Prehistoric Earthworks. *Ohio Archaeological and Historical Quarterly* 35(1):227.

    1930 *The Mound Builders*. Appleton, New York.

Shetrone, H. C., and E. F. Greenman

    1931 Explorations of the Seip Group of Prehistoric Earthworks. *Ohio Archaeological and Historical Quarterly* 40:343–509.

Smith, B. D.

    1985 The Role of *Chenopodium* as a Domesticate in Pre-Maize Garden Systems of the Eastern United States. *Southeastern Archaeology* 4:107–133.

    1992 Prehistoric Plant Husbandry in Eastern North America. In *The Origins of Agriculture: An International Perspective,* edited by C. W. Cowan and P. J. Watson, pp. 101–119. Smithsonian Institution Press, Washington, D.C.

Struever, S., and G. L. Houart

    1972 An Analysis of the Hopewell Interaction Sphere. In *Social Exchange and Interaction,* edited by E. N. Wilmsen, pp. 47–79. Anthropological Papers 46. Museum of Anthropology, University of Michigan, Ann Arbor.

Taylor, W. W., Jr.

    1948 *A Study of Archaeology*. Memoir 69. American Anthropological Association, Washington, D.C.

Willoughby, C. C., and E. A. Hooton

    1922 *The Turner Group of Earthworks, Hamilton County, Ohio*. Paper 8(3). Peabody Museum of Archaeology and Ethnology, Cambridge, Massachesetts.

Contributors

Jeff Carskadden received a B.A. in geology from Denison University in 1969 and attended graduate school at The Ohio State University working toward an M.A. in anthropology. His graduate career was interrupted by the military draft, however, and he served with the U.S. Army in Vietnam as an aerial photo analyst in 1970–71. He has been an avocational archaeologist since the 1970s and received the Society of American Archaeology's Crabtree Award in 1995. He currently resides in Zanesville, Ohio, directs the Muskingum Valley Archaeological Survey, and serves as a consultant for the optical industry.

Flora Church received her Ph.D. from The Ohio State University in 1987 and is currently a Principal Investigator for the ASC Group, Inc., Columbus, Ohio, and is director of the Midwest Faunal and Microwear Labs. Her research interests include prehistoric archaeology of the Eastern Woodlands with emphasis on the Late Woodland and Late Prehistoric periods.

Robert P. Connolly is Station Archaeologist at the Poverty Point State Commemorative Area, Epps, Louisiana, and has an adjunct appointment at Northeast Louisiana University in Monroe, Louisiana. He has a master's degree from the University of Cincinnati (1991) and a Ph.D. from the University of Illinois (1996). Both degrees were based on a decade of field research at Fort Ancient.

Sean Coughlin is a Ph.D. student in the Department of Anthropology at the University of Tennessee, Knoxville. He received his master's degree in anthropology from the University of Tennessee and his bachelors degree from Kent State University, also in anthropology. His current research includes the analysis of faunal remains from historic and prehistoric sites in the southeastern and midwestern United States.

WILLIAM S. DANCEY received his Ph.D. from the University of Washington, Seattle, in 1973, and since then he has been on the faculty of The Ohio State University, Columbus, where he is an associate professor of anthropology. Among his publications are *Archaeological Field Methods: An Introduction* (1981) and *First Discovery of America: Archaeological Evidence of the Early Inhabitants of the Ohio Area* (1994), an edited collection of papers on the Paleoindian and Early Archaic periods. His current research focuses on the prehistory of the Middle Ohio River Valley, with particular emphasis on the Woodland period. He serves on the editorial advisory board of *American Archaeology.*

ANNETTE G. ERICKSEN received her Ph.D. from The Ohio State University and currently serves as Principal Investigator for the ASC Group, Inc., Columbus, Ohio, and as director of the ADS Paleoethnobotanical laboratory. As a member of the Archaeological and Historic Textiles Materials Program, she has helped establish the Comparative Plant Fiber Collection at The Ohio State University. Her principal research interests are the prehistoric archaeology of the Eastern Woodlands, paleoethnobotany, and prehistoric and historic textiles.

ROBERT A. GENHEIMER is the Archaeological Collections Manager at the Museum of Natural History and Science of the Cincinnati Museum Center. He holds both a B.A. and M.A. in anthropology from the University of Cincinnati. He has had an active interest in the nonmortuary aspects of Hopewell and has conducted investigations at several sites in the middle to lower reaches of the Little Miami River Valley. His master's thesis was on the use of flint bladelets in the interpretation of Hopewell settlement systems.

N'OMI B. GREBER, Curator of Archaeology at the Cleveland Museum of Natural History and Adjunct Associate Professor in the Department of Anthropology, Case Western Reserve, holds a Ph.D. in anthropology from Case Western Reserve University. She has conducted long-term research centered on Ohio Hopewell combining data from archived materials with modern field data obtained using traditional and geophysical remote sensing techniques. Her work has been published in visual media, slides, and CD, in addition to being presented in various papers and other publications.

JAMES B. GRIFFIN has been a contributor to American prehistory for over sixty years. At the University of Michigan, Ann Arbor, and the Museum of Natural History, Washington, D.C., he is now a Bethesda, Maryland, resident.

SUE ELLEN KOZAREK received her master's degree from the University of Cincinnati in 1987 and currently is a Principle Investigator with Gray & Pape, Inc., Cultural Resources Consultants, Cincinnati.

BRADLEY T. LEPPER is Curator of Archaeology for the Ohio Historical Society and an Affiliated Scholar (and sometimes Visiting Assistant Professor) in the Department of Sociology and Anthropology at Denison University in Granville, Ohio. He served as Curator and Site Archaeologist for the Newark Earthworks State Memorials and Flint Ridge State Memorial from 1988 until 1994. He has some experience in highway archaeology, having served as a graduate student intern with ODOT's Bureau of Environmental Services during the summers of 1979, 1985, and 1986.

MARK E. MADSEN is a Ph.D. student at the University of Washington, Seattle. Among his interests are the application of evolutionary theory to archaeology. He is assistant Webmaster for Technical Operations at Progressive Networks, Inc., Seattle.

JAMES MORTON received a B.A. in art history from the University of Wisconsin in 1969. His graduate career includes earning a master's in art history in 1971 and a master's in fine arts in 1973, also from the University of Wisconsin. He has pursued avocational archaeology in eastern Ohio since the 1970s and is co-founder of the Muskingum Valley Archaeological Survey. He has been a practicing artist in Columbus, Ohio, for the last twenty-three years.

PAUL J. PACHECO received his Ph.D. from The Ohio State University in 1993 and has taught as an instructor at Kent State University and Heidelberg College. He is a Research Archaeologist with the Muskingum Valley Archaeological Survey, Zanesville, Ohio, and is editor of *A View from the Core: A Synthesis of Ohio Hopewell Archaeology* (1997), a special publication of the Ohio Archaeological Council.

OLAF H. PRUFER, Professor of Anthropology, Kent State University, earned his B.A. (1956), M.A. (1958), and Ph.D. (1961) at Harvard University and has conducted archaeological fieldwork in India, Germany, and Ohio. His major specializations are Hopewell and Paleoindian archaeology along with psychological anthropology. Among his many publications in Ohio archaeology are *The McGraw Site: A Study in Hopewellian Dynamics* and *Studies in Ohio Archaeology* (co-edited with D. H. McKenzie).

MARK F. SEEMAN received his Ph.D. from Indiana University in 1977. He is currently a Professor of Anthropology at Kent State University and Associate Editor of *Midcontinental Journal of Archaeology*. Current research interests include Ohio Valley systematics, style and identity, and interregional relations. In the area of Hopewell studies, his most recent publication is "When Words Are Not Enough: Hopewell Interregionalism and the Use of Material Symbols at the GE Mound" (1995) in *Native American Interactions,* edited by M. Nassany and K. Sassaman.

DEE ANNE WYMER received her Ph.D. from The Ohio State University in 1987 and is an Associate Professor in the Department of Anthropology at Bloomsburg University, Pennsylvania. She has been conducting paleoethnobotanical research since the early 1980s, focusing on the Middle and Late Woodland periods. Her research interests include the analysis of the shift from the Eastern Agricultural Complex to maize agriculture, the impact of humans on their landscape, and the Hopewell ceremonial utilization of plants. She has directed or participated in excavations in Ohio, West Virginia, Kentucky, Pennsylvania, Colorado, Arizona, and England.

RICHARD W. YERKES, his Ph.D. from the University of Wisconsin-Madison, is Associate

Professor of Anthropology at The Ohio State University. He has over twenty years of excavation and survey experience with Archaic, Woodland, and Late Prehistoric cultures in eastern North America and numerous publications on his specializations in environmental archaeology, craft specialization and ancient economies, and lithic artifact analysis.

Index

Abrams, E. M., 379
Adena mound, 409
Ayrshire Mound, 238

Baby, R. S., 110
Baum site: domestic sites near, 216–17; enclo-
   sure (Hopewell) at, 208, 218, 219, 418;
   Hopewell habitation debris at, 217, 221;
   village (Fort Ancient) at, 120, 208
Bentley site, 240
Bernhardt, J. E., 375–76
Bethel mound, 343
Black Dog Mound, 373
Blain Village, 120
Blitz, J. H., 217–18
Bolte site, 343
Braun, D. P., 9
Brown mounds, 343
Brown's Bottom site, 118, 239, 362

Caldwell, J. R., 116, 410–11
Caldwell mound, 344
Caldwell's Bottom and Bluff sites, 341, 342
Campbell Hollow site, 136
Campus site, 157
Childers site, 158, 240

Converse, R. N., 16
Cox sites, 371, 372, 374

Daines Mound 2, 115, 119, 415–16
Dancey, W. S., 332
Davis, E. H., 367, 405–6
De Boer, W. R., 217–18
Dodson "Village," 375
Drake's Lower Terrace and Corn Crib sites, 342
Dresden Circle, 372, 374
Duncan Falls site, 379
Dunnell, R. C., 92, 95–96

Edwin Harness mound, 219
Essenpreis, P. S., 251, 252, 253, 254
Etowah site, 409

Fairport Harbor site, 120
Feurt village, 409
Fischer, F. W., 316
Ford, J. A., 410
Ford, R. I., 119
Fort Ancient, 41, 252, 408, 409, 410, 416; con-
   struction stages at, 219, 258–60, 314–15, 316;
   Hopewellian artifacts from, 313, 314, 419;
   lithics from, 260–68; pavement at, 255–58,

Ohio Hopewell Community Organization

was designed by Will Underwood;

composed in 10/13 Adobe Minion with subheads set in Syntax

by Cornerstone Composition Services;

printed by sheet-fed offset on 50-pound Glatfelter Smooth Natural acid-free stock,

notch case bound over 88-point binder's boards in Arrestox B-grade cloth,

and wrapped in dustjackets printed in two colors

on 100-pound enamel stock finished with matte film lamination

by Braun-Brumfield, Inc.;

and published by

The Kent State University Press

KENT, OHIO 44242